☩OLDMAN

PART 2

⊕OLDMAN

PART 2

Story and Art:
Chang Sheng

Adaptation:
Xiuying Zhang

Editor:
Austin Osueke

Published by:
eigoMANGA
PO Box 2071
San Jose, CA 95109
eigoMANGA.com

Distributed by:
SCB Distributors

ISBN:
978-0578988801
Printed in the USA

CONTENTS

This publication reads
from right to left.

☩OLDMAN

PART 2

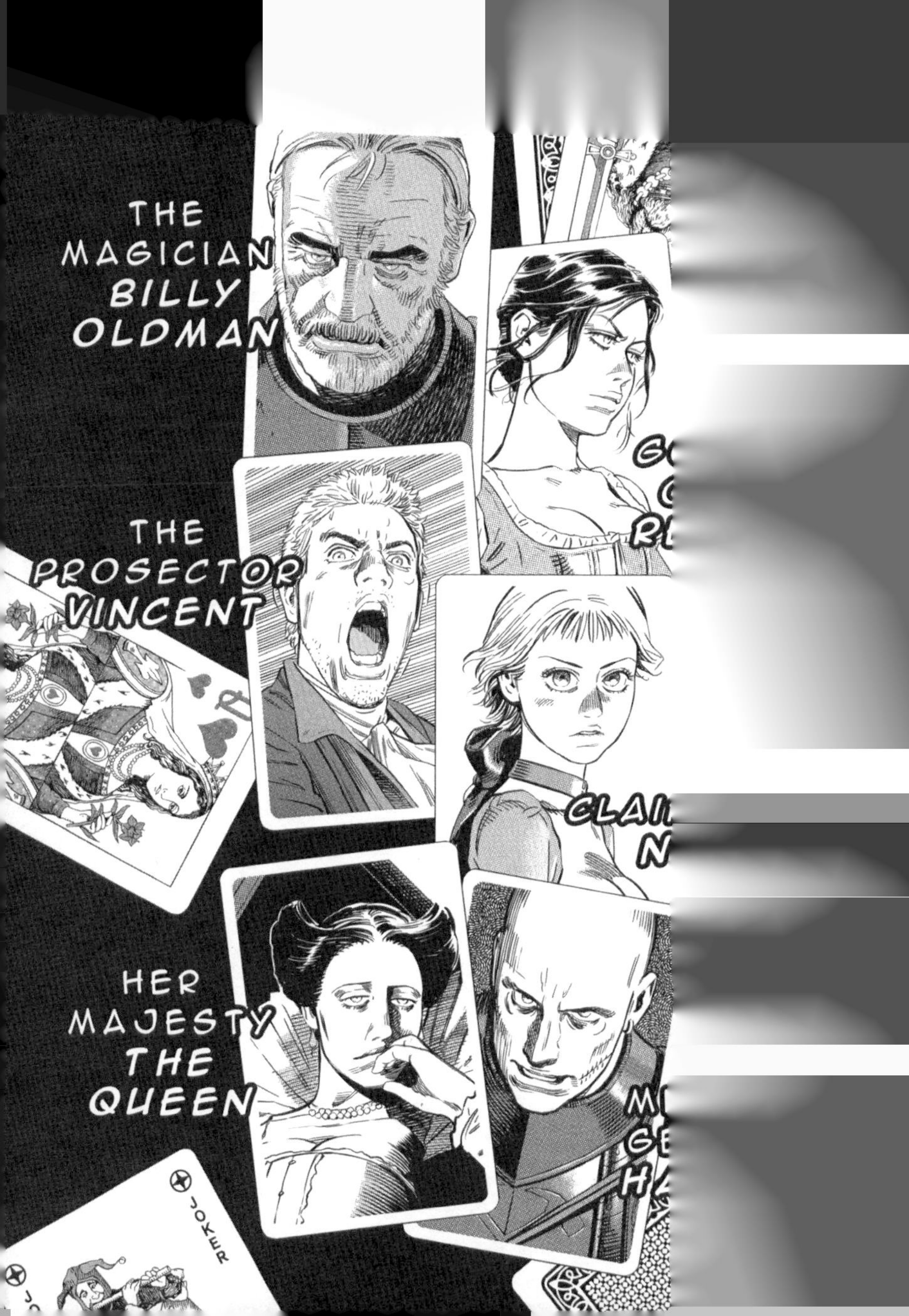
THE MAGICIAN BILLY OLDMAN
THE PROSECTOR VINCENT
HER MAJESTY THE QUEEN
JOKER

PREVIOUSLY...

A RUTHLESS QUEEN RULED HER LAND. SHE WAS UNMARRIED QUEEN WITH NO CHILDREN; SHE ADOPTED ORPHANS TO PROVE TO HER SUBJECTS THAT ONE DAY A COMMONER COULD RULE THE THRONE. AS THE YEARS PASSED, THE QUEEN SOMEHOW RETAINED HER YOUTH. ONLY ONE MAN KNOWS THE QUEEN'S DARK SECRET; OLDMAN WHOM THE QUEEN HAD LOCKED AWAY IN THE PALACE'S PRISON.

ONE NIGHT OLDMAN STAGES HIS ESCAPE AND RESCUES A NEIGHBORING PRISONER, WHO IS A MAIMED SWORDSWOMAN. THE QUEEN THEN DISPATCHES HER ROYAL GUARDS TO APPREHEND OLDMAN AND HIS PARTY. THEY WERE ATTACKED BUT MANAGED TO REPEL THE SOLDIERS. BUT NOW, OLDMAN MUST RETURN TO THE PALACE IN ORDER TO CONFRONT THE SECRETS OF HIS PAST.

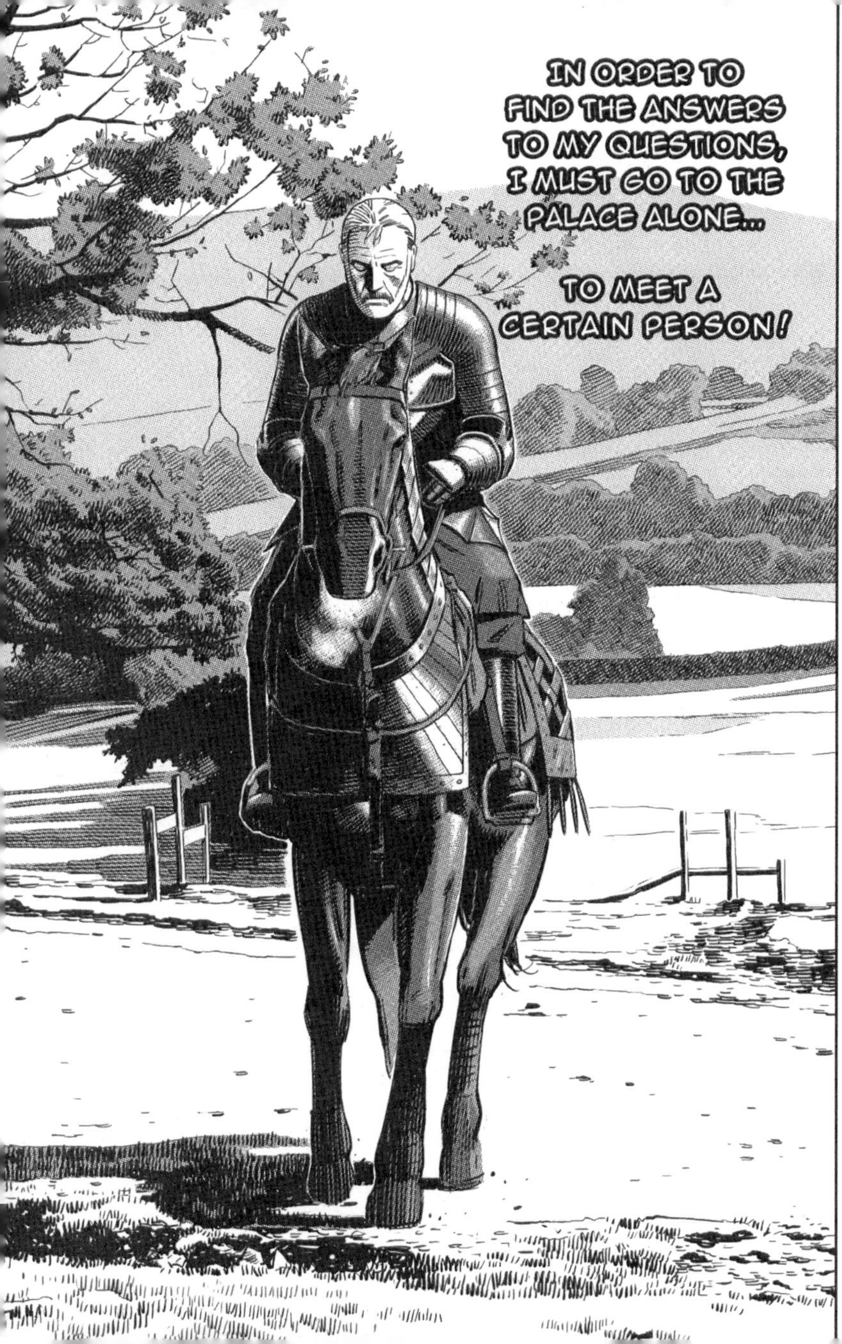
IN ORDER TO FIND THE ANSWERS TO MY QUESTIONS, I MUST GO TO THE PALACE ALONE...
TO MEET A CERTAIN PERSON!

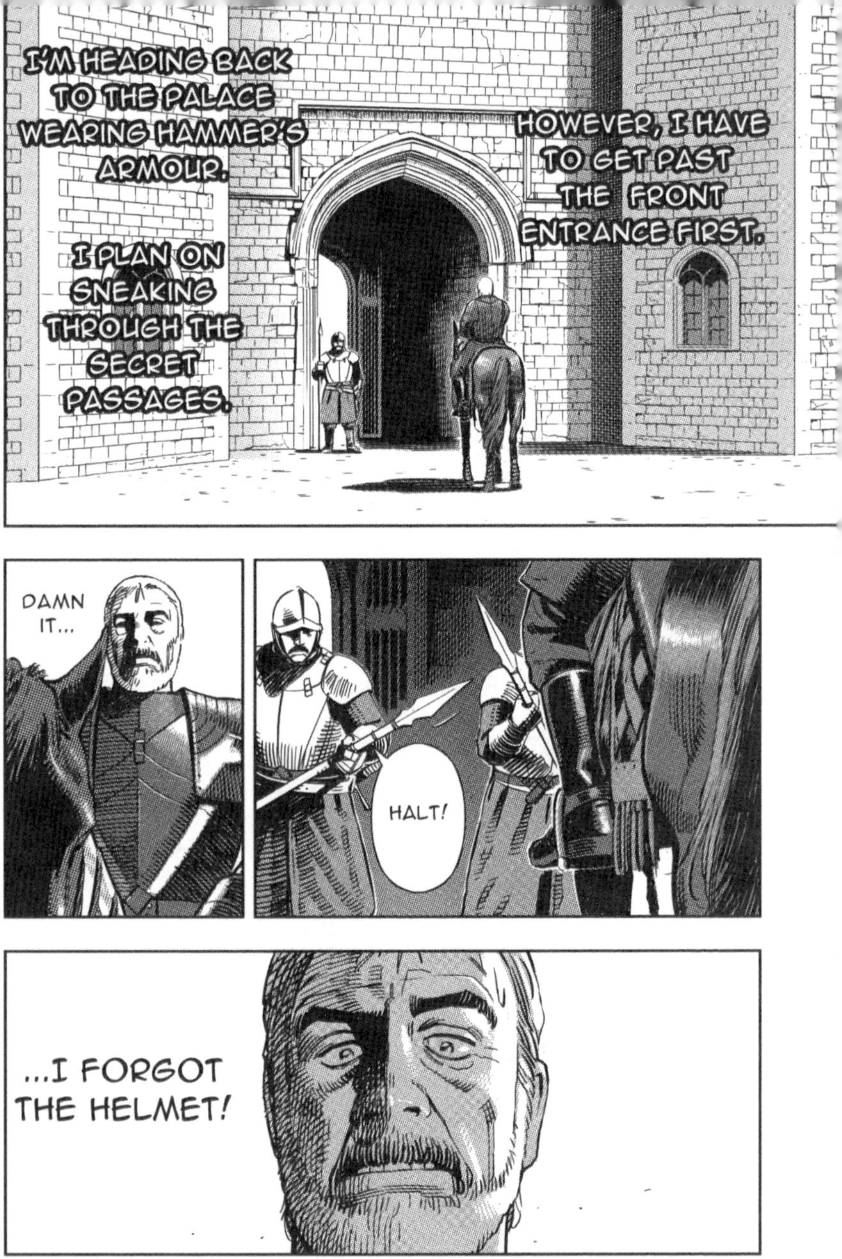
I'M HEADING BACK TO THE PALACE WEARING HAMMER'S ARMOUR.
I PLAN ON SNEAKING THROUGH THE SECRET PASSAGES.
HOWEVER, I HAVE TO GET PAST THE FRONT ENTRANCE FIRST.
HALT!
DAMN IT...
...I FORGOT THE HELMET!

CHAPTER 5
EIDE'S TIME MAGIC

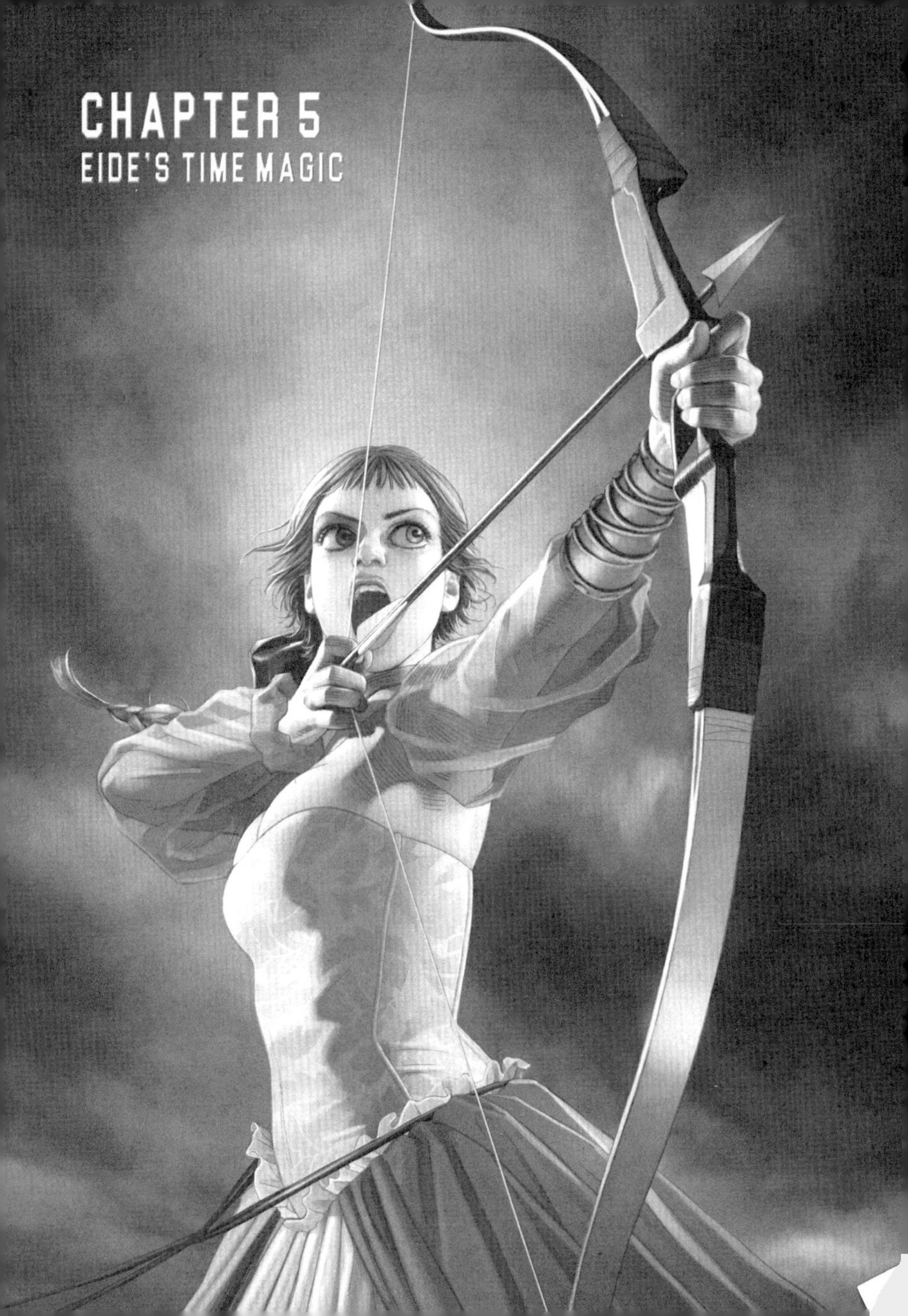

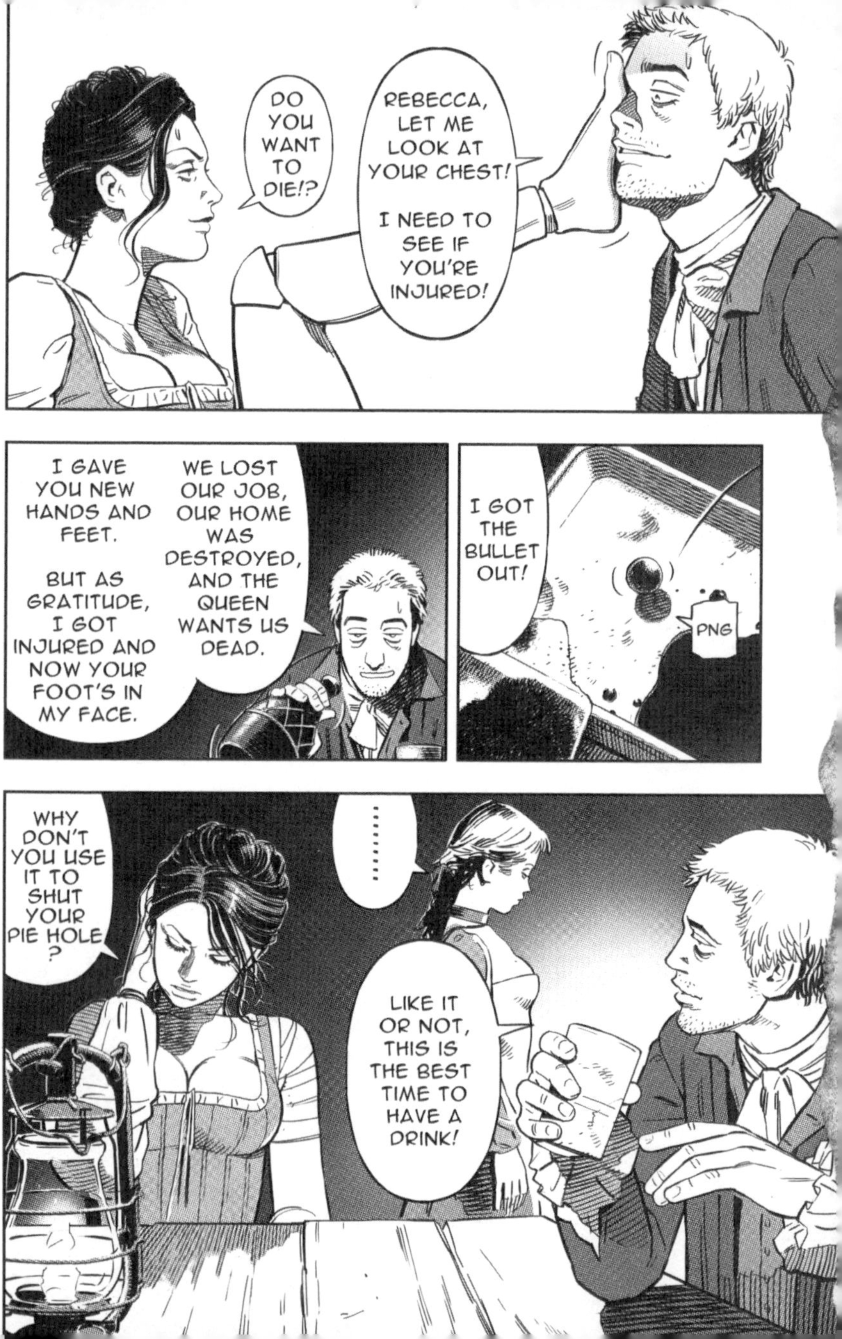

REBECCA, LET ME LOOK AT YOUR CHEST!
I NEED TO SEE IF YOU'RE INJURED!
DO YOU WANT TO DIE!?
I GOT THE BULLET OUT!
PNG
WE LOST OUR JOB, OUR HOME WAS DESTROYED, AND THE QUEEN WANTS US DEAD.
I GAVE YOU NEW HANDS AND FEET.
BUT AS GRATITUDE, I GOT INJURED AND NOW YOUR FOOT'S IN MY FACE.
....
WHY DON'T YOU USE IT TO SHUT YOUR PIE HOLE?
LIKE IT OR NOT, THIS IS THE BEST TIME TO HAVE A DRINK!

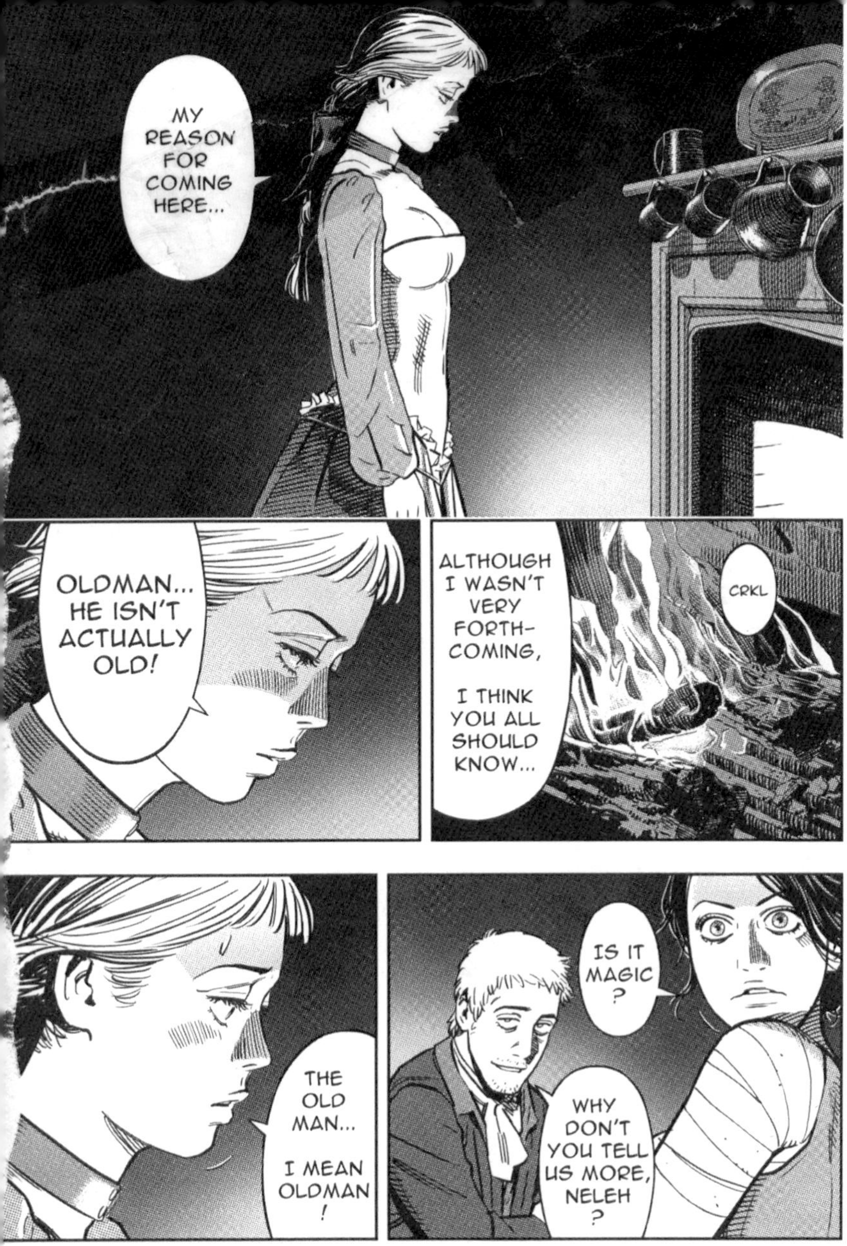
MY REASON FOR COMING HERE...
CRKL
ALTHOUGH I WASN'T VERY FORTH-COMING,
I THINK YOU ALL SHOULD KNOW...
OLDMAN... HE ISN'T ACTUALLY OLD!
IS IT MAGIC?
WHY DON'T YOU TELL US MORE, NELEH?
THE OLD MAN...
I MEAN OLDMAN!

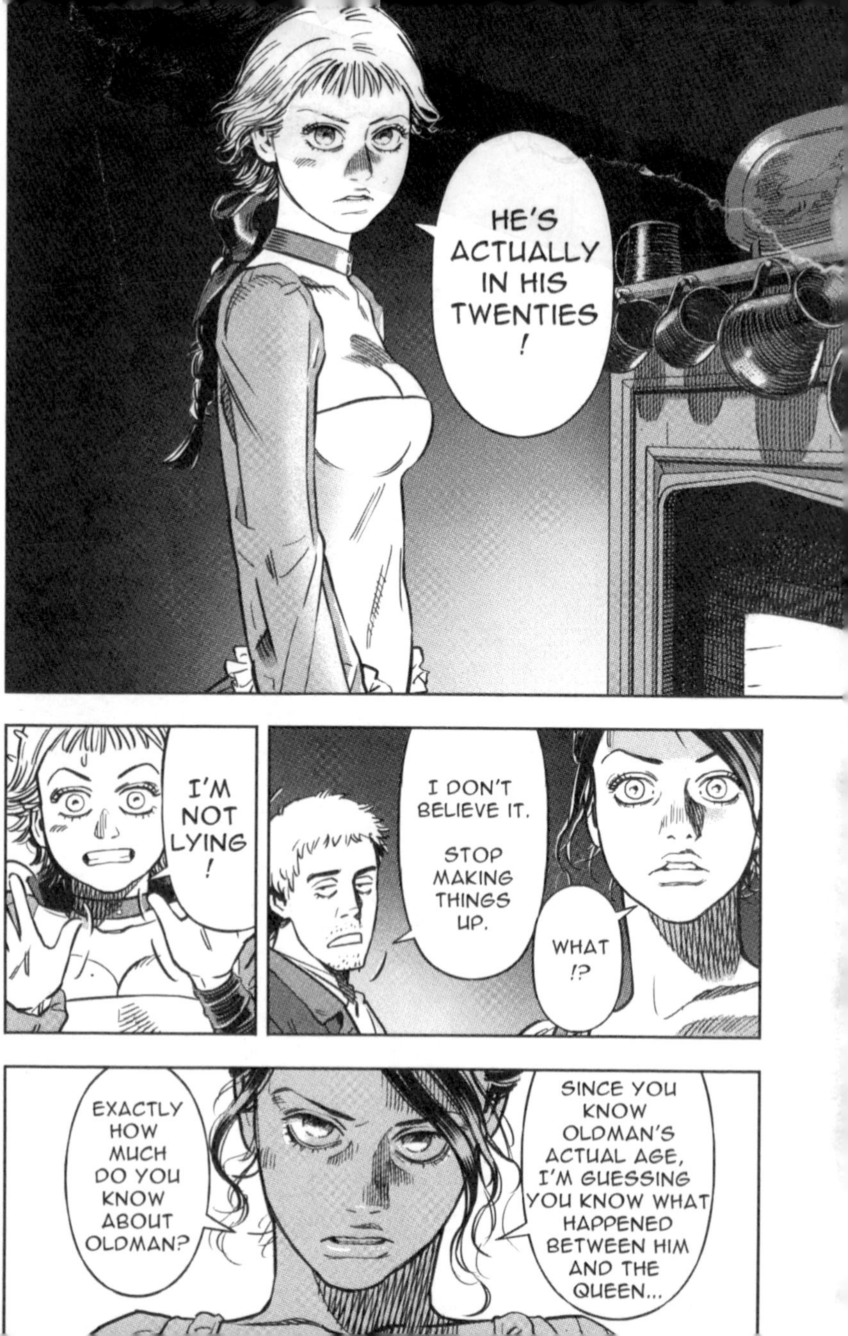
HE'S ACTUALLY IN HIS TWENTIES!
WHAT!?
I DON'T BELIEVE IT. STOP MAKING THINGS UP.
I'M NOT LYING!
SINCE YOU KNOW OLDMAN'S ACTUAL AGE, I'M GUESSING YOU KNOW WHAT HAPPENED BETWEEN HIM AND THE QUEEN...
EXACTLY HOW MUCH DO YOU KNOW ABOUT OLDMAN?

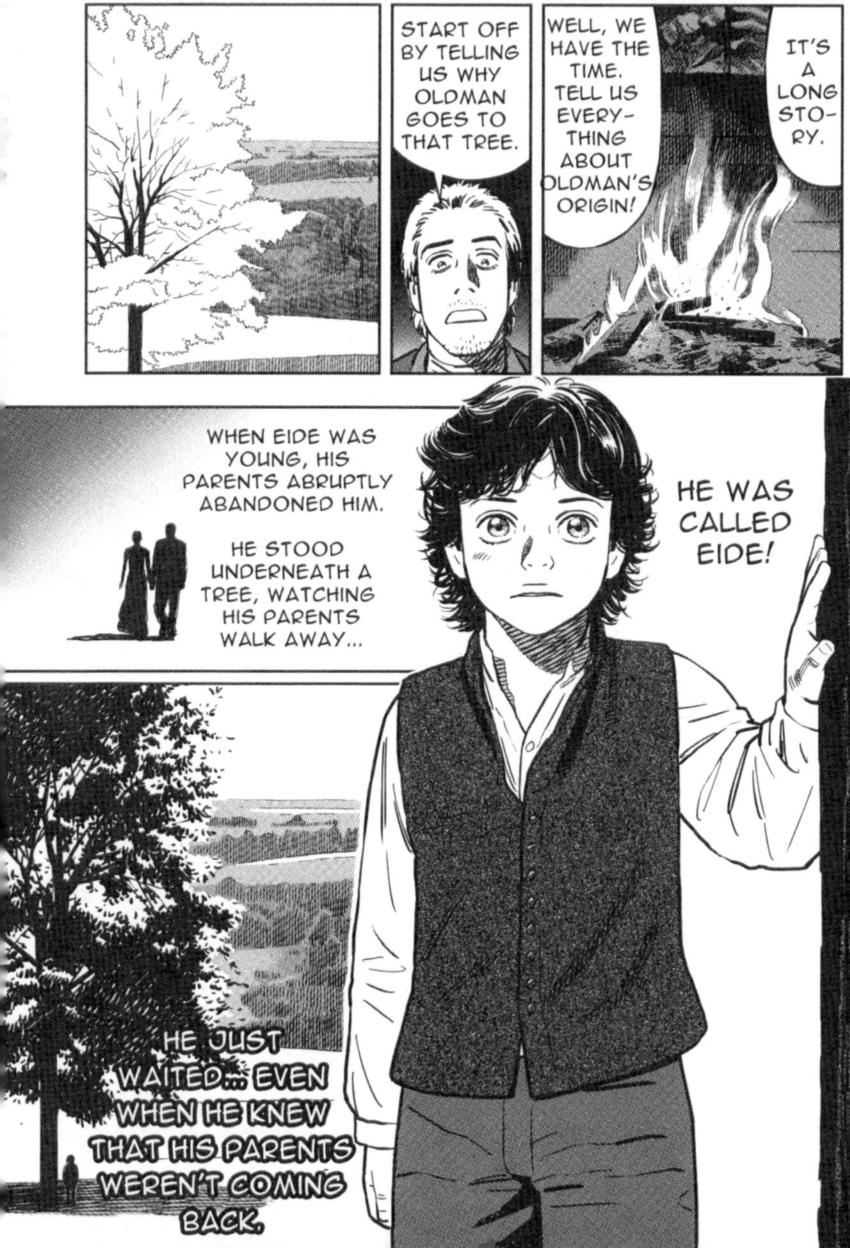
IT'S A LONG STORY.
WELL, WE HAVE THE TIME. TELL US EVERYTHING ABOUT OLDMAN'S ORIGIN!
START OFF BY TELLING US WHY OLDMAN GOES TO THAT TREE.
HE WAS CALLED EIDE!
WHEN EIDE WAS YOUNG, HIS PARENTS ABRUPTLY ABANDONED HIM.
HE STOOD UNDERNEATH A TREE, WATCHING HIS PARENTS WALK AWAY...
HE JUST WAITED... EVEN WHEN HE KNEW THAT HIS PARENTS WEREN'T COMING BACK.

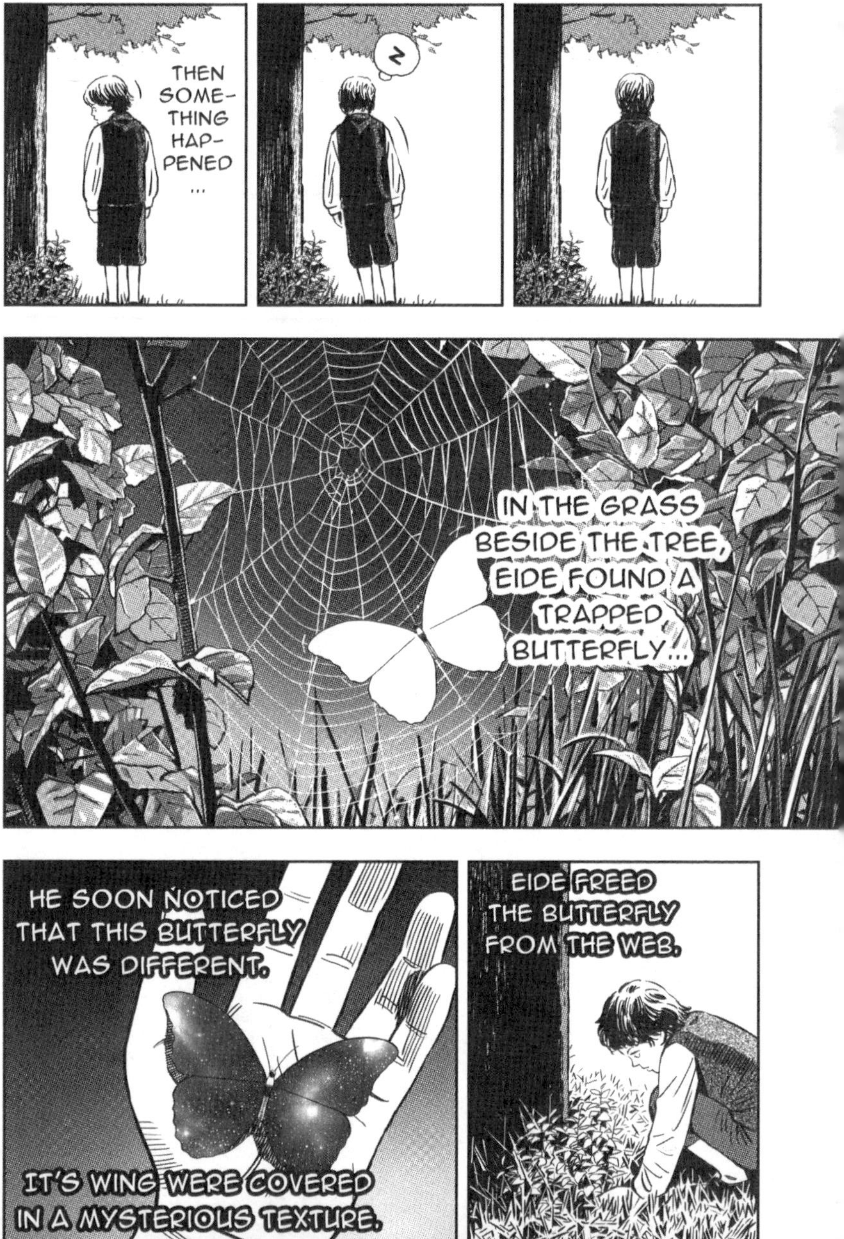

Z
THEN SOMETHING HAPPENED ...
IN THE GRASS BESIDE THE TREE, EIDE FOUND A TRAPPED BUTTERFLY...
EIDE FREED THE BUTTERFLY FROM THE WEB.
HE SOON NOTICED THAT THIS BUTTERFLY WAS DIFFERENT.
IT'S WING WERE COVERED IN A MYSTERIOUS TEXTURE.

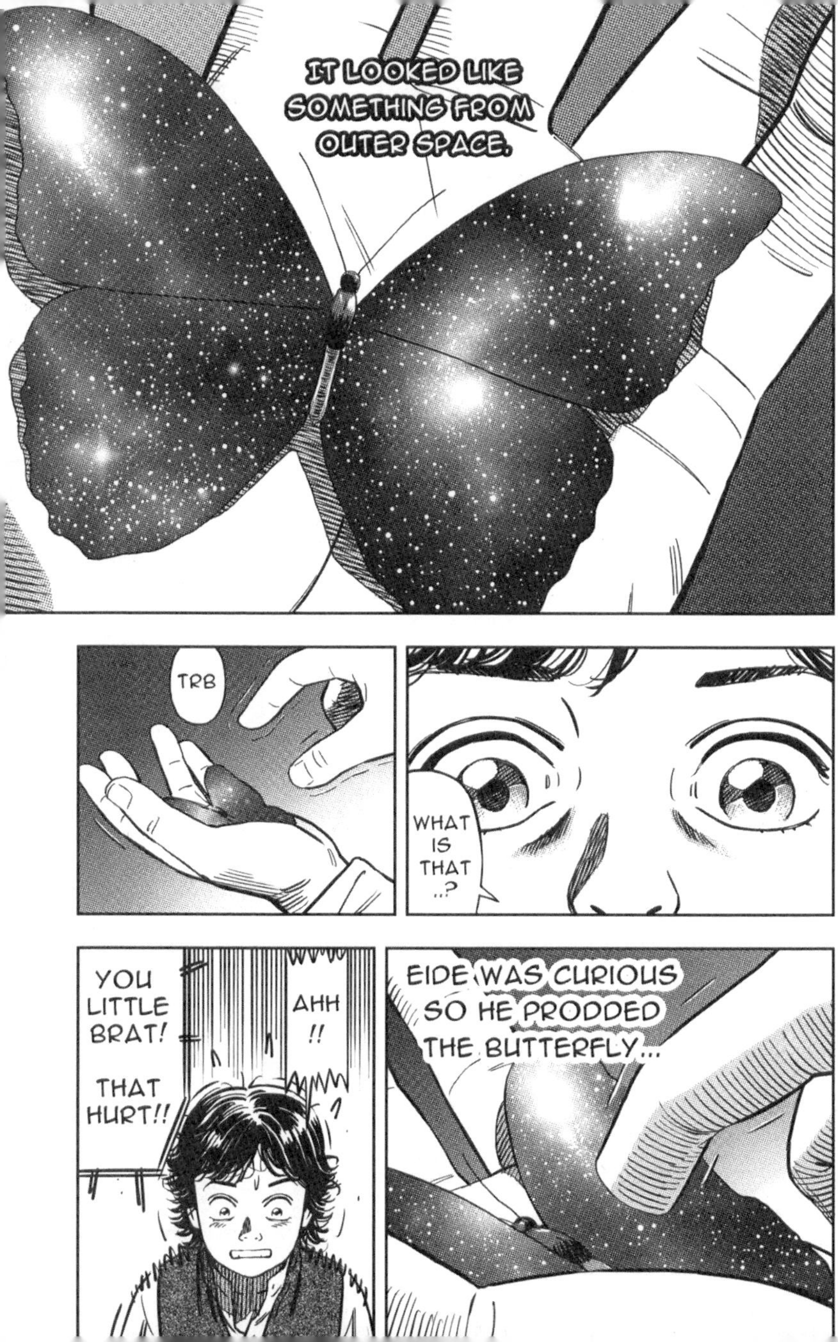
IT LOOKED LIKE SOMETHING FROM OUTER SPACE.
WHAT IS THAT ..?
TRB
EIDE WAS CURIOUS SO HE PRODDED THE BUTTERFLY...
AHH !!
YOU LITTLE BRAT!
THAT HURT!!

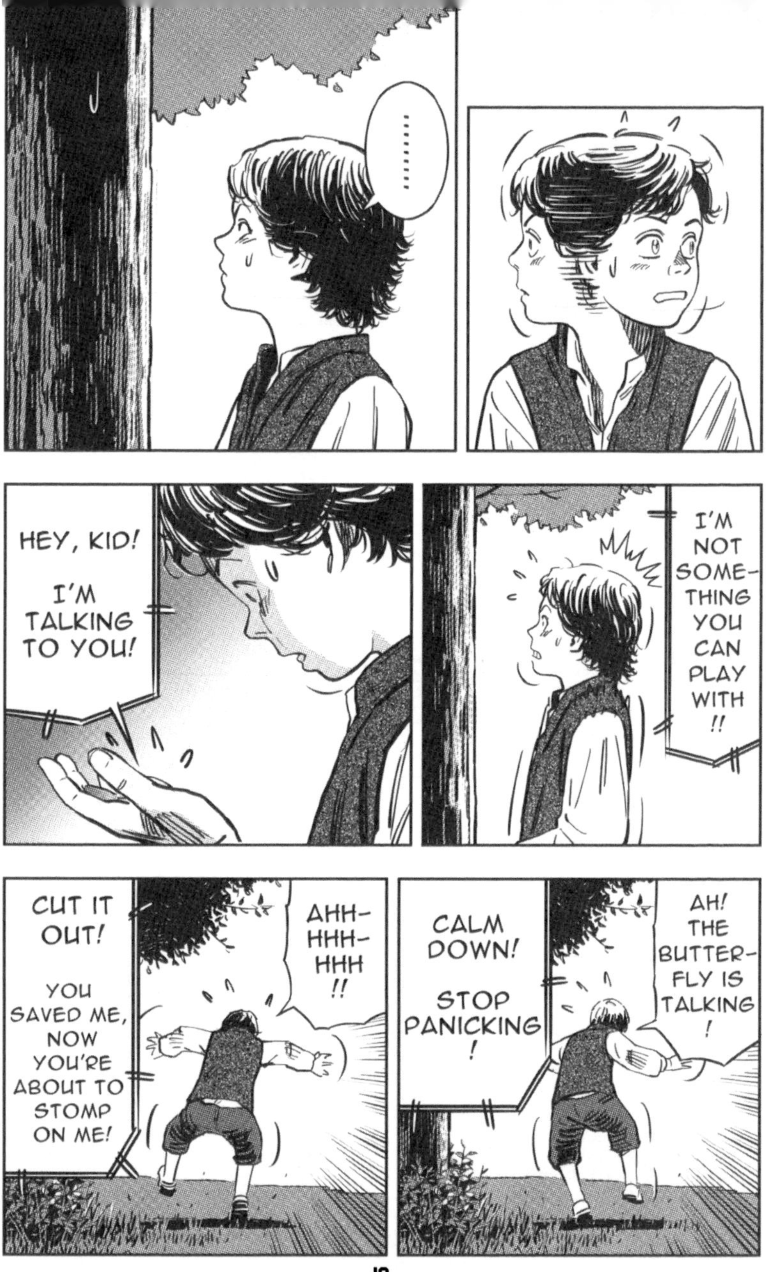
......
I'M NOT SOMETHING YOU CAN PLAY WITH!!
HEY, KID!
I'M TALKING TO YOU!
AH! THE BUTTERFLY IS TALKING!
CALM DOWN!
STOP PANICKING!
AHHHHHHHH!!
CUT IT OUT!
YOU SAVED ME, NOW YOU'RE ABOUT TO STOMP ON ME!

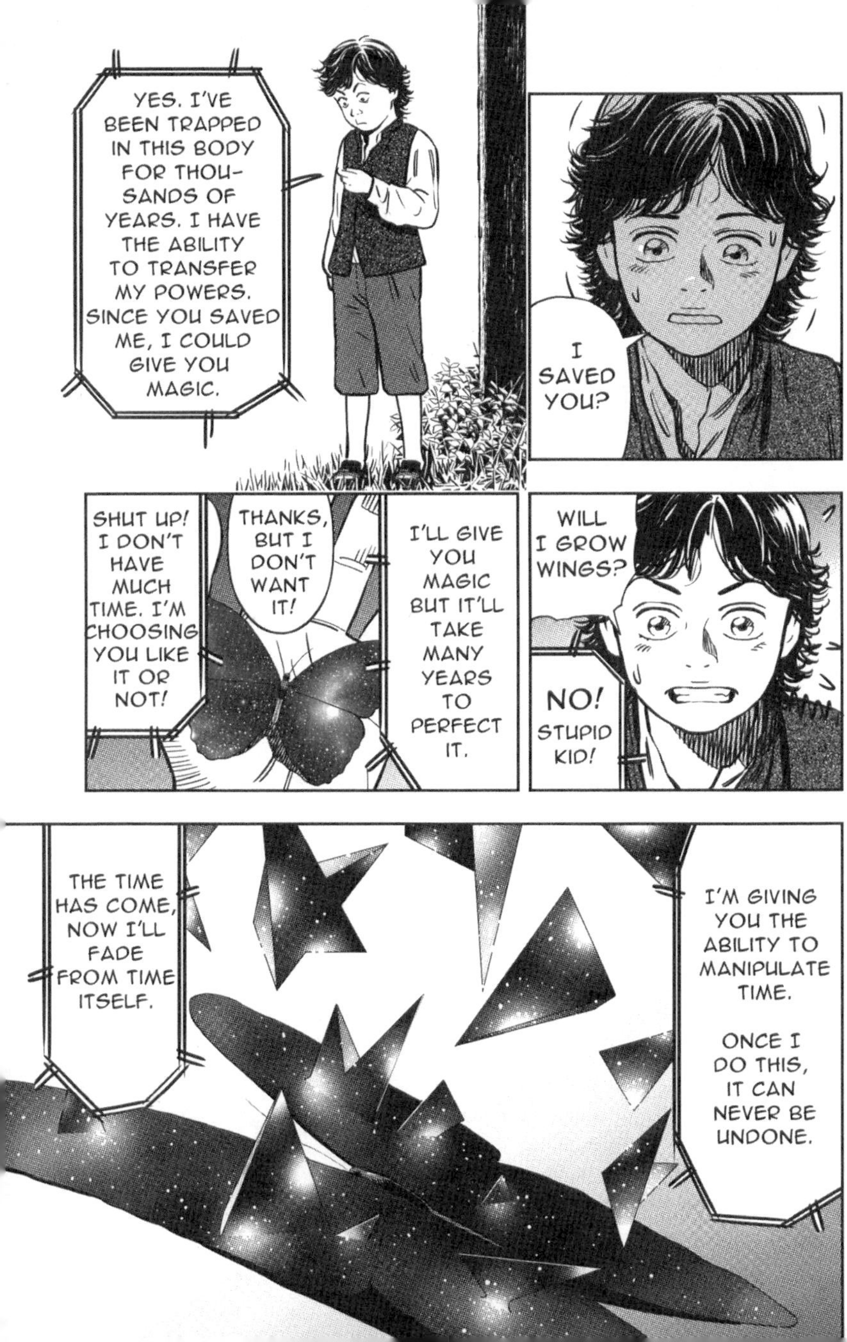
I SAVED YOU?
YES. I'VE BEEN TRAPPED IN THIS BODY FOR THOU-SANDS OF YEARS. I HAVE THE ABILITY TO TRANSFER MY POWERS. SINCE YOU SAVED ME, I COULD GIVE YOU MAGIC.
WILL I GROW WINGS?
NO! STUPID KID!
I'LL GIVE YOU MAGIC BUT IT'LL TAKE MANY YEARS TO PERFECT IT.
THANKS, BUT I DON'T WANT IT!
SHUT UP! I DON'T HAVE MUCH TIME. I'M CHOOSING YOU LIKE IT OR NOT!
I'M GIVING YOU THE ABILITY TO MANIPULATE TIME.
ONCE I DO THIS, IT CAN NEVER BE UNDONE.
THE TIME HAS COME, NOW I'LL FADE FROM TIME ITSELF.

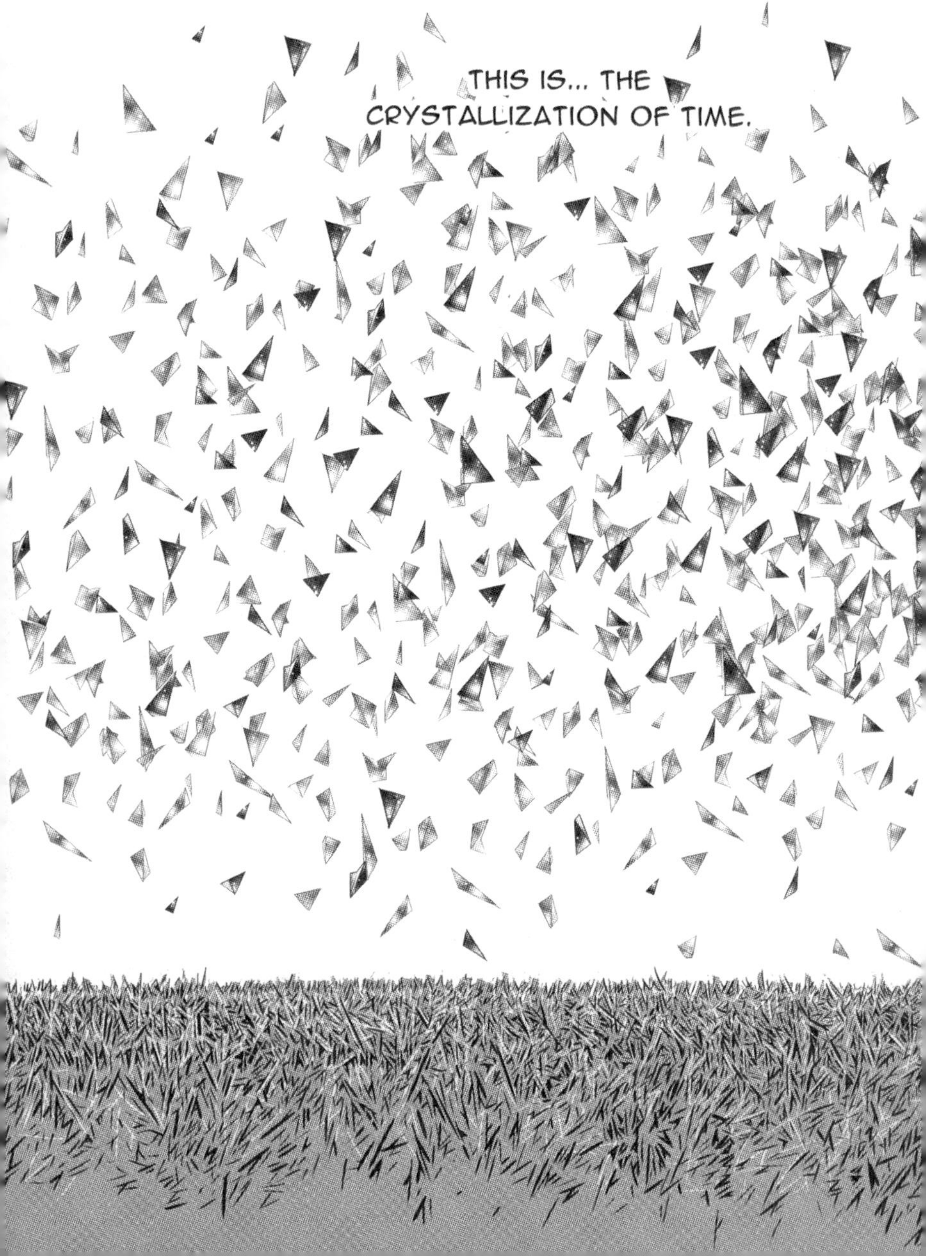
THIS IS... THE CRYSTALLIZATION OF TIME.

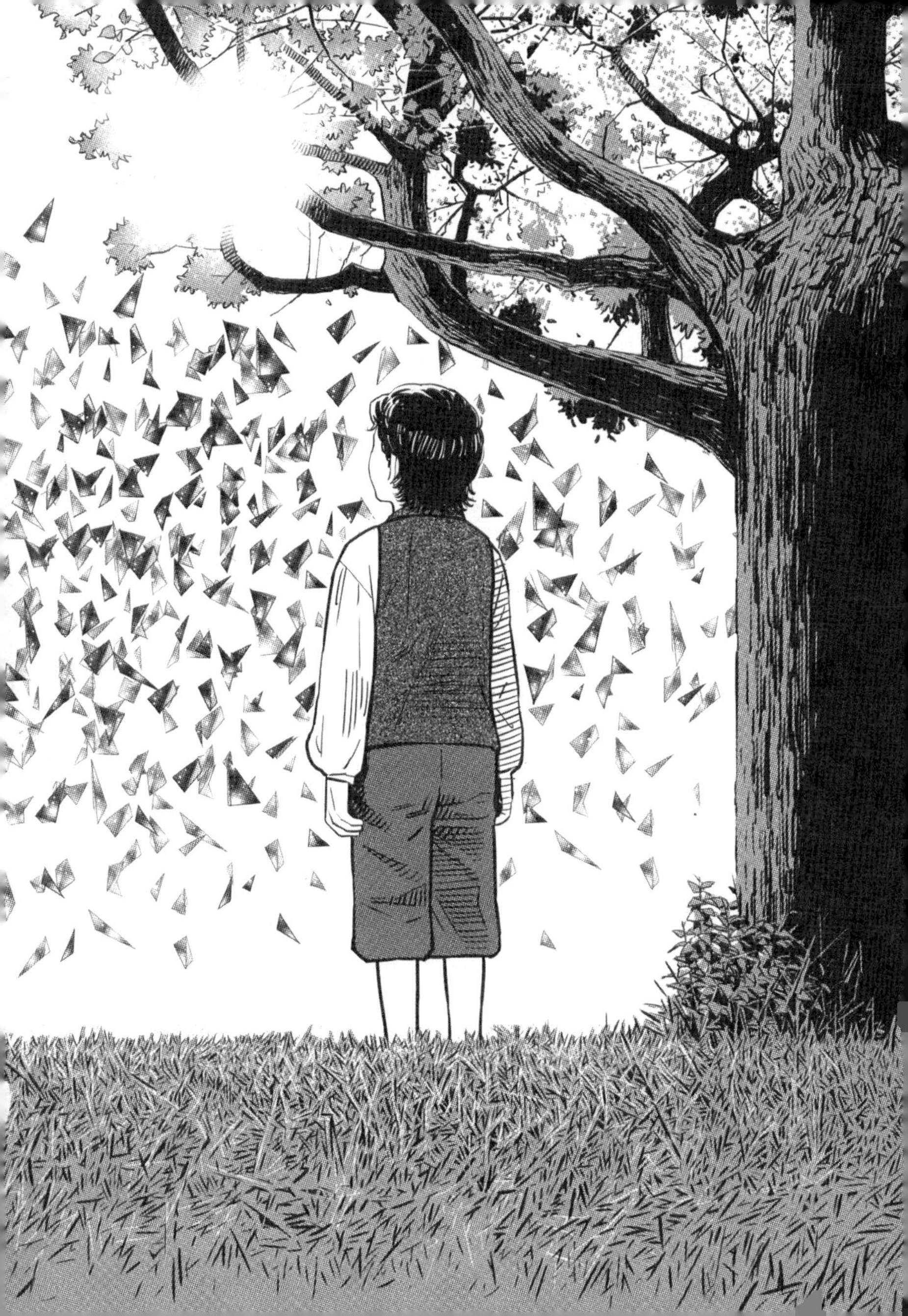

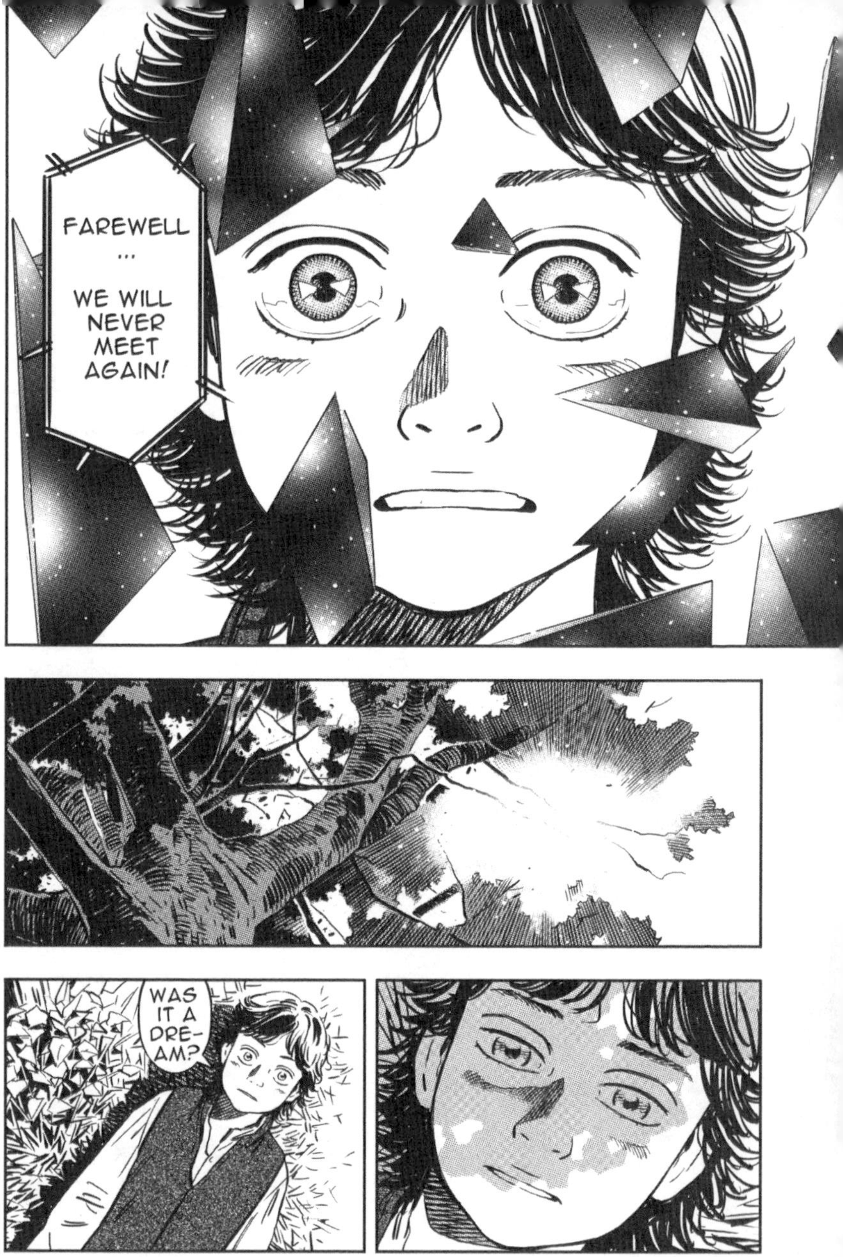
FAREWELL ... WE WILL NEVER MEET AGAIN!
WAS IT A DRE-AM?

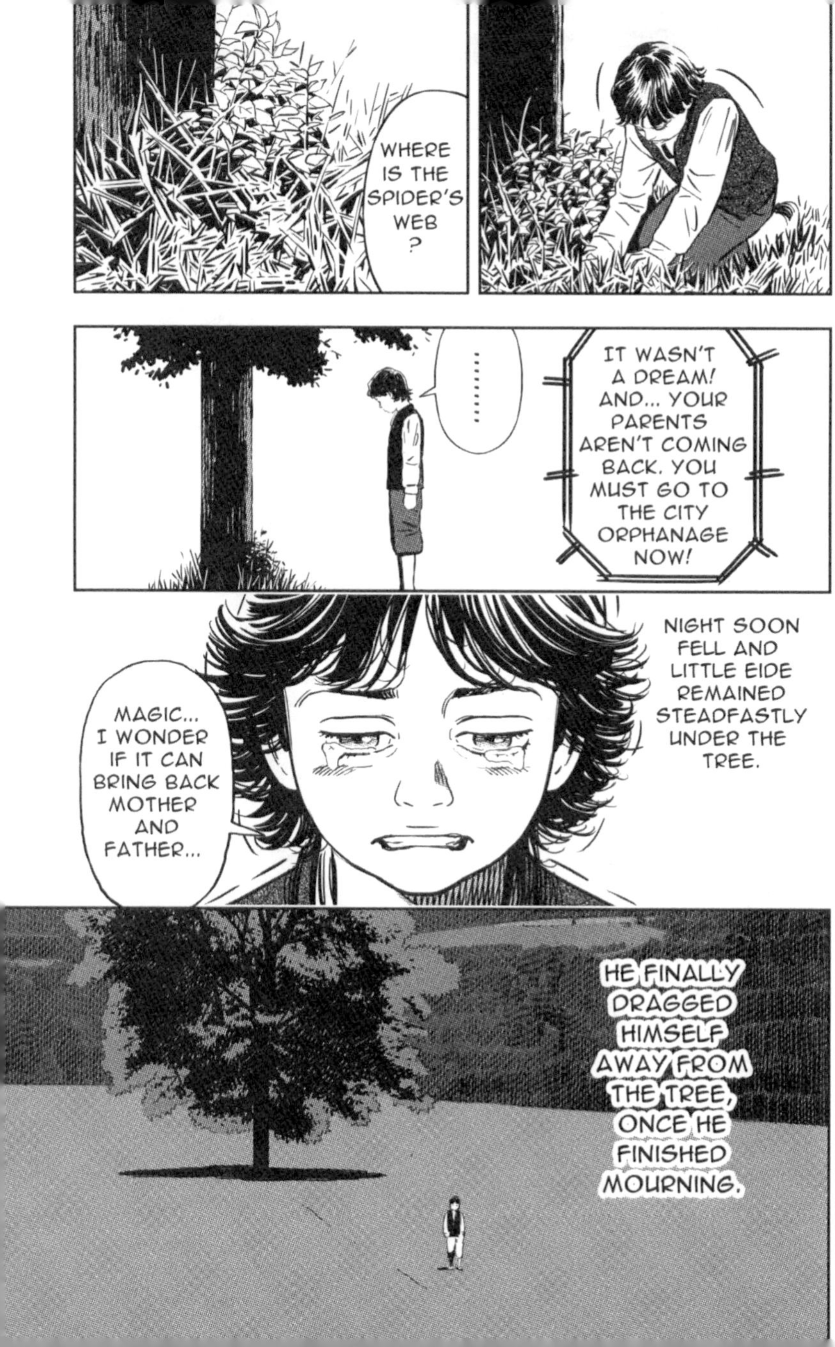
WHERE IS THE SPIDER'S WEB ?
IT WASN'T A DREAM! AND... YOUR PARENTS AREN'T COMING BACK. YOU MUST GO TO THE CITY ORPHANAGE NOW!
....
NIGHT SOON FELL AND LITTLE EIDE REMAINED STEADFASTLY UNDER THE TREE.
MAGIC... I WONDER IF IT CAN BRING BACK MOTHER AND FATHER...
HE FINALLY DRAGGED HIMSELF AWAY FROM THE TREE, ONCE HE FINISHED MOURNING.

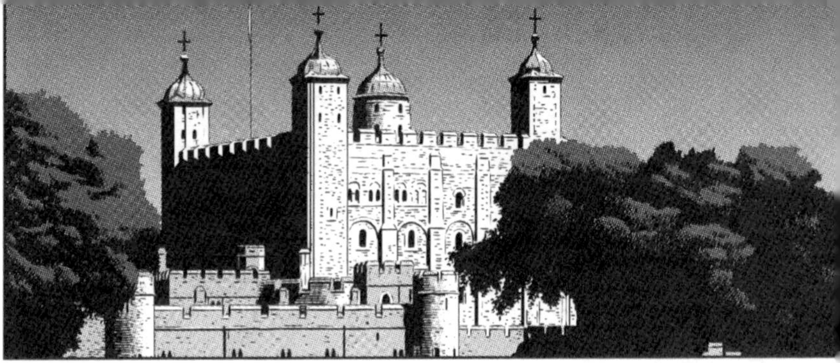

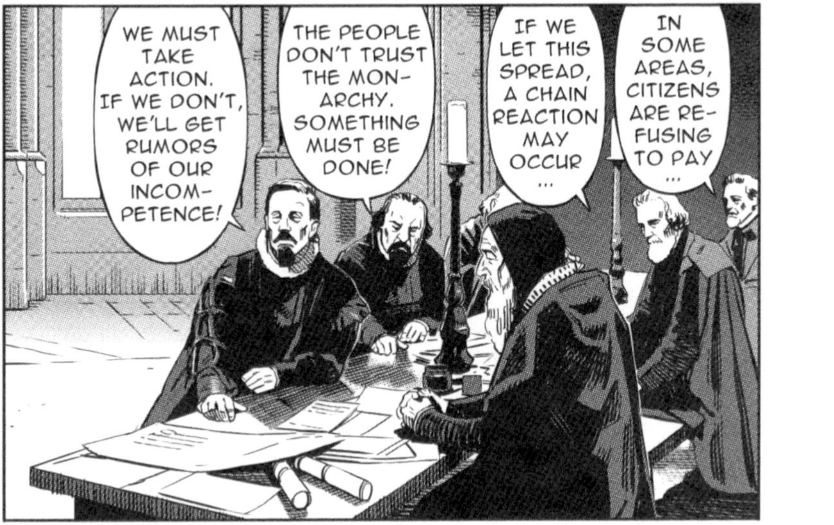
IN SOME AREAS, CITIZENS ARE RE-FUSING TO PAY ...
IF WE LET THIS SPREAD, A CHAIN REACTION MAY OCCUR ...
THE PEOPLE DON'T TRUST THE MON-ARCHY. SOMETHING MUST BE DONE!
WE MUST TAKE ACTION. IF WE DON'T, WE'LL GET RUMORS OF OUR INCOM-PETENCE!

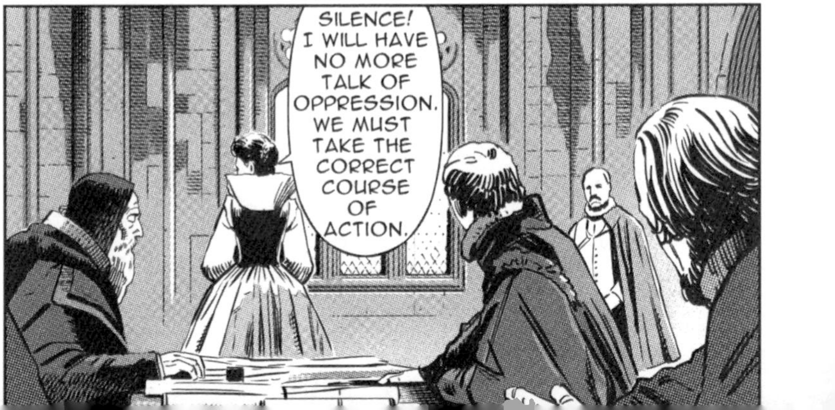
SILENCE! I WILL HAVE NO MORE TALK OF OPPRESSION. WE MUST TAKE THE CORRECT COURSE OF ACTION.

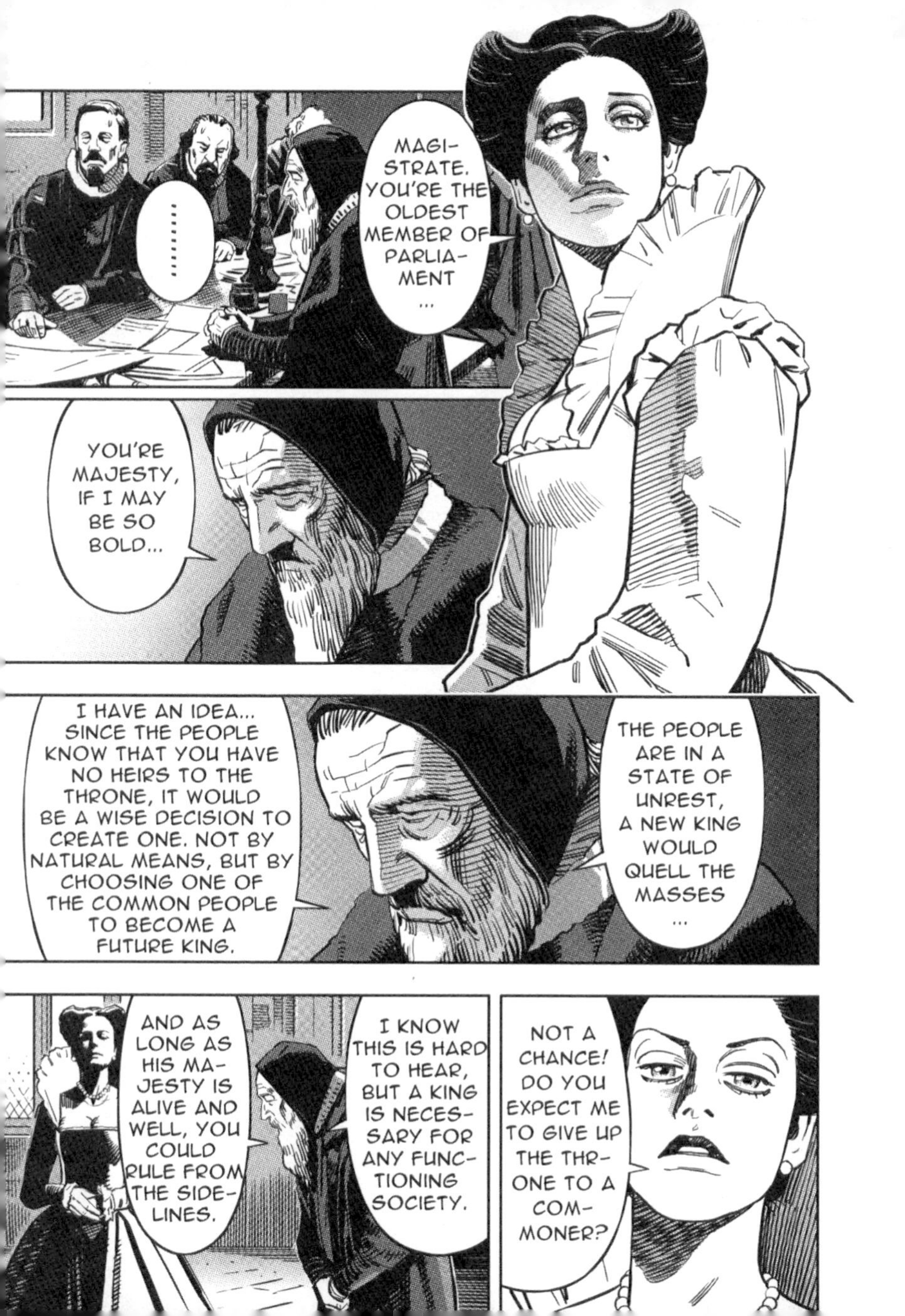
MAGI-STRATE. YOU'RE THE OLDEST MEMBER OF PARLIA-MENT ...
......
YOU'RE MAJESTY, IF I MAY BE SO BOLD...
THE PEOPLE ARE IN A STATE OF UNREST, A NEW KING WOULD QUELL THE MASSES ...
I HAVE AN IDEA... SINCE THE PEOPLE KNOW THAT YOU HAVE NO HEIRS TO THE THRONE, IT WOULD BE A WISE DECISION TO CREATE ONE. NOT BY NATURAL MEANS, BUT BY CHOOSING ONE OF THE COMMON PEOPLE TO BECOME A FUTURE KING.
NOT A CHANCE! DO YOU EXPECT ME TO GIVE UP THE THR-ONE TO A COM-MONER?
I KNOW THIS IS HARD TO HEAR, BUT A KING IS NECES-SARY FOR ANY FUNC-TIONING SOCIETY.
AND AS LONG AS HIS MA-JESTY IS ALIVE AND WELL, YOU COULD RULE FROM THE SIDE-LINES.

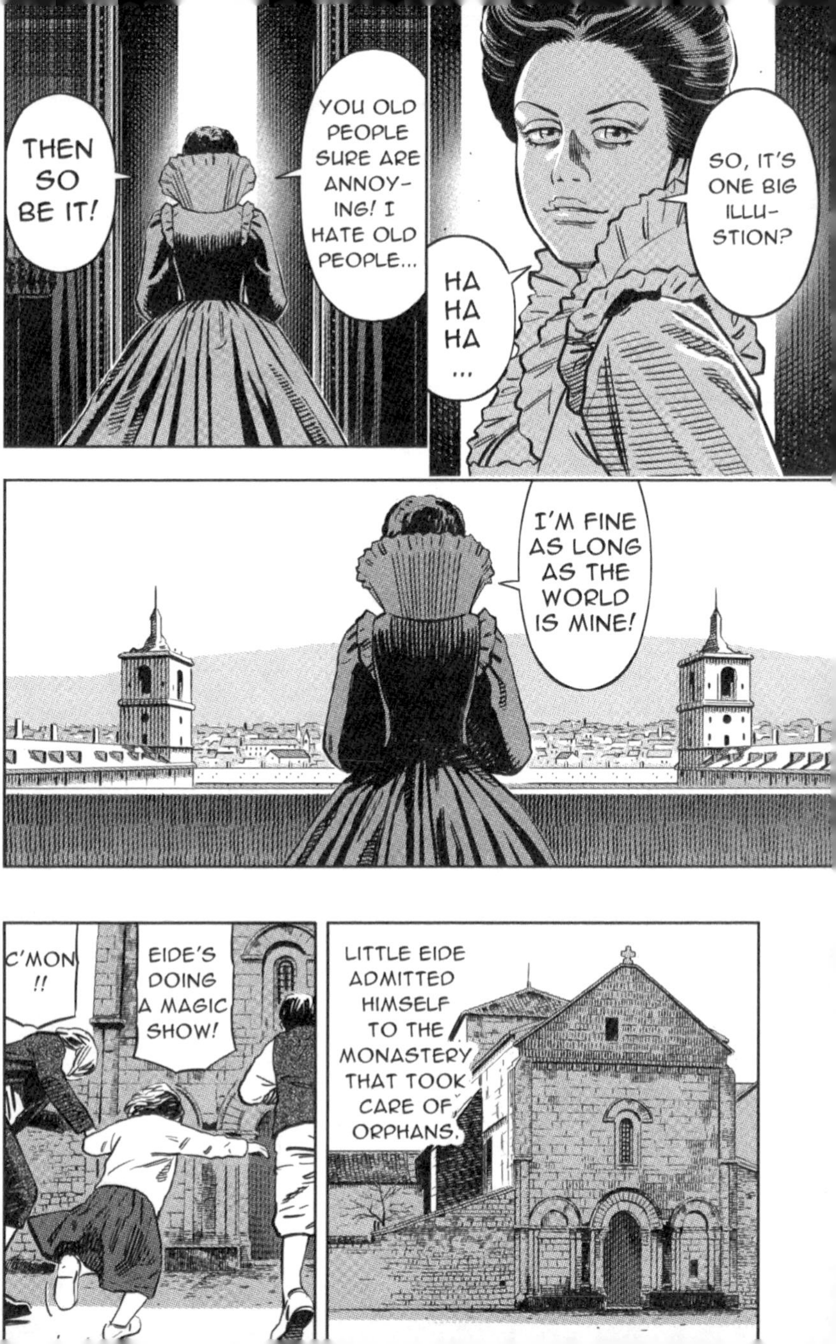
SO, IT'S ONE BIG ILLU-STION?
HA HA HA ...
YOU OLD PEOPLE SURE ARE ANNOY-ING! I HATE OLD PEOPLE...
THEN SO BE IT!
I'M FINE AS LONG AS THE WORLD IS MINE!
LITTLE EIDE ADMITTED HIMSELF TO THE MONASTERY THAT TOOK CARE OF ORPHANS.
EIDE'S DOING A MAGIC SHOW!
C'MON !!

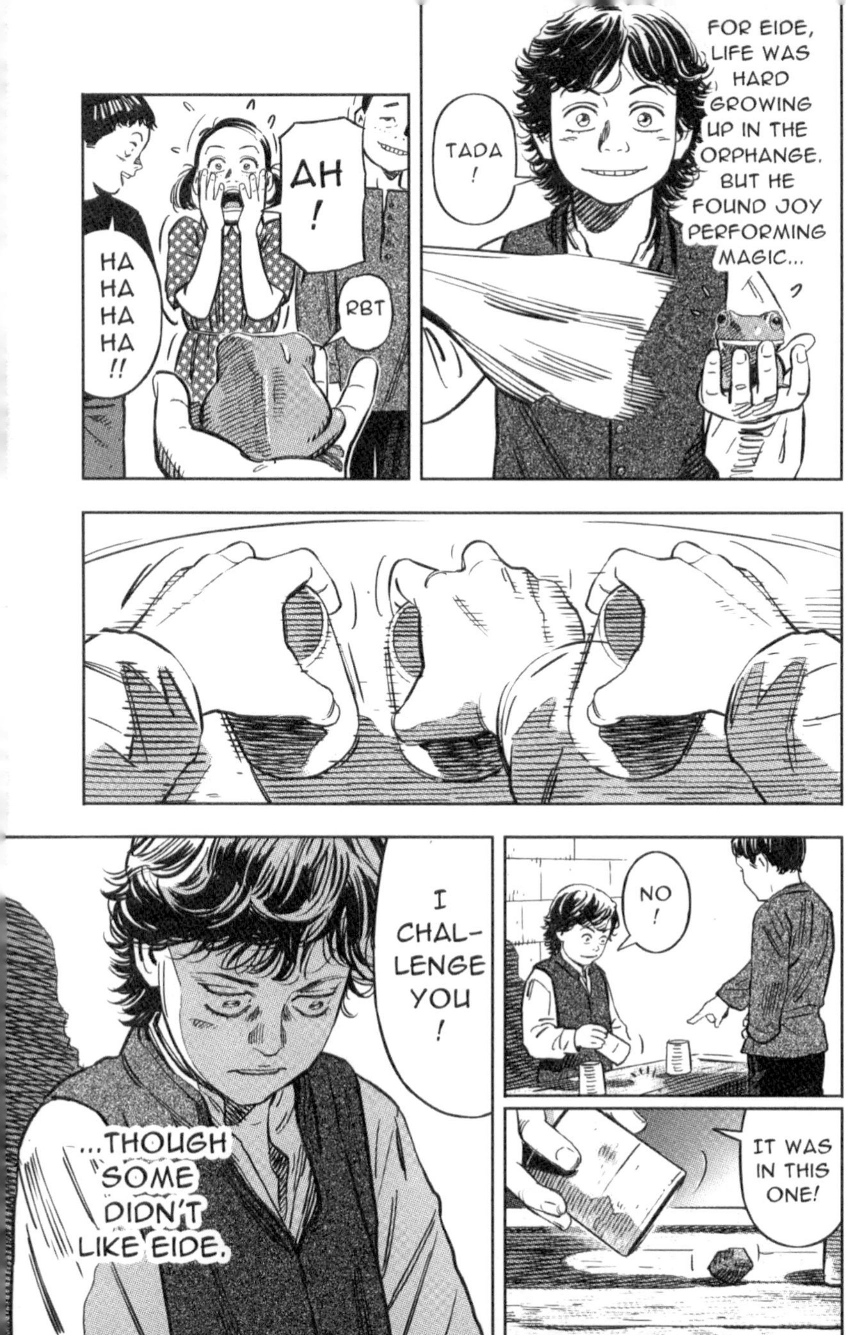
FOR EIDE, LIFE WAS HARD GROWING UP IN THE ORPHANGE. BUT HE FOUND JOY PERFORMING MAGIC...
TADA!
AH!
RBT
HA HA HA HA!!
NO!
IT WAS IN THIS ONE!
I CHAL- LENGE YOU!
...THOUGH SOME DIDN'T LIKE EIDE.

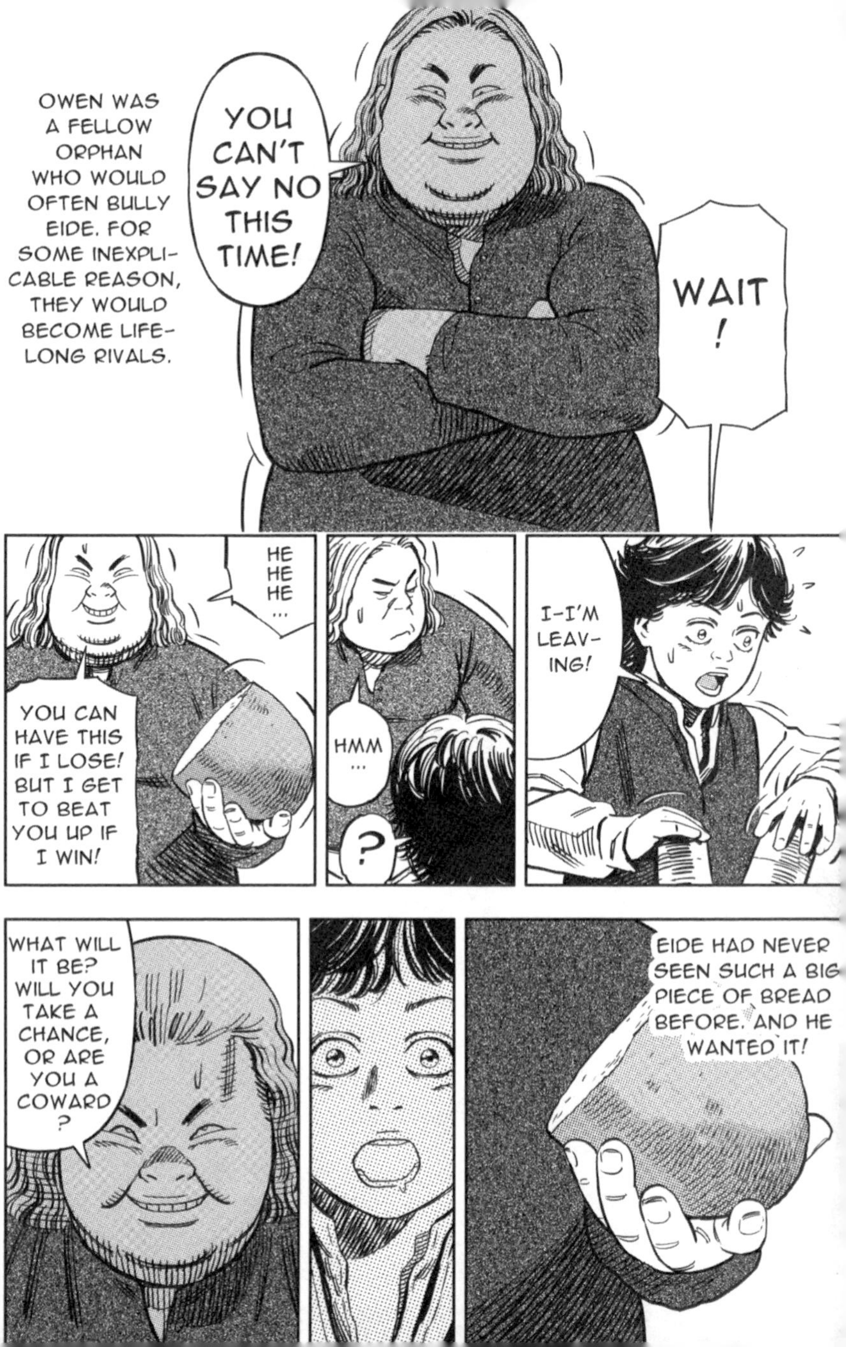
WAIT!
YOU CAN'T SAY NO THIS TIME!
OWEN WAS A FELLOW ORPHAN WHO WOULD OFTEN BULLY EIDE. FOR SOME INEXPLICABLE REASON, THEY WOULD BECOME LIFELONG RIVALS.
I-I'M LEAVING!
HMM...
?
HE HE HE...
YOU CAN HAVE THIS IF I LOSE! BUT I GET TO BEAT YOU UP IF I WIN!
EIDE HAD NEVER SEEN SUCH A BIG PIECE OF BREAD BEFORE. AND HE WANTED IT!
WHAT WILL IT BE? WILL YOU TAKE A CHANCE, OR ARE YOU A COWARD?

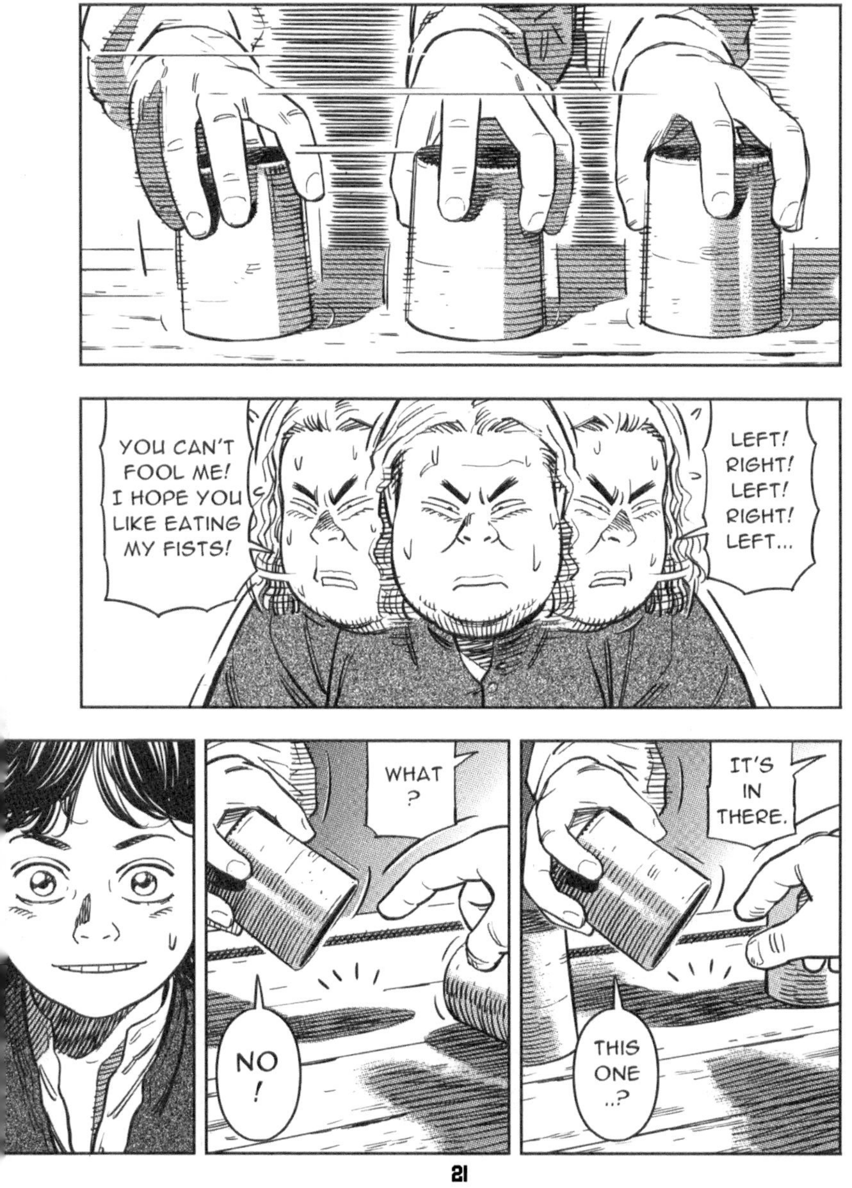
LEFT! RIGHT! LEFT! RIGHT! LEFT...
YOU CAN'T FOOL ME! I HOPE YOU LIKE EATING MY FISTS!
IT'S IN THERE.
THIS ONE ..?
WHAT ?
NO !

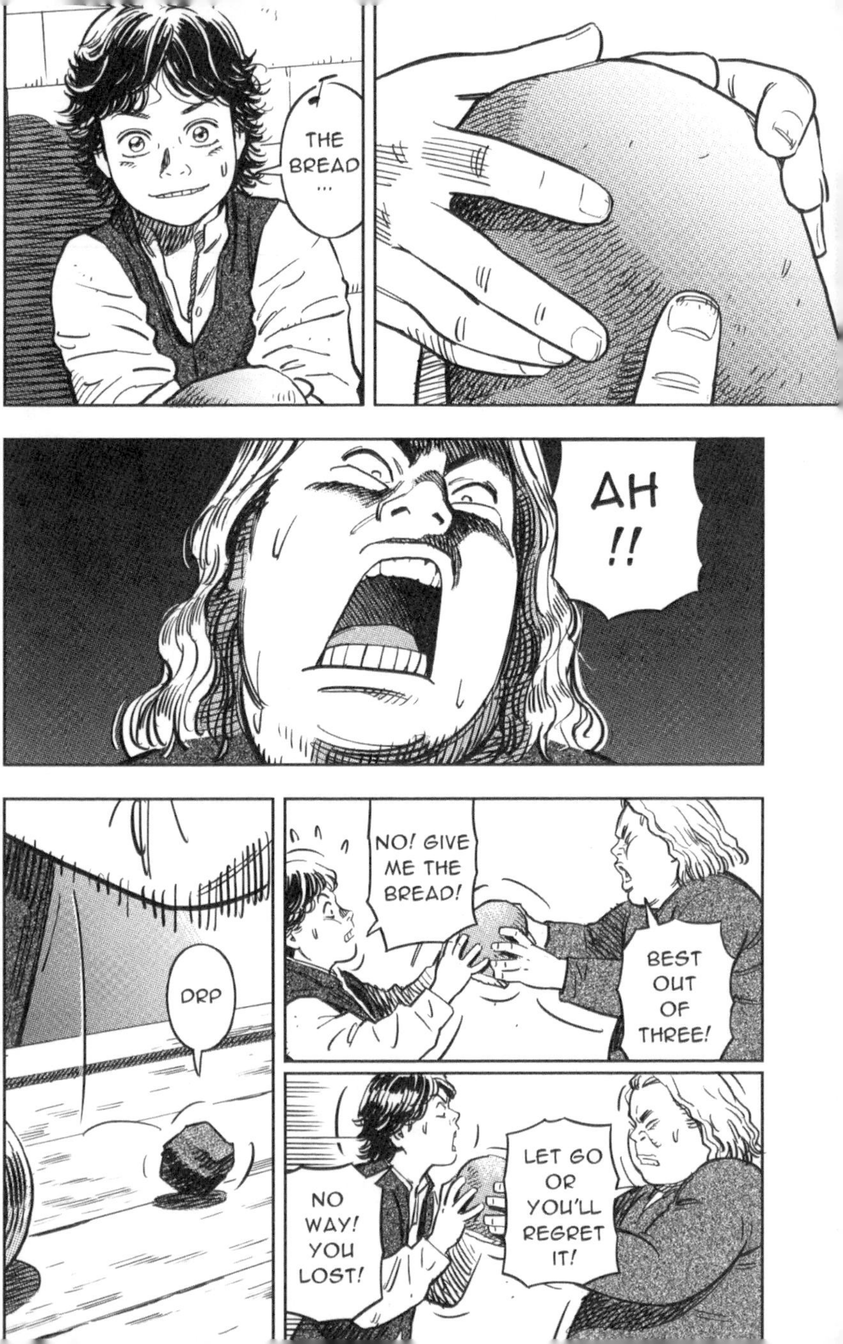
THE BREAD ...
AH !!
NO! GIVE ME THE BREAD!
BEST OUT OF THREE!
LET GO OR YOU'LL REGRET IT!
NO WAY! YOU LOST!
DRP

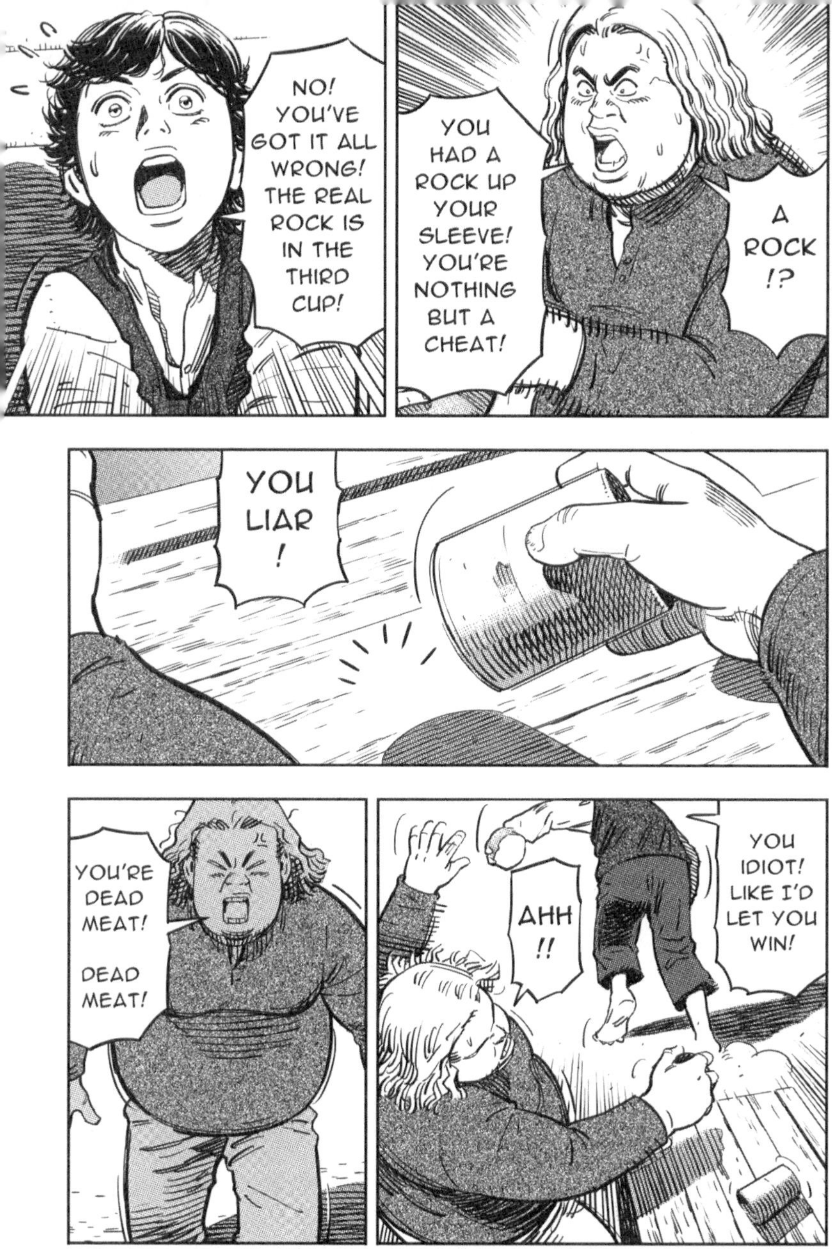
A ROCK !?
YOU HAD A ROCK UP YOUR SLEEVE! YOU'RE NOTHING BUT A CHEAT!
NO! YOU'VE GOT IT ALL WRONG! THE REAL ROCK IS IN THE THIRD CUP!
YOU LIAR !
YOU IDIOT! LIKE I'D LET YOU WIN!
AHH !!
YOU'RE DEAD MEAT!
DEAD MEAT!

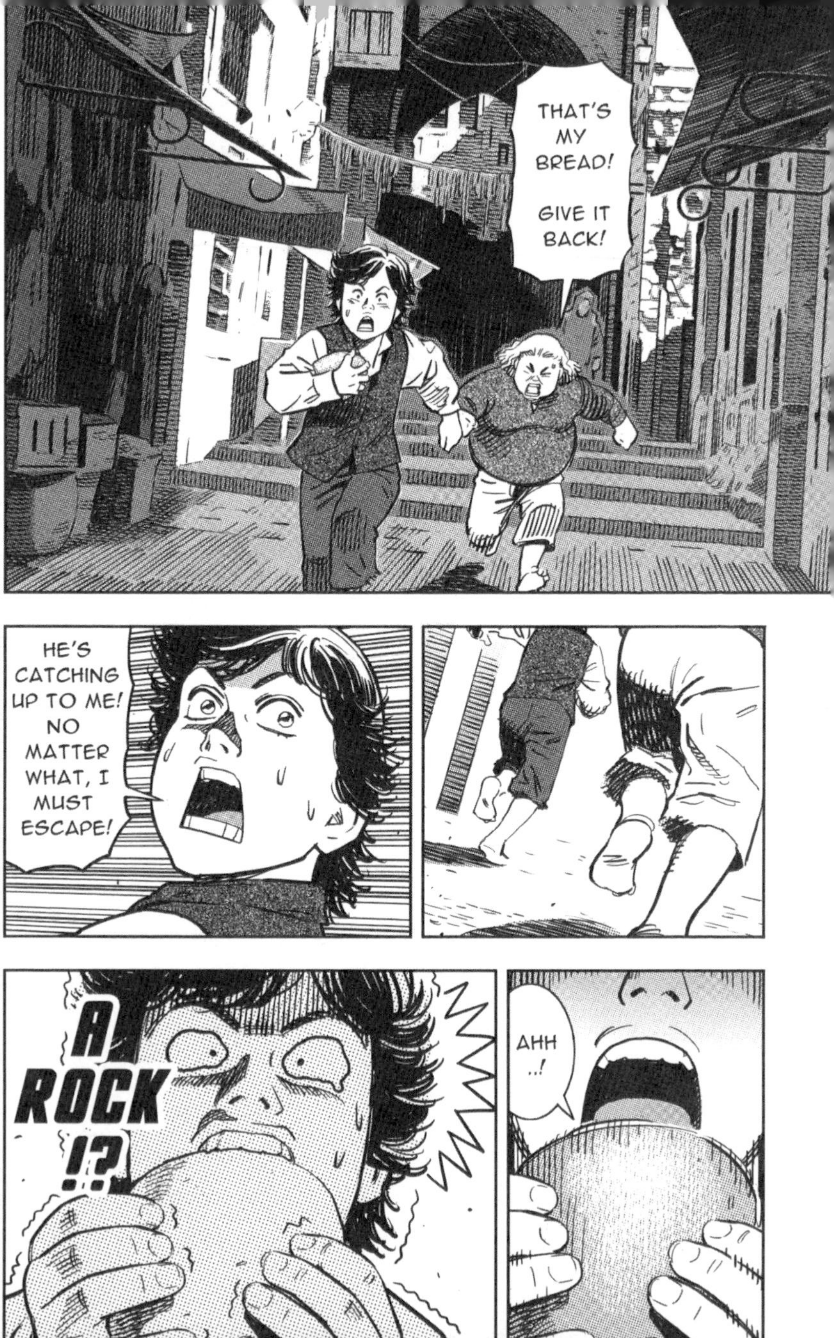
THAT'S MY BREAD!
GIVE IT BACK!
HE'S CATCHING UP TO ME! NO MATTER WHAT, I MUST ESCAPE!
AHH ..!
A ROCK !?

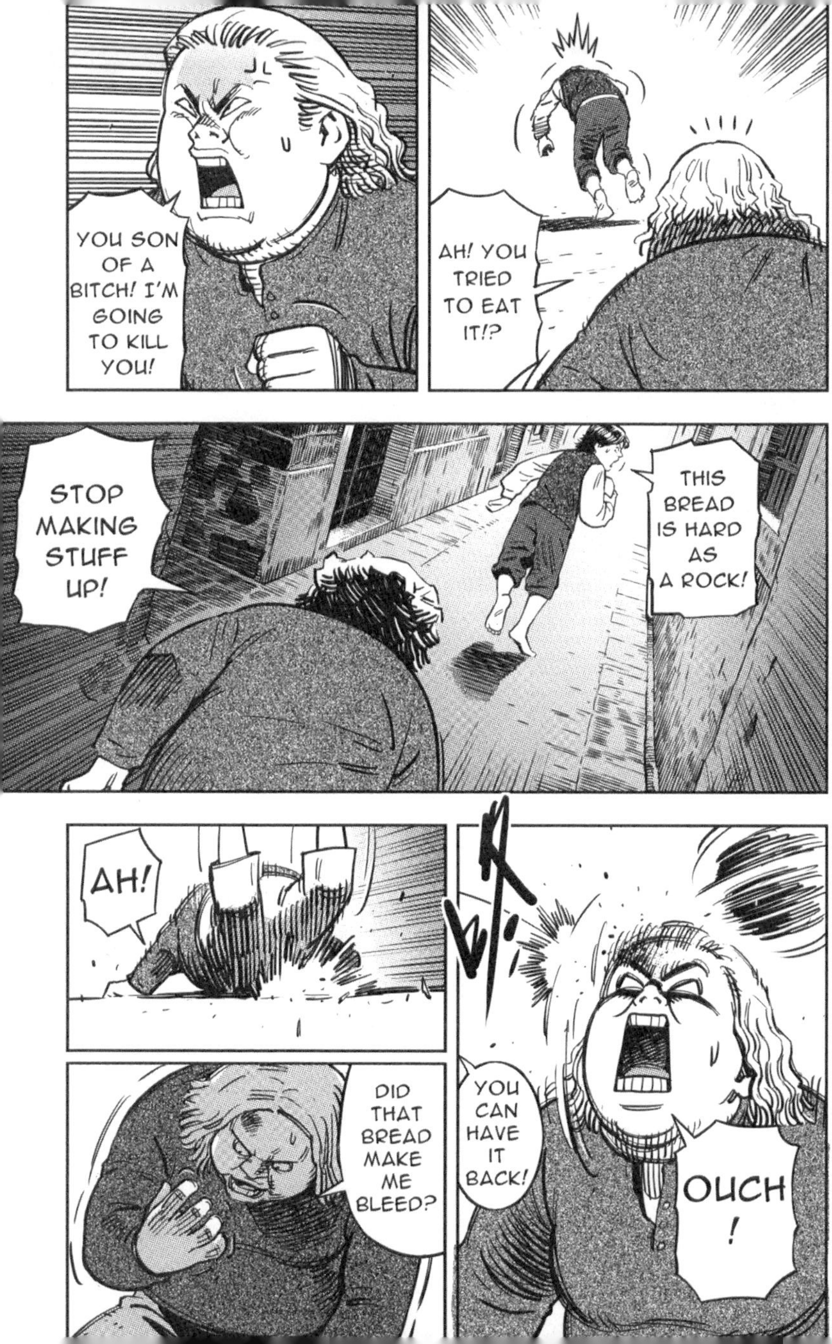
AH! YOU TRIED TO EAT IT!?
YOU SON OF A BITCH! I'M GOING TO KILL YOU!
THIS BREAD IS HARD AS A ROCK!
STOP MAKING STUFF UP!
YOU CAN HAVE IT BACK!
OUCH!
AH!
DID THAT BREAD MAKE ME BLEED?

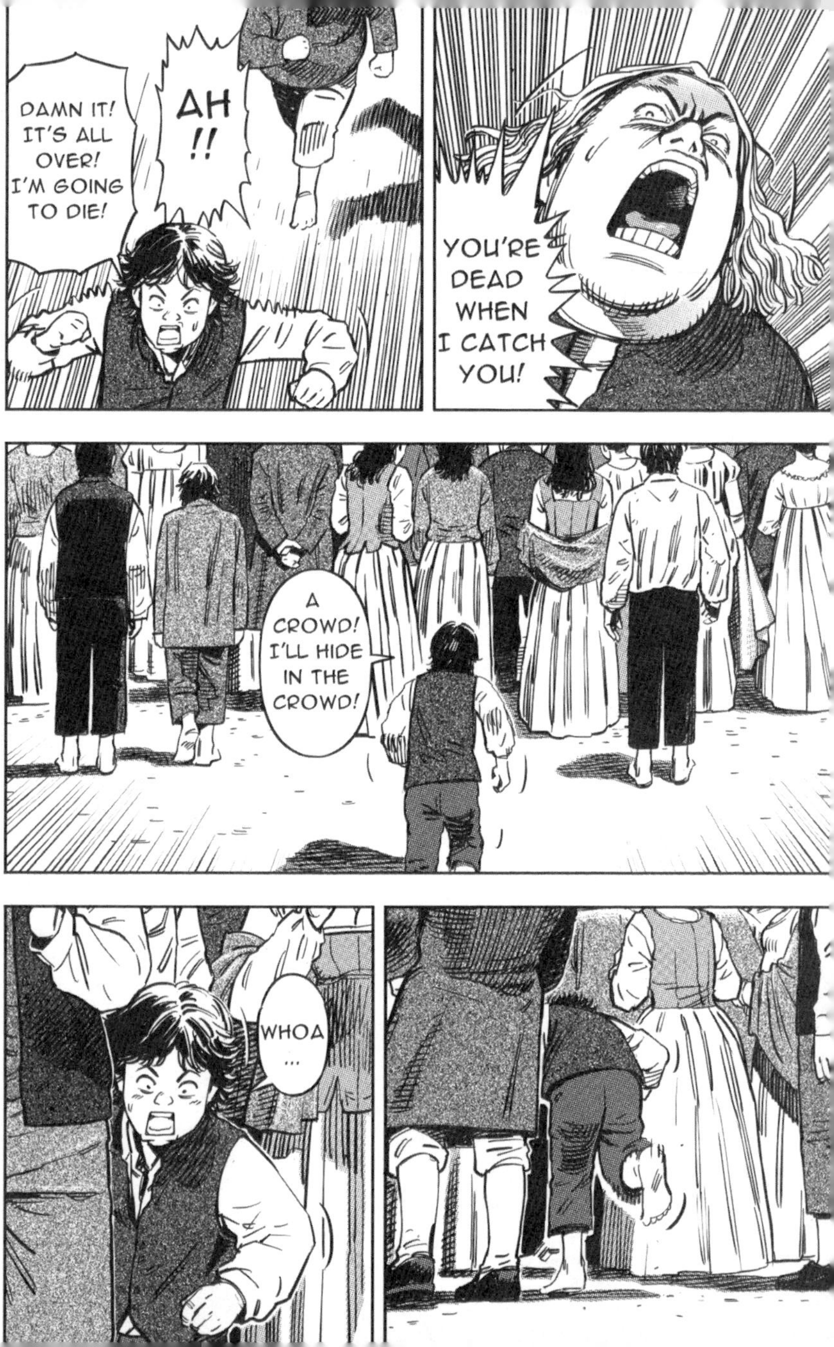
YOU'RE DEAD WHEN I CATCH YOU!
AH !!
DAMN IT! IT'S ALL OVER! I'M GOING TO DIE!
A CROWD! I'LL HIDE IN THE CROWD!
WHOA ...

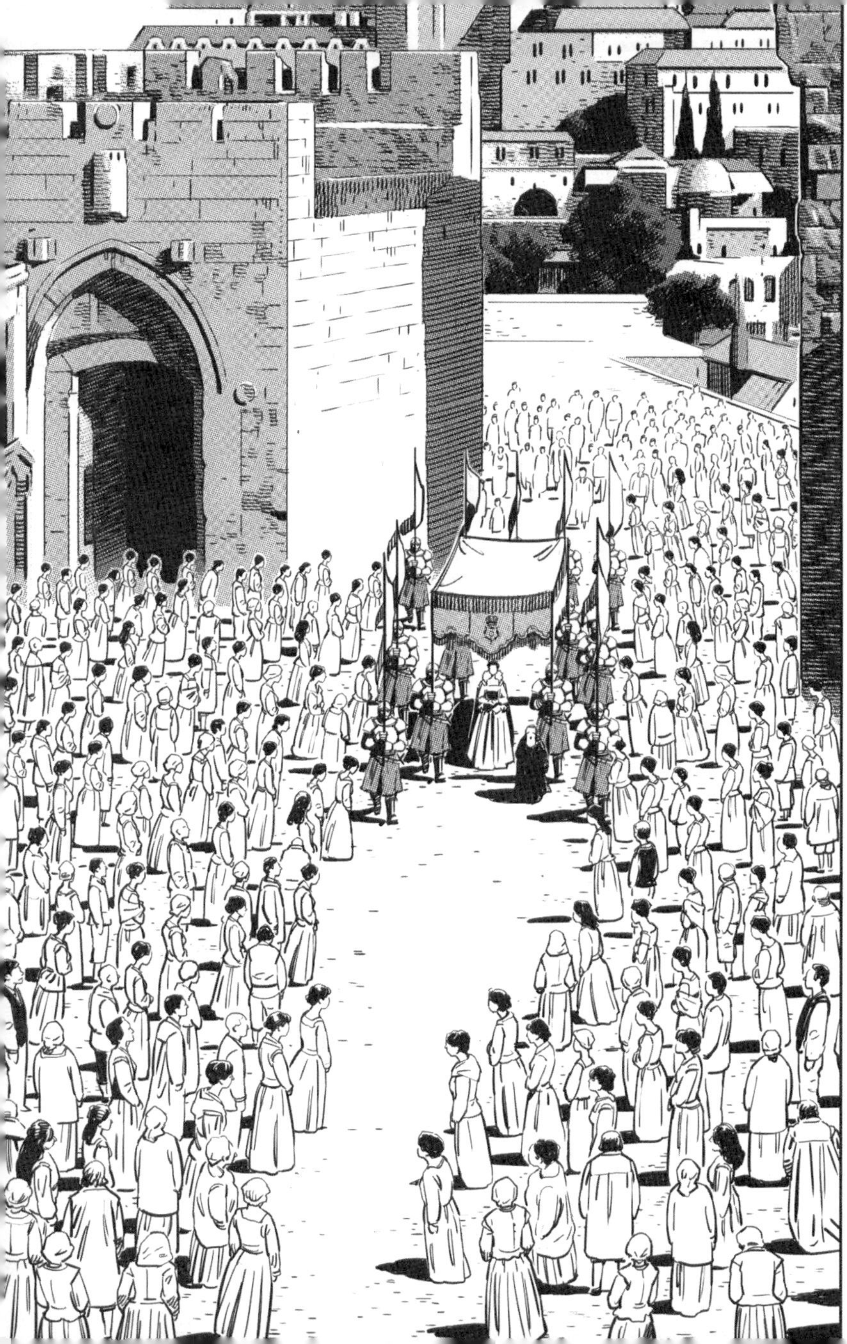

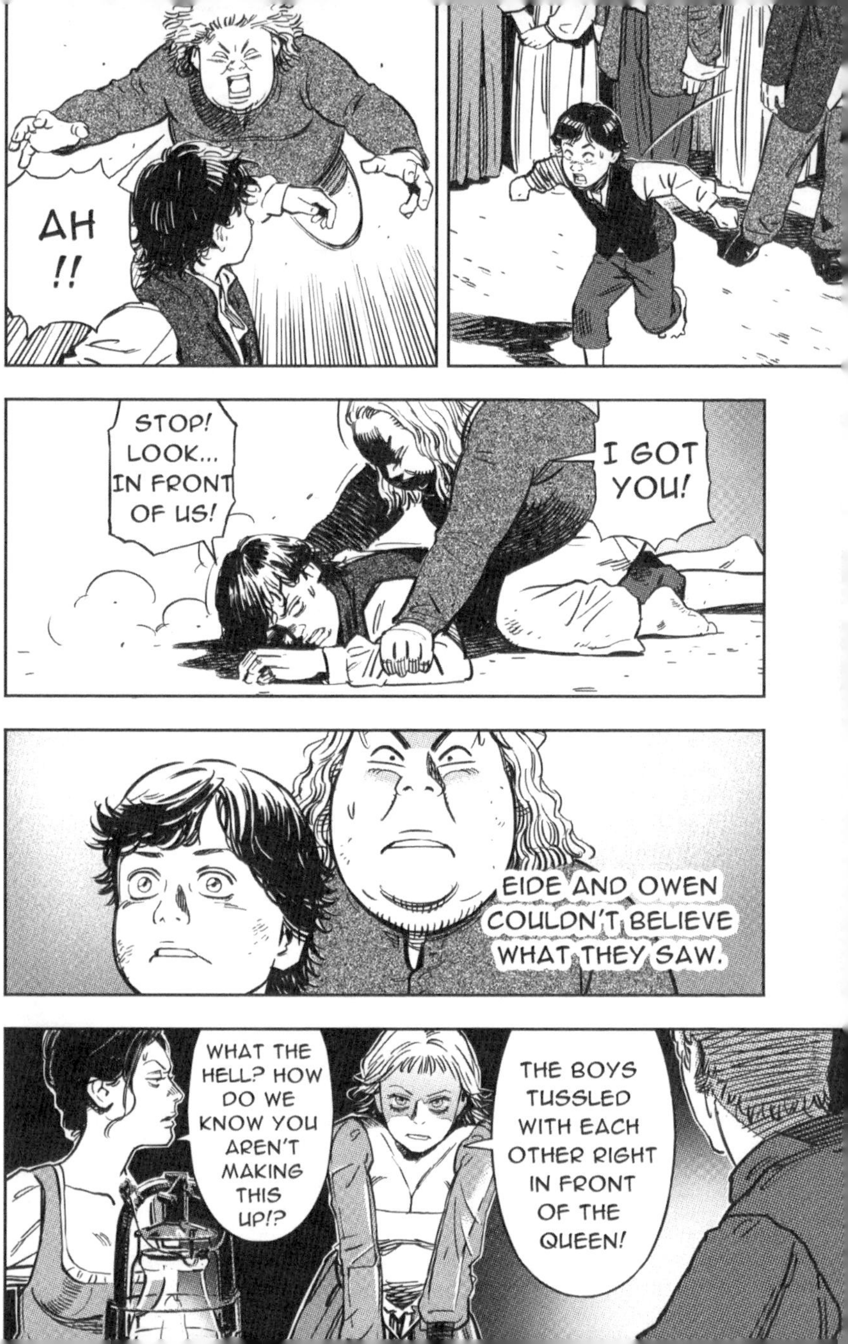
AH !!
I GOT YOU!
STOP! LOOK... IN FRONT OF US!
EIDE AND OWEN COULDN'T BELIEVE WHAT THEY SAW.
THE BOYS TUSSLED WITH EACH OTHER RIGHT IN FRONT OF THE QUEEN!
WHAT THE HELL? HOW DO WE KNOW YOU AREN'T MAKING THIS UP!?

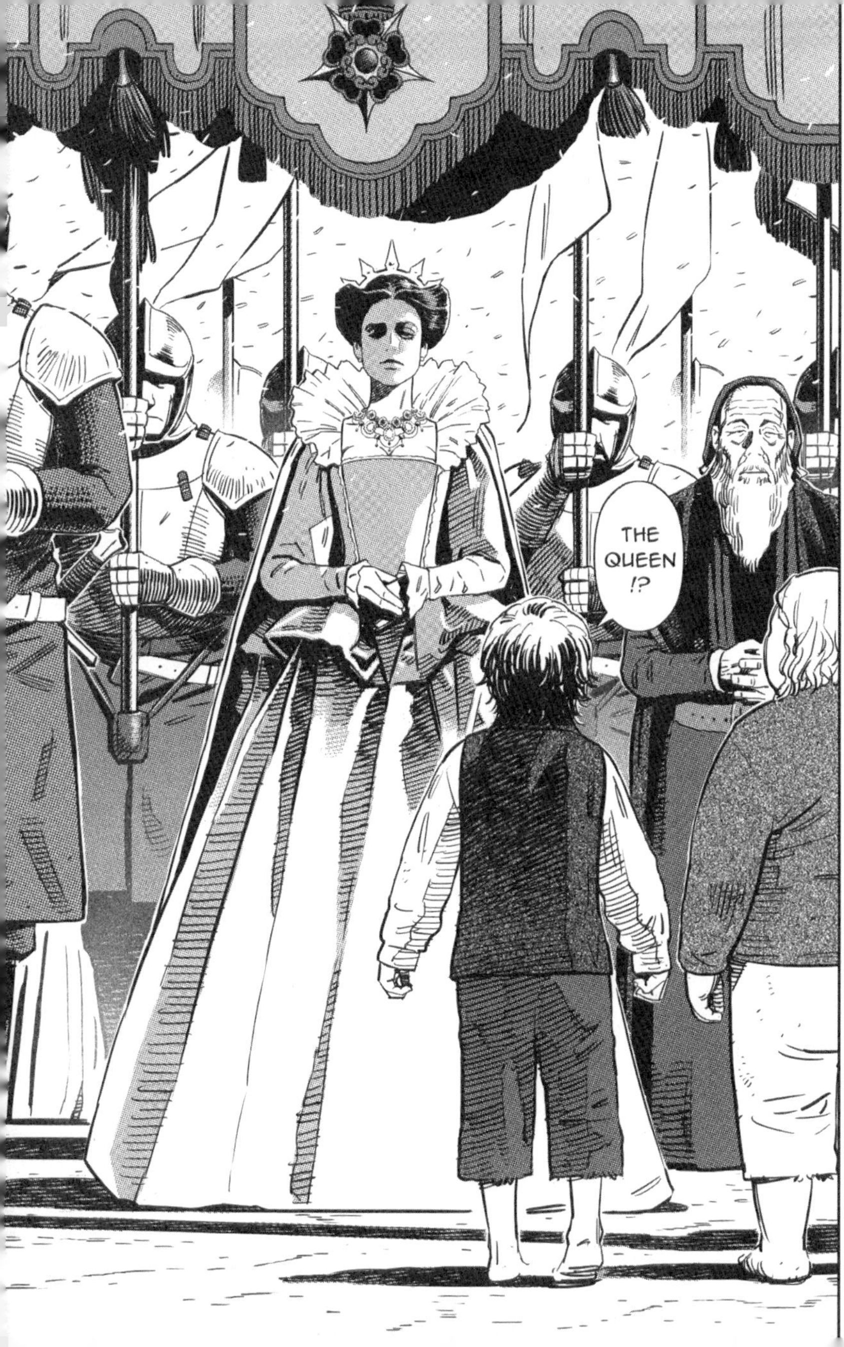
THE QUEEN !?

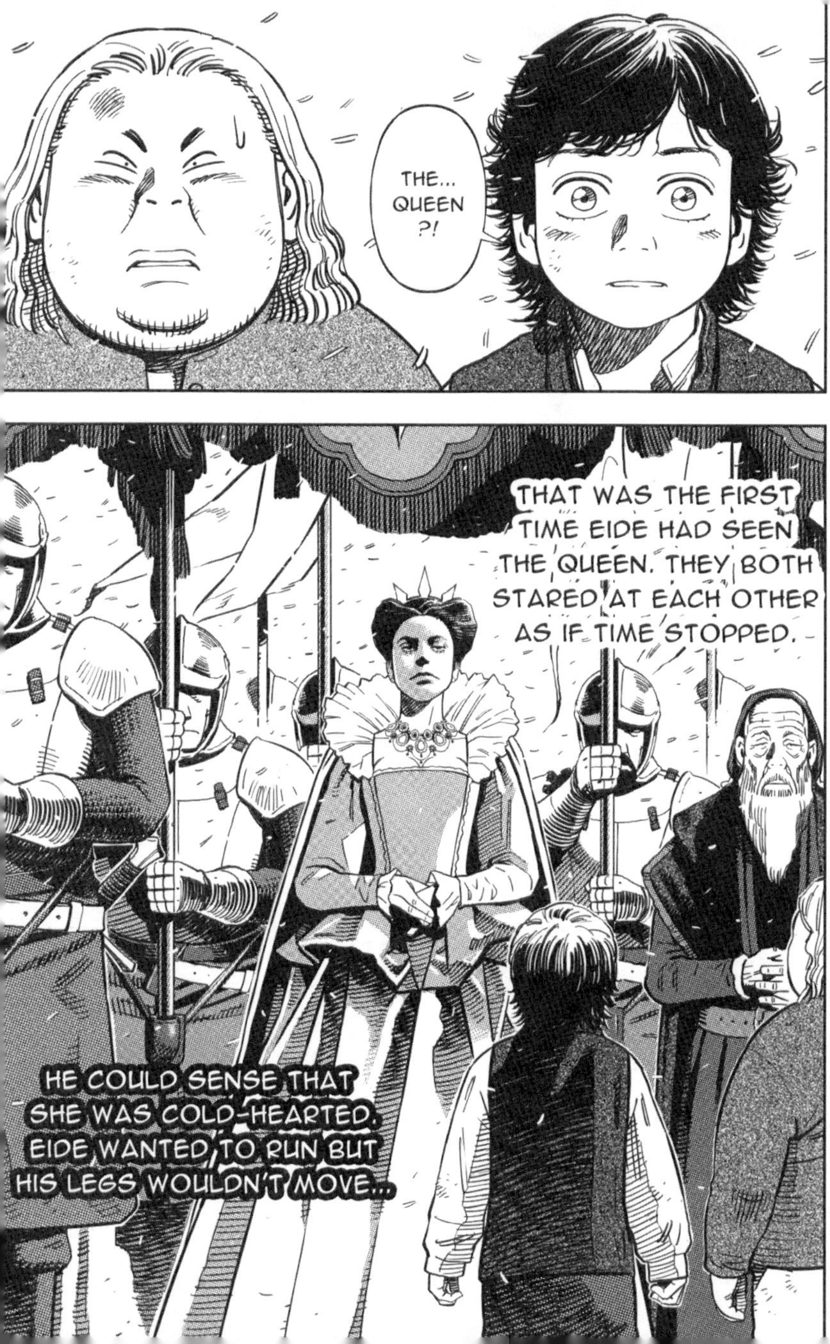
THE... QUEEN ?!
THAT WAS THE FIRST TIME EIDE HAD SEEN THE QUEEN. THEY BOTH STARED AT EACH OTHER AS IF TIME STOPPED.
HE COULD SENSE THAT SHE WAS COLD-HEARTED. EIDE WANTED TO RUN BUT HIS LEGS WOULDN'T MOVE...

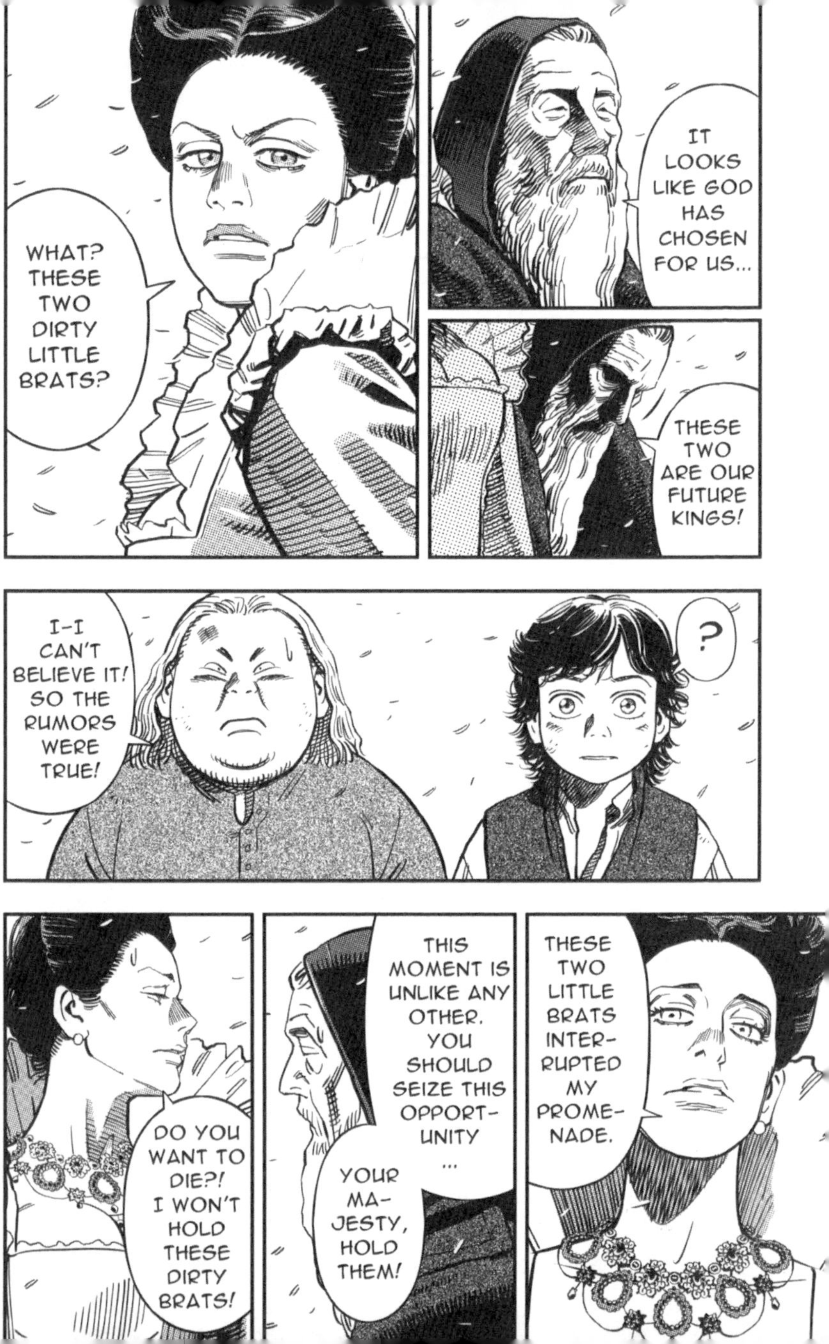
IT LOOKS LIKE GOD HAS CHOSEN FOR US...
THESE TWO ARE OUR FUTURE KINGS!
WHAT? THESE TWO DIRTY LITTLE BRATS?
?
I-I CAN'T BELIEVE IT! SO THE RUMORS WERE TRUE!
THESE TWO LITTLE BRATS INTERRUPTED MY PROMENADE.
THIS MOMENT IS UNLIKE ANY OTHER. YOU SHOULD SEIZE THIS OPPORTUNITY ...
YOUR MAJESTY, HOLD THEM!
DO YOU WANT TO DIE?! I WON'T HOLD THESE DIRTY BRATS!

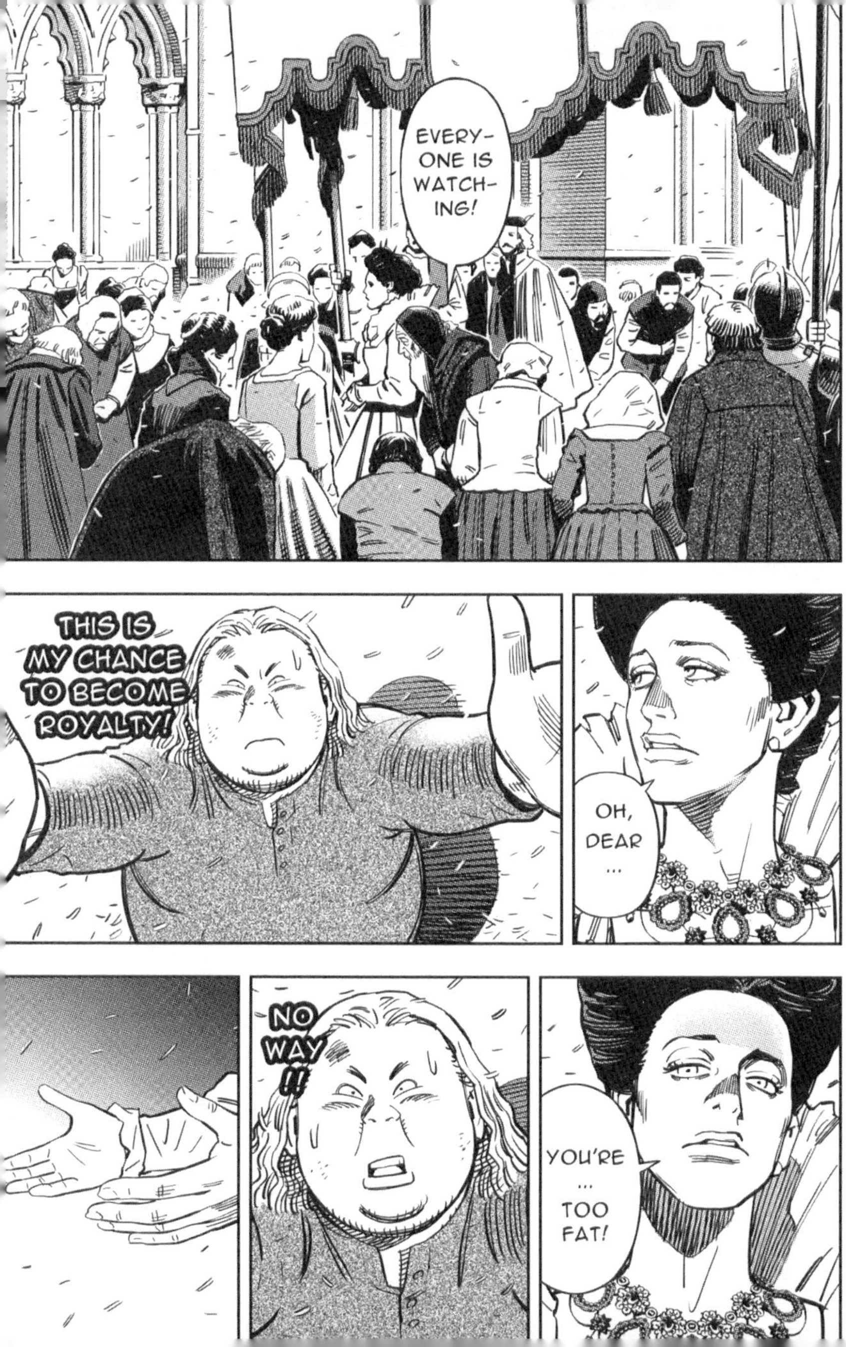
EVERY-ONE IS WATCHING!
OH, DEAR ...
THIS IS MY CHANCE TO BECOME ROYALTY!
YOU'RE ... TOO FAT!
NO WAY !!

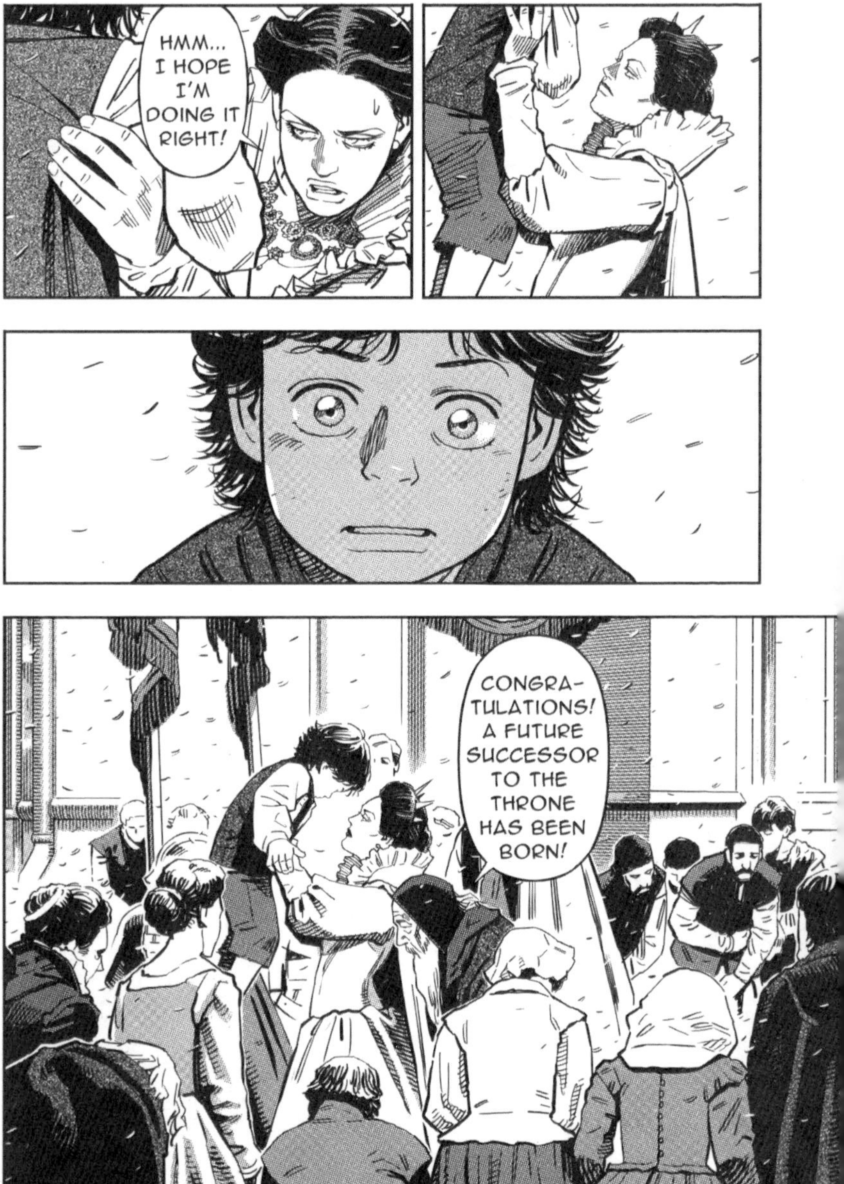
HMM... I HOPE I'M DOING IT RIGHT!
CONGRATULATIONS! A FUTURE SUCCESSOR TO THE THRONE HAS BEEN BORN!

CHAPTER 6
ROAD TO THE PALACE

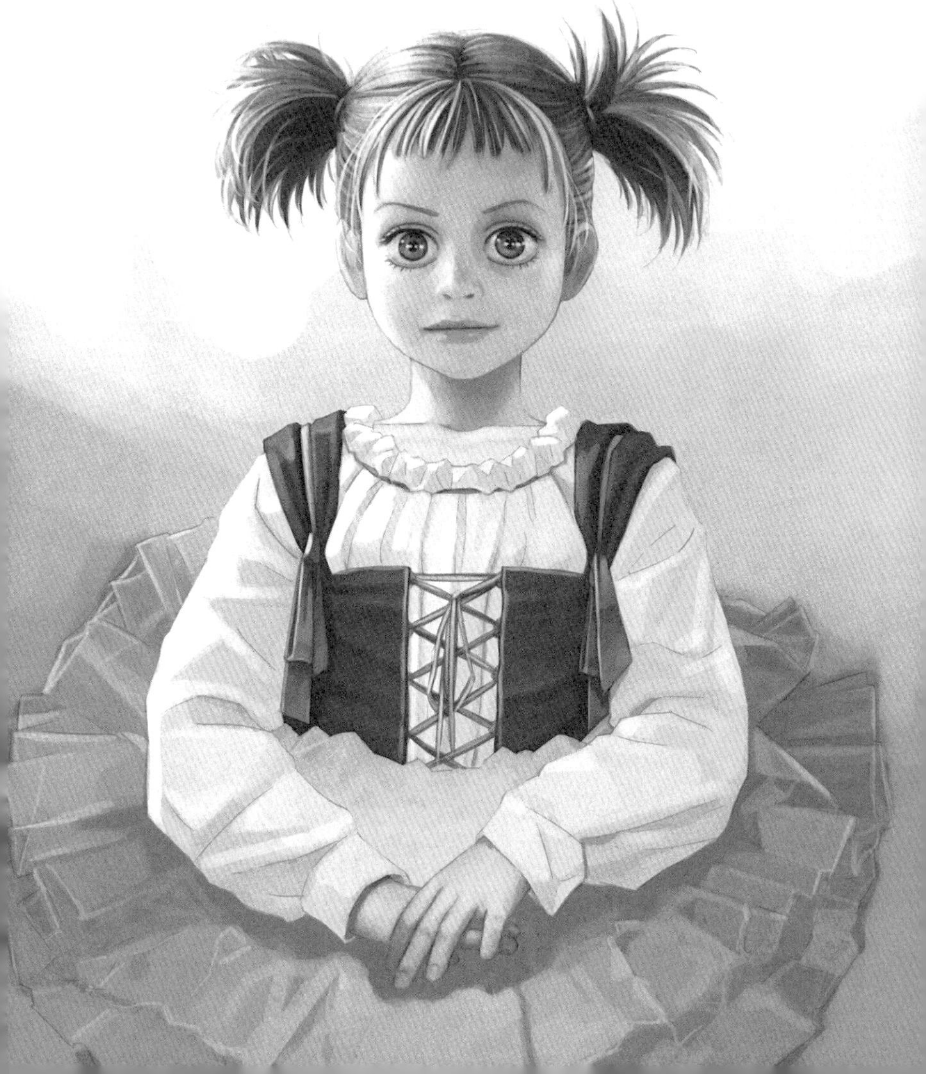

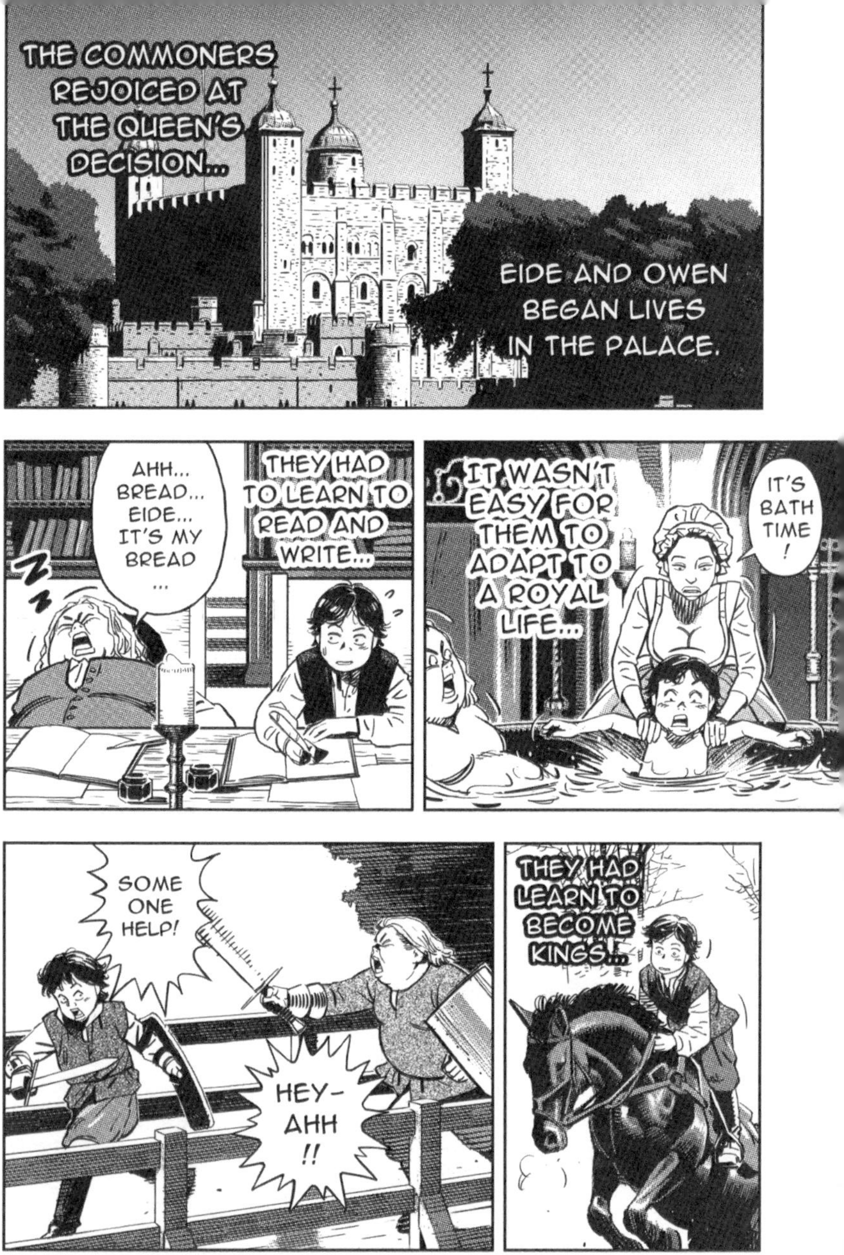
THE COMMONERS REJOICED AT THE QUEEN'S DECISION...
EIDE AND OWEN BEGAN LIVES IN THE PALACE.
IT WASN'T EASY FOR THEM TO ADAPT TO A ROYAL LIFE...
IT'S BATH TIME!
THEY HAD TO LEARN TO READ AND WRITE...
AHH... BREAD... EIDE... IT'S MY BREAD ...
THEY HAD LEARN TO BECOME KINGS...
SOME ONE HELP!
HEY-AHH !!

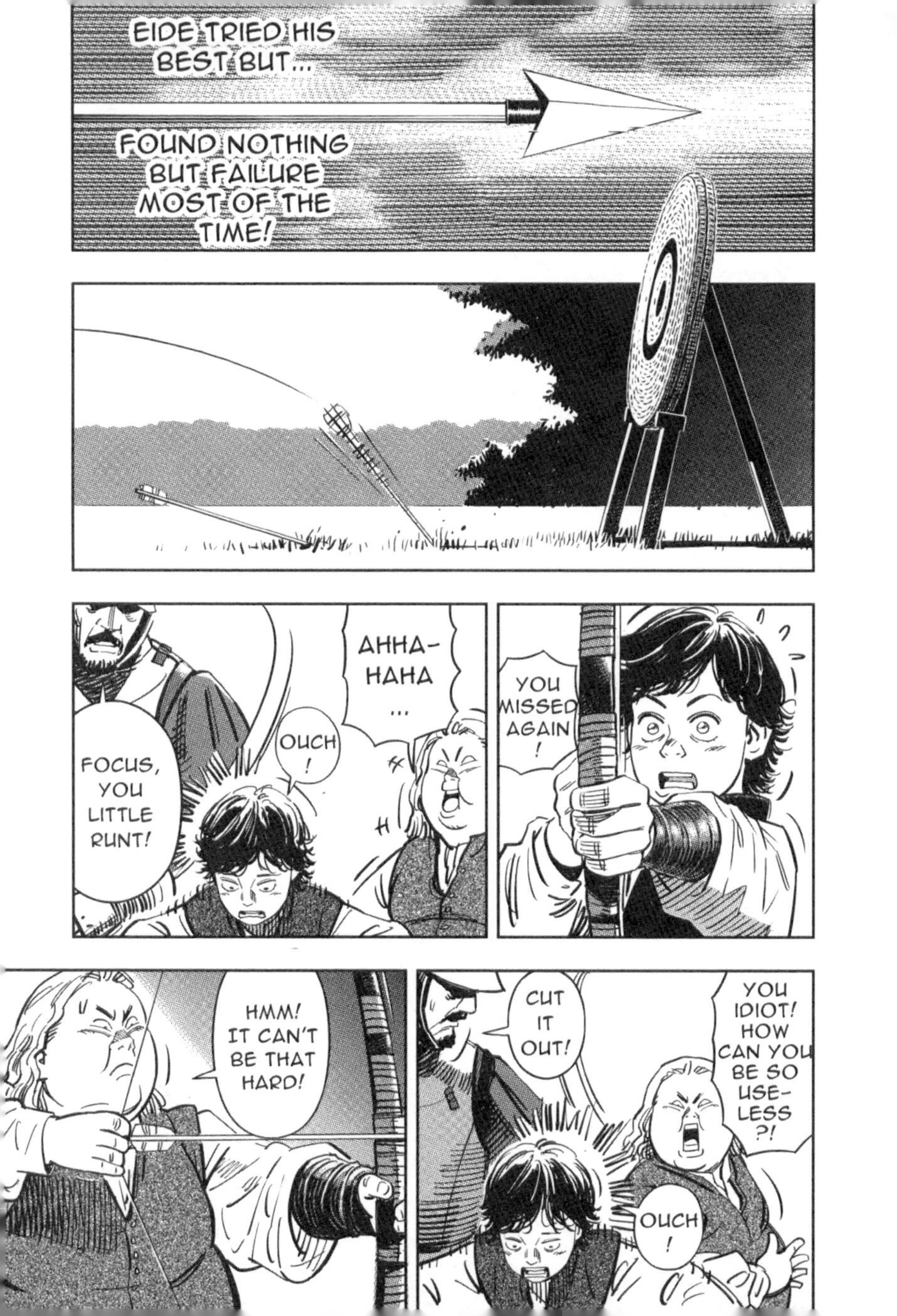
EIDE TRIED HIS BEST BUT...
FOUND NOTHING BUT FAILURE MOST OF THE TIME!
YOU MISSED AGAIN!
AHHA-HAHA ...
OUCH!
FOCUS, YOU LITTLE RUNT!
YOU IDIOT! HOW CAN YOU BE SO USE-LESS?!
CUT IT OUT!
OUCH!
HMM! IT CAN'T BE THAT HARD!

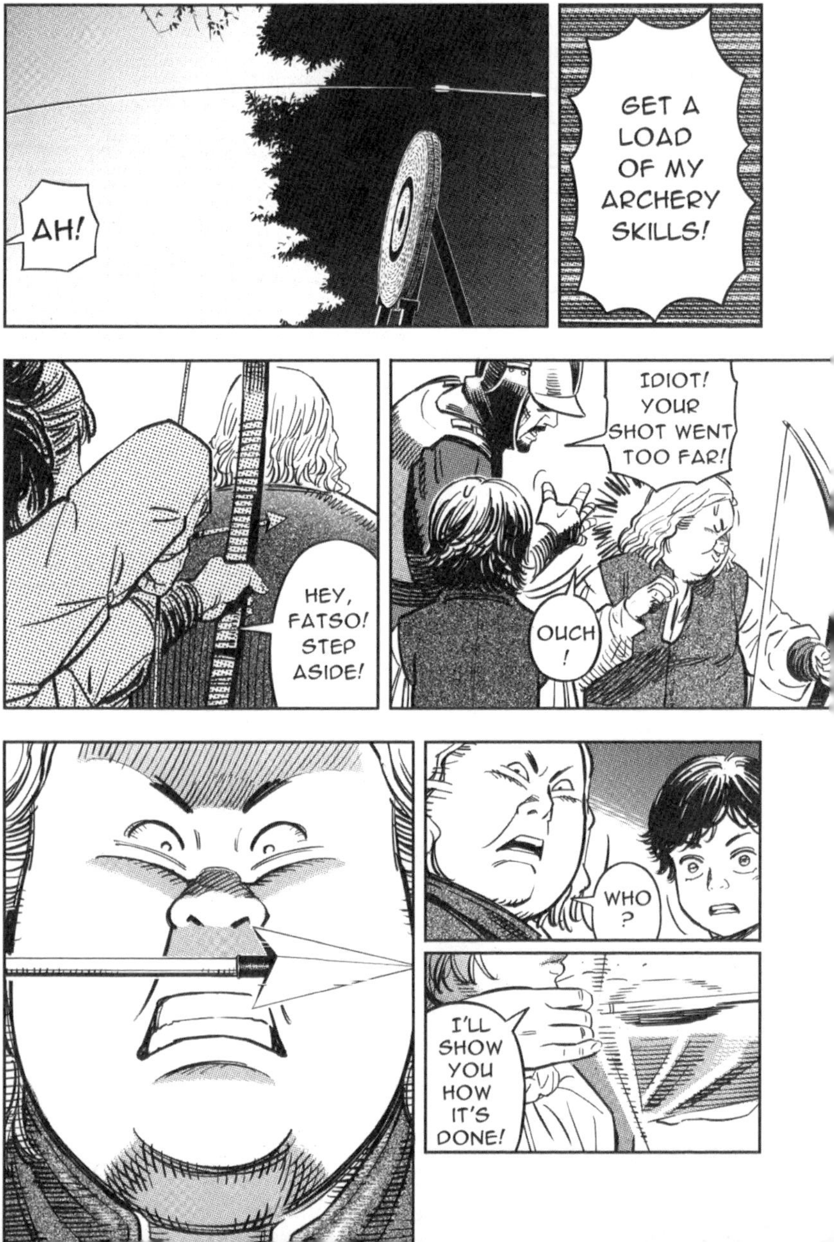
GET A LOAD OF MY ARCHERY SKILLS!
AH!
IDIOT! YOUR SHOT WENT TOO FAR!
OUCH!
HEY, FATSO! STEP ASIDE!
WHO?
I'LL SHOW YOU HOW IT'S DONE!

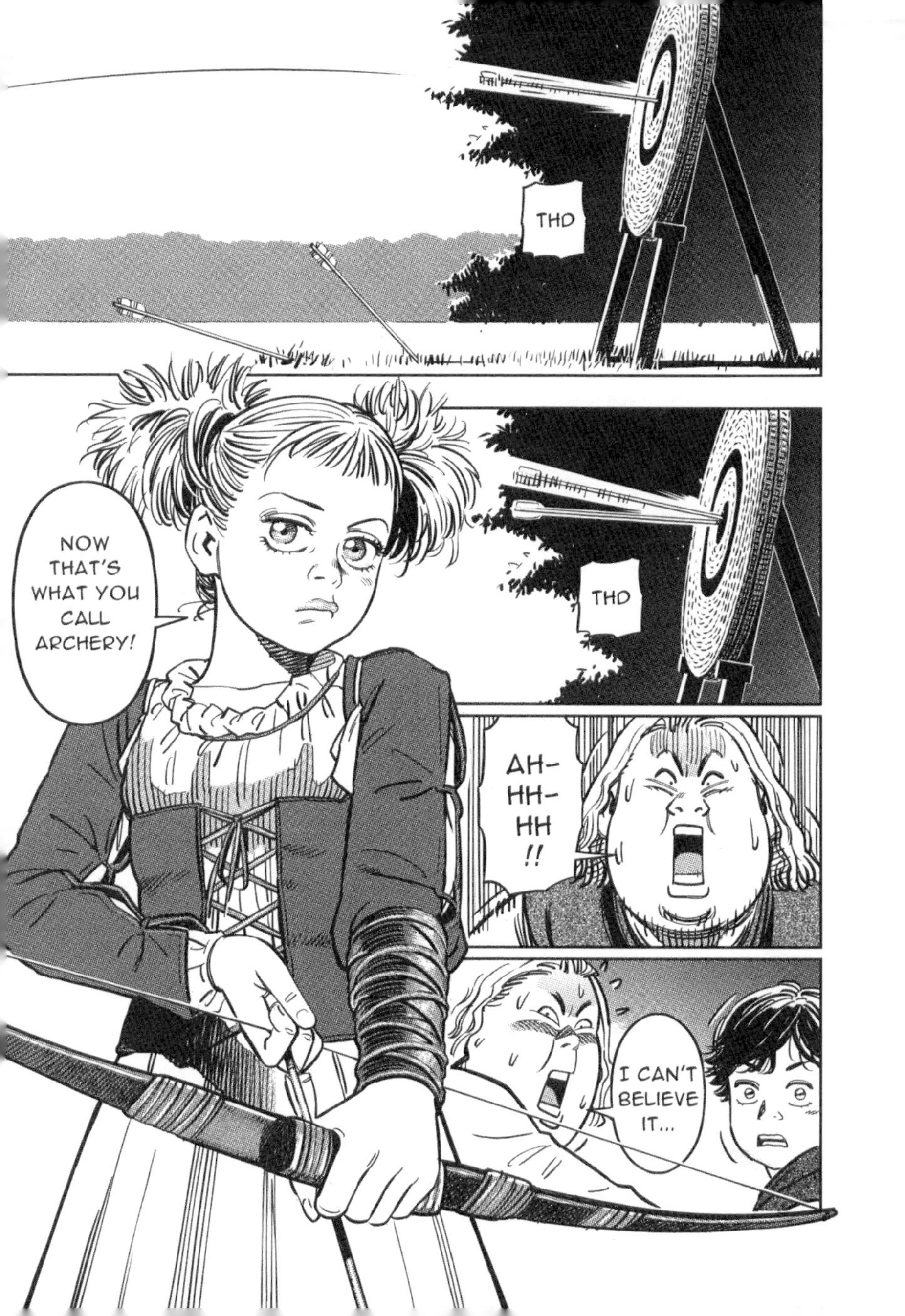
THD
THD
AH-HH-HH!!
I CAN'T BELIEVE IT...
NOW THAT'S WHAT YOU CALL ARCHERY!

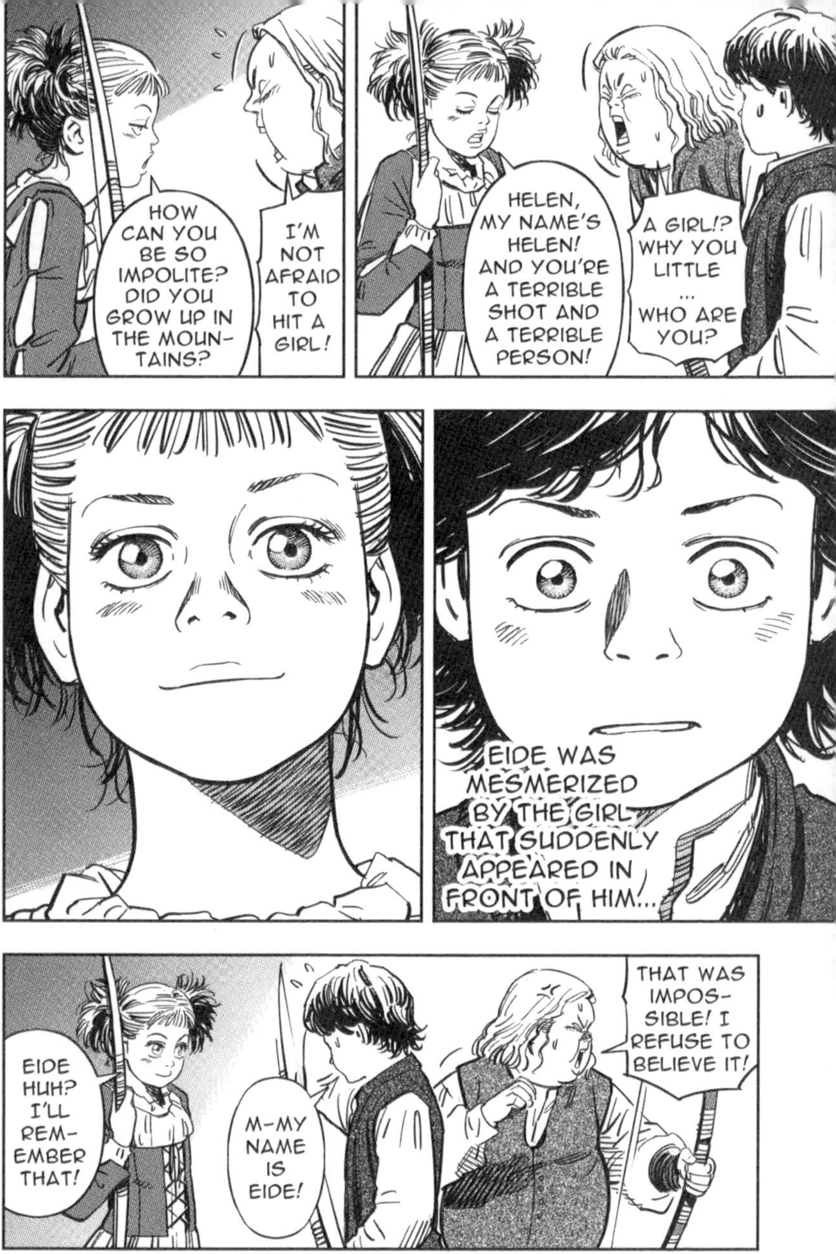
A GIRL!? WHY YOU LITTLE ... WHO ARE YOU?
HELEN, MY NAME'S HELEN! AND YOU'RE A TERRIBLE SHOT AND A TERRIBLE PERSON!
I'M NOT AFRAID TO HIT A GIRL!
HOW CAN YOU BE SO IMPOLITE? DID YOU GROW UP IN THE MOUNTAINS?
EIDE WAS MESMERIZED BY THE GIRL THAT SUDDENLY APPEARED IN FRONT OF HIM...
THAT WAS IMPOSSIBLE! I REFUSE TO BELIEVE IT!
M-MY NAME IS EIDE!
EIDE HUH? I'LL REMEMBER THAT!

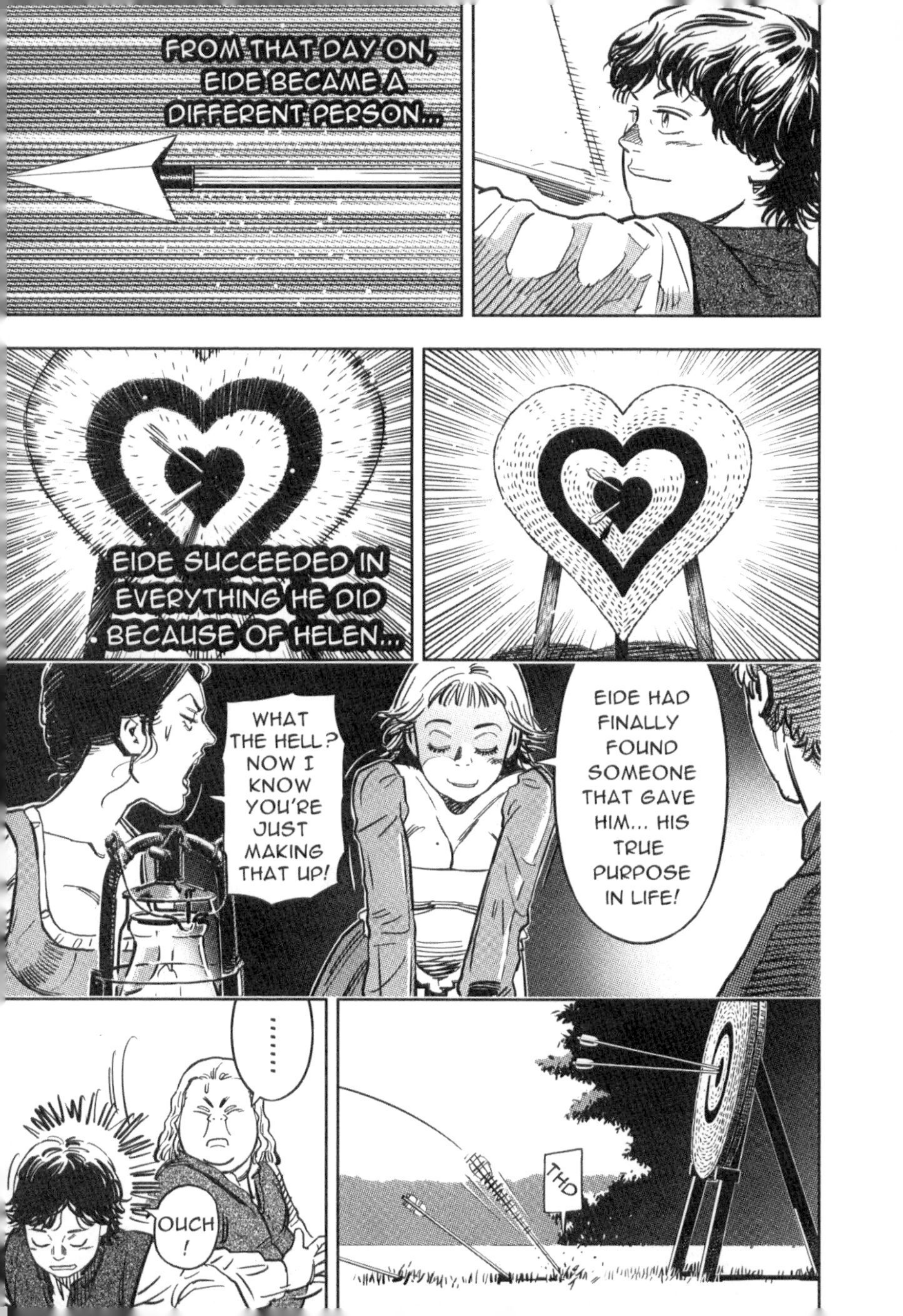
FROM THAT DAY ON, EIDE BECAME A DIFFERENT PERSON...
EIDE SUCCEEDED IN EVERYTHING HE DID BECAUSE OF HELEN...
EIDE HAD FINALLY FOUND SOMEONE THAT GAVE HIM... HIS TRUE PURPOSE IN LIFE!
WHAT THE HELL? NOW I KNOW YOU'RE JUST MAKING THAT UP!
THD
......
OUCH!

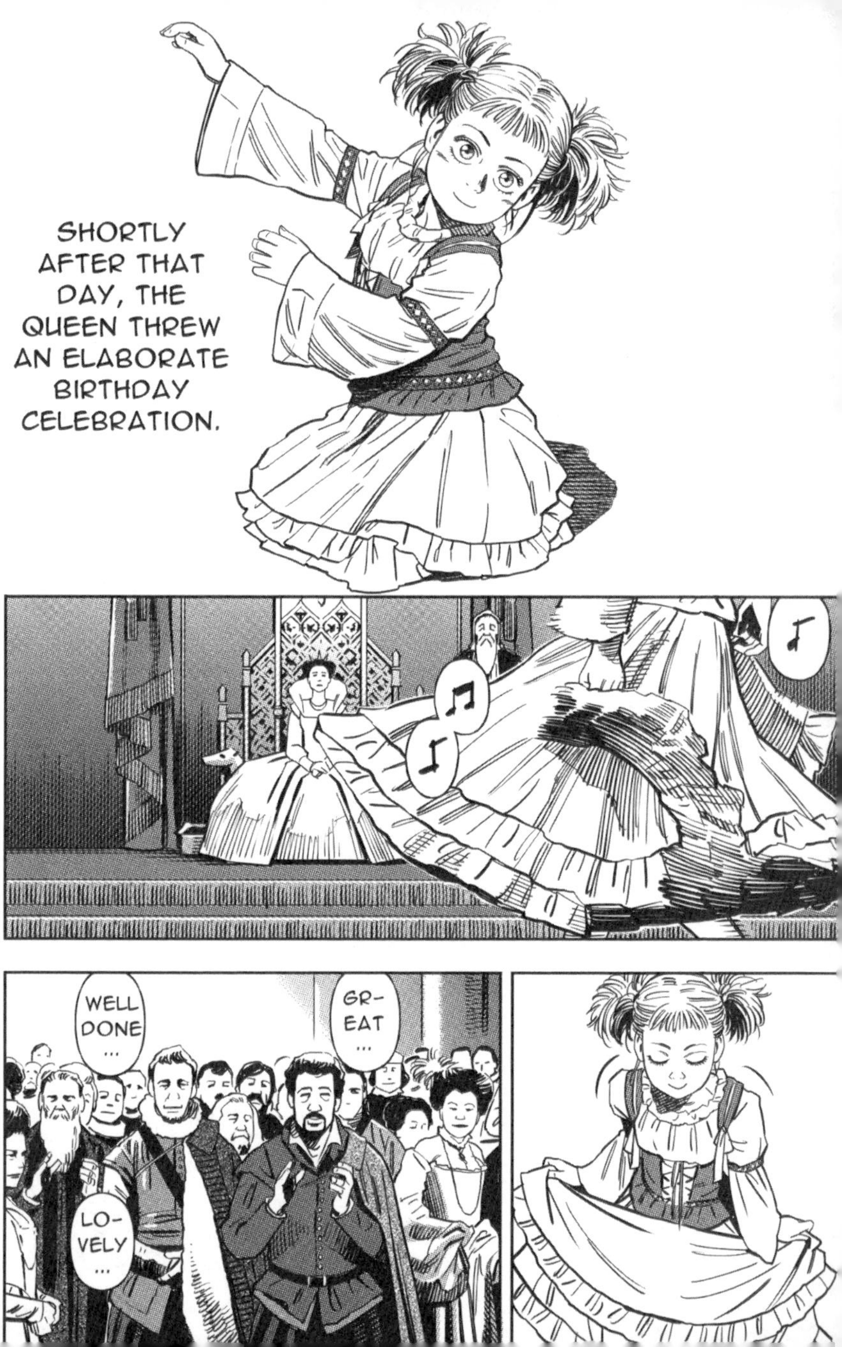
SHORTLY AFTER THAT DAY, THE QUEEN THREW AN ELABORATE BIRTHDAY CELEBRATION.
GR-EAT ...
WELL DONE ...
LO-VELY ...

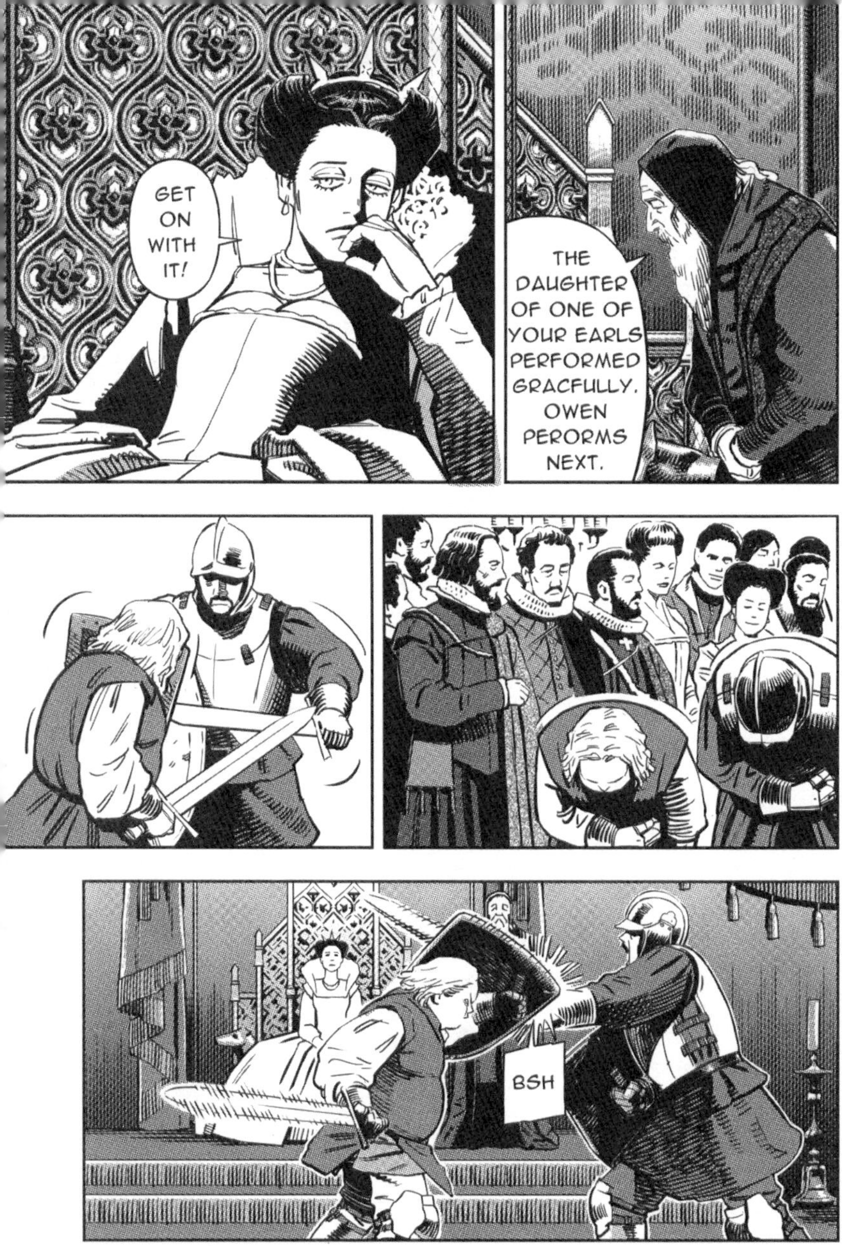
THE DAUGHTER OF ONE OF YOUR EARLS PERFORMED GRACFULLY. OWEN PERORMS NEXT.
GET ON WITH IT!
BSH

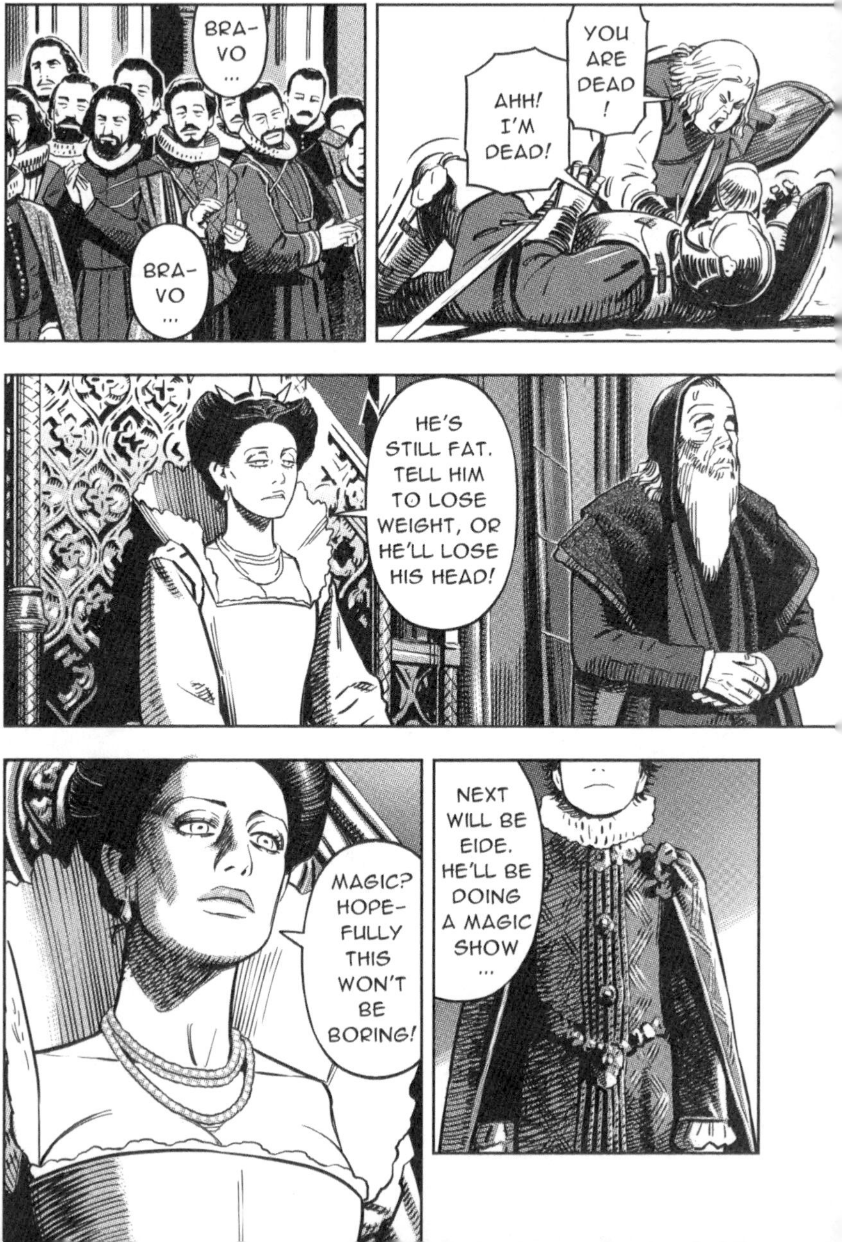
YOU ARE DEAD!
AHH! I'M DEAD!
BRA-VO ...
BRA-VO ...
HE'S STILL FAT. TELL HIM TO LOSE WEIGHT, OR HE'LL LOSE HIS HEAD!
NEXT WILL BE EIDE. HE'LL BE DOING A MAGIC SHOW ...
MAGIC? HOPE-FULLY THIS WON'T BE BORING!

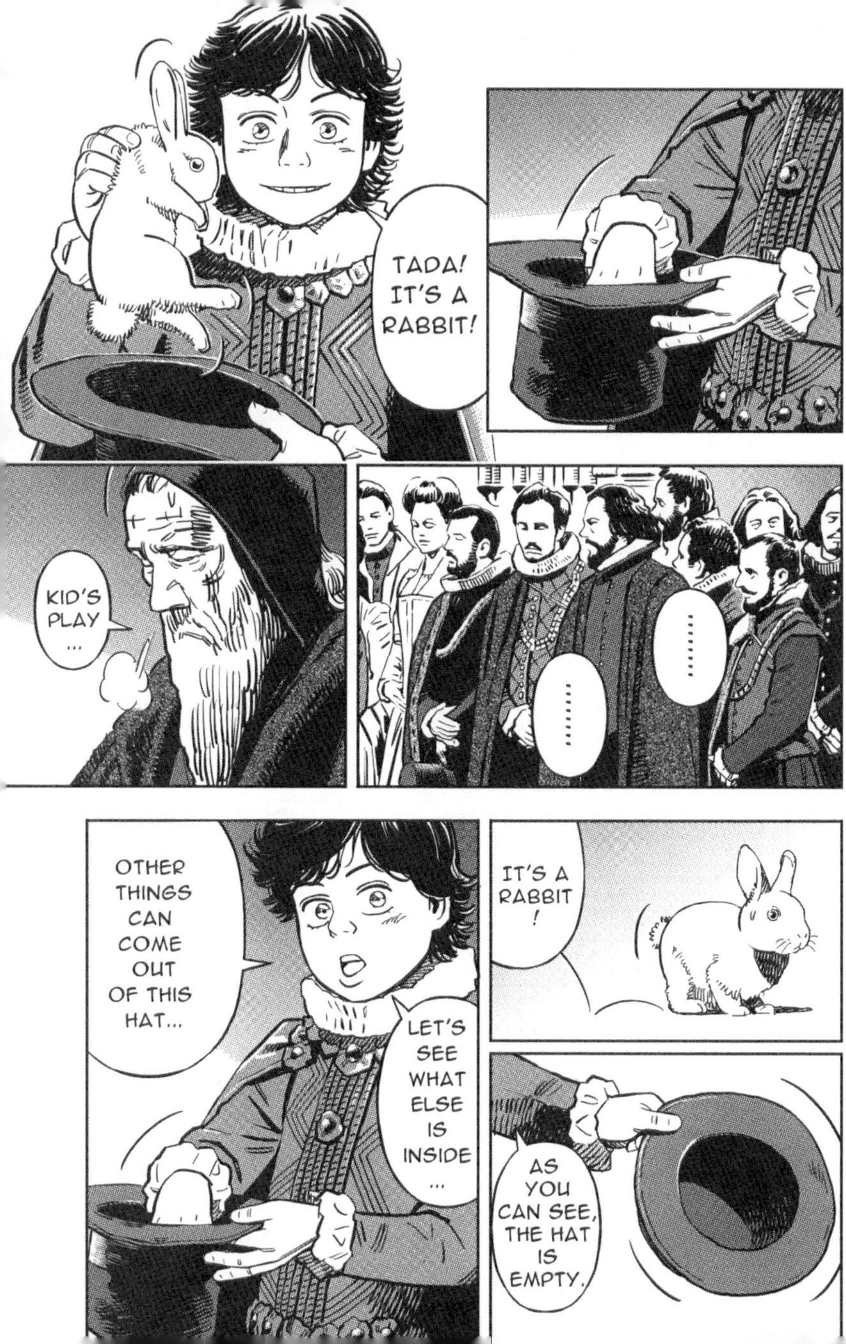
TADA! IT'S A RABBIT!
....
....
KID'S PLAY ...
IT'S A RABBIT !
AS YOU CAN SEE, THE HAT IS EMPTY.
OTHER THINGS CAN COME OUT OF THIS HAT...
LET'S SEE WHAT ELSE IS INSIDE ...

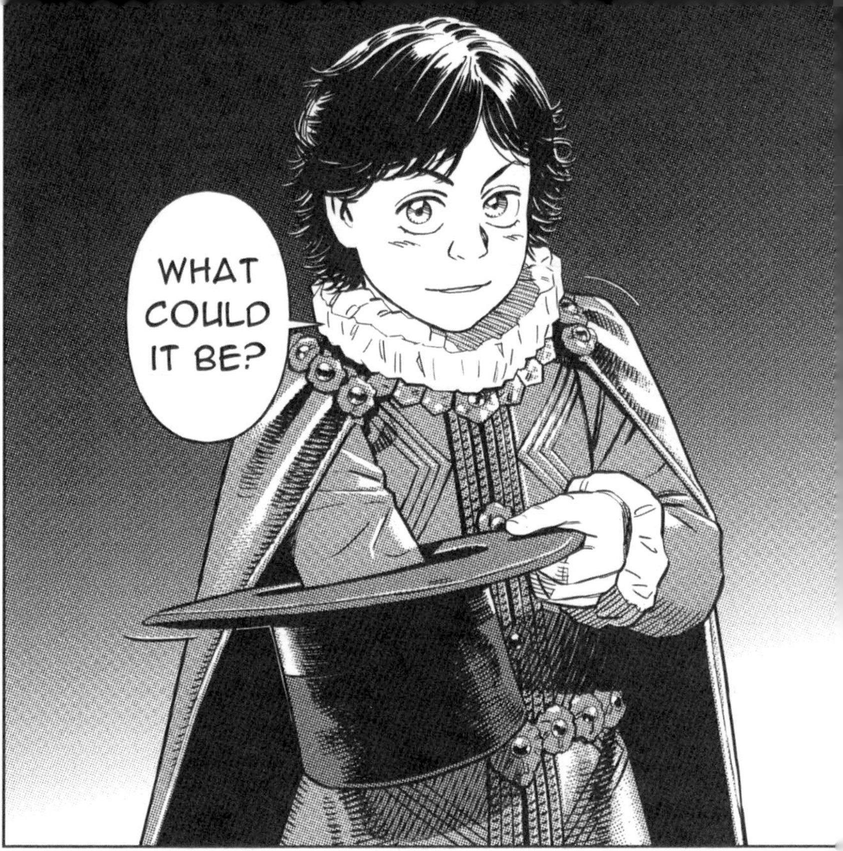
WHAT COULD IT BE?

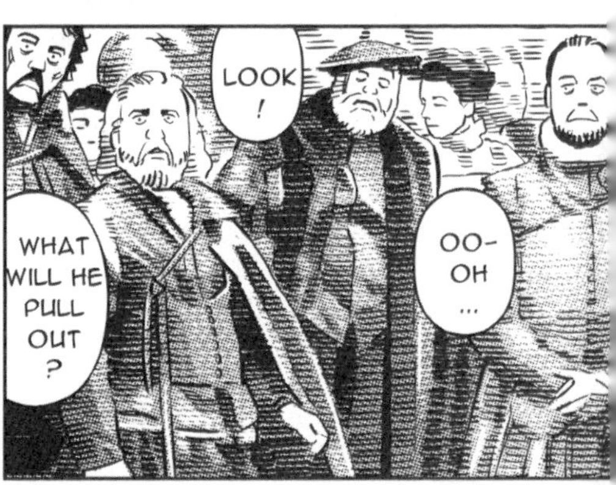
LOOK!
OO-OH...
WHAT WILL HE PULL OUT?

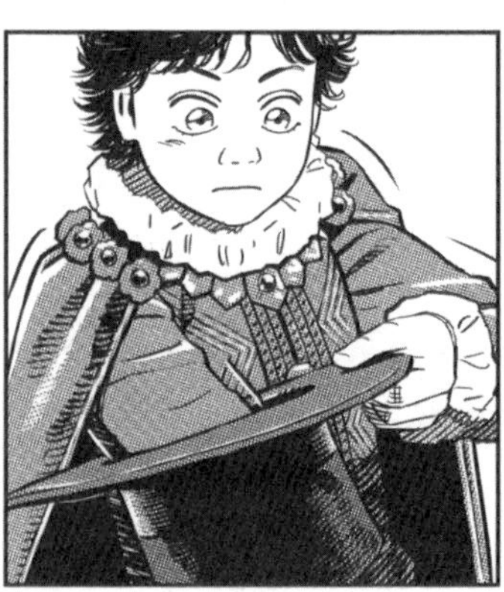

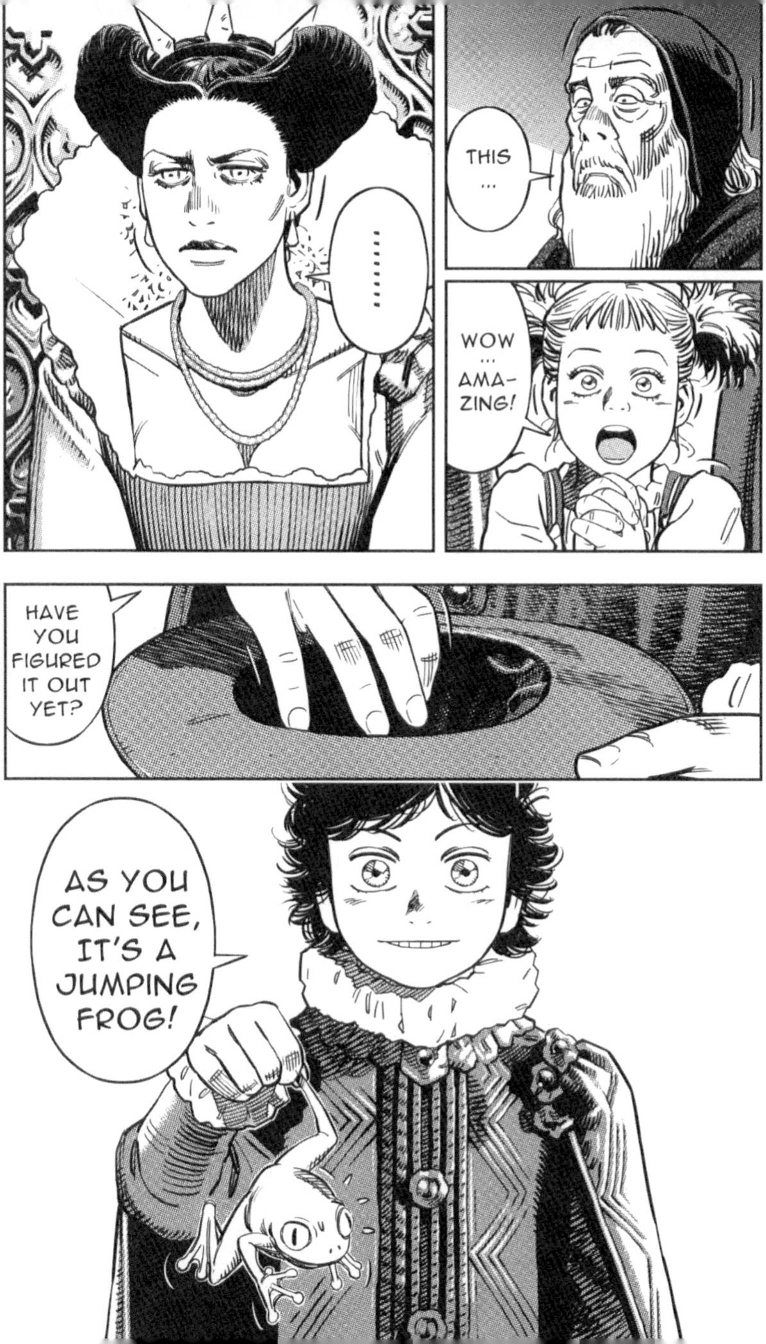
THIS ...
WOW ... AMA-ZING!
......
HAVE YOU FIGURED IT OUT YET?
AS YOU CAN SEE, IT'S A JUMPING FROG!

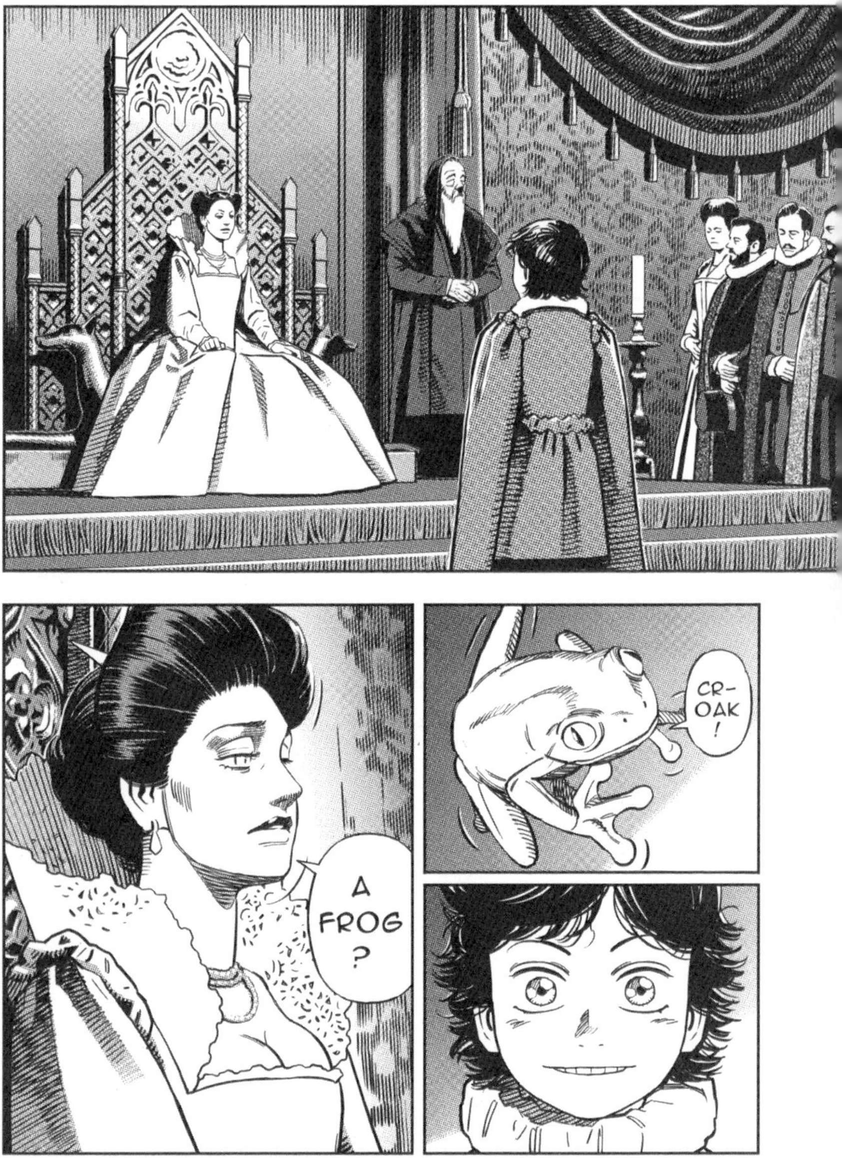
CR-OAK!
A FROG?

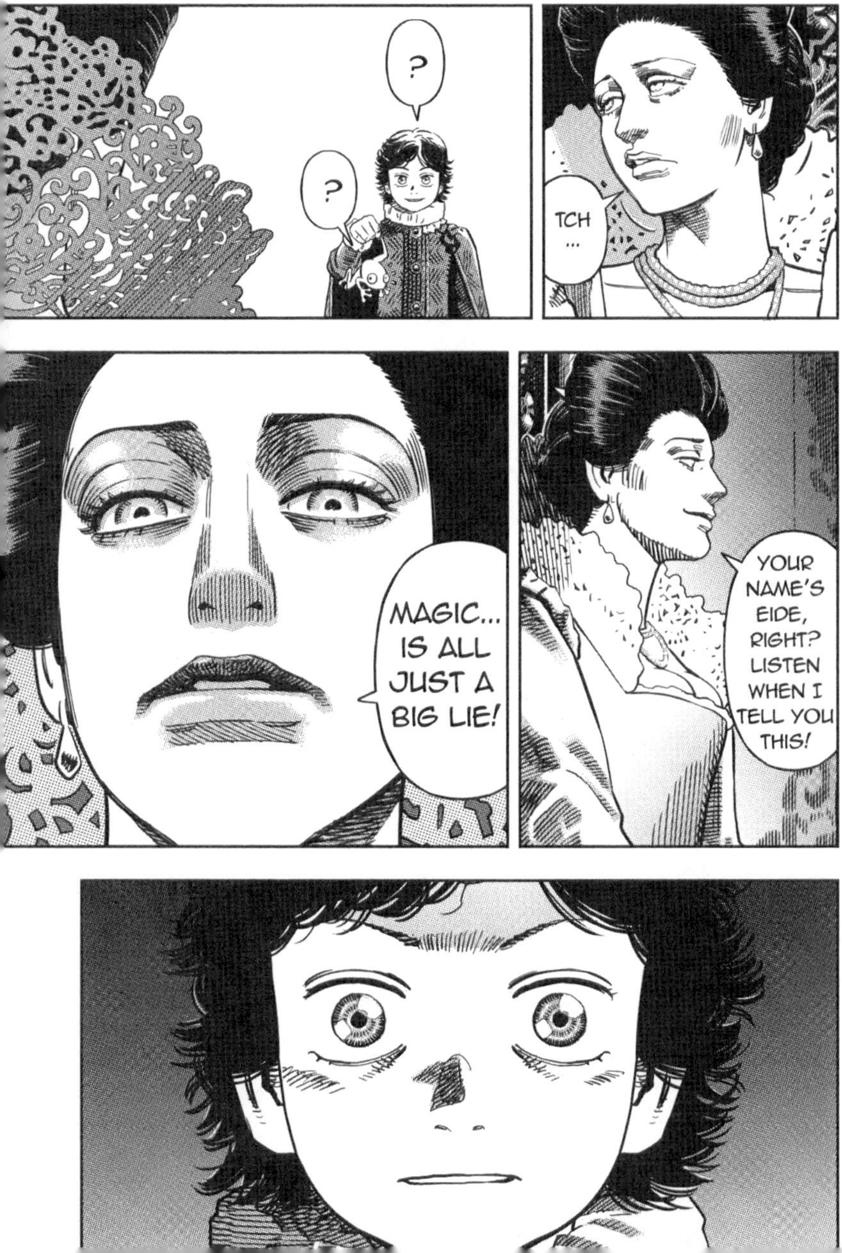
TCH ...
?
?
YOUR NAME'S EIDE, RIGHT? LISTEN WHEN I TELL YOU THIS!
MAGIC... IS ALL JUST A BIG LIE!

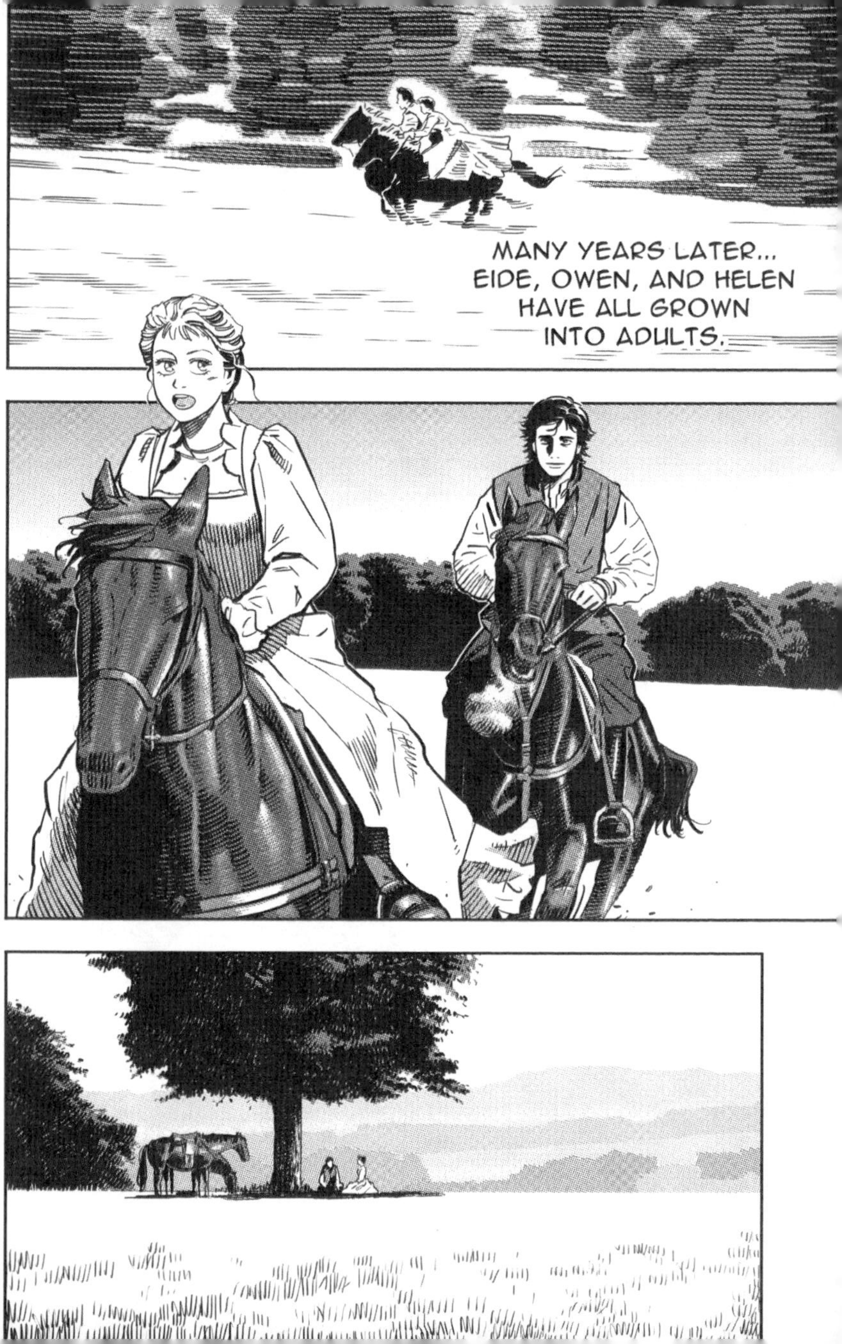
MANY YEARS LATER... EIDE, OWEN, AND HELEN HAVE ALL GROWN INTO ADULTS.

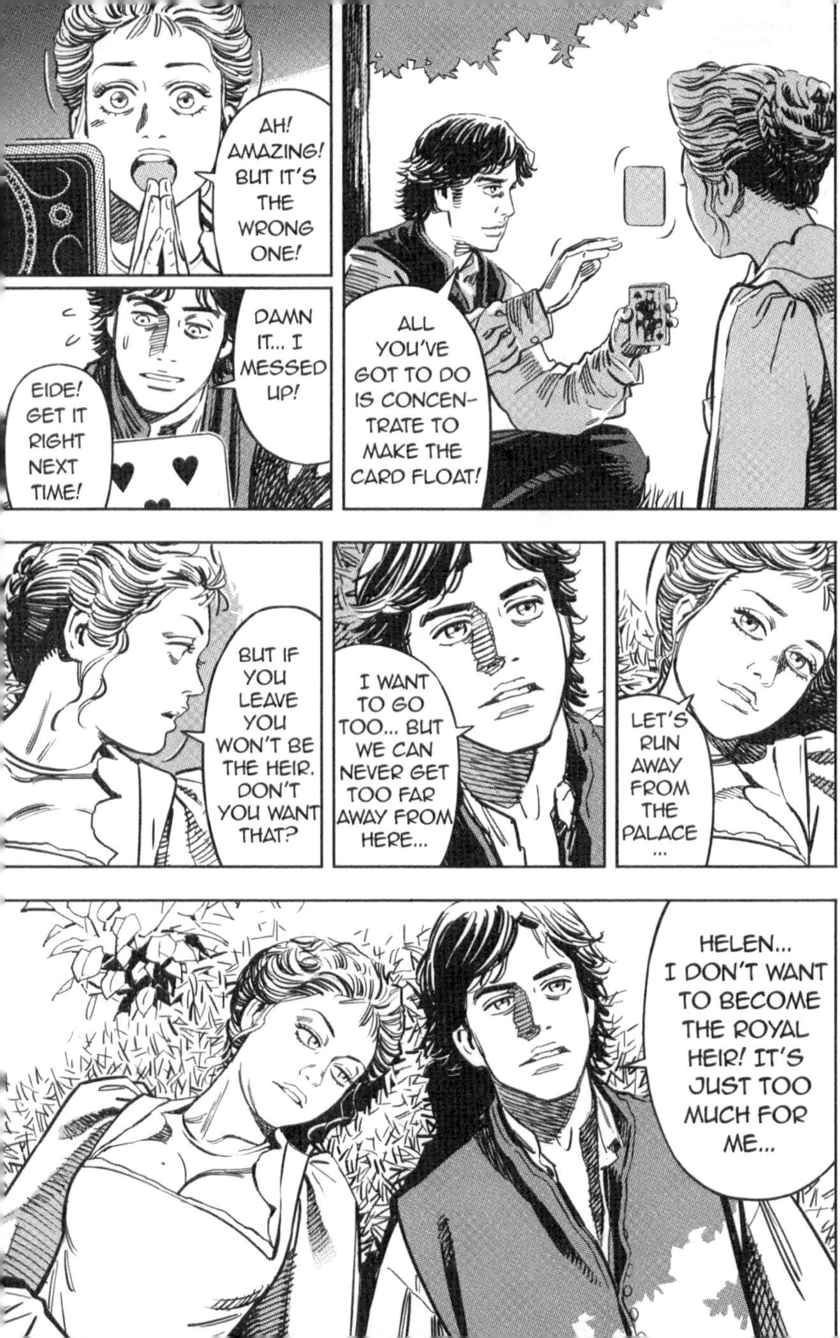
ALL YOU'VE GOT TO DO IS CONCENTRATE TO MAKE THE CARD FLOAT!
AH! AMAZING! BUT IT'S THE WRONG ONE!
DAMN IT... I MESSED UP!
EIDE! GET IT RIGHT NEXT TIME!
LET'S RUN AWAY FROM THE PALACE ...
I WANT TO GO TOO... BUT WE CAN NEVER GET TOO FAR AWAY FROM HERE...
BUT IF YOU LEAVE YOU WON'T BE THE HEIR. DON'T YOU WANT THAT?
HELEN... I DON'T WANT TO BECOME THE ROYAL HEIR! IT'S JUST TOO MUCH FOR ME...

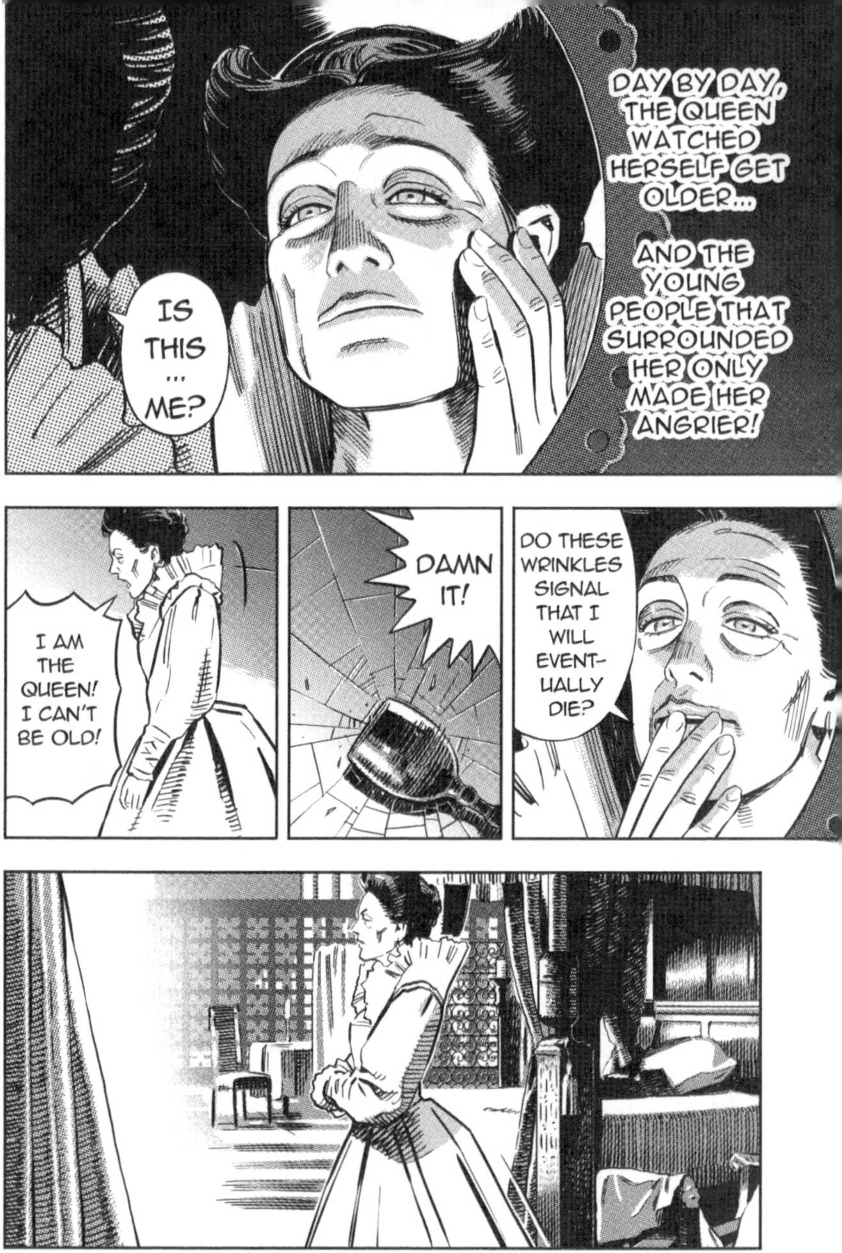
DAY BY DAY, THE QUEEN WATCHED HERSELF GET OLDER...
AND THE YOUNG PEOPLE THAT SURROUNDED HER ONLY MADE HER ANGRIER!
IS THIS ... ME?
DO THESE WRINKLES SIGNAL THAT I WILL EVENT-UALLY DIE?
DAMN IT!
I AM THE QUEEN! I CAN'T BE OLD!

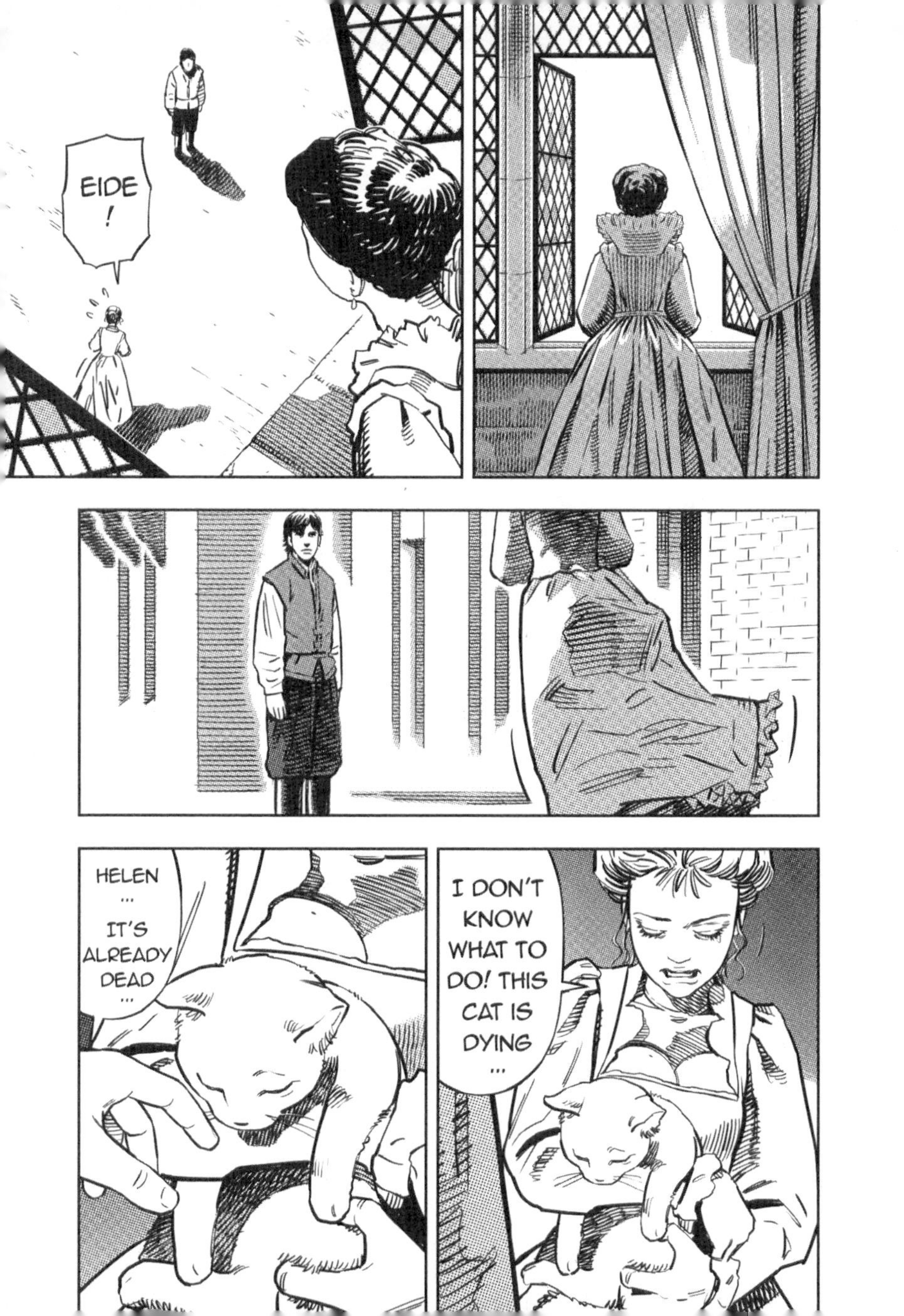
EIDE!
I DON'T KNOW WHAT TO DO! THIS CAT IS DYING ...
HELEN ... IT'S ALREADY DEAD ...

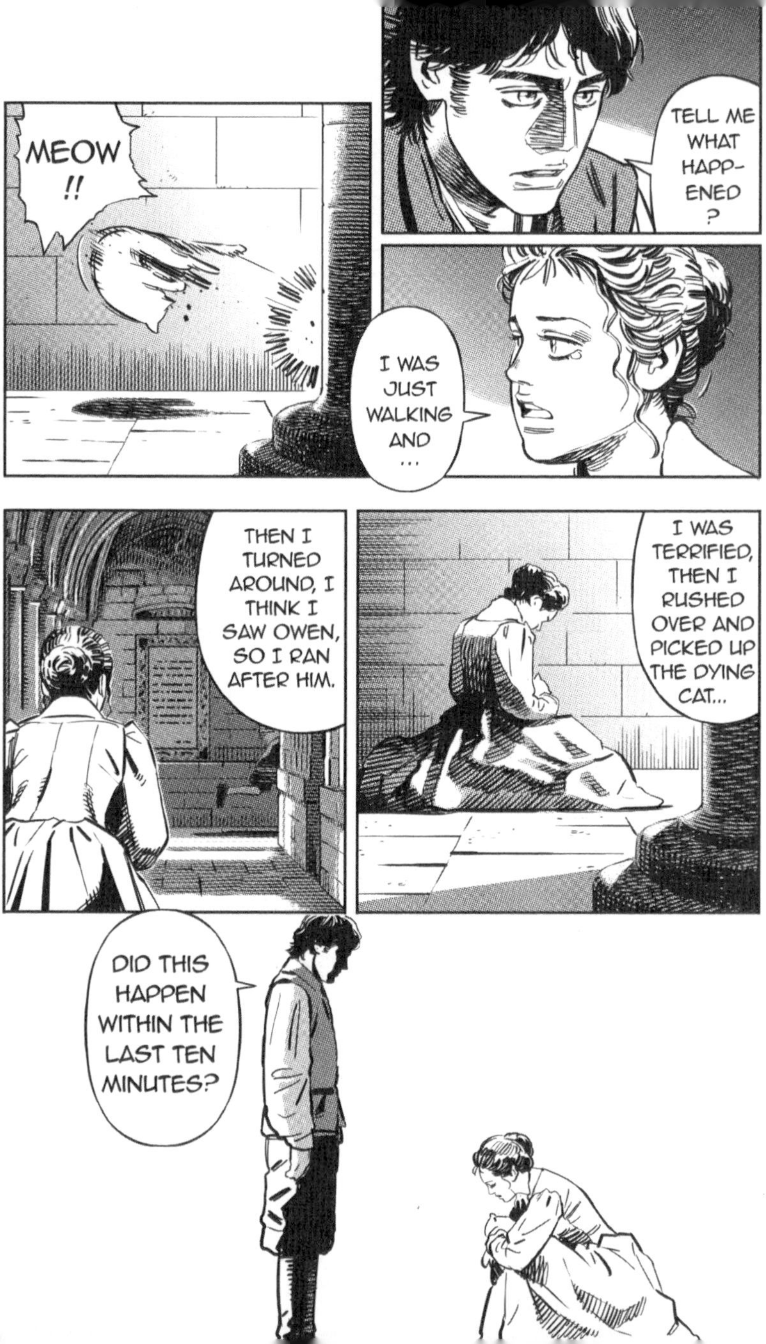
TELL ME WHAT HAPP-ENED ?
I WAS JUST WALKING AND ...
MEOW !!
I WAS TERRIFIED, THEN I RUSHED OVER AND PICKED UP THE DYING CAT...
THEN I TURNED AROUND, I THINK I SAW OWEN, SO I RAN AFTER HIM.
DID THIS HAPPEN WITHIN THE LAST TEN MINUTES?

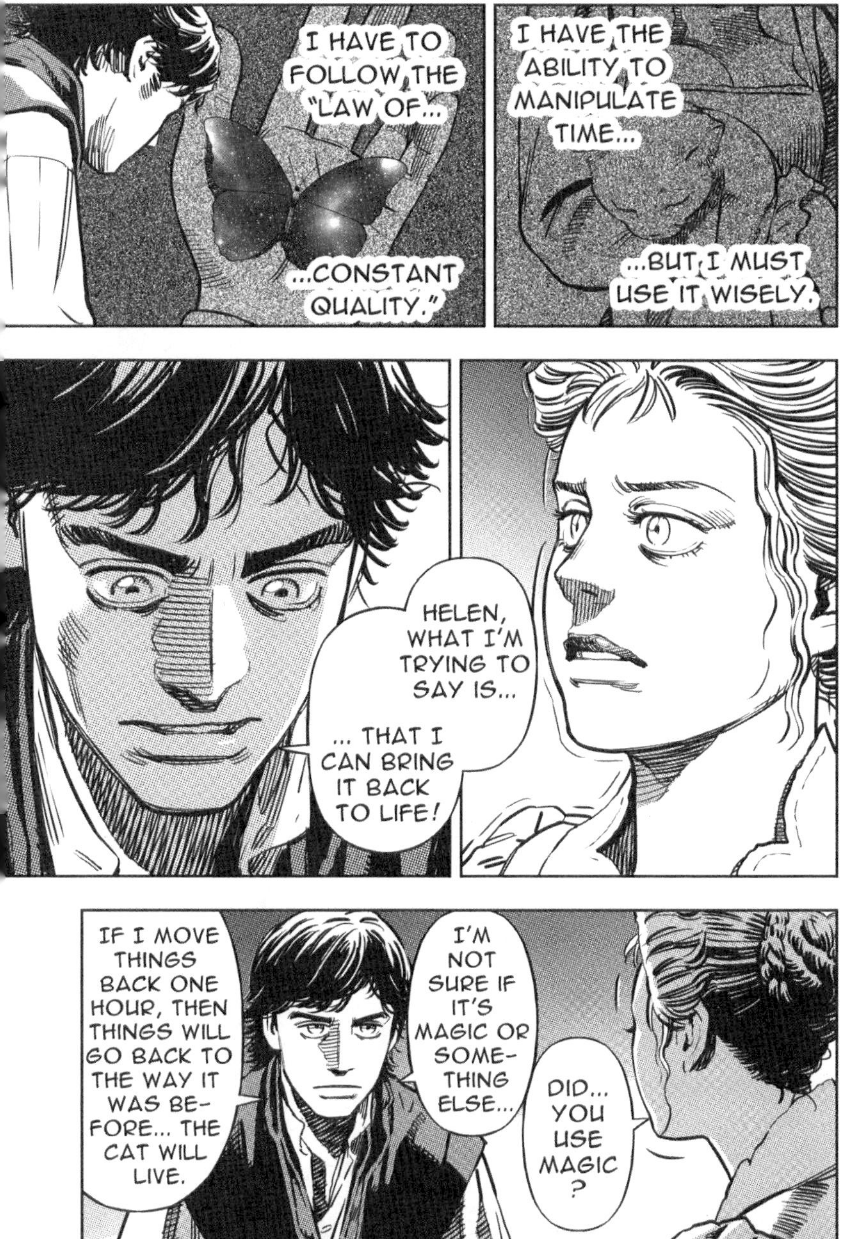
I HAVE THE ABILITY TO MANIPULATE TIME...
...BUT I MUST USE IT WISELY.
I HAVE TO FOLLOW THE "LAW OF...
...CONSTANT QUALITY."
HELEN, WHAT I'M TRYING TO SAY IS...
... THAT I CAN BRING IT BACK TO LIFE!
DID... YOU USE MAGIC ?
I'M NOT SURE IF IT'S MAGIC OR SOME-THING ELSE...
IF I MOVE THINGS BACK ONE HOUR, THEN THINGS WILL GO BACK TO THE WAY IT WAS BE-FORE... THE CAT WILL LIVE.

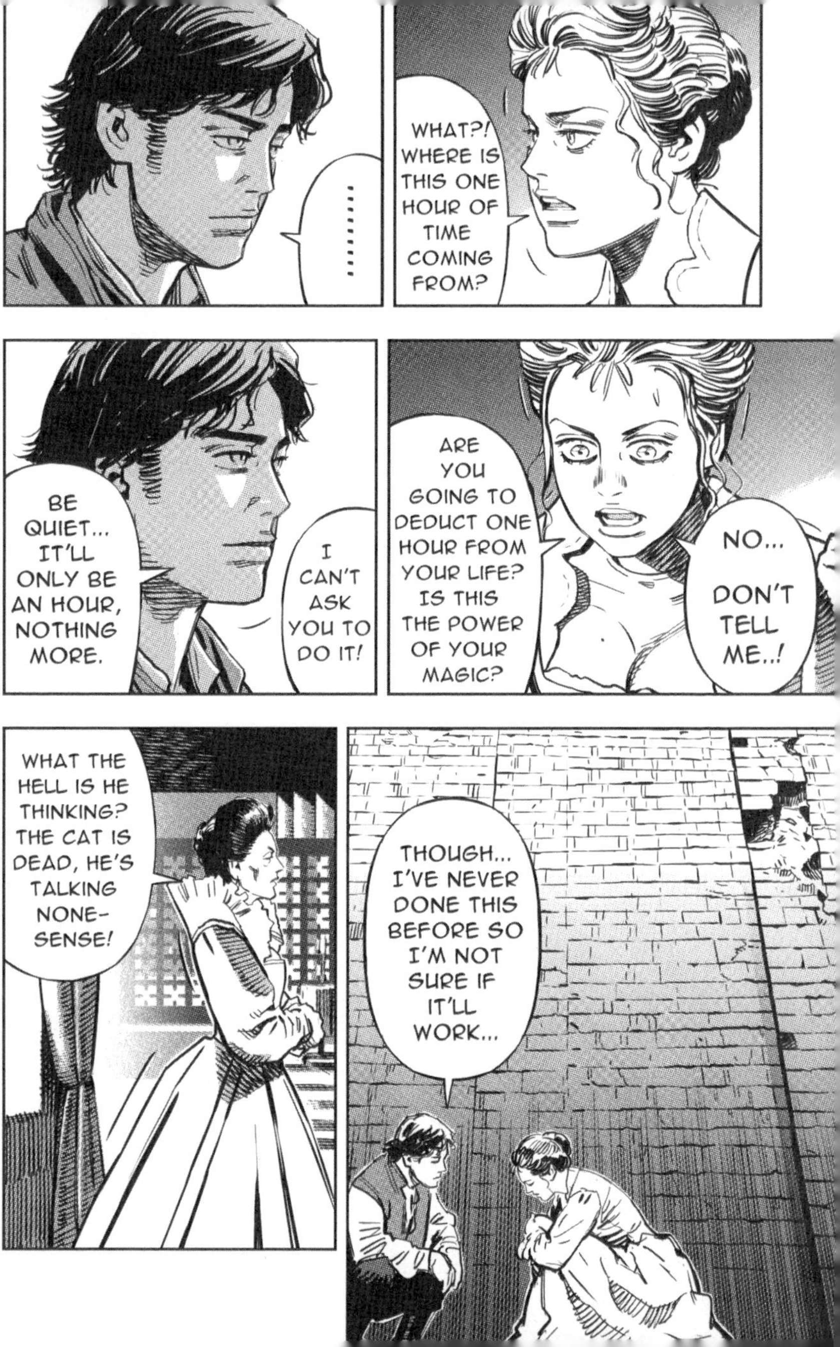
WHAT?! WHERE IS THIS ONE HOUR OF TIME COMING FROM?
....
ARE YOU GOING TO DEDUCT ONE HOUR FROM YOUR LIFE? IS THIS THE POWER OF YOUR MAGIC?
NO... DON'T TELL ME..!
I CAN'T ASK YOU TO DO IT!
BE QUIET... IT'LL ONLY BE AN HOUR, NOTHING MORE.
THOUGH... I'VE NEVER DONE THIS BEFORE SO I'M NOT SURE IF IT'LL WORK...
WHAT THE HELL IS HE THINKING? THE CAT IS DEAD, HE'S TALKING NONE-SENSE!

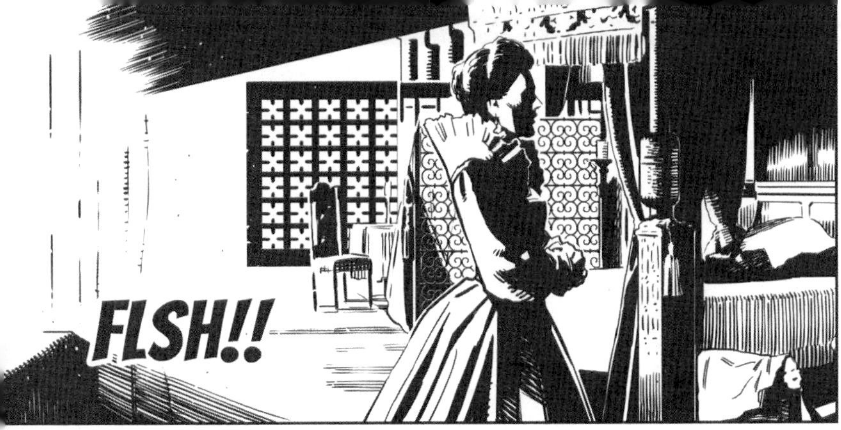
FLSH!!
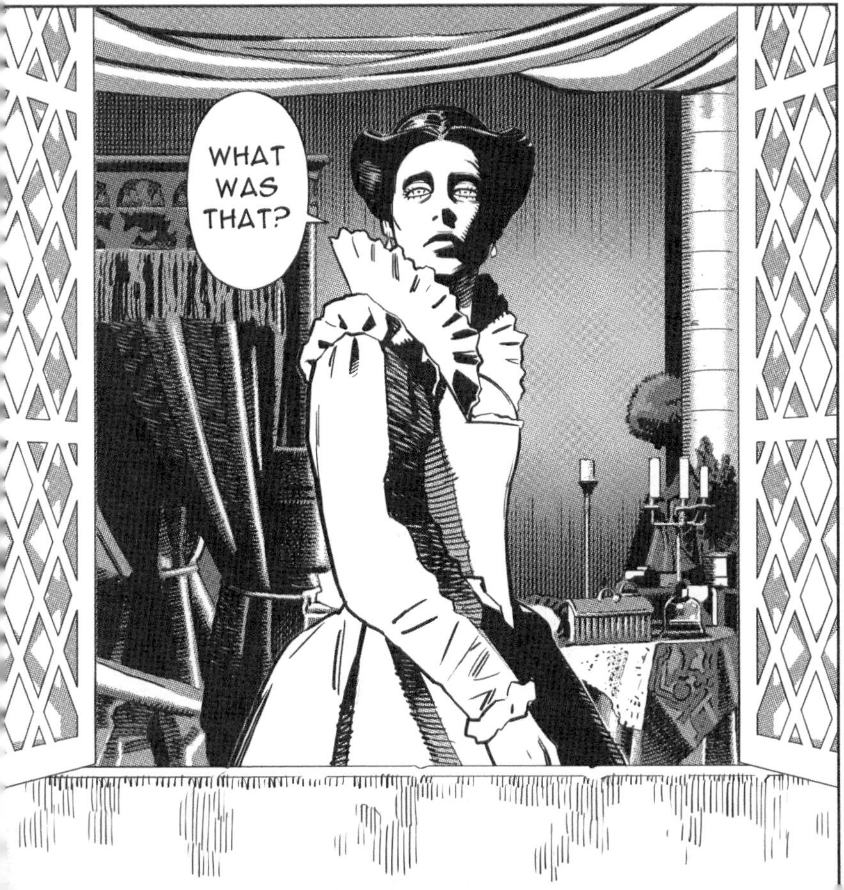
WHAT WAS THAT?

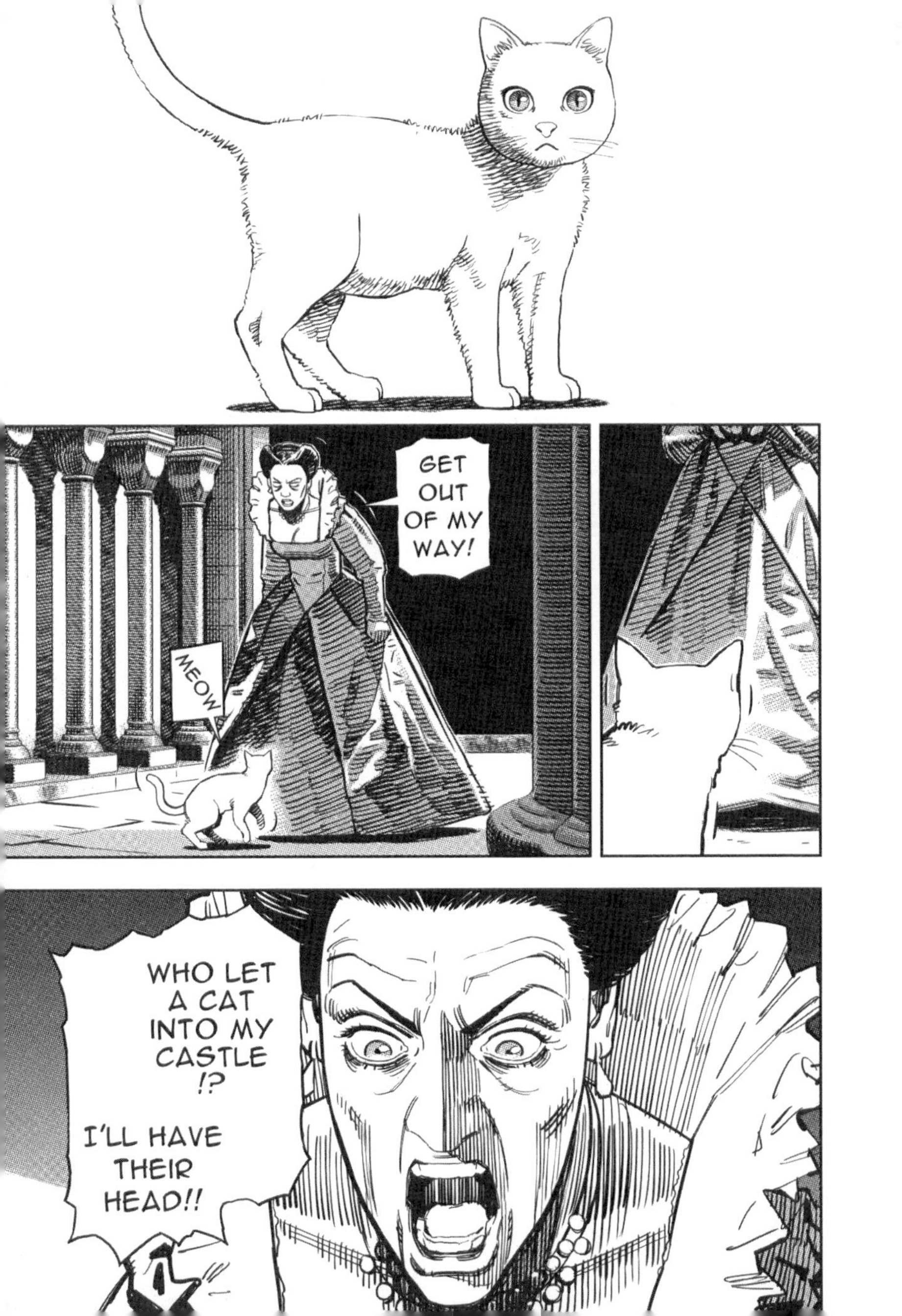
GET OUT OF MY WAY!
MEOW
WHO LET A CAT INTO MY CASTLE !?
I'LL HAVE THEIR HEAD!!

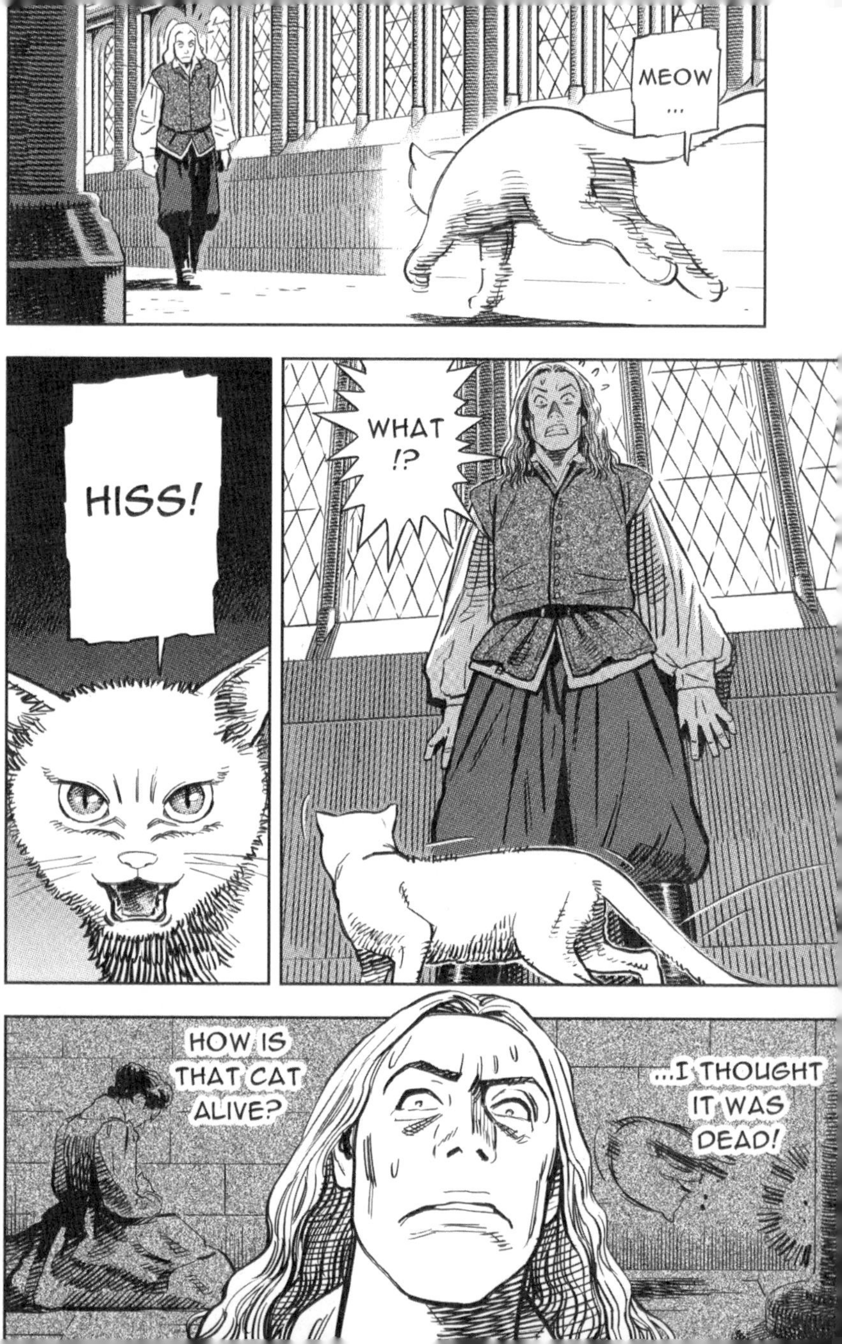
MEOW ...
WHAT !?
HISS!
HOW IS THAT CAT ALIVE?
...I THOUGHT IT WAS DEAD!

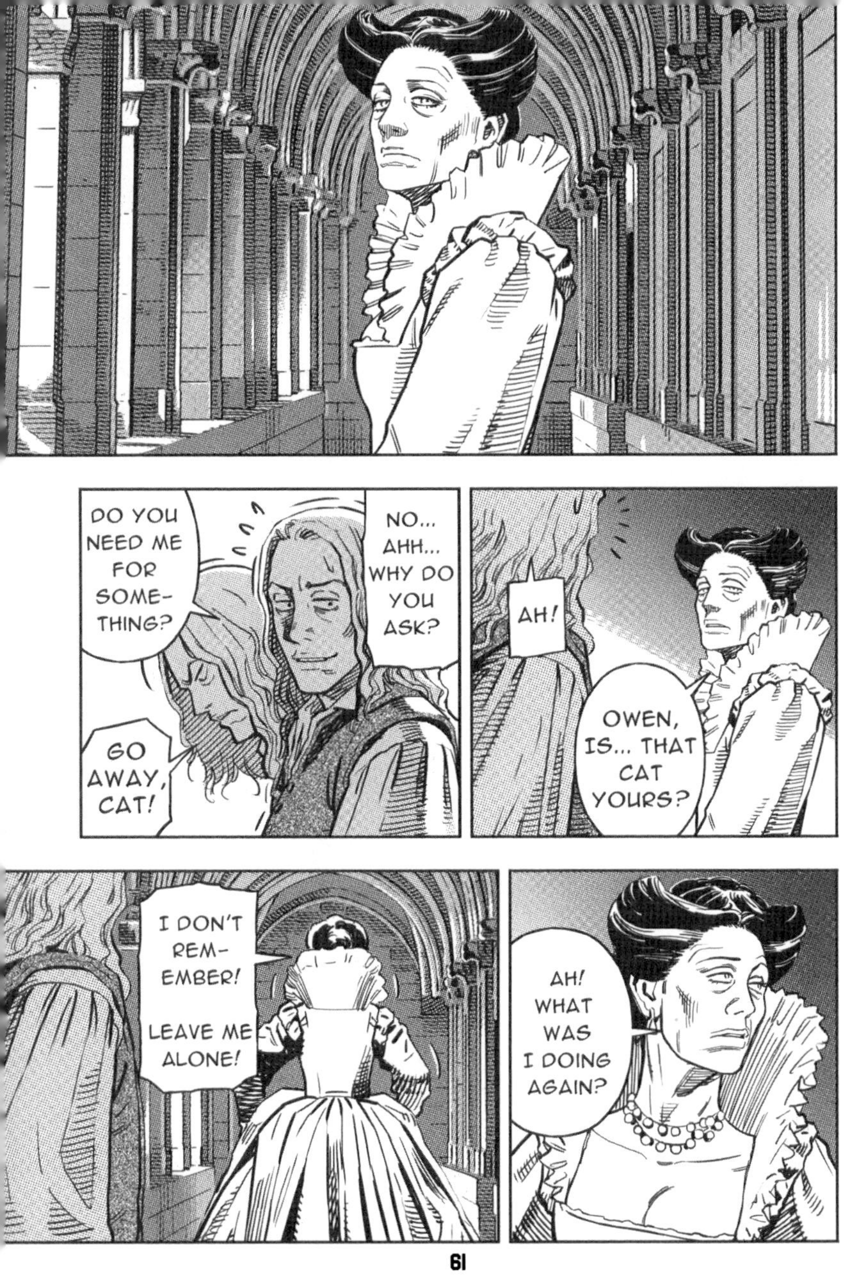
AH!
OWEN, IS... THAT CAT YOURS?
NO... AHH... WHY DO YOU ASK?
DO YOU NEED ME FOR SOME-THING?
GO AWAY, CAT!
AH! WHAT WAS I DOING AGAIN?
I DON'T REM-EMBER!
LEAVE ME ALONE!

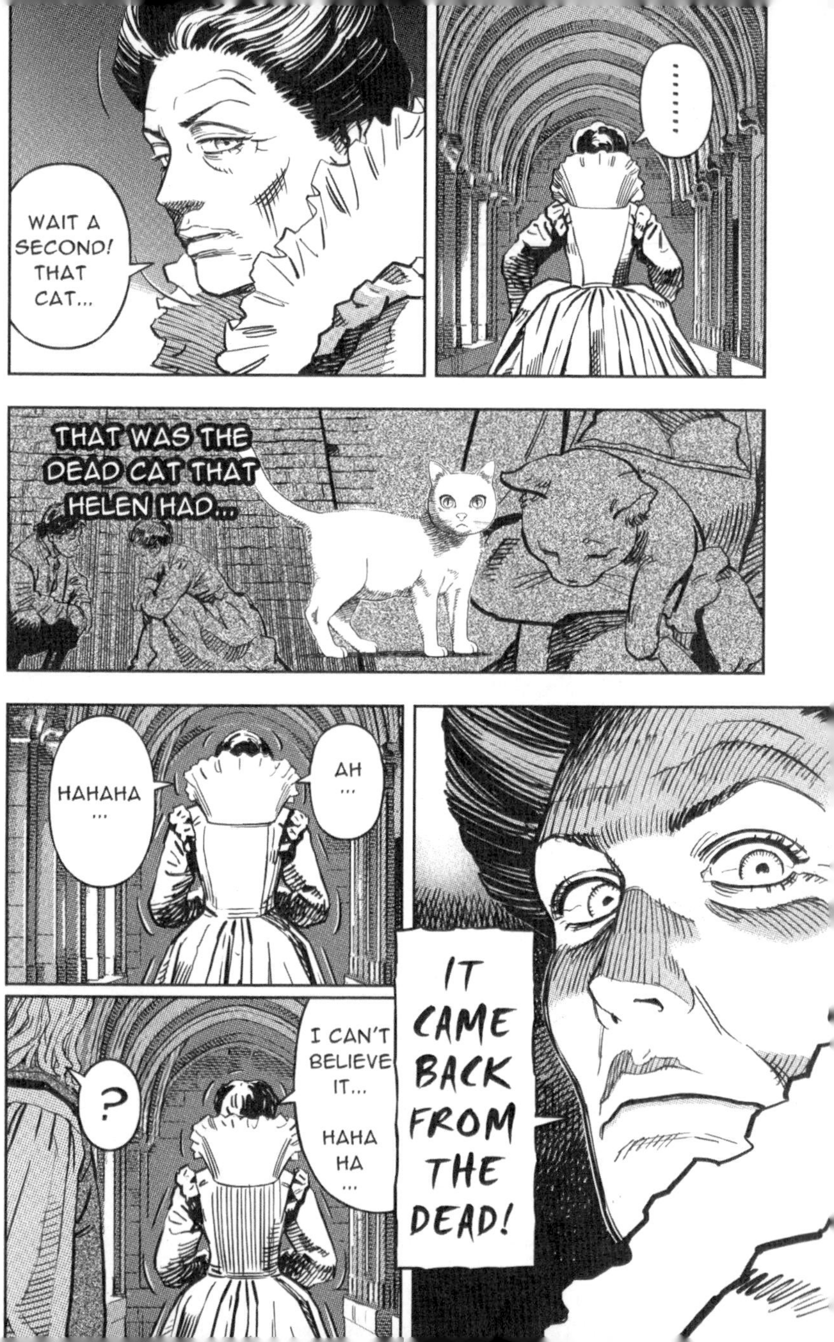

......
WAIT A SECOND! THAT CAT...
THAT WAS THE DEAD CAT THAT HELEN HAD...
IT CAME BACK FROM THE DEAD!
AH ...
HAHAHA ...
I CAN'T BELIEVE IT...
HAHA HA ...
?

CHAPTER 7
AN OLD QUEEN NO LONGER!

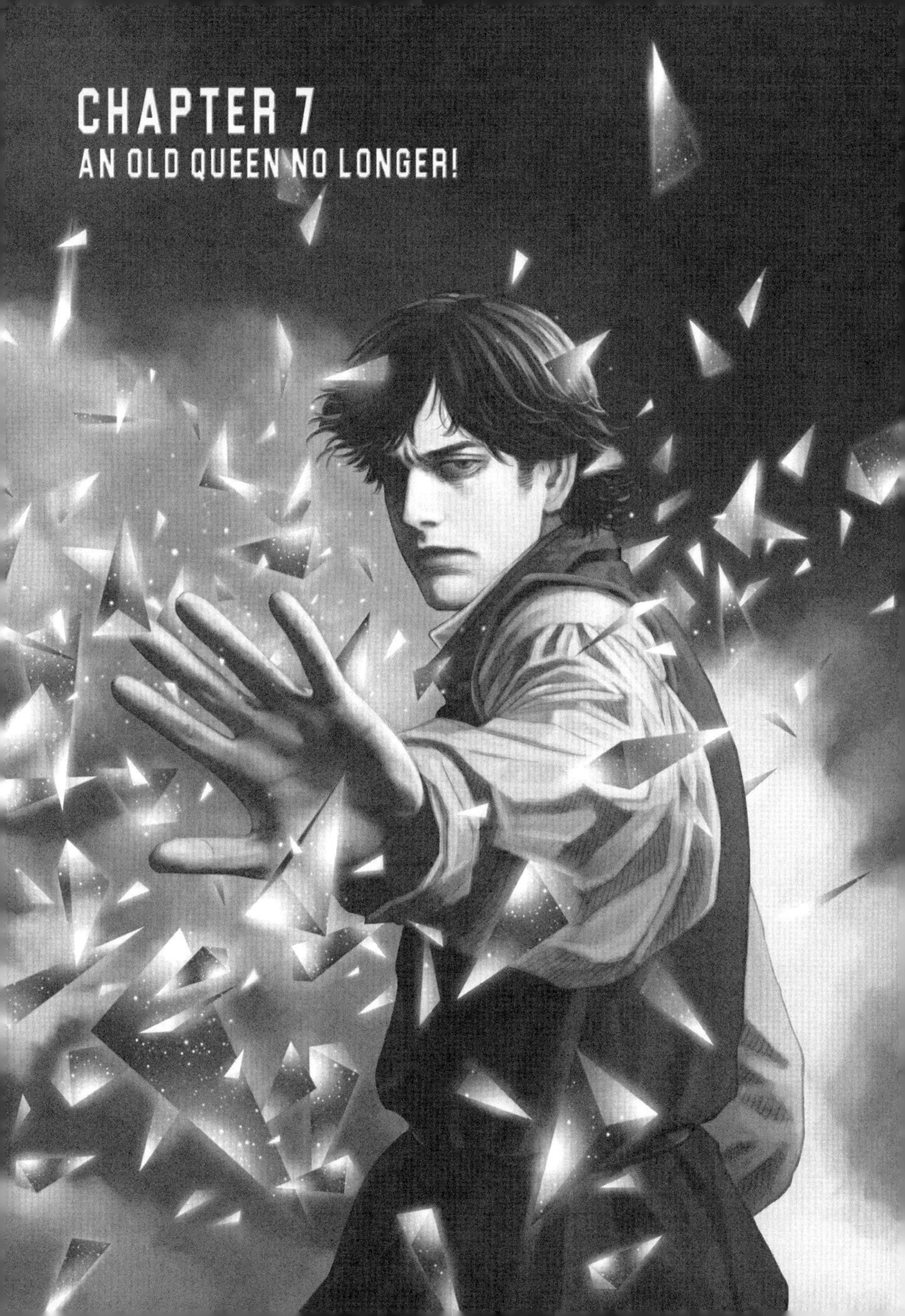

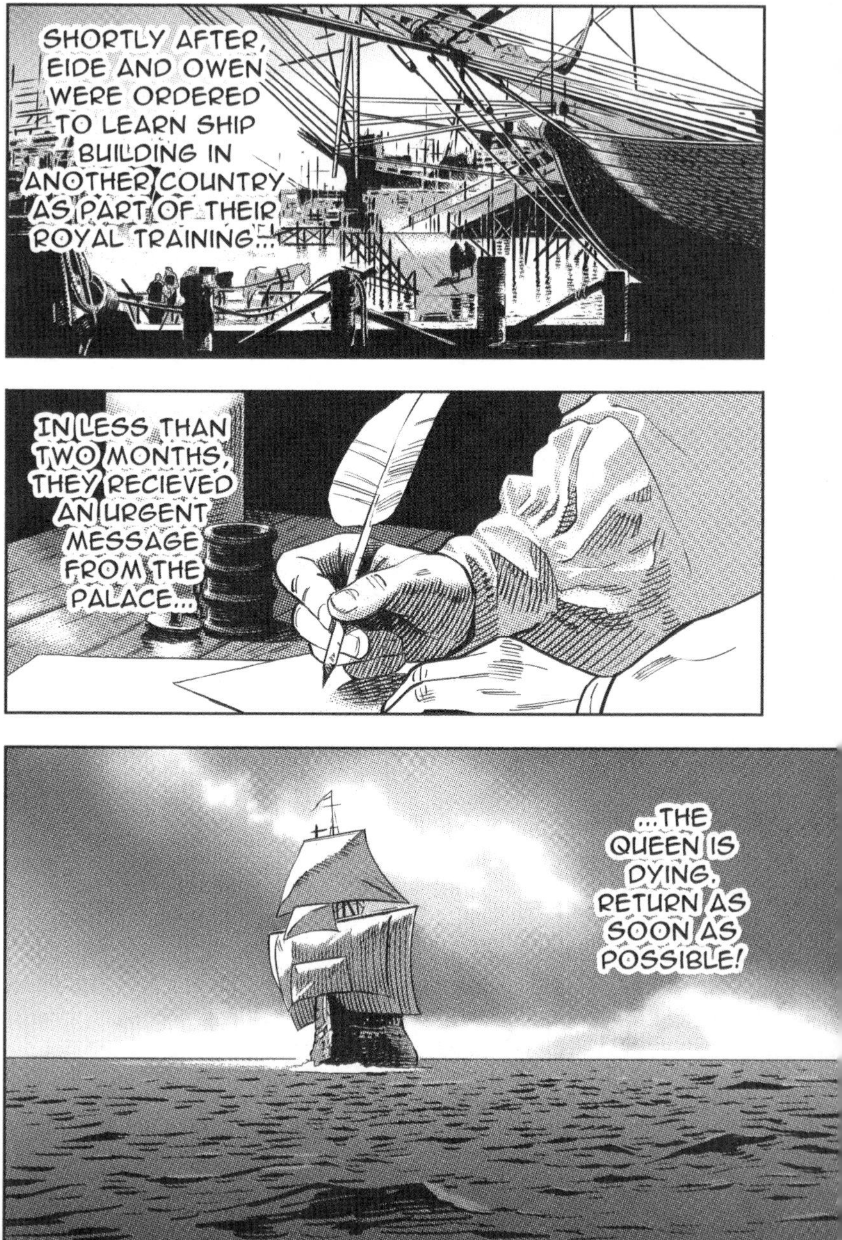
SHORTLY AFTER, EIDE AND OWEN WERE ORDERED TO LEARN SHIP BUILDING IN ANOTHER COUNTRY AS PART OF THEIR ROYAL TRAINING...
IN LESS THAN TWO MONTHS, THEY RECIEVED AN URGENT MESSAGE FROM THE PALACE...
...THE QUEEN IS DYING. RETURN AS SOON AS POSSIBLE!

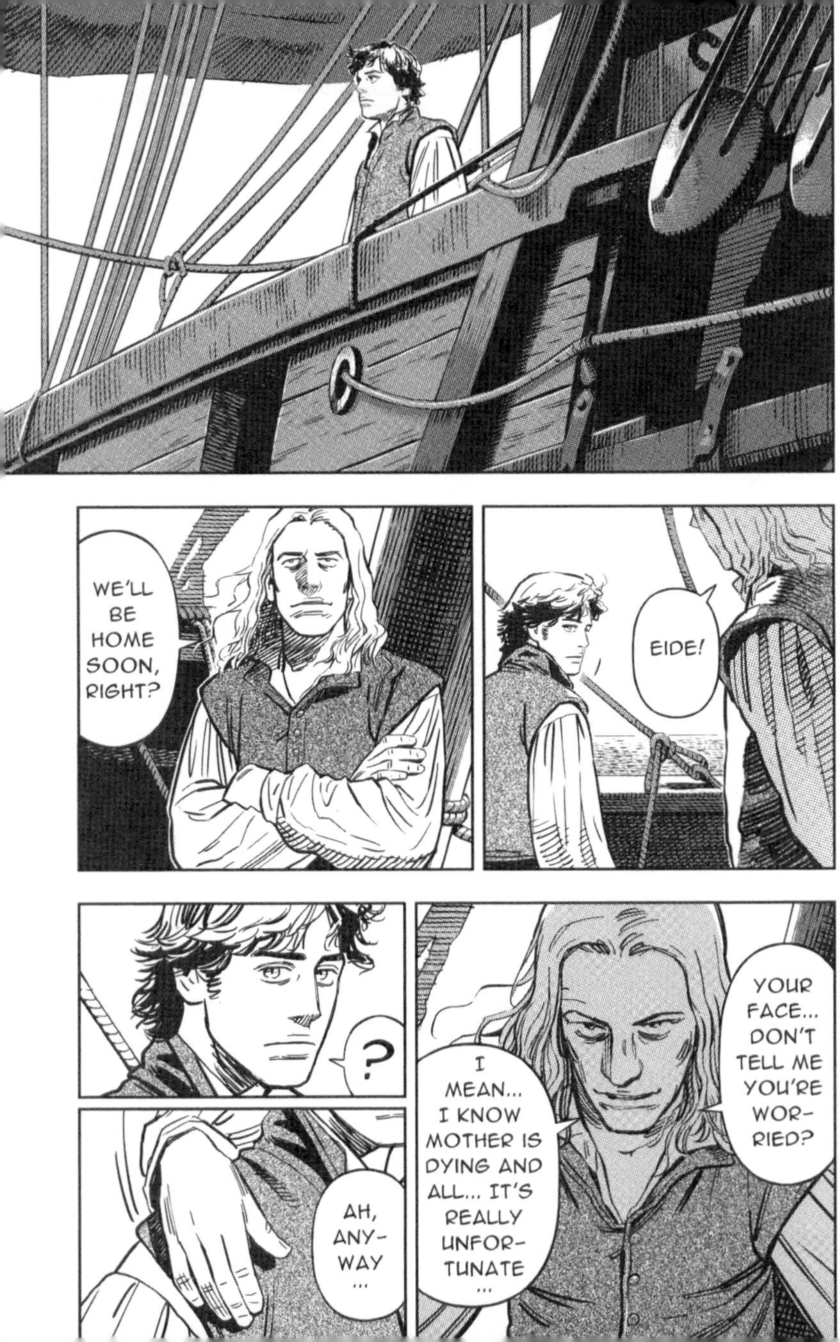
EIDE!
WE'LL BE HOME SOON, RIGHT?
YOUR FACE... DON'T TELL ME YOU'RE WOR-RIED?
I MEAN... I KNOW MOTHER IS DYING AND ALL... IT'S REALLY UNFOR-TUNATE ...
?
AH, ANY-WAY ...

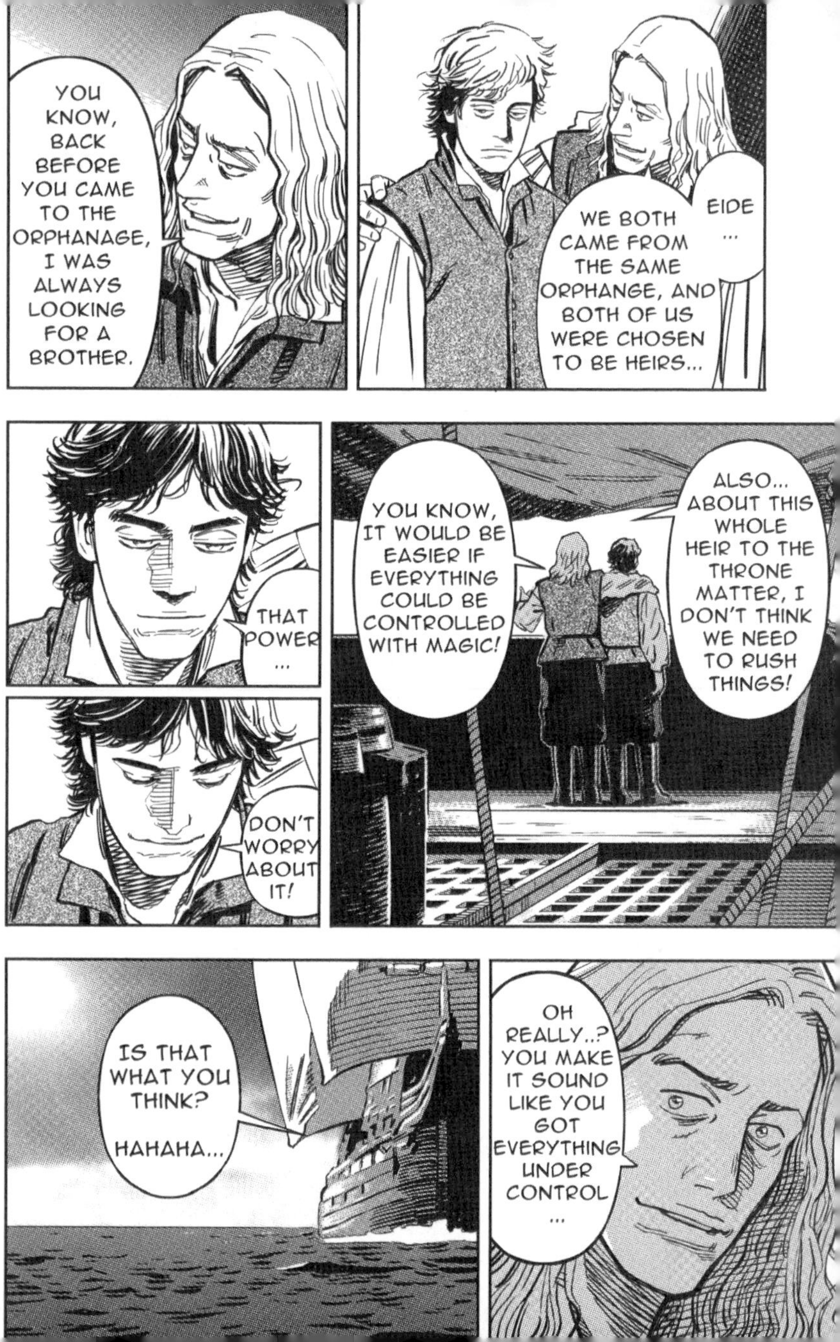
EIDE ...
WE BOTH CAME FROM THE SAME ORPHANGE, AND BOTH OF US WERE CHOSEN TO BE HEIRS...
YOU KNOW, BACK BEFORE YOU CAME TO THE ORPHANAGE, I WAS ALWAYS LOOKING FOR A BROTHER.
ALSO... ABOUT THIS WHOLE HEIR TO THE THRONE MATTER, I DON'T THINK WE NEED TO RUSH THINGS!
YOU KNOW, IT WOULD BE EASIER IF EVERYTHING COULD BE CONTROLLED WITH MAGIC!
THAT POWER ...
DON'T WORRY ABOUT IT!
OH REALLY..? YOU MAKE IT SOUND LIKE YOU GOT EVERYTHING UNDER CONTROL ...
IS THAT WHAT YOU THINK?
HAHAHA...

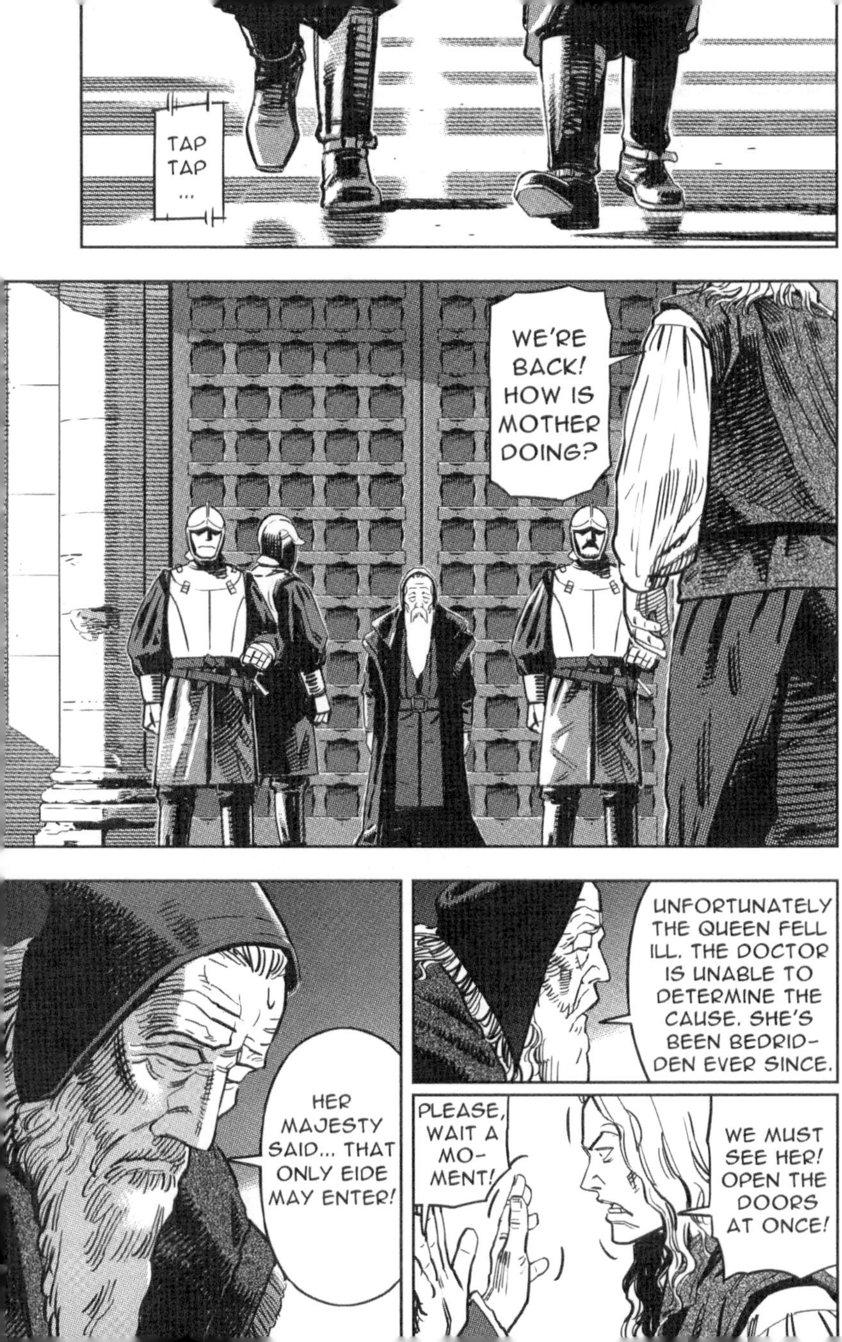
TAP TAP ...
WE'RE BACK! HOW IS MOTHER DOING?
UNFORTUNATELY THE QUEEN FELL ILL. THE DOCTOR IS UNABLE TO DETERMINE THE CAUSE. SHE'S BEEN BEDRID-DEN EVER SINCE.
WE MUST SEE HER! OPEN THE DOORS AT ONCE!
PLEASE, WAIT A MO-MENT!
HER MAJESTY SAID... THAT ONLY EIDE MAY ENTER!

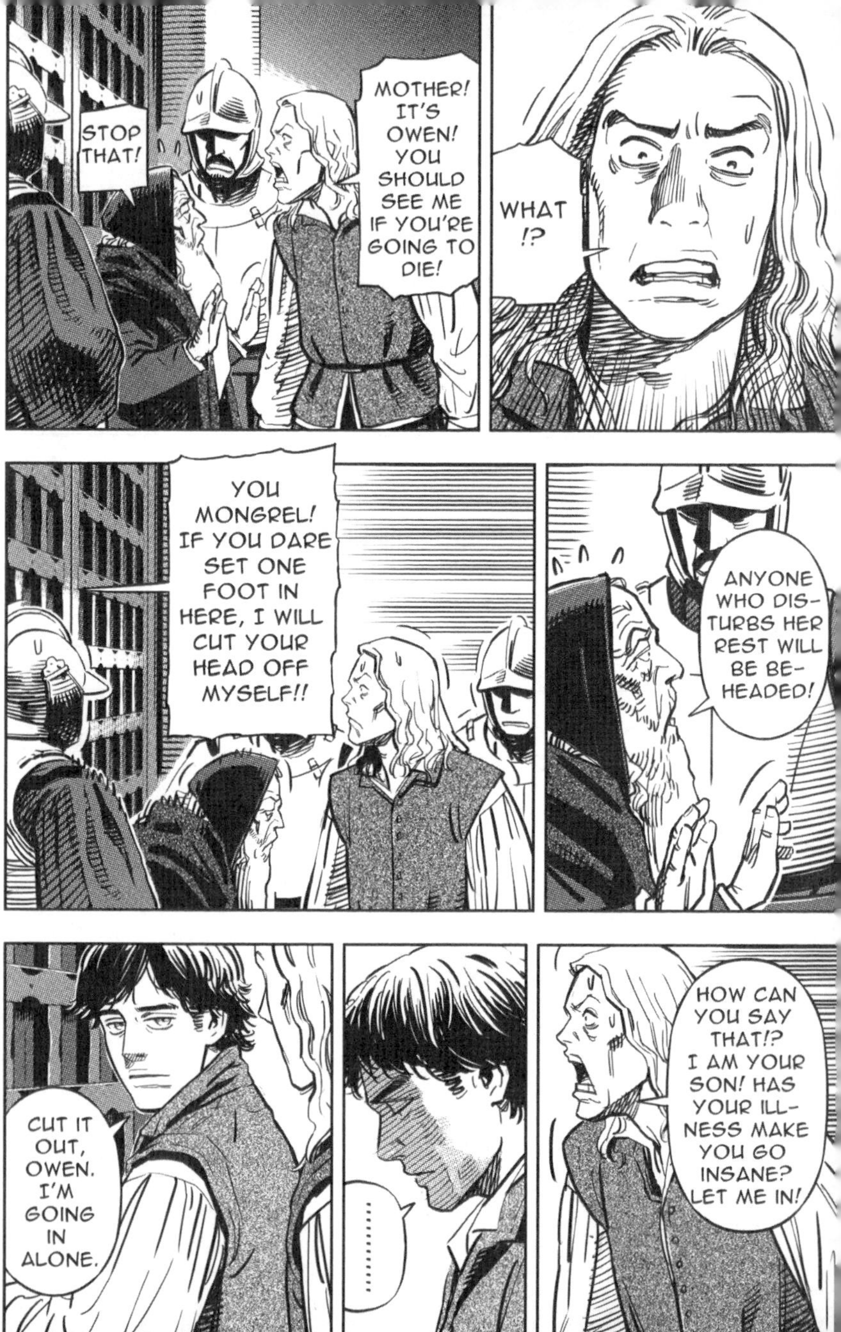
WHAT !?
MOTHER! IT'S OWEN! YOU SHOULD SEE ME IF YOU'RE GOING TO DIE!
STOP THAT!
ANYONE WHO DIS- TURBS HER REST WILL BE BE- HEADED!
YOU MONGREL! IF YOU DARE SET ONE FOOT IN HERE, I WILL CUT YOUR HEAD OFF MYSELF!!
HOW CAN YOU SAY THAT!? I AM YOUR SON! HAS YOUR ILL- NESS MAKE YOU GO INSANE? LET ME IN!
......
CUT IT OUT, OWEN. I'M GOING IN ALONE.

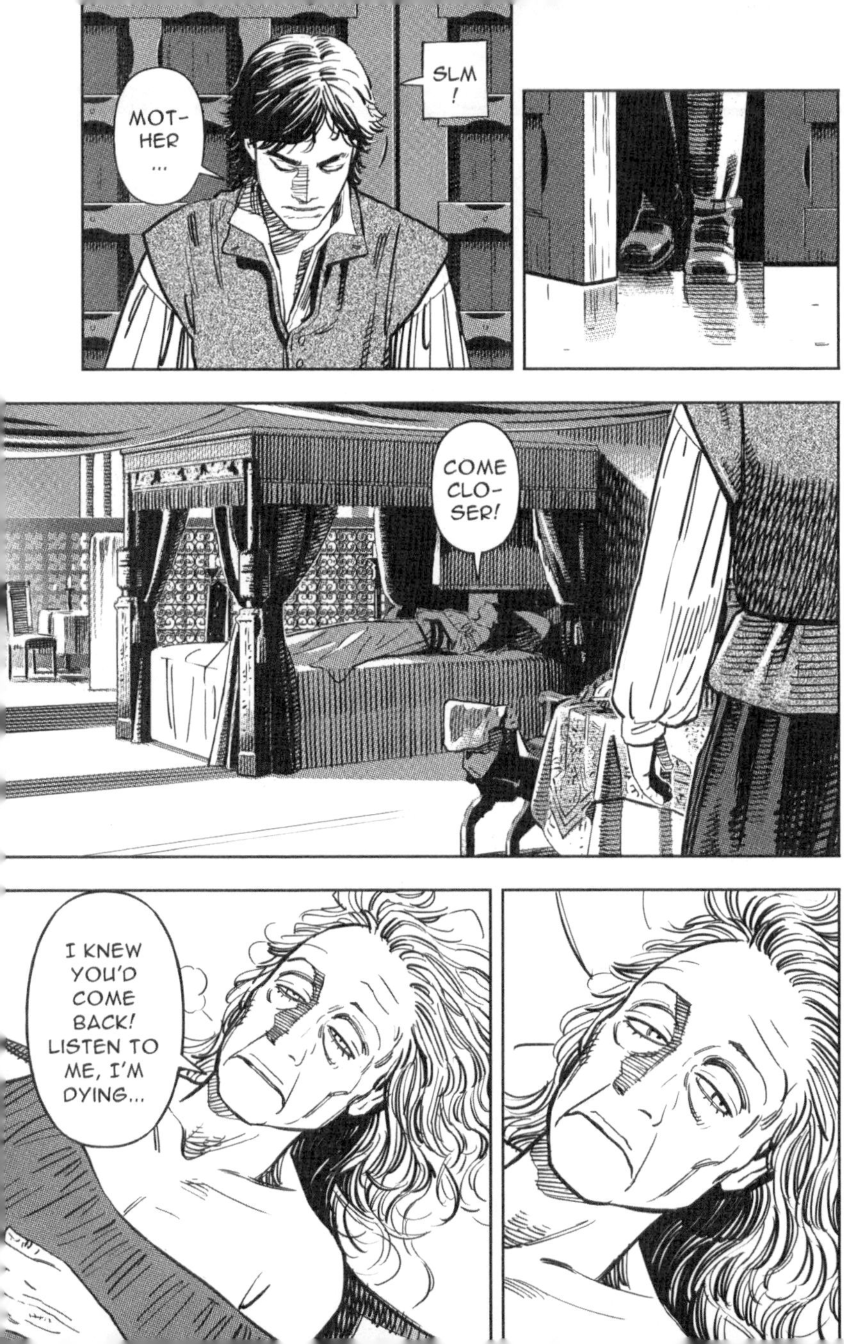
SLM!
MOT-HER...
COME CLO-SER!
I KNEW YOU'D COME BACK! LISTEN TO ME, I'M DYING...

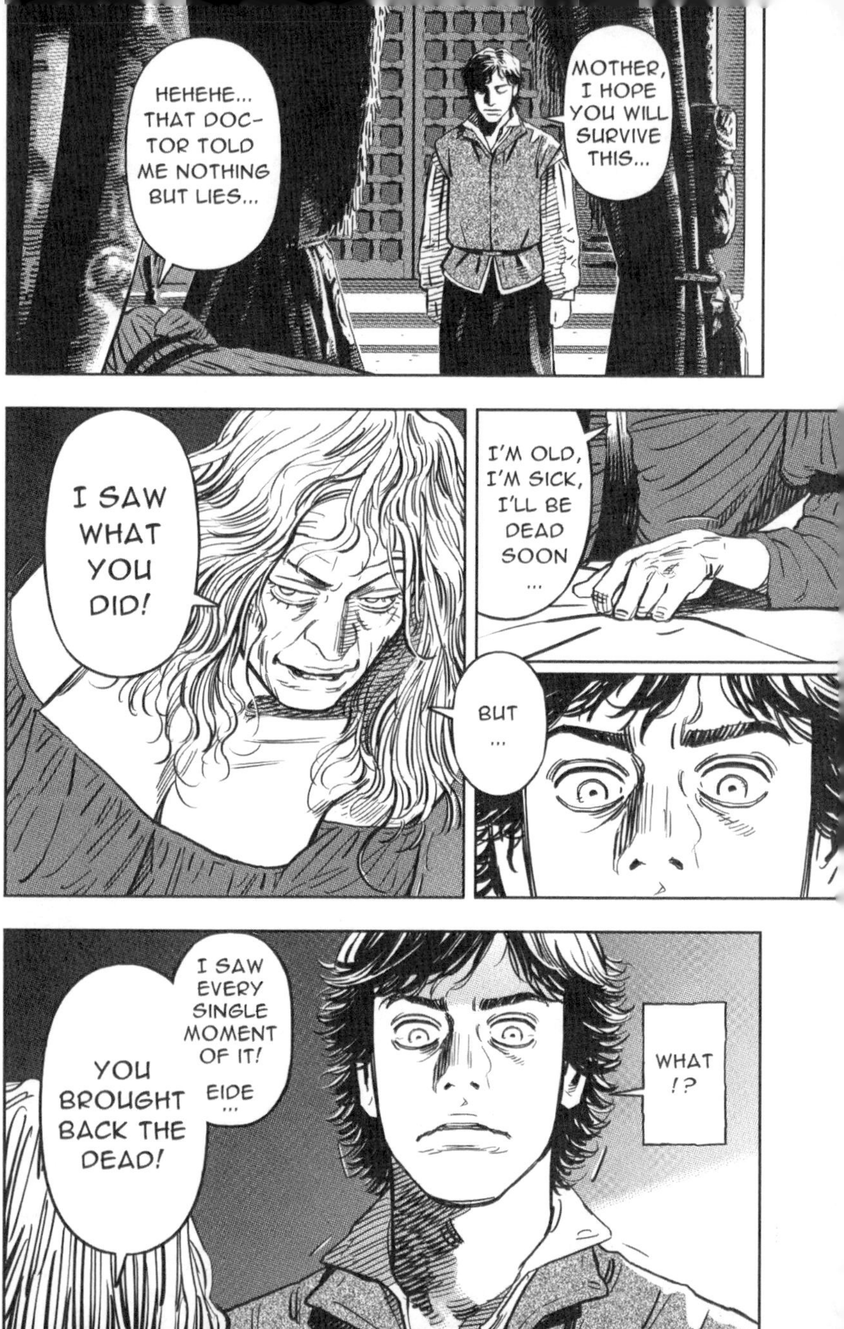
MOTHER, I HOPE YOU WILL SURVIVE THIS...
HEHEHE... THAT DOC-TOR TOLD ME NOTHING BUT LIES...
I'M OLD, I'M SICK, I'LL BE DEAD SOON ...
BUT ...
I SAW WHAT YOU DID!
WHAT !?
I SAW EVERY SINGLE MOMENT OF IT!
EIDE ...
YOU BROUGHT BACK THE DEAD!

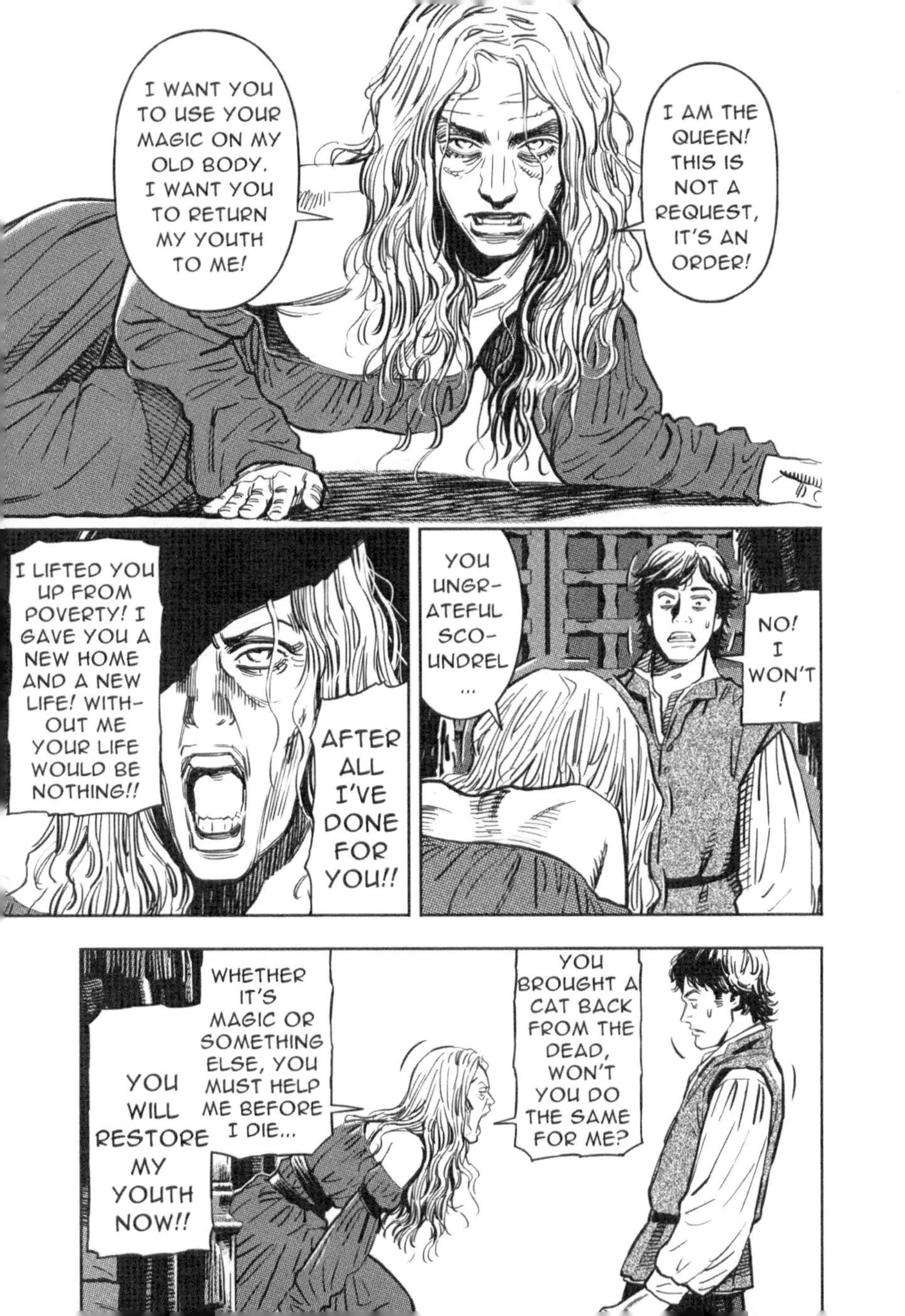
I AM THE QUEEN! THIS IS NOT A REQUEST, IT'S AN ORDER!
I WANT YOU TO USE YOUR MAGIC ON MY OLD BODY. I WANT YOU TO RETURN MY YOUTH TO ME!
NO! I WON'T!
YOU UNGRATEFUL SCOUNDREL...
I LIFTED YOU UP FROM POVERTY! I GAVE YOU A NEW HOME AND A NEW LIFE! WITHOUT ME YOUR LIFE WOULD BE NOTHING!!
AFTER ALL I'VE DONE FOR YOU!!
YOU BROUGHT A CAT BACK FROM THE DEAD, WON'T YOU DO THE SAME FOR ME?
WHETHER IT'S MAGIC OR SOMETHING ELSE, YOU MUST HELP ME BEFORE I DIE...
YOU WILL RESTORE MY YOUTH NOW!!

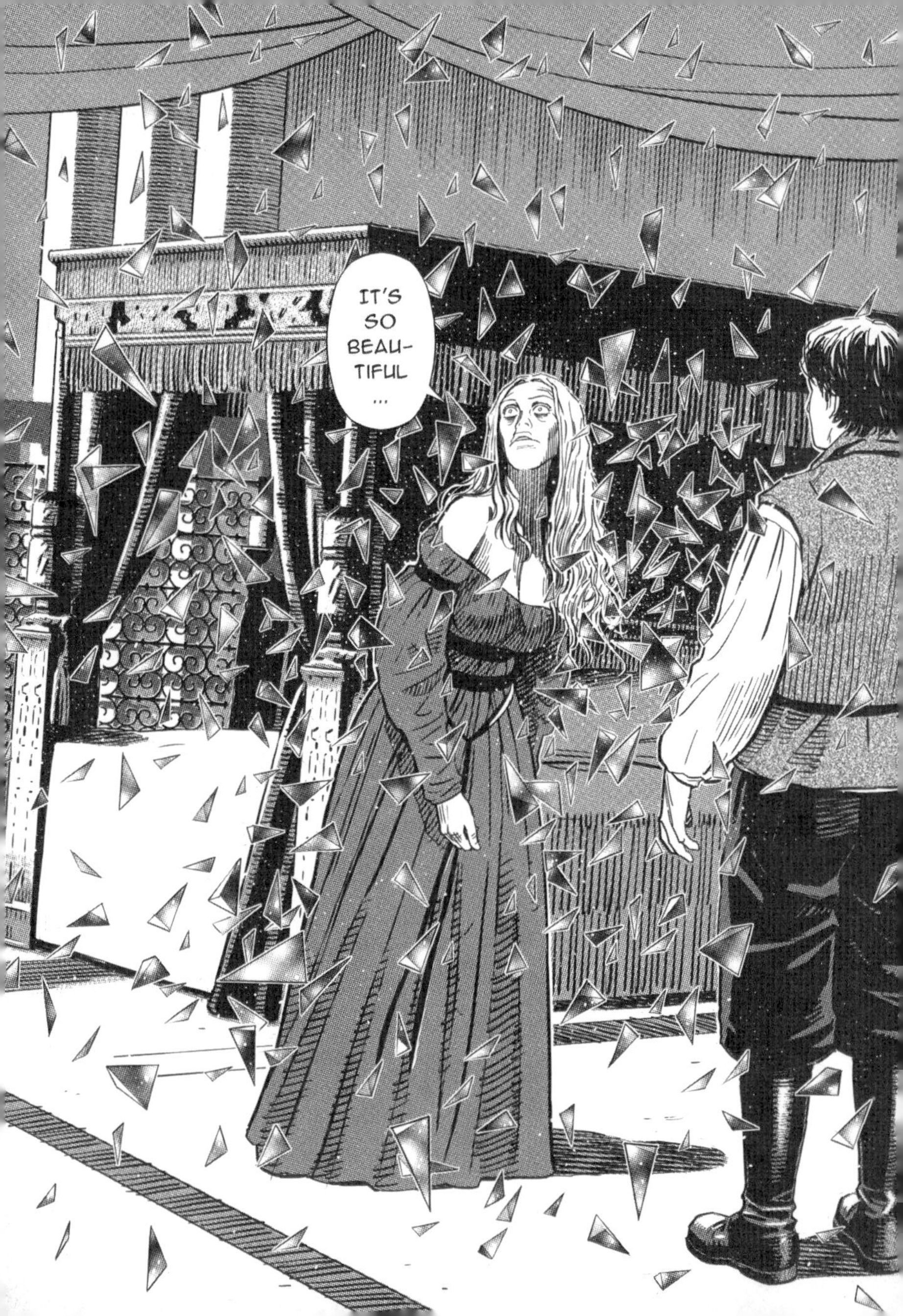
IT'S SO BEAU- TIFUL ...

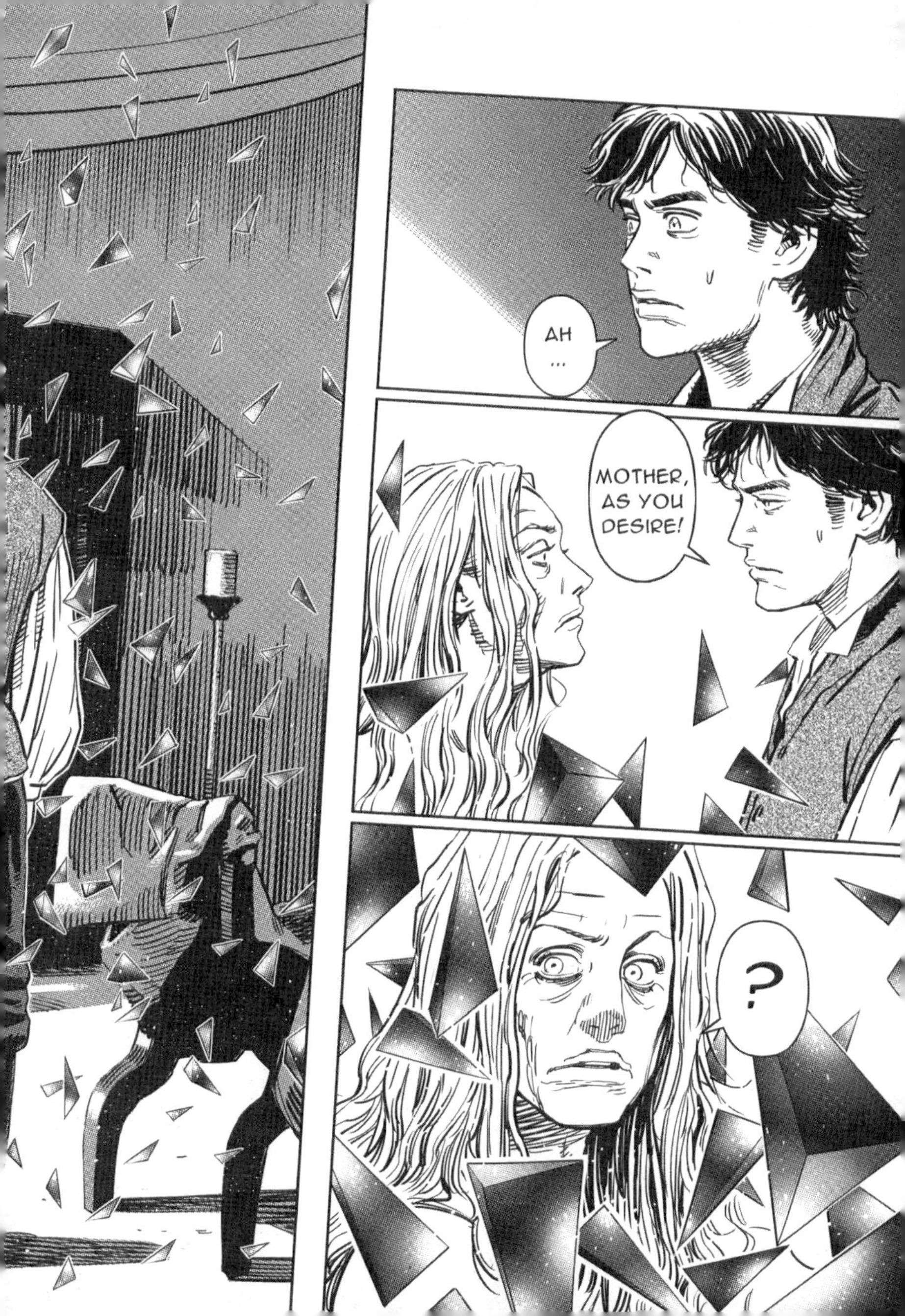
AH ...
MOTHER, AS YOU DESIRE!
?

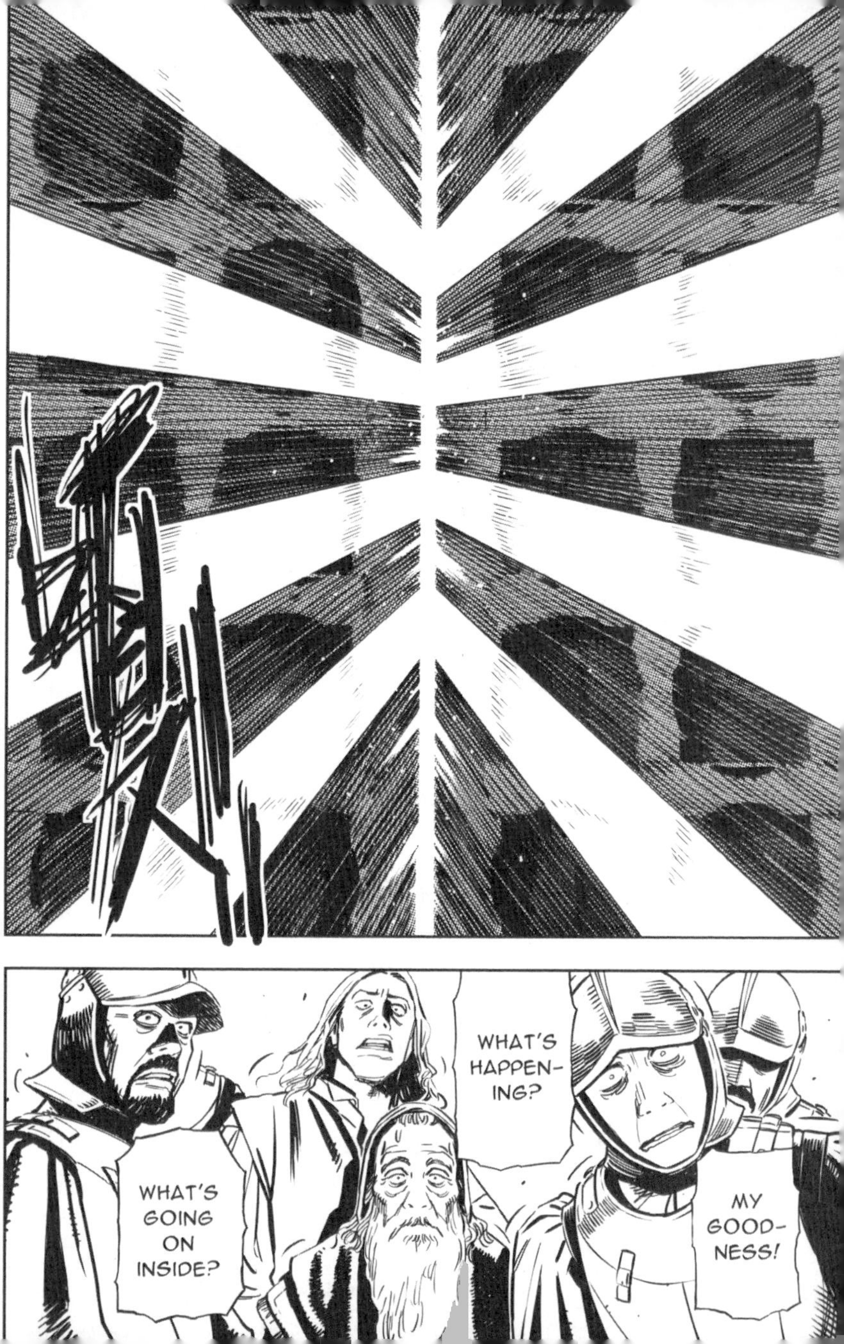
MY GOODNESS!
WHAT'S HAPPENING?
WHAT'S GOING ON INSIDE?

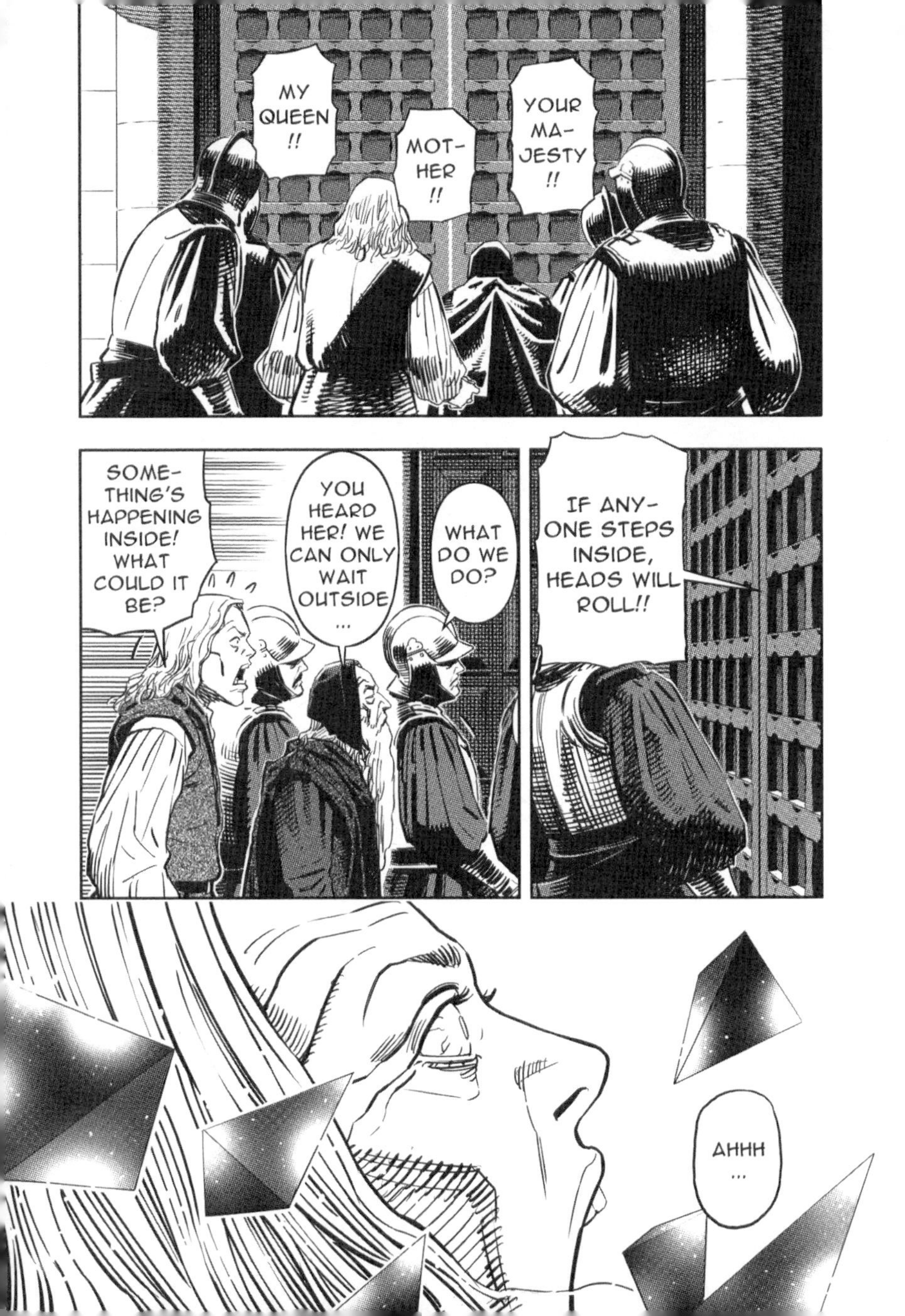
YOUR MA- JESTY !!
MOT- HER !!
MY QUEEN !!
IF ANY- ONE STEPS INSIDE, HEADS WILL ROLL!!
WHAT DO WE DO?
YOU HEARD HER! WE CAN ONLY WAIT OUTSIDE ...
SOME- THING'S HAPPENING INSIDE! WHAT COULD IT BE?
AHHH ...

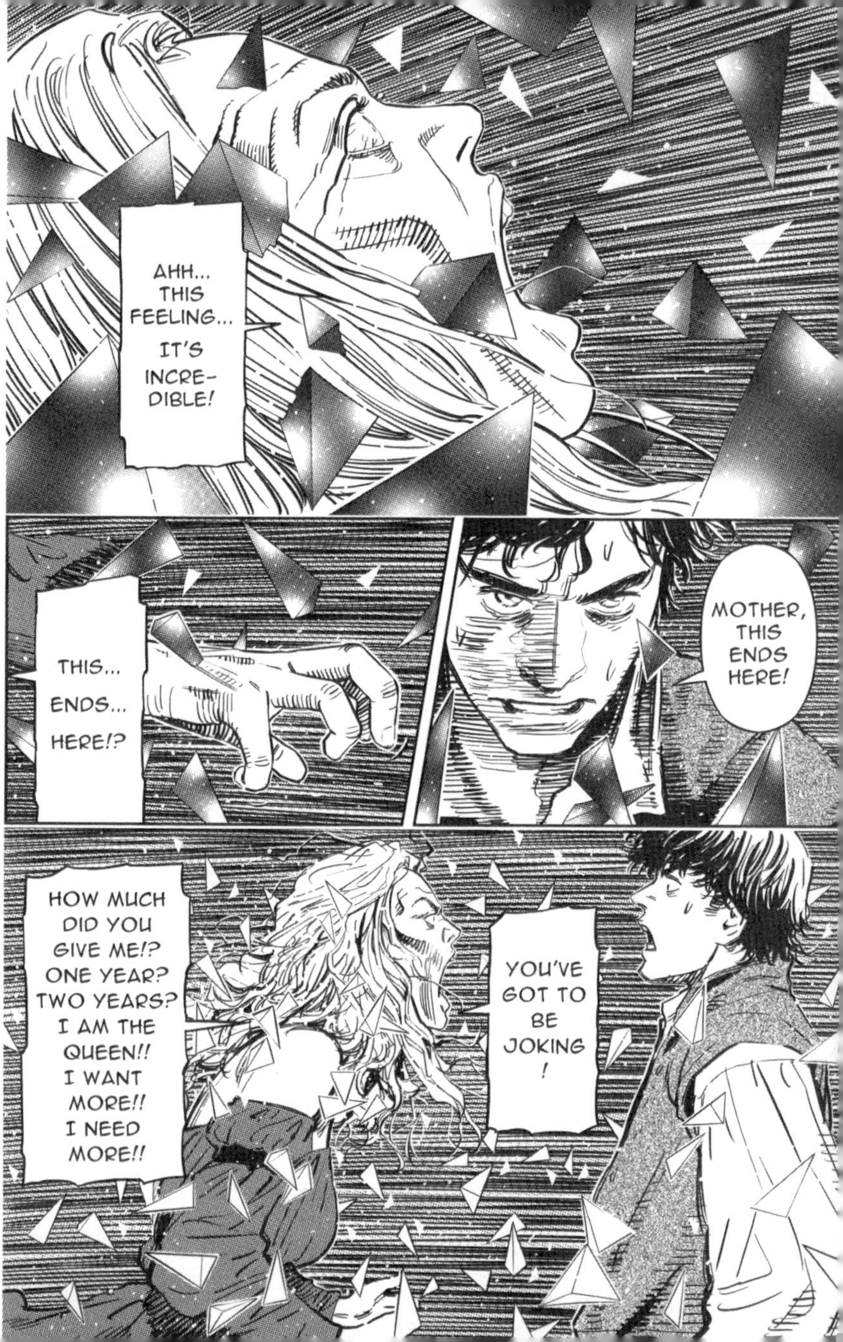
AHH... THIS FEELING... IT'S INCRE-DIBLE!
MOTHER, THIS ENDS HERE!
THIS... ENDS... HERE!?
YOU'VE GOT TO BE JOKING!
HOW MUCH DID YOU GIVE ME!? ONE YEAR? TWO YEARS? I AM THE QUEEN!! I WANT MORE!! I NEED MORE!!

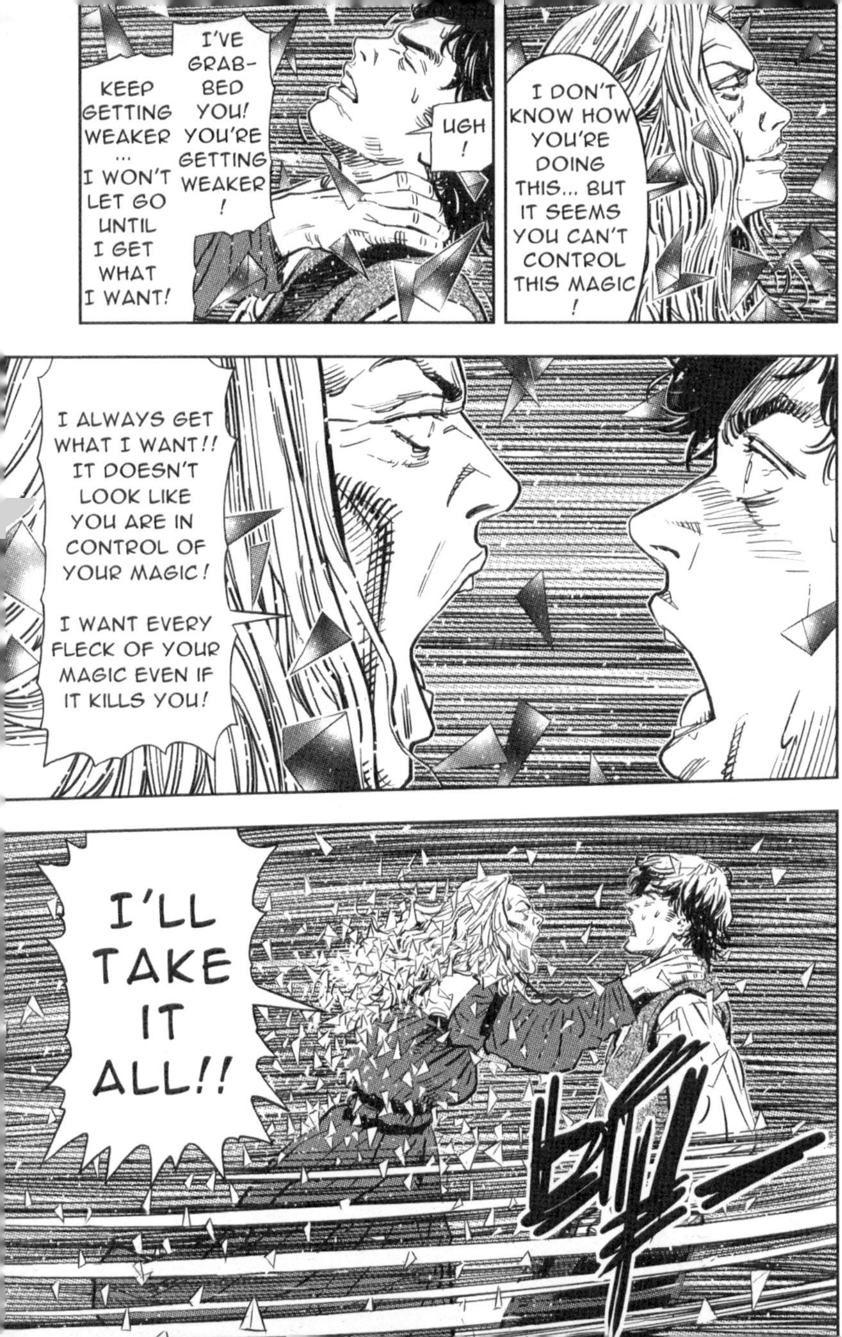
I DON'T KNOW HOW YOU'RE DOING THIS... BUT IT SEEMS YOU CAN'T CONTROL THIS MAGIC!
UGH!
I'VE GRAB-BED YOU! YOU'RE GETTING WEAKER!
KEEP GETTING WEAKER... I WON'T LET GO UNTIL I GET WHAT I WANT!
I ALWAYS GET WHAT I WANT!! IT DOESN'T LOOK LIKE YOU ARE IN CONTROL OF YOUR MAGIC!
I WANT EVERY FLECK OF YOUR MAGIC EVEN IF IT KILLS YOU!
I'LL TAKE IT ALL!!

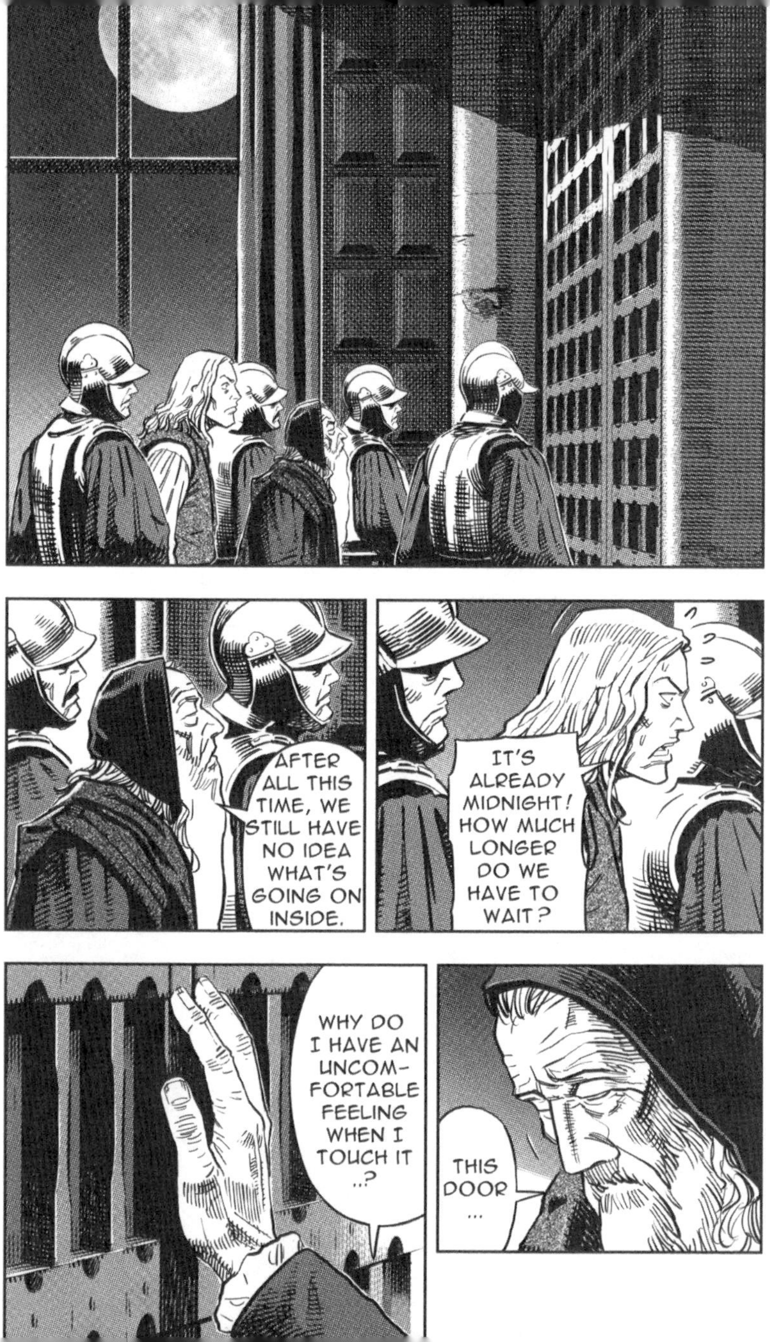
IT'S ALREADY MIDNIGHT! HOW MUCH LONGER DO WE HAVE TO WAIT?
AFTER ALL THIS TIME, WE STILL HAVE NO IDEA WHAT'S GOING ON INSIDE.
THIS DOOR ...
WHY DO I HAVE AN UNCOM-FORTABLE FEELING WHEN I TOUCH IT ..?

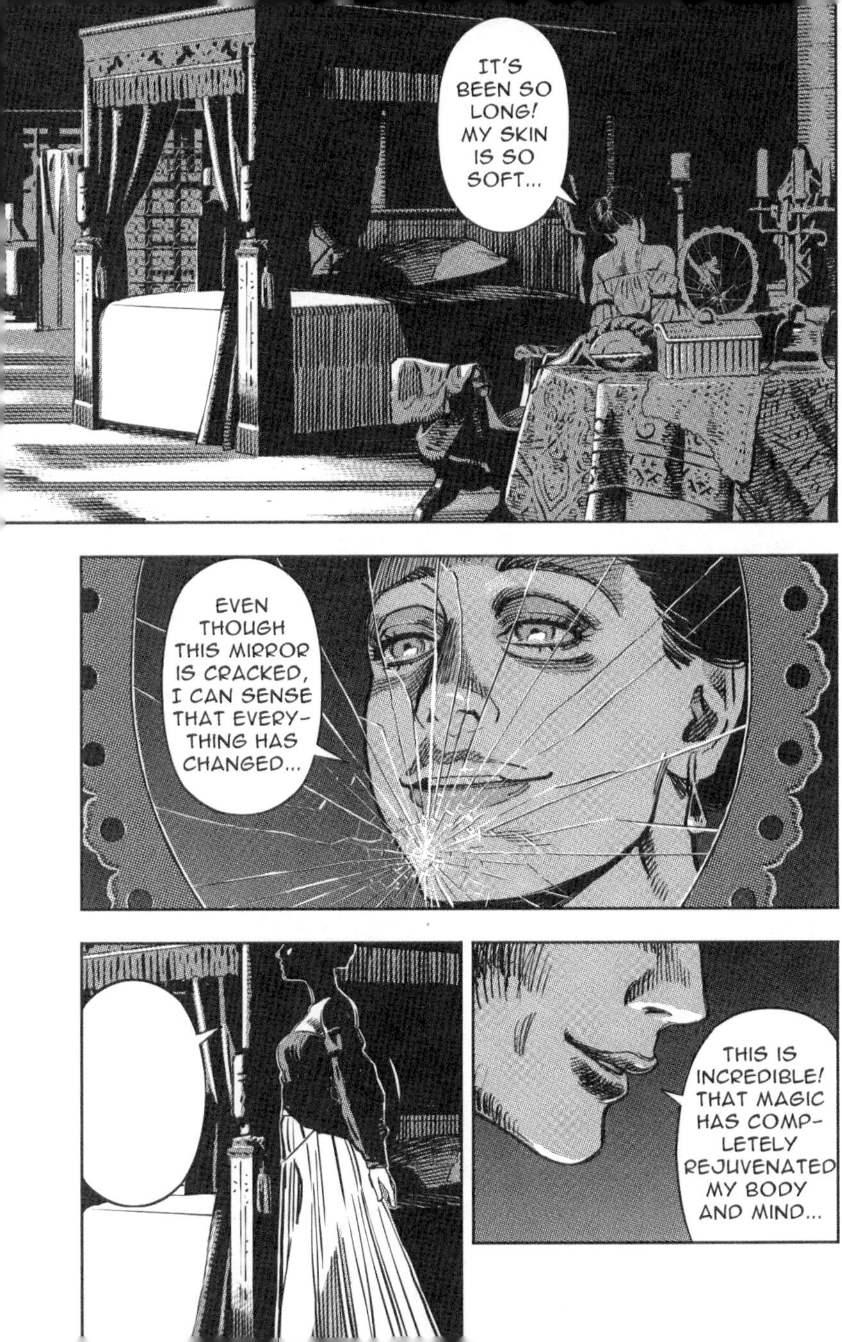
IT'S BEEN SO LONG! MY SKIN IS SO SOFT...
EVEN THOUGH THIS MIRROR IS CRACKED, I CAN SENSE THAT EVERY-THING HAS CHANGED...
THIS IS INCREDIBLE! THAT MAGIC HAS COMP-LETELY REJUVENATED MY BODY AND MIND...

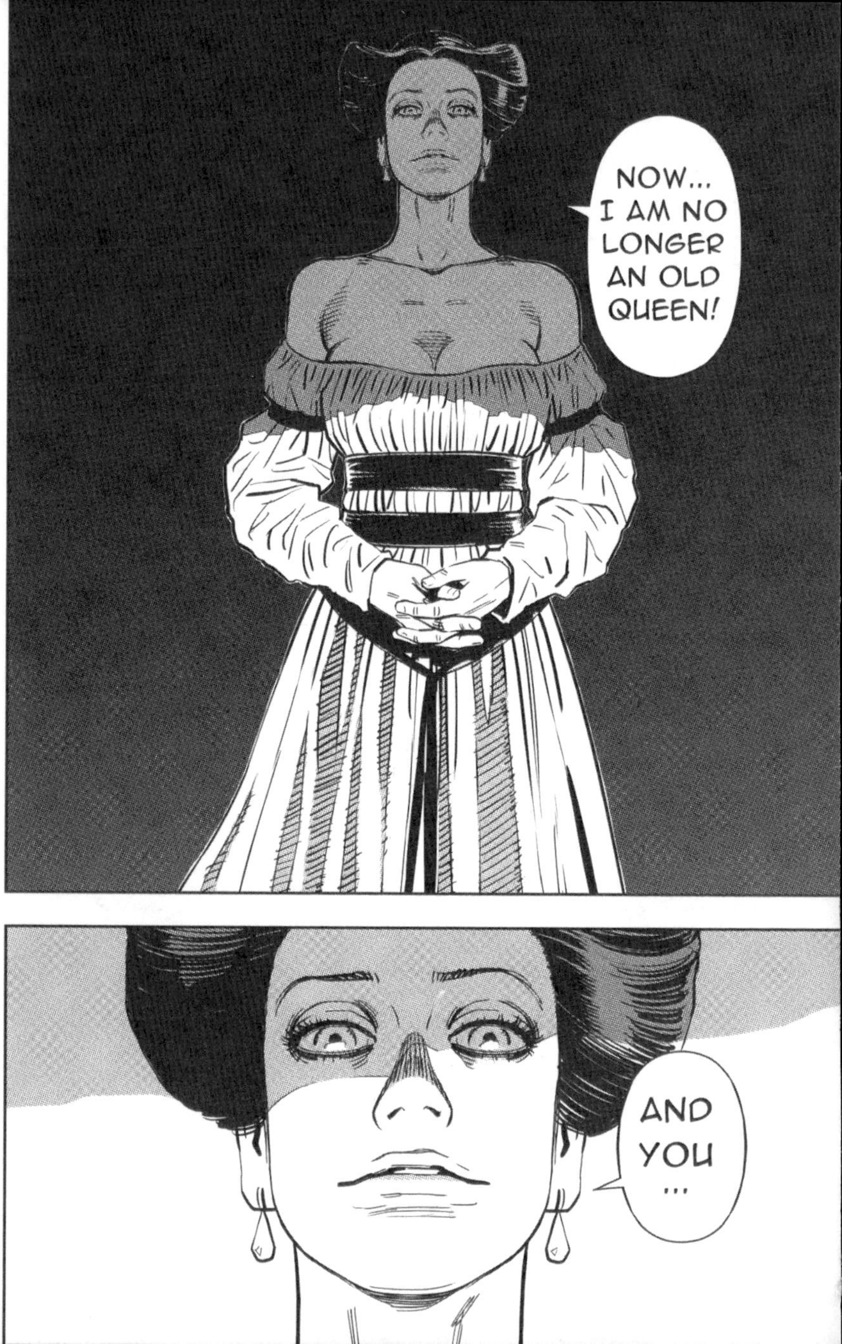
NOW... I AM NO LONGER AN OLD QUEEN!
AND YOU ...

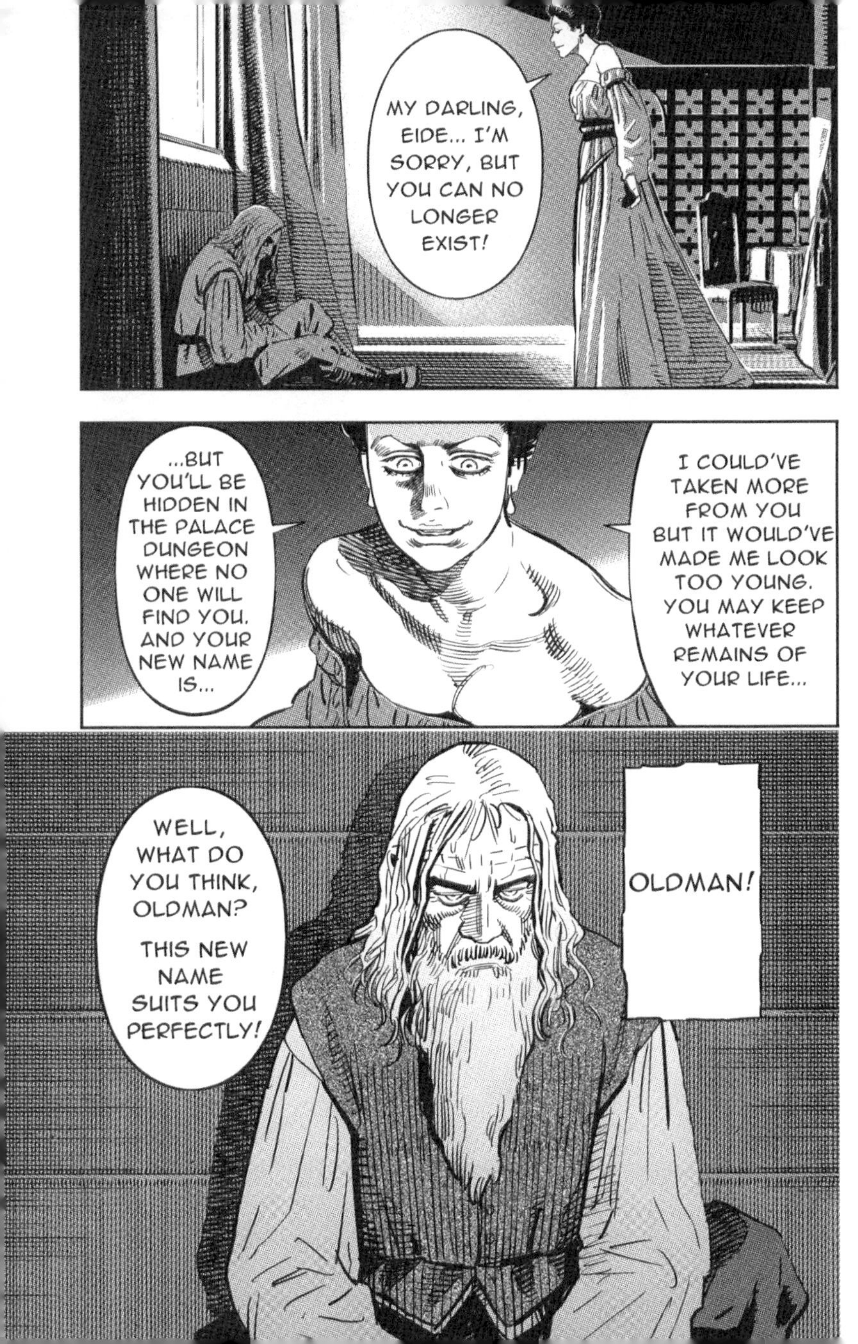
MY DARLING, EIDE... I'M SORRY, BUT YOU CAN NO LONGER EXIST!
I COULD'VE TAKEN MORE FROM YOU BUT IT WOULD'VE MADE ME LOOK TOO YOUNG. YOU MAY KEEP WHATEVER REMAINS OF YOUR LIFE...
...BUT YOU'LL BE HIDDEN IN THE PALACE DUNGEON WHERE NO ONE WILL FIND YOU. AND YOUR NEW NAME IS...
OLDMAN!
WELL, WHAT DO YOU THINK, OLDMAN?
THIS NEW NAME SUITS YOU PERFECTLY!

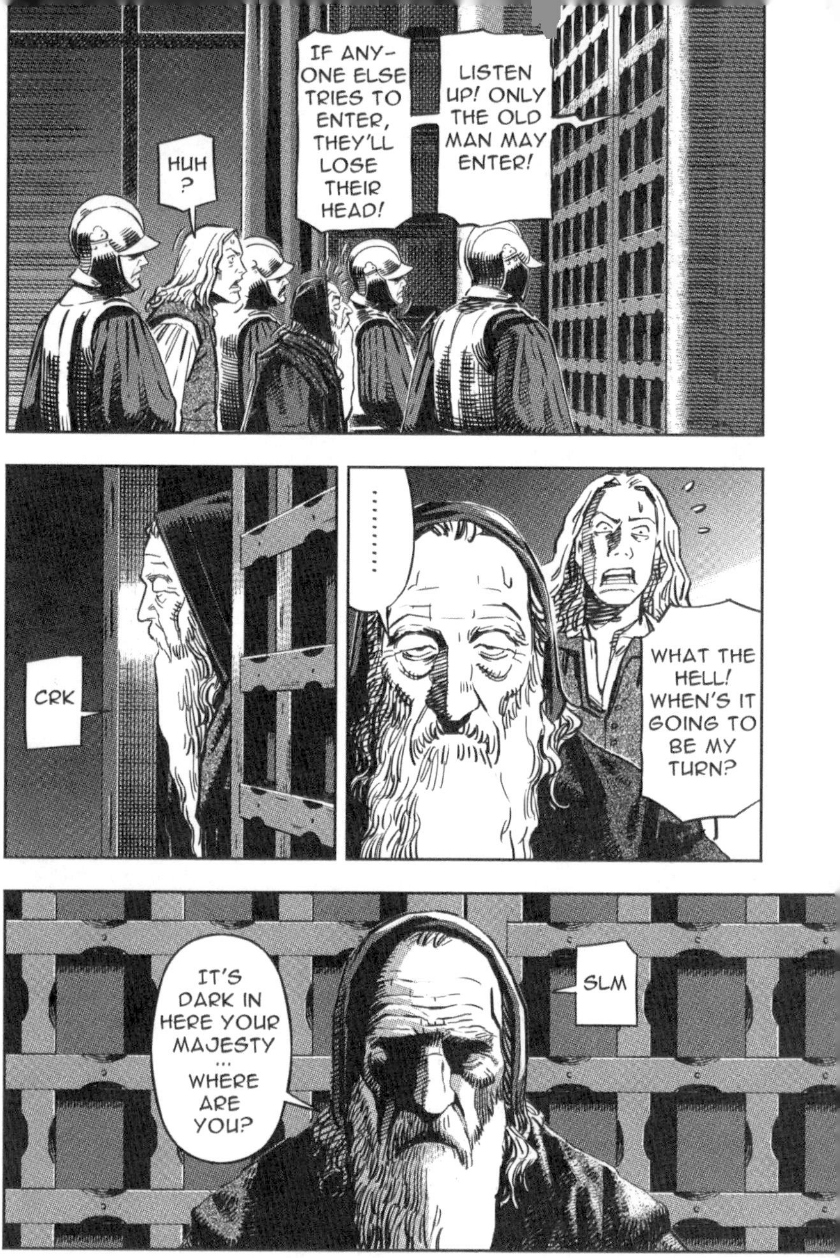
LISTEN UP! ONLY THE OLD MAN MAY ENTER!
IF ANY-ONE ELSE TRIES TO ENTER, THEY'LL LOSE THEIR HEAD!
HUH?
......
WHAT THE HELL! WHEN'S IT GOING TO BE MY TURN?
CRK
SLM
IT'S DARK IN HERE YOUR MAJESTY ... WHERE ARE YOU?

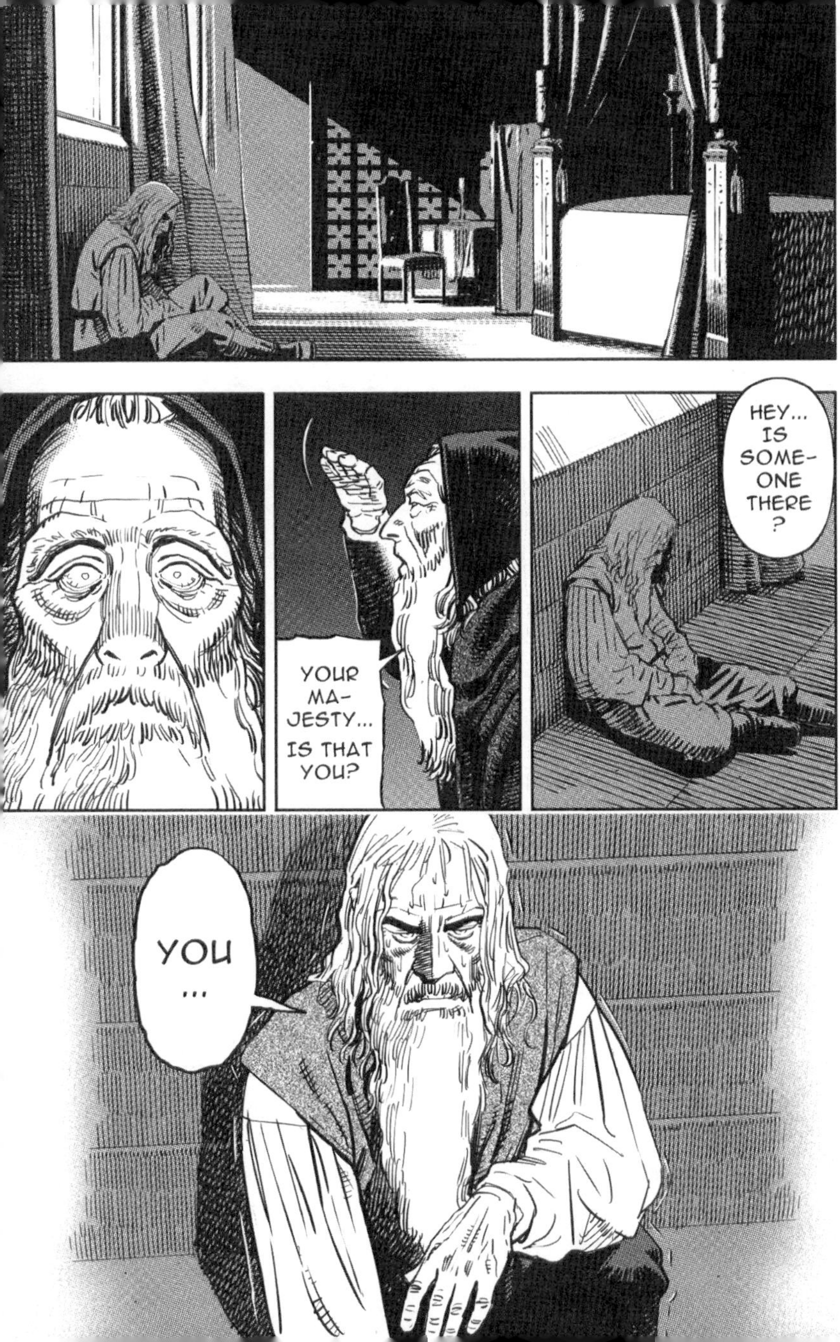
HEY... IS SOMEONE-ONE THERE?
YOUR MA-JESTY... IS THAT YOU?
YOU ...

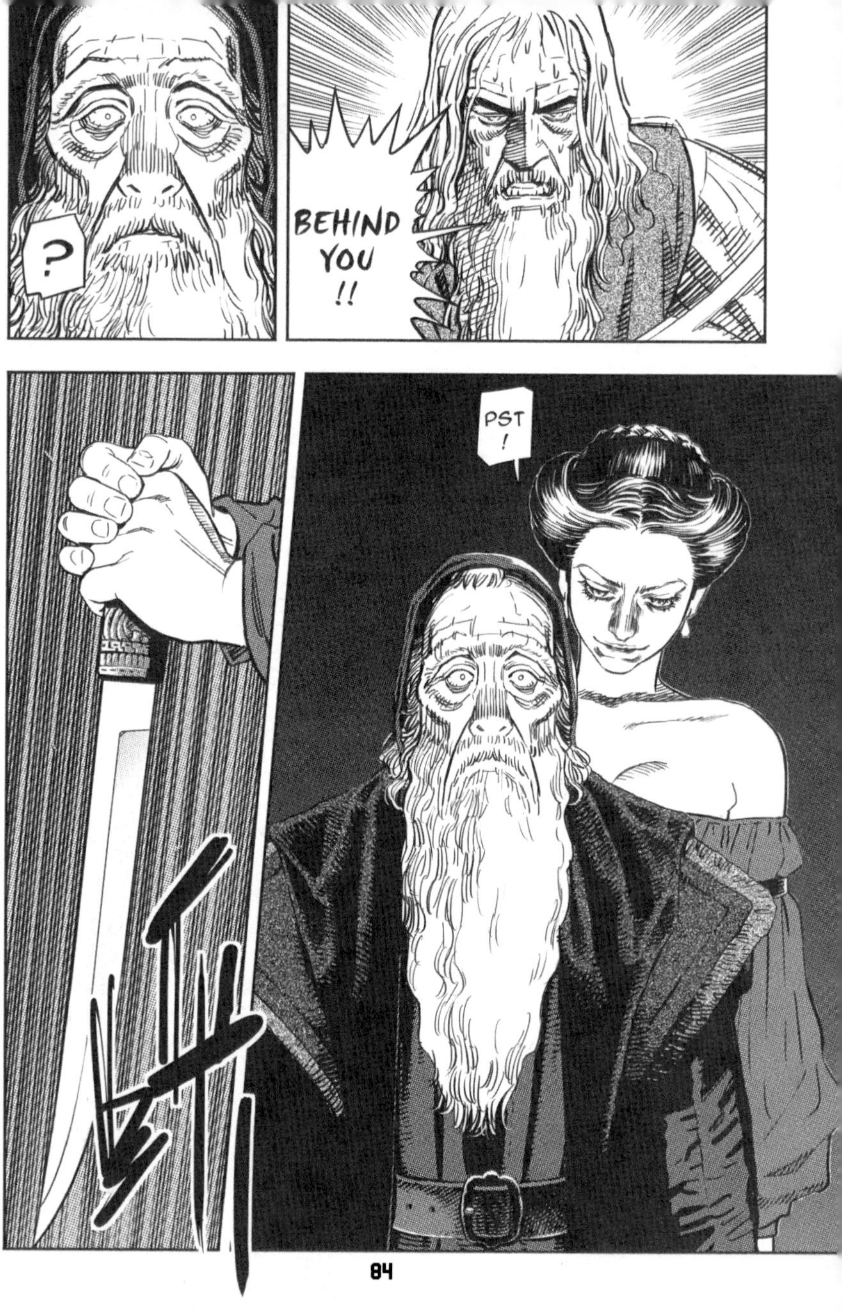
BEHIND YOU !!
?
PST !

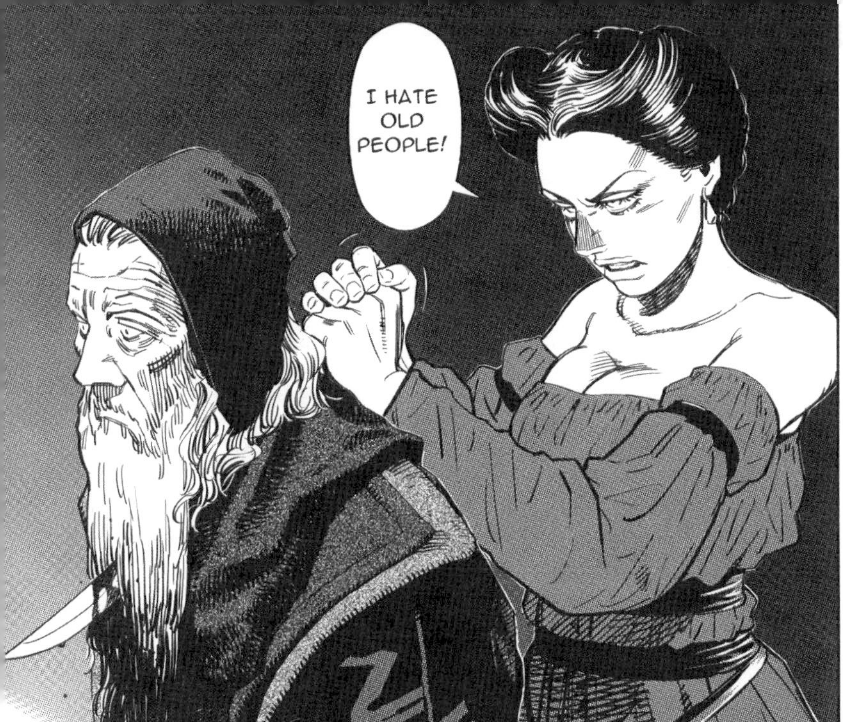
I HATE OLD PEOPLE!
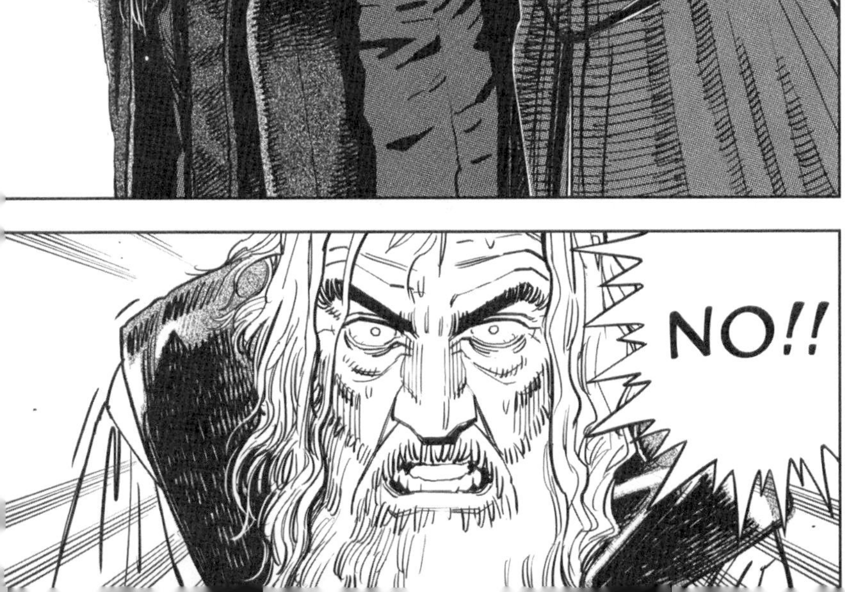
NO!!

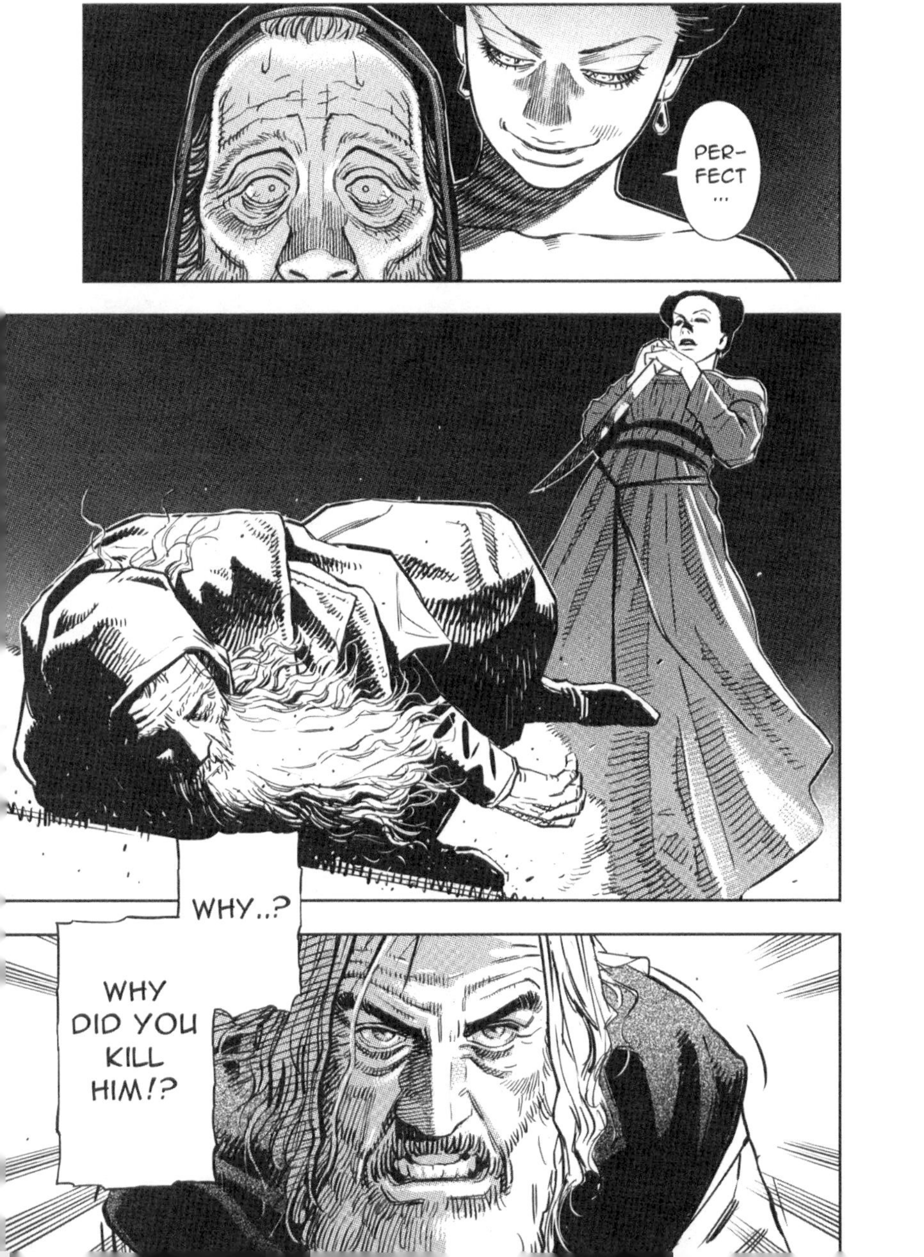
PER-
FECT
...
WHY..?
WHY
DID YOU
KILL
HIM!?

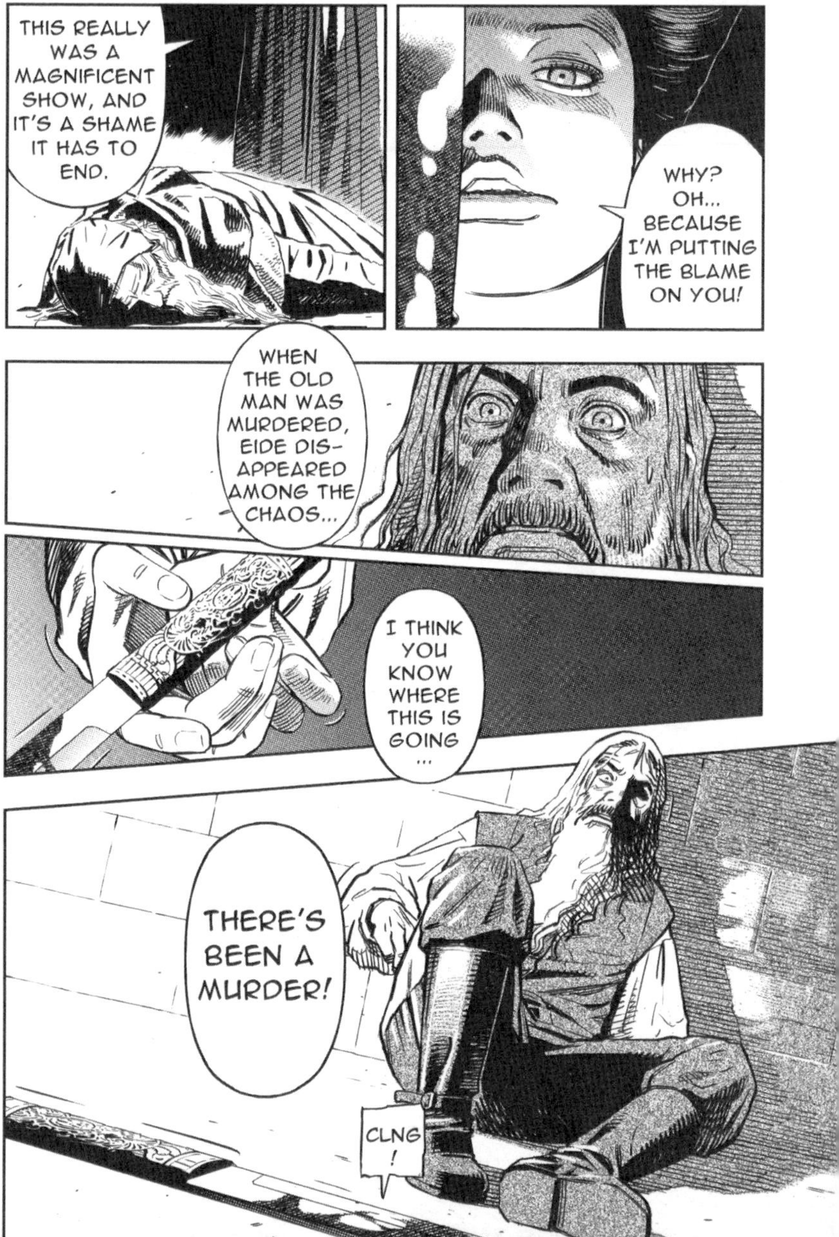
THIS REALLY WAS A MAGNIFICENT SHOW, AND IT'S A SHAME IT HAS TO END.
WHY? OH... BECAUSE I'M PUTTING THE BLAME ON YOU!
WHEN THE OLD MAN WAS MURDERED, EIDE DIS-APPEARED AMONG THE CHAOS...
I THINK YOU KNOW WHERE THIS IS GOING ...
THERE'S BEEN A MURDER!
CLNG !

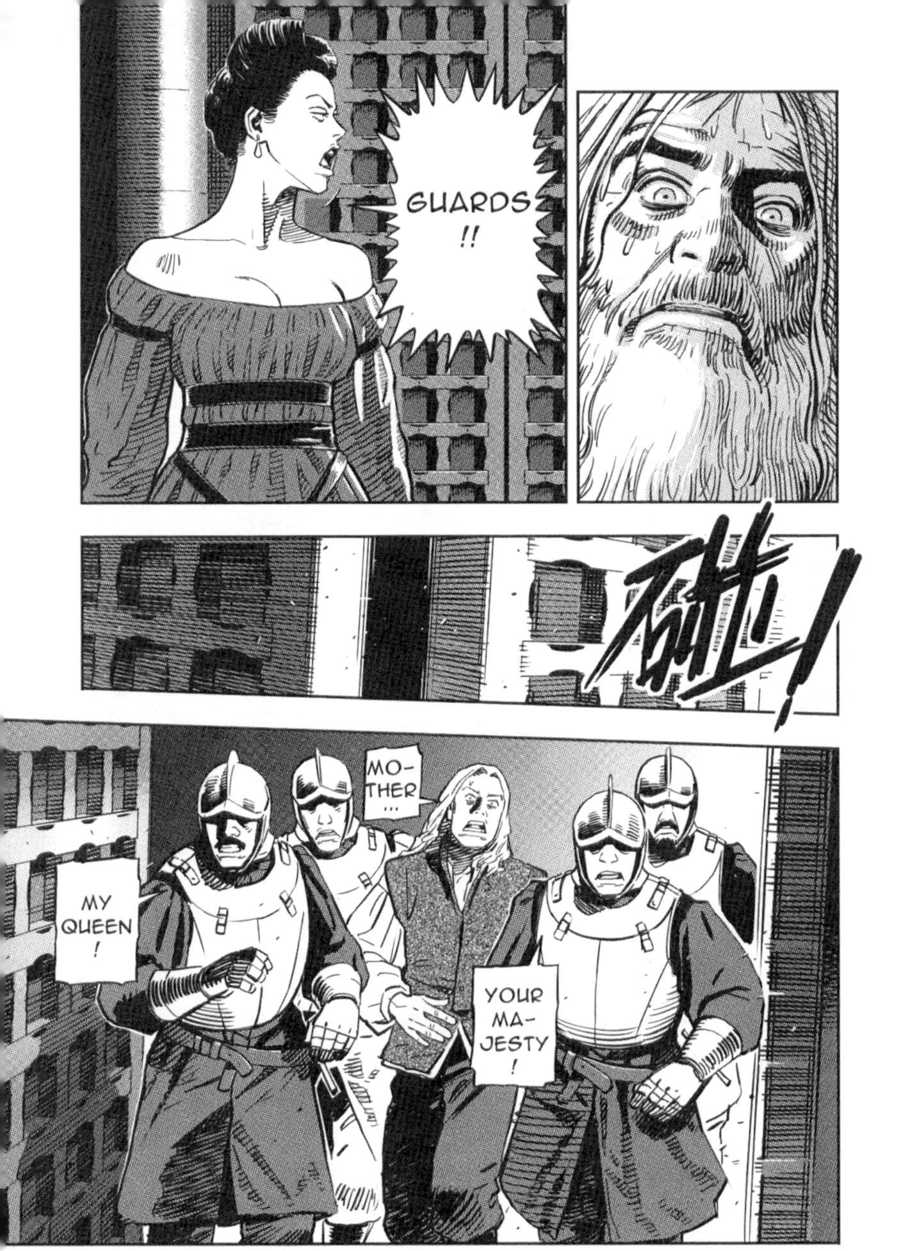
GUARDS !!
MO-THER ...
YOUR MA-JESTY !
MY QUEEN !

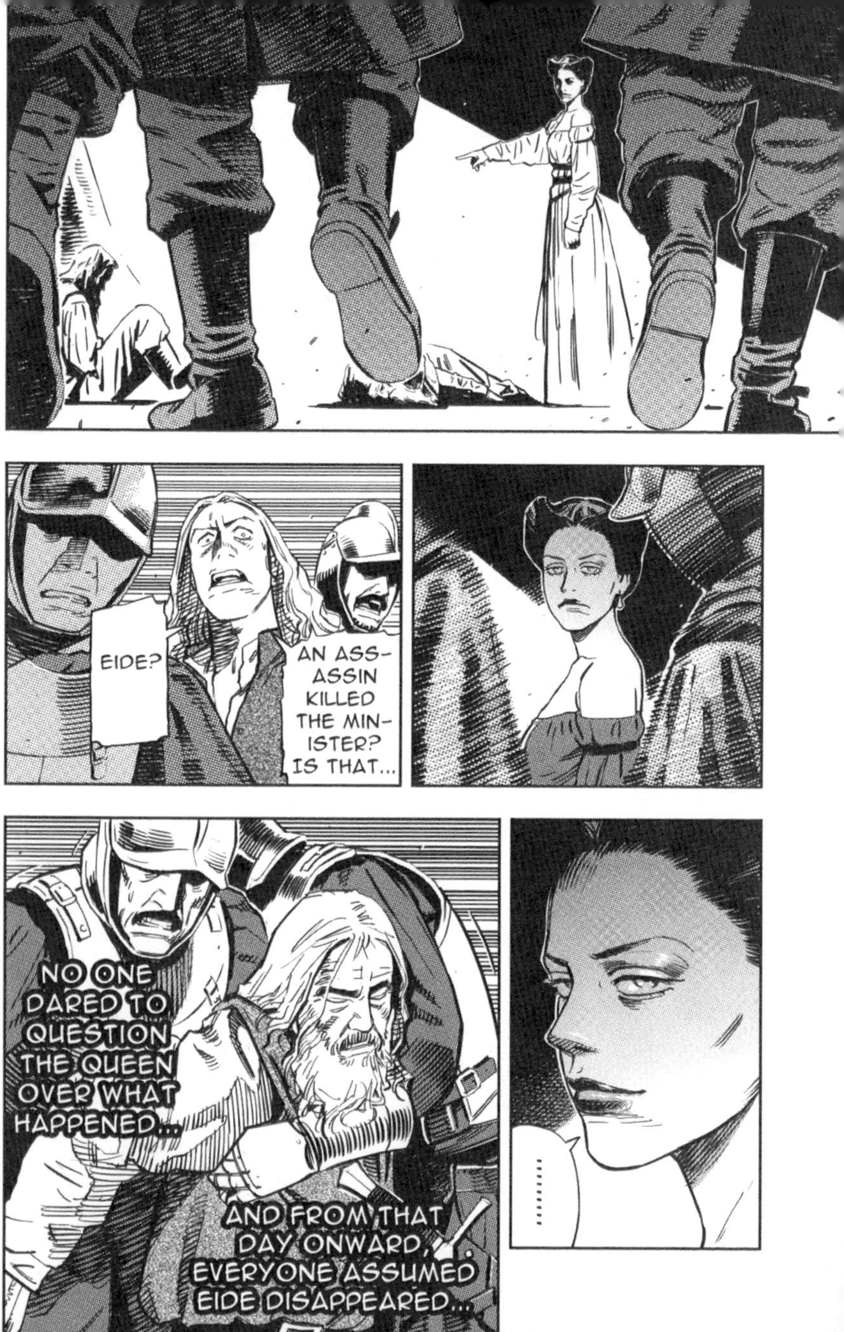
AN ASS-ASSIN KILLED THE MIN-ISTER? IS THAT...
EIDE?
......
NO ONE DARED TO QUESTION THE QUEEN OVER WHAT HAPPENED...
AND FROM THAT DAY ONWARD, EVERYONE ASSUMED EIDE DISAPPEARED...

CHAPTER 8
ILLUSION

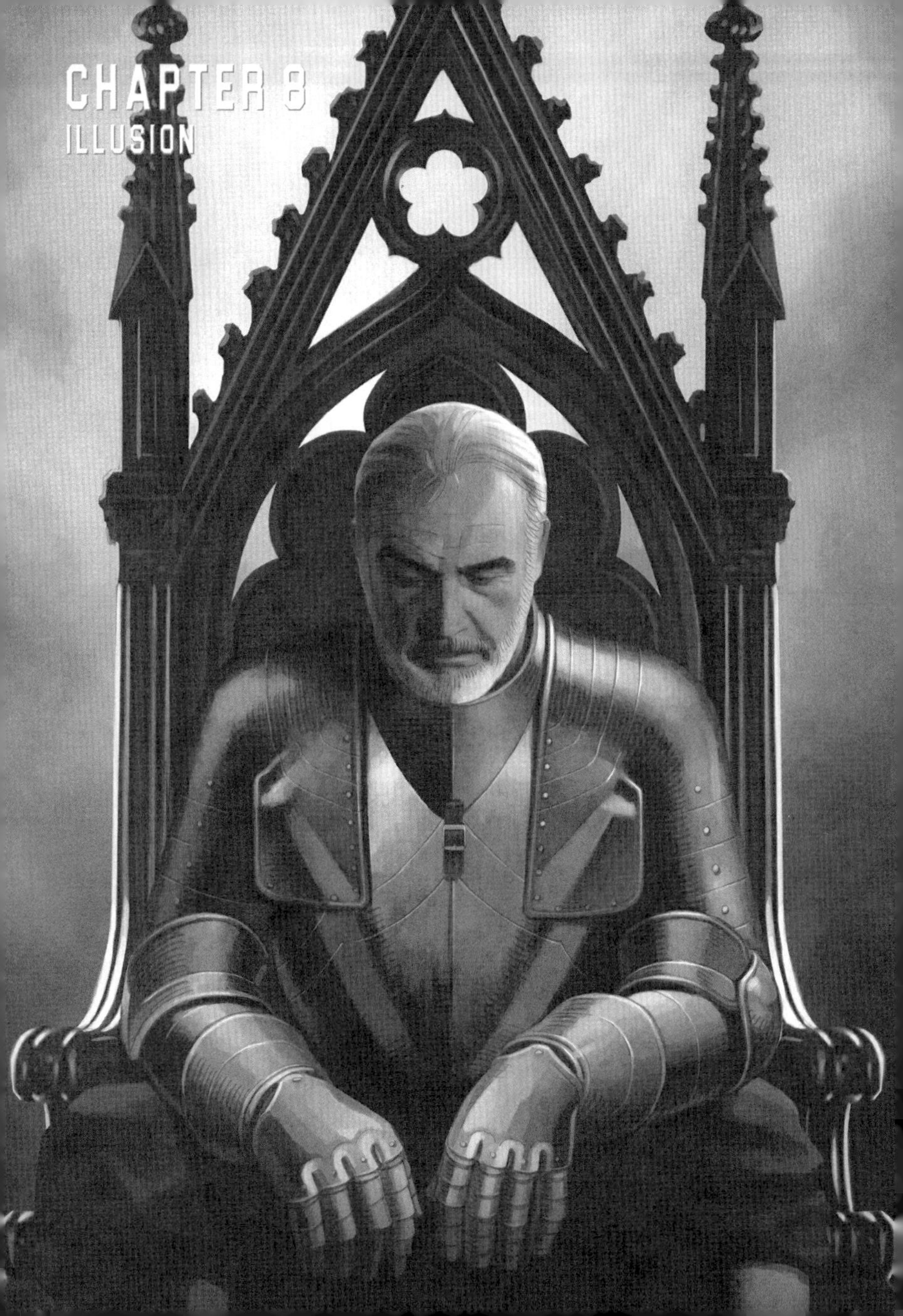

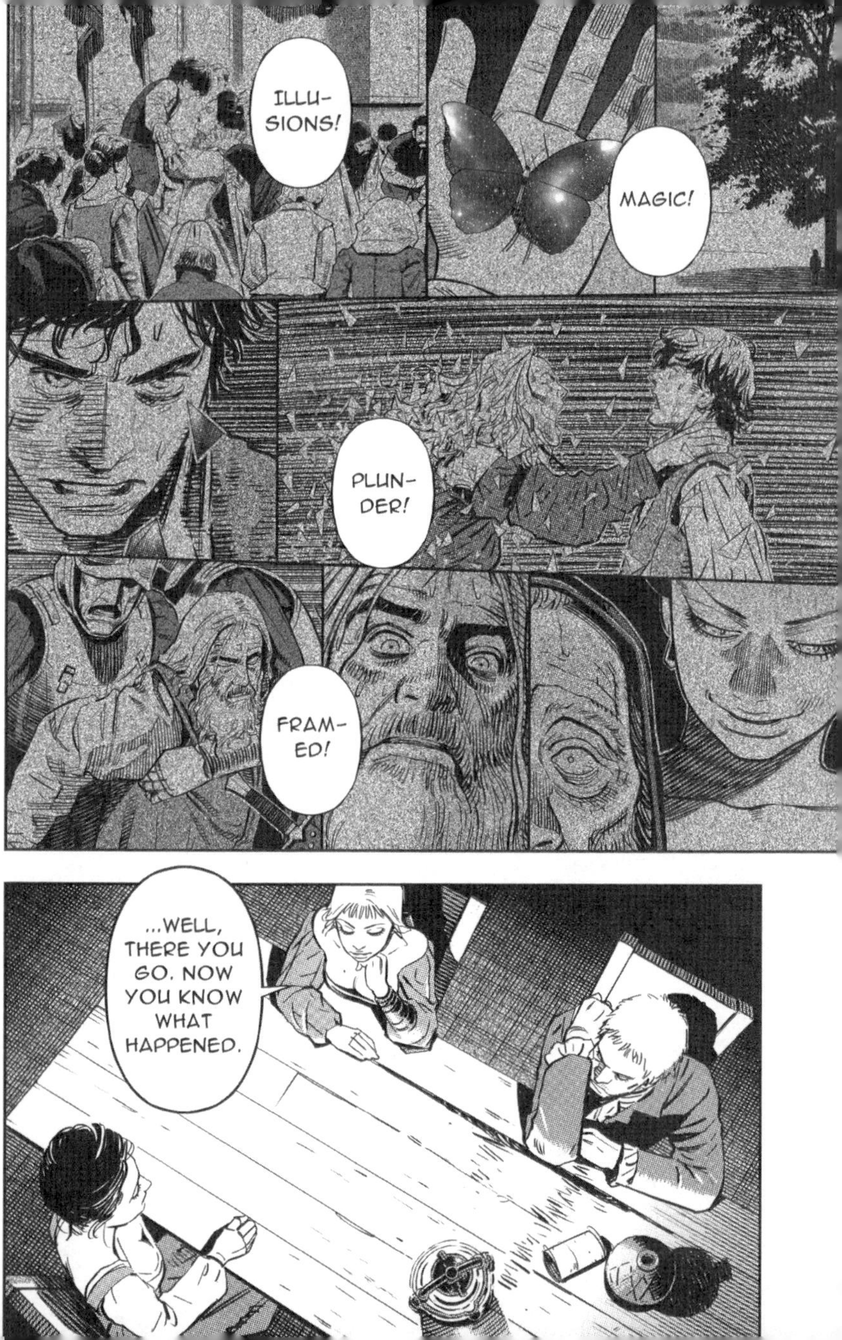
MAGIC!
ILLU-SIONS!
PLUN-DER!
FRAM-ED!
...WELL, THERE YOU GO. NOW YOU KNOW WHAT HAPPENED.

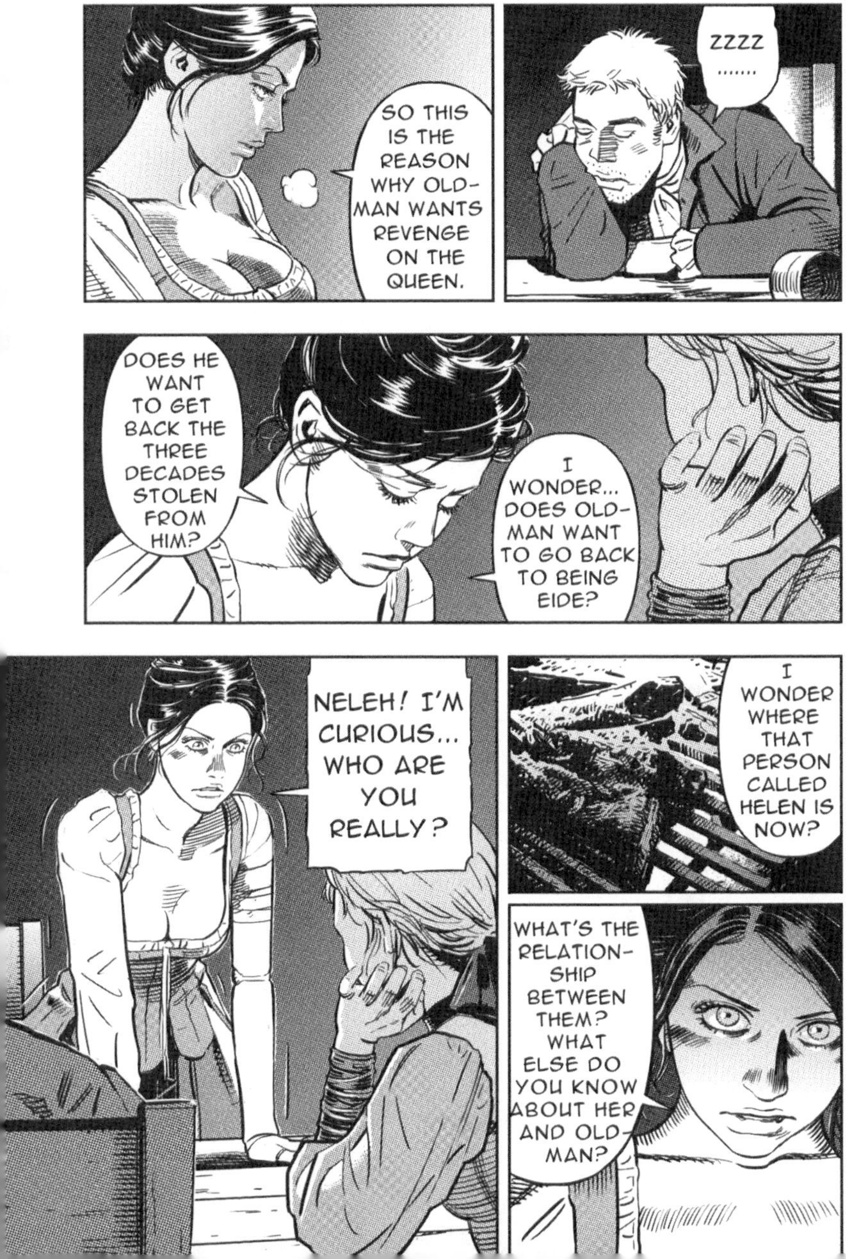
SO THIS IS THE REASON WHY OLD-MAN WANTS REVENGE ON THE QUEEN.
ZZZZ ......
DOES HE WANT TO GET BACK THE THREE DECADES STOLEN FROM HIM?
I WONDER... DOES OLD-MAN WANT TO GO BACK TO BEING EIDE?
NELEH! I'M CURIOUS... WHO ARE YOU REALLY?
I WONDER WHERE THAT PERSON CALLED HELEN IS NOW?
WHAT'S THE RELATION-SHIP BETWEEN THEM? WHAT ELSE DO YOU KNOW ABOUT HER AND OLD-MAN?

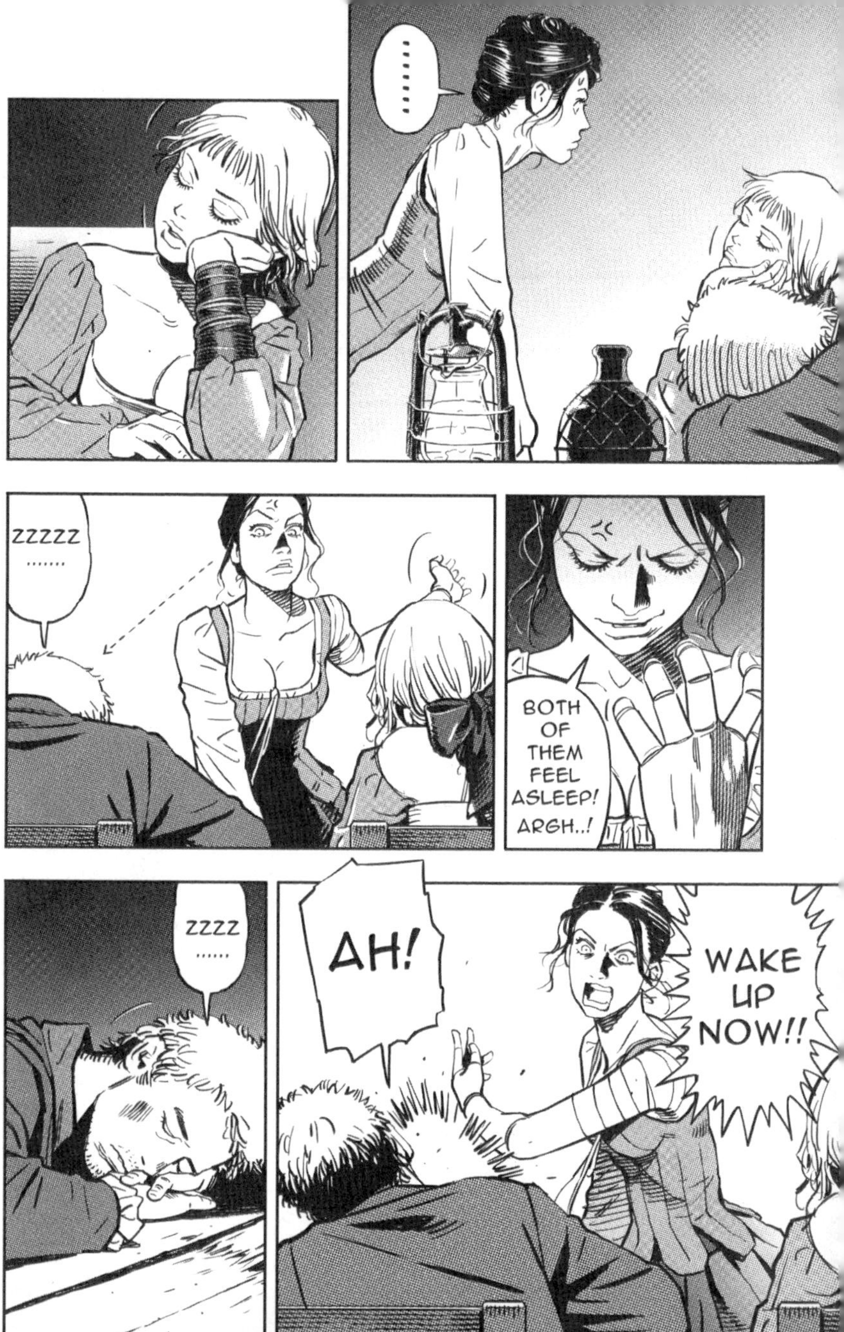
......
BOTH OF THEM FEEL ASLEEP! ARGH..!
ZZZZZ ....
WAKE UP NOW!!
AH!
ZZZZ ......

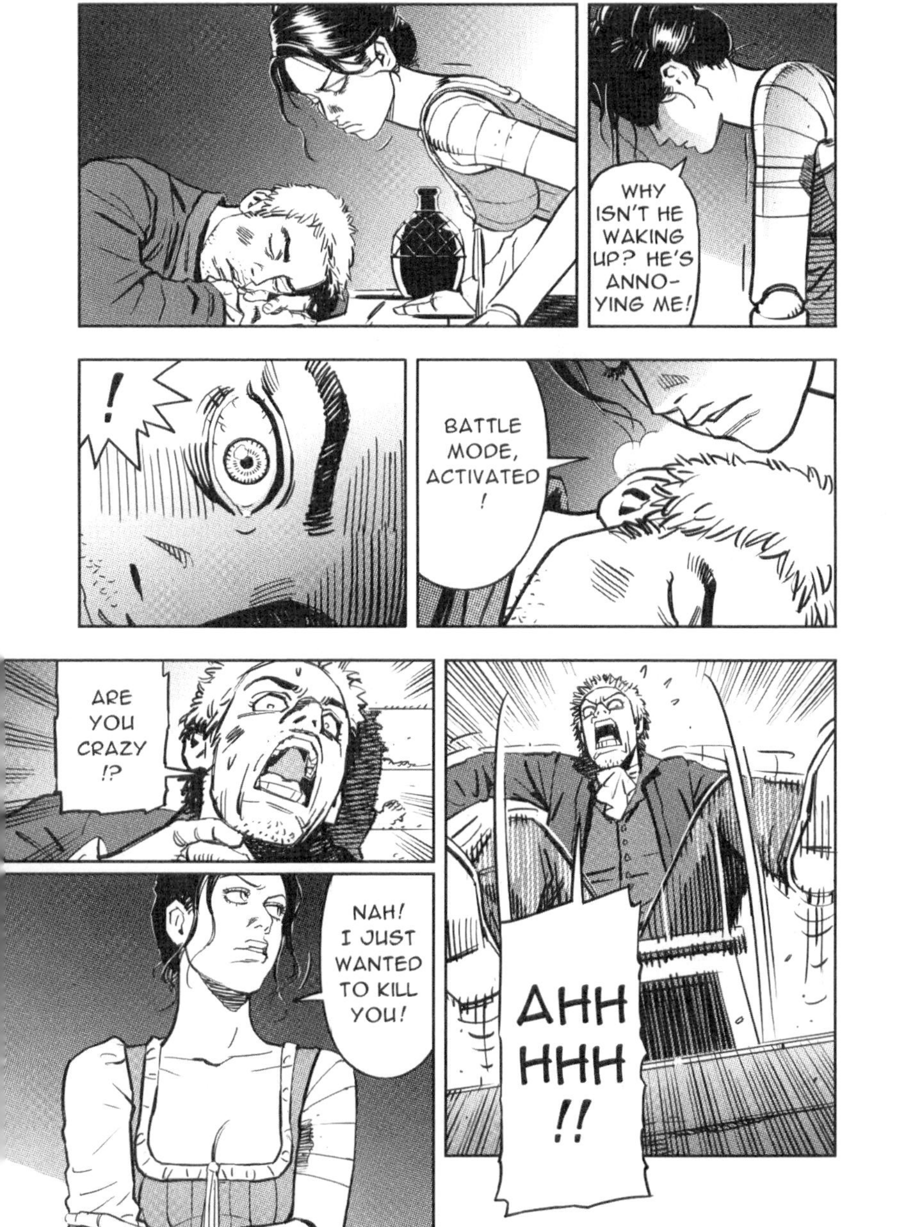
WHY ISN'T HE WAKING UP? HE'S ANNOYING ME!
!
BATTLE MODE, ACTIVATED!
AHHHHH!!
ARE YOU CRAZY!?
NAH! I JUST WANTED TO KILL YOU!

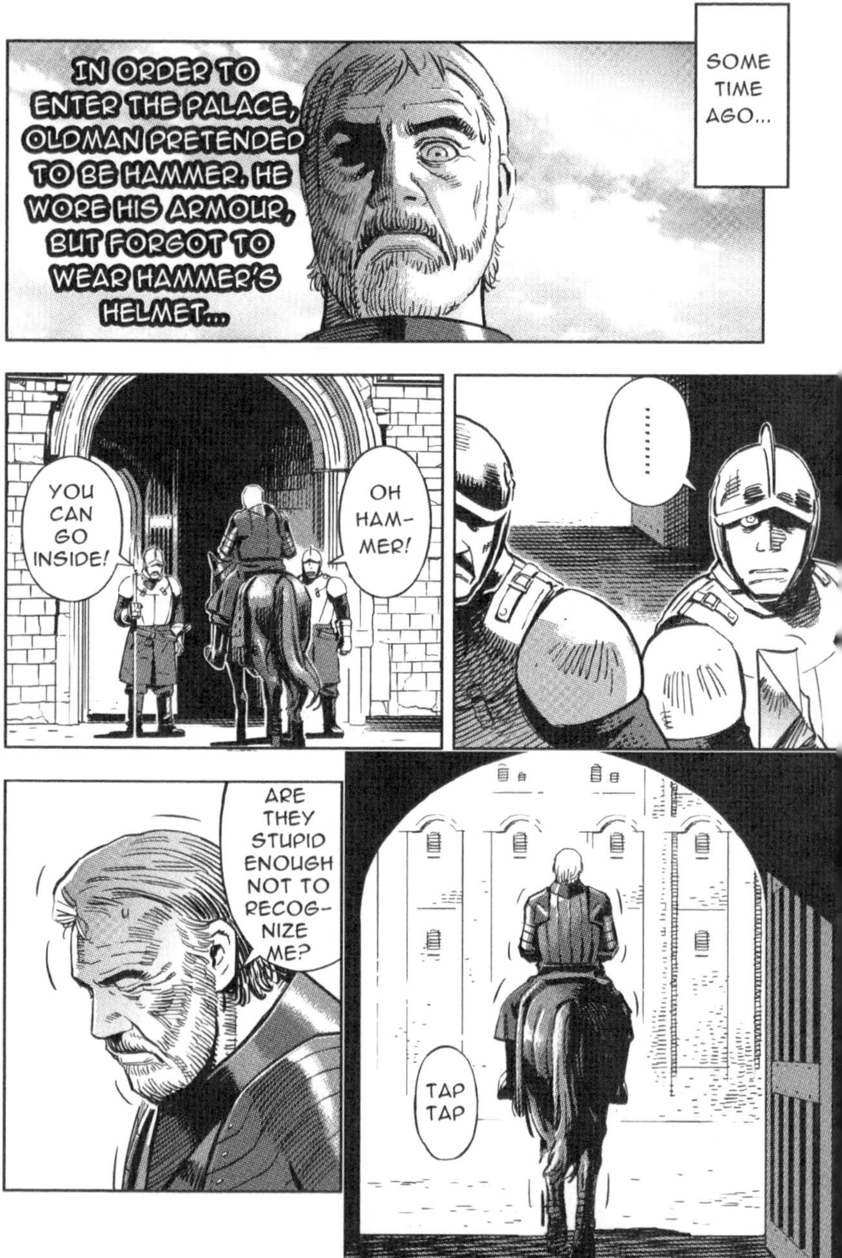
SOME TIME AGO...
IN ORDER TO ENTER THE PALACE, OLDMAN PRETENDED TO BE HAMMER. HE WORE HIS ARMOUR, BUT FORGOT TO WEAR HAMMER'S HELMET...
....
OH HAM-MER!
YOU CAN GO INSIDE!
TAP TAP
ARE THEY STUPID ENOUGH NOT TO RECOG-NIZE ME?

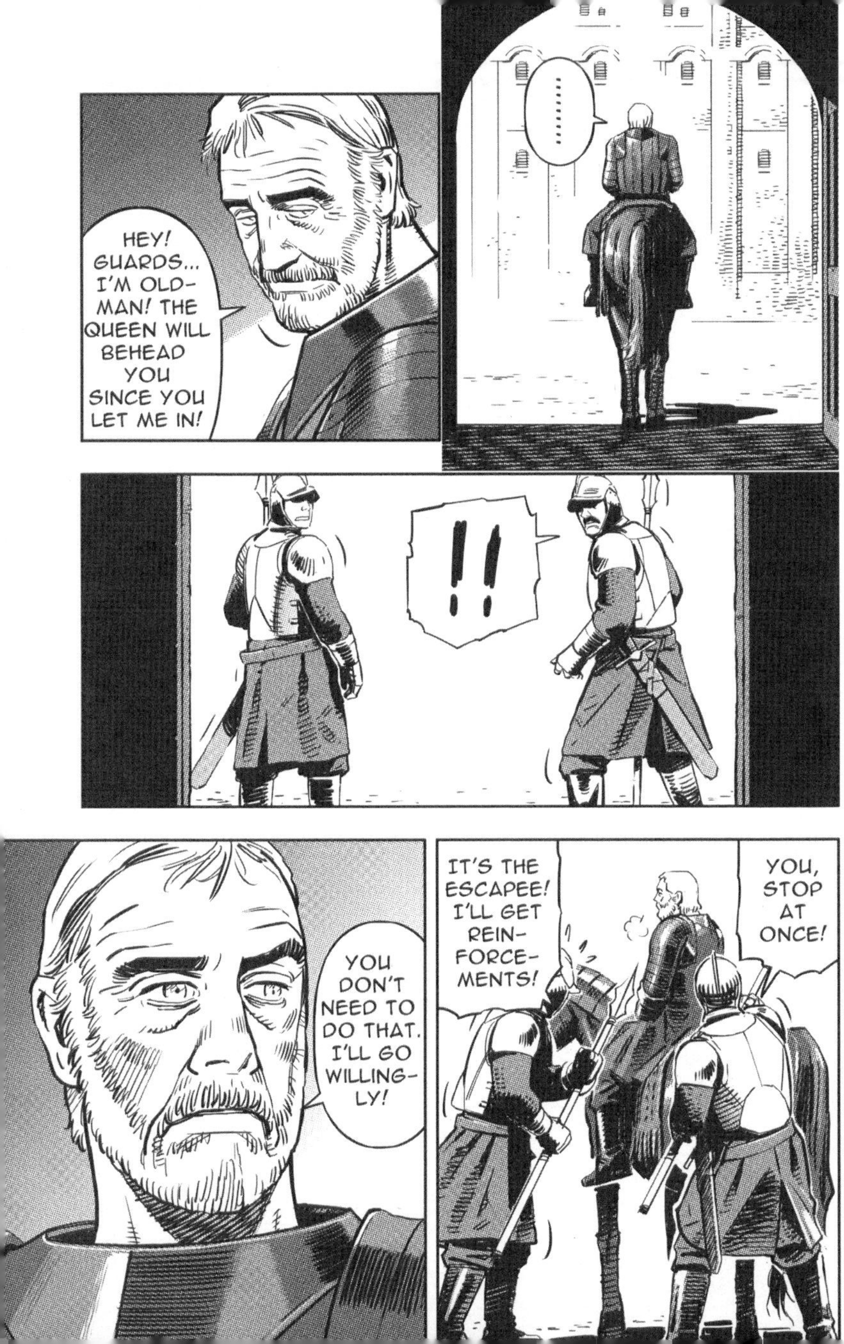
......
HEY! GUARDS... I'M OLD-MAN! THE QUEEN WILL BEHEAD YOU SINCE YOU LET ME IN!
!!
YOU, STOP AT ONCE!
IT'S THE ESCAPEE! I'LL GET REIN-FORCE-MENTS!
YOU DON'T NEED TO DO THAT. I'LL GO WILLING-LY!

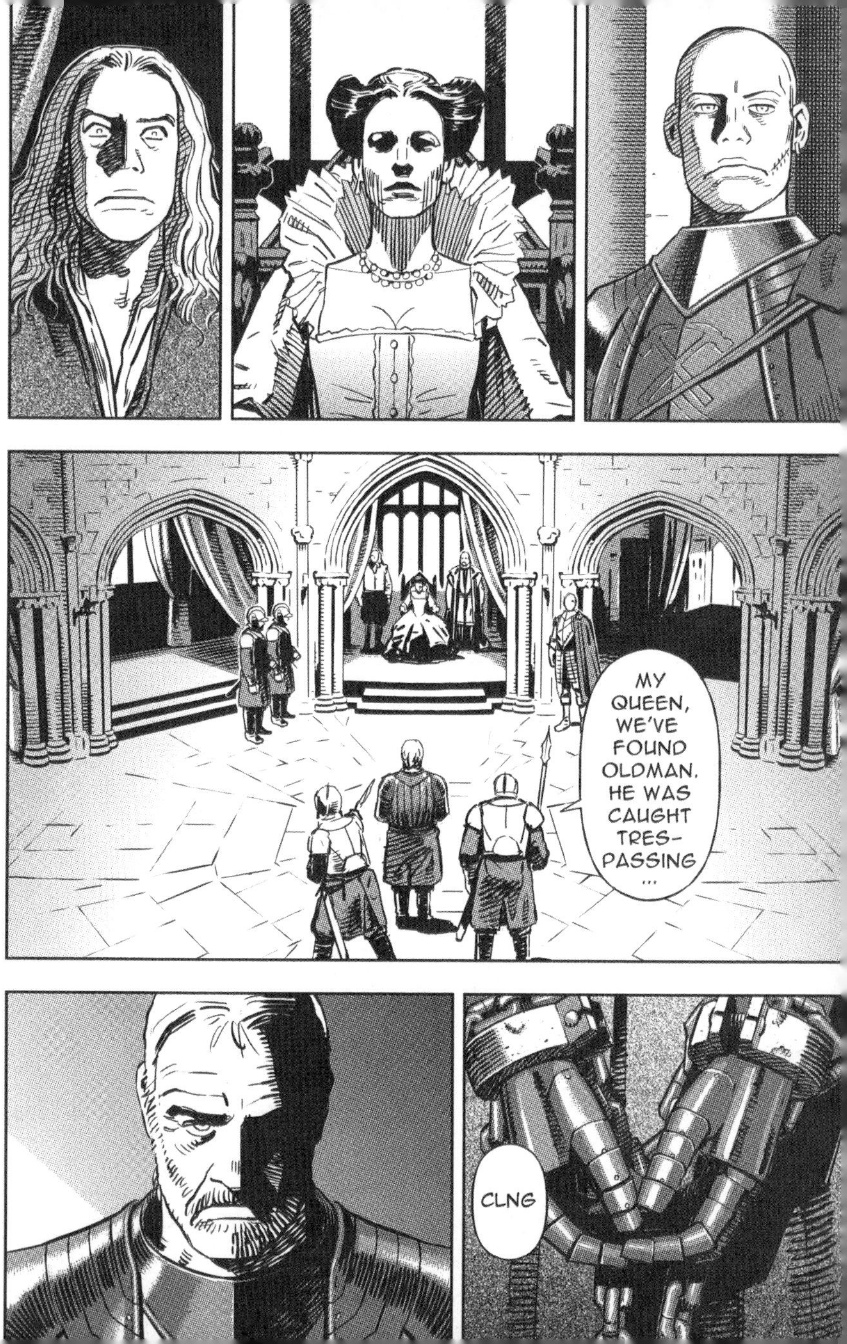
MY QUEEN, WE'VE FOUND OLDMAN. HE WAS CAUGHT TRES-PASSING ...
CLNG

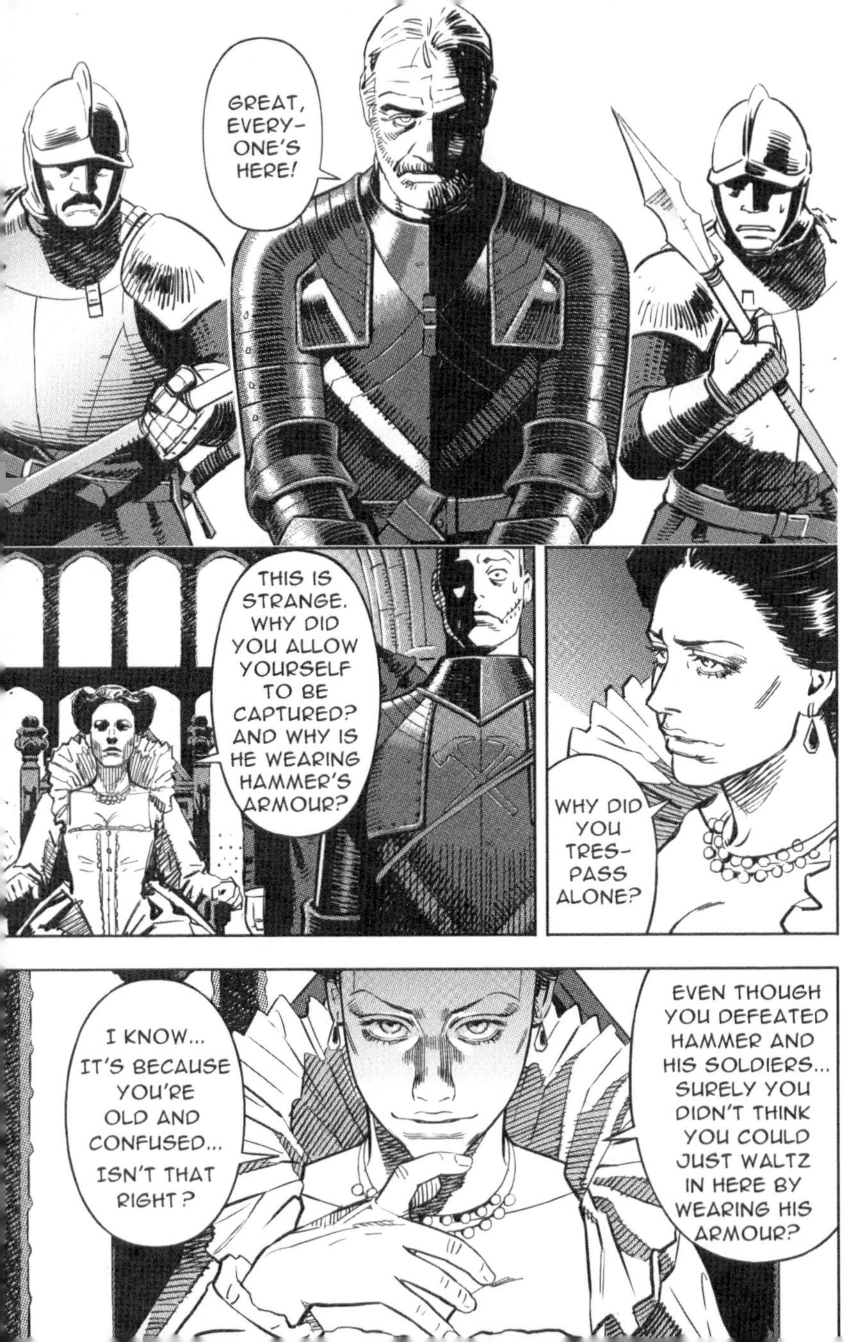
GREAT, EVERY-ONE'S HERE!
WHY DID YOU TRES-PASS ALONE?
THIS IS STRANGE. WHY DID YOU ALLOW YOURSELF TO BE CAPTURED? AND WHY IS HE WEARING HAMMER'S ARMOUR?
EVEN THOUGH YOU DEFEATED HAMMER AND HIS SOLDIERS... SURELY YOU DIDN'T THINK YOU COULD JUST WALTZ IN HERE BY WEARING HIS ARMOUR?
I KNOW... IT'S BECAUSE YOU'RE OLD AND CONFUSED... ISN'T THAT RIGHT?

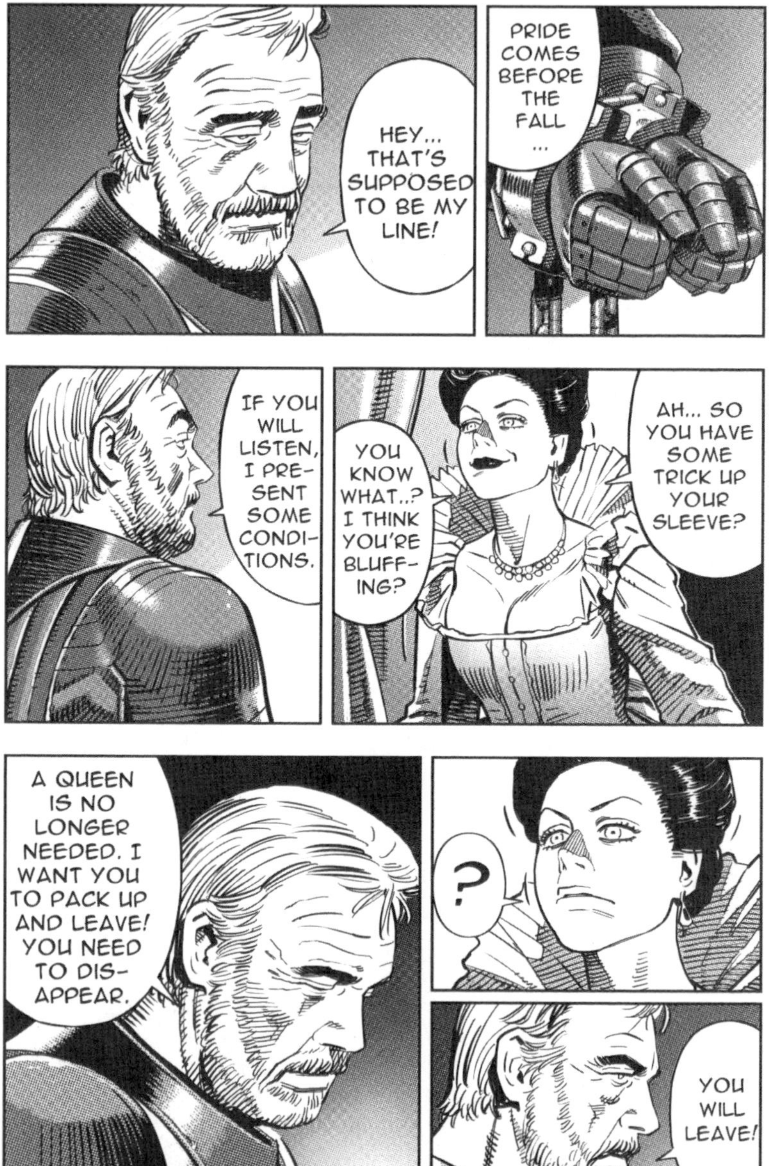
PRIDE COMES BEFORE THE FALL ...
HEY... THAT'S SUPPOSED TO BE MY LINE!
AH... SO YOU HAVE SOME TRICK UP YOUR SLEEVE?
YOU KNOW WHAT..? I THINK YOU'RE BLUFFING?
IF YOU WILL LISTEN, I PRESENT SOME CONDITIONS.
?
YOU WILL LEAVE!
A QUEEN IS NO LONGER NEEDED. I WANT YOU TO PACK UP AND LEAVE! YOU NEED TO DISAPPEAR.

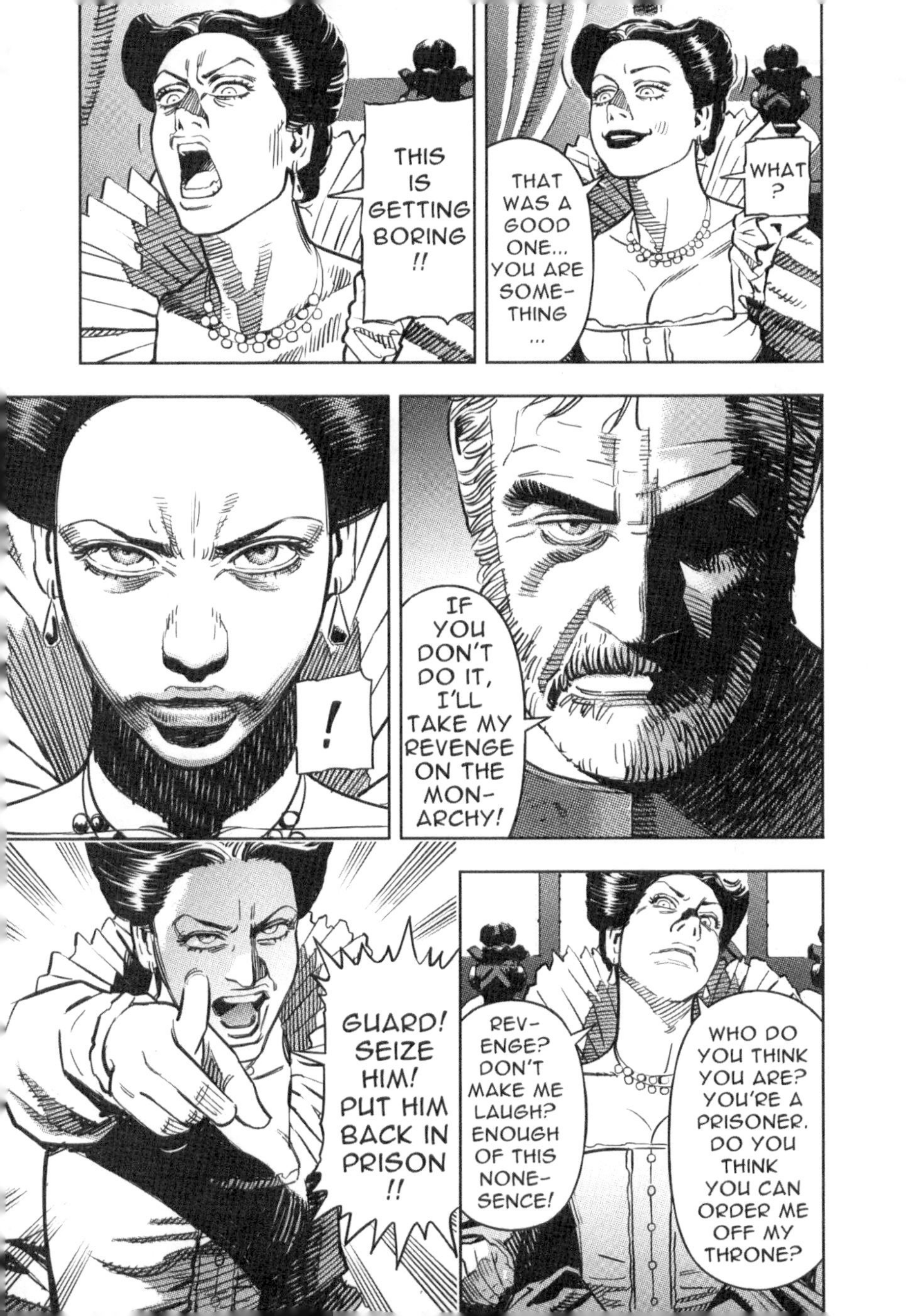
WHAT?
THAT WAS A GOOD ONE... YOU ARE SOME-THING ...
THIS IS GETTING BORING !!
IF YOU DON'T DO IT, I'LL TAKE MY REVENGE ON THE MON-ARCHY!
!
WHO DO YOU THINK YOU ARE? YOU'RE A PRISONER. DO YOU THINK YOU CAN ORDER ME OFF MY THRONE?
REV-ENGE? DON'T MAKE ME LAUGH? ENOUGH OF THIS NONE-SENCE!
GUARD! SEIZE HIM! PUT HIM BACK IN PRISON !!

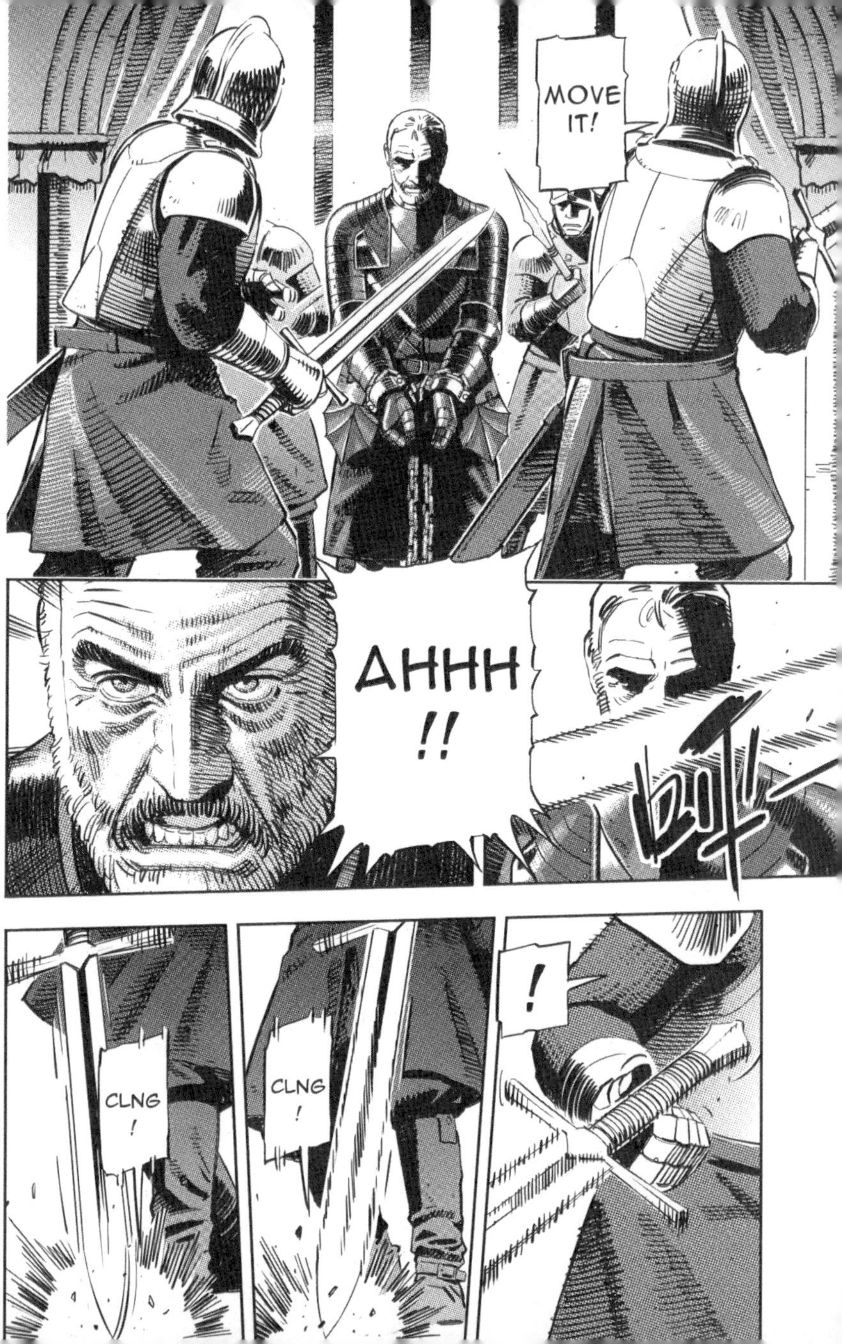
MOVE IT!
AHHH !!
!
CLNG !
CLNG !

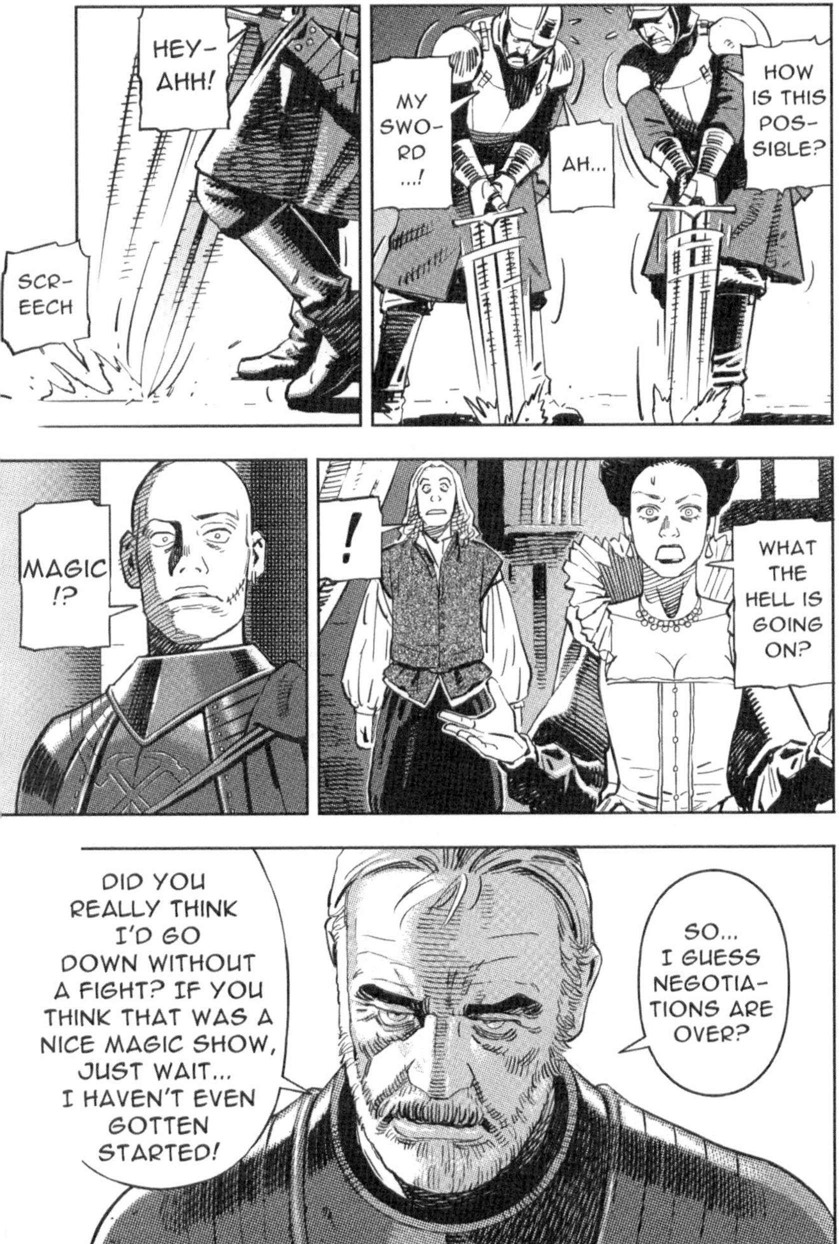
HOW IS THIS POSSIBLE?
MY SWORD...!
AH...
HEY-AHH!
SCREECH
WHAT THE HELL IS GOING ON?
!
MAGIC!?
SO... I GUESS NEGOTIATIONS ARE OVER?
DID YOU REALLY THINK I'D GO DOWN WITHOUT A FIGHT? IF YOU THINK THAT WAS A NICE MAGIC SHOW, JUST WAIT... I HAVEN'T EVEN GOTTEN STARTED!

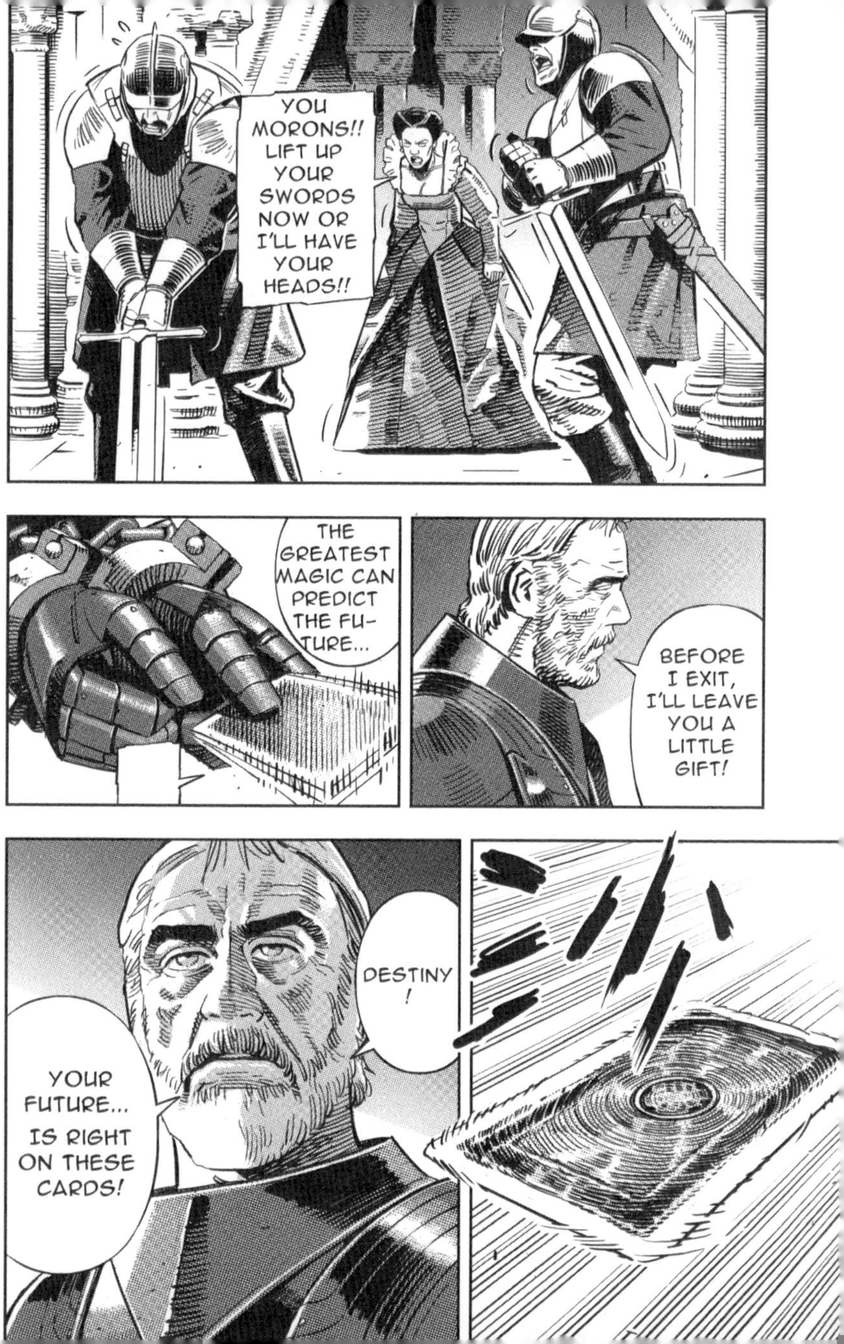
YOU MORONS!! LIFT UP YOUR SWORDS NOW OR I'LL HAVE YOUR HEADS!!
BEFORE I EXIT, I'LL LEAVE YOU A LITTLE GIFT!
THE GREATEST MAGIC CAN PREDICT THE FU-TURE...
DESTINY!
YOUR FUTURE... IS RIGHT ON THESE CARDS!

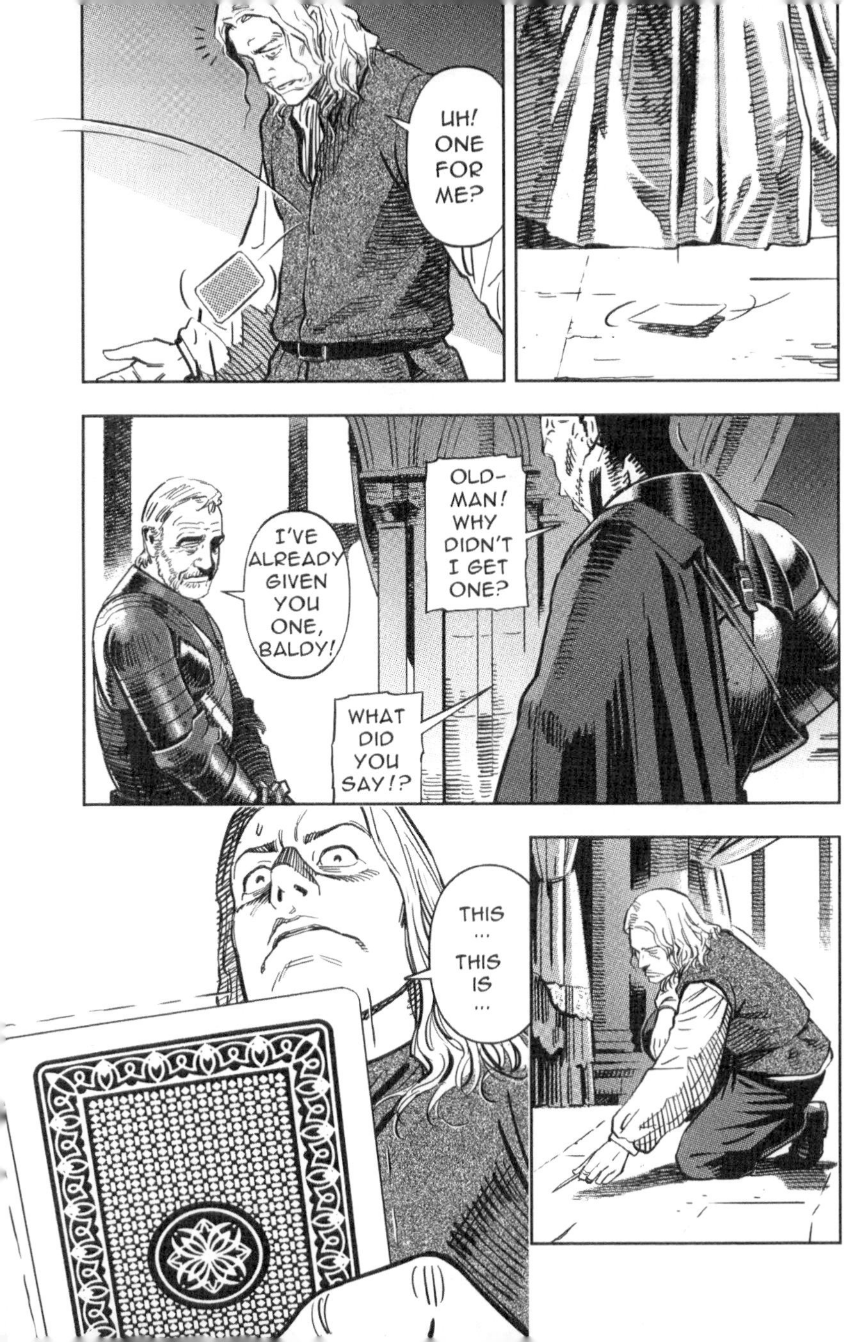
UH! ONE FOR ME?
OLD-MAN! WHY DIDN'T I GET ONE?
I'VE ALREADY GIVEN YOU ONE, BALDY!
WHAT DID YOU SAY!?
THIS ... THIS IS ...

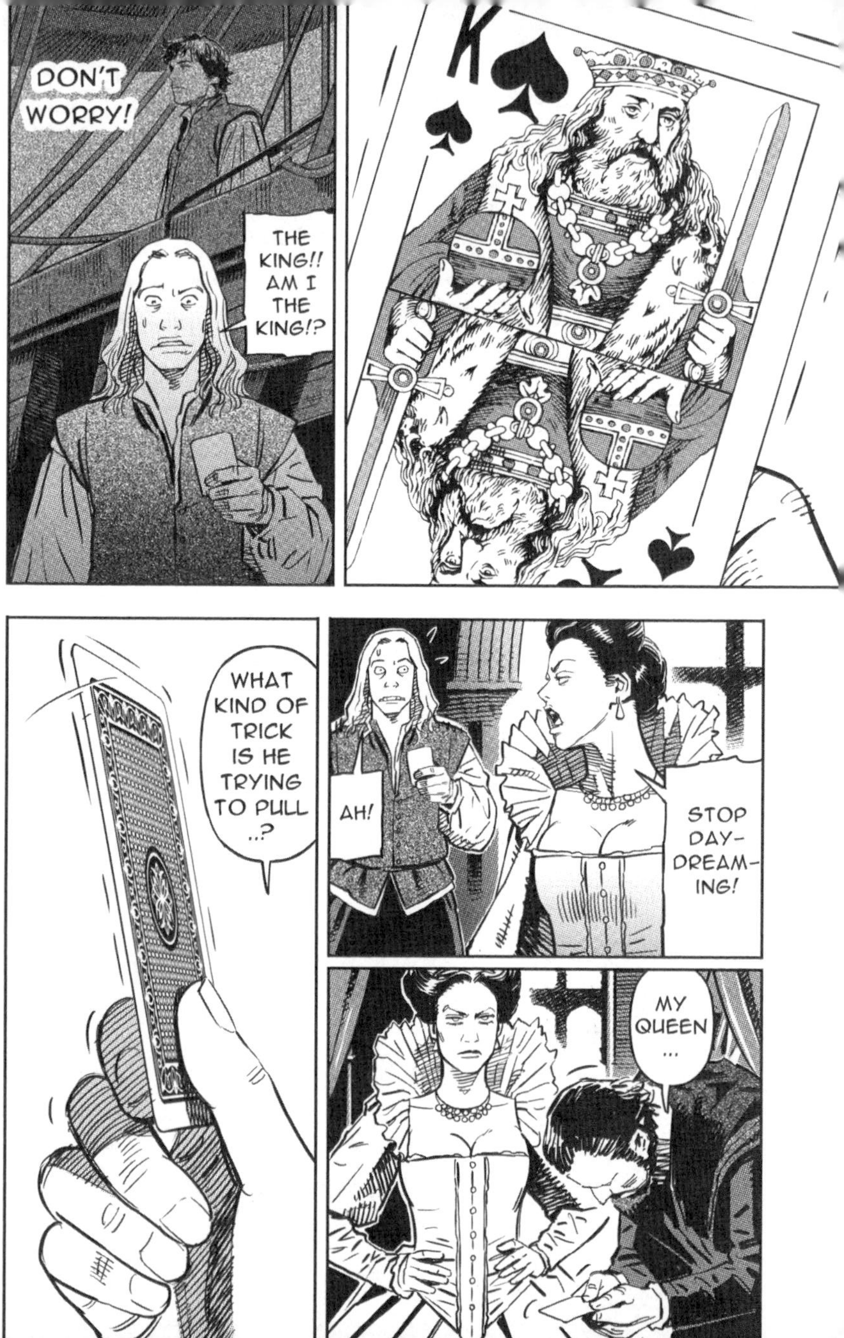
DON'T WORRY!
THE KING!! AM I THE KING!?
STOP DAY-DREAMING!
AH!
MY QUEEN ...
WHAT KIND OF TRICK IS HE TRYING TO PULL ..?

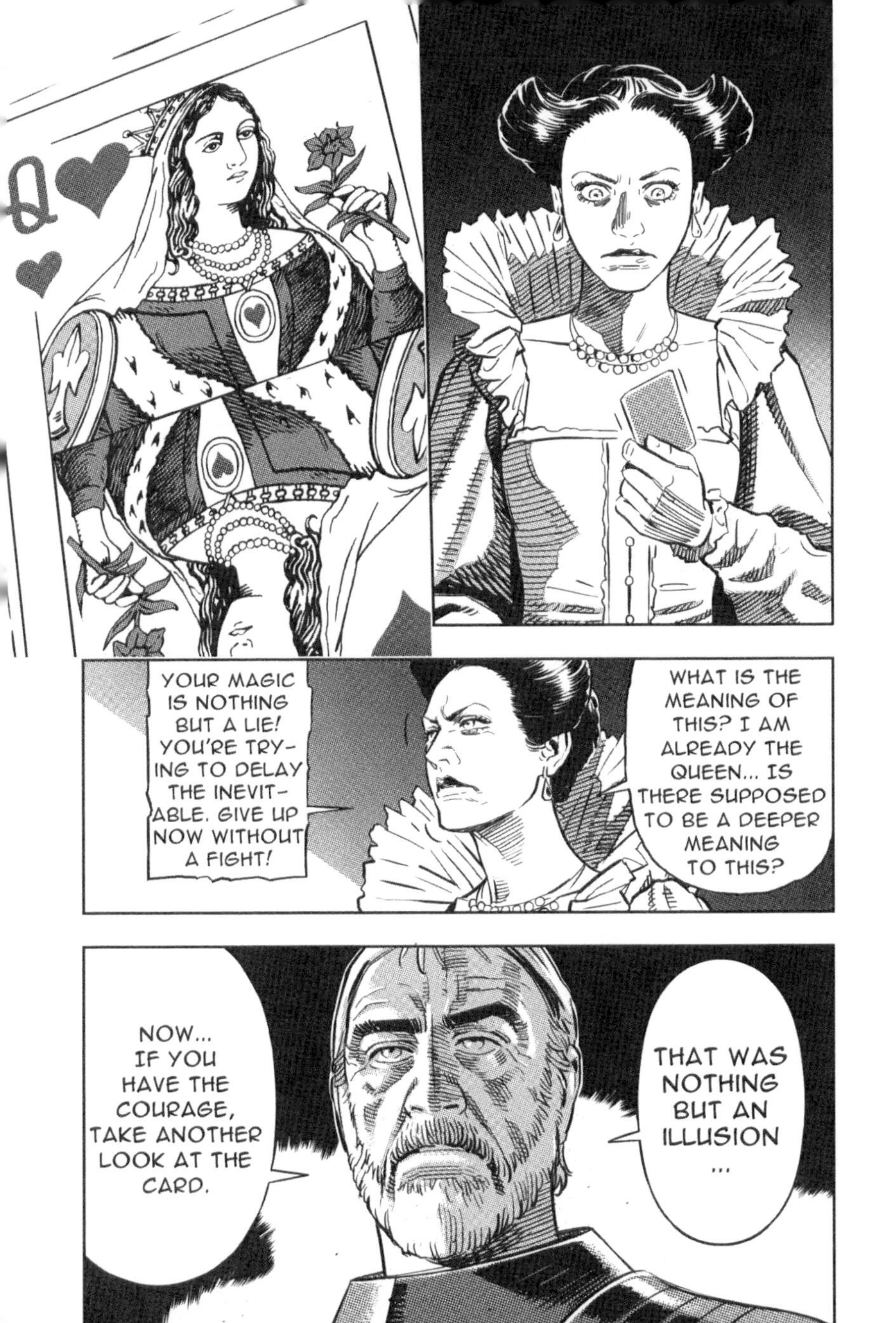
WHAT IS THE MEANING OF THIS? I AM ALREADY THE QUEEN... IS THERE SUPPOSED TO BE A DEEPER MEANING TO THIS?
YOUR MAGIC IS NOTHING BUT A LIE! YOU'RE TRYING TO DELAY THE INEVITABLE. GIVE UP NOW WITHOUT A FIGHT!
THAT WAS NOTHING BUT AN ILLUSION ...
NOW... IF YOU HAVE THE COURAGE, TAKE ANOTHER LOOK AT THE CARD.

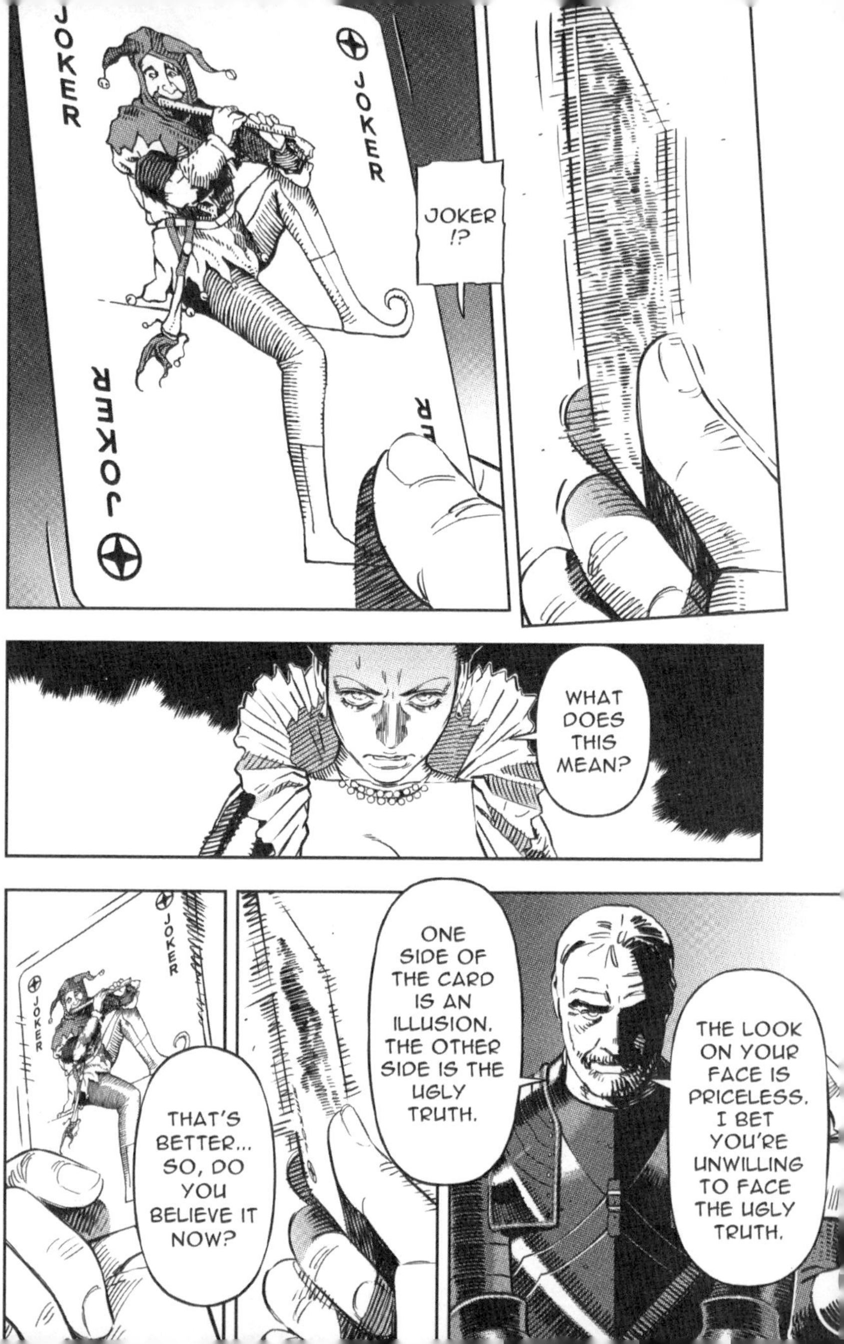
JOKER !?
WHAT DOES THIS MEAN?
THE LOOK ON YOUR FACE IS PRICELESS. I BET YOU'RE UNWILLING TO FACE THE UGLY TRUTH.
ONE SIDE OF THE CARD IS AN ILLUSION. THE OTHER SIDE IS THE UGLY TRUTH.
THAT'S BETTER... SO, DO YOU BELIEVE IT NOW?

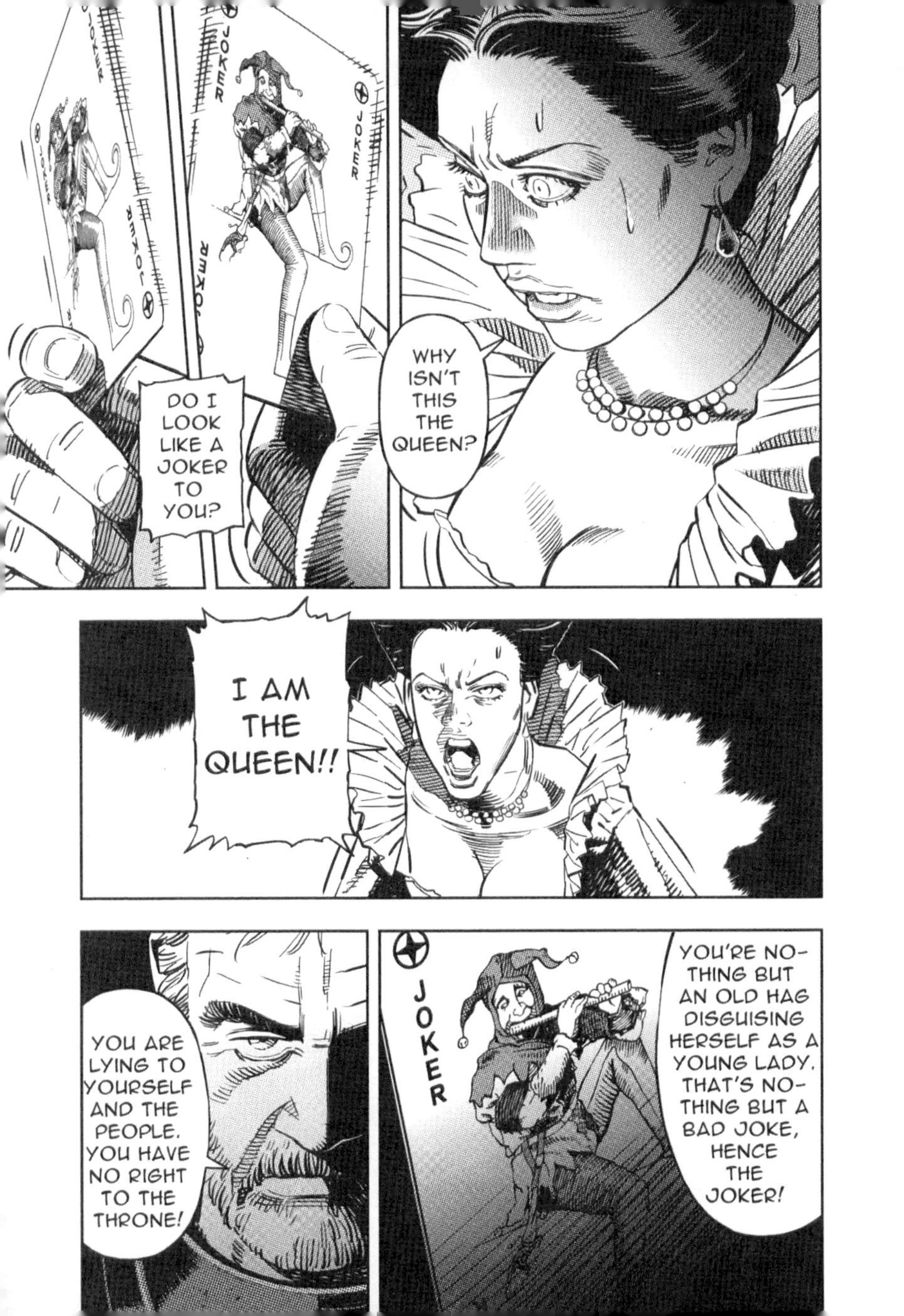
WHY ISN'T THIS THE QUEEN?
JOKER
DO I LOOK LIKE A JOKER TO YOU?
I AM THE QUEEN!!
JOKER
YOU'RE NO-THING BUT AN OLD HAG DISGUISING HERSELF AS A YOUNG LADY. THAT'S NO-THING BUT A BAD JOKE, HENCE THE JOKER!
YOU ARE LYING TO YOURSELF AND THE PEOPLE. YOU HAVE NO RIGHT TO THE THRONE!

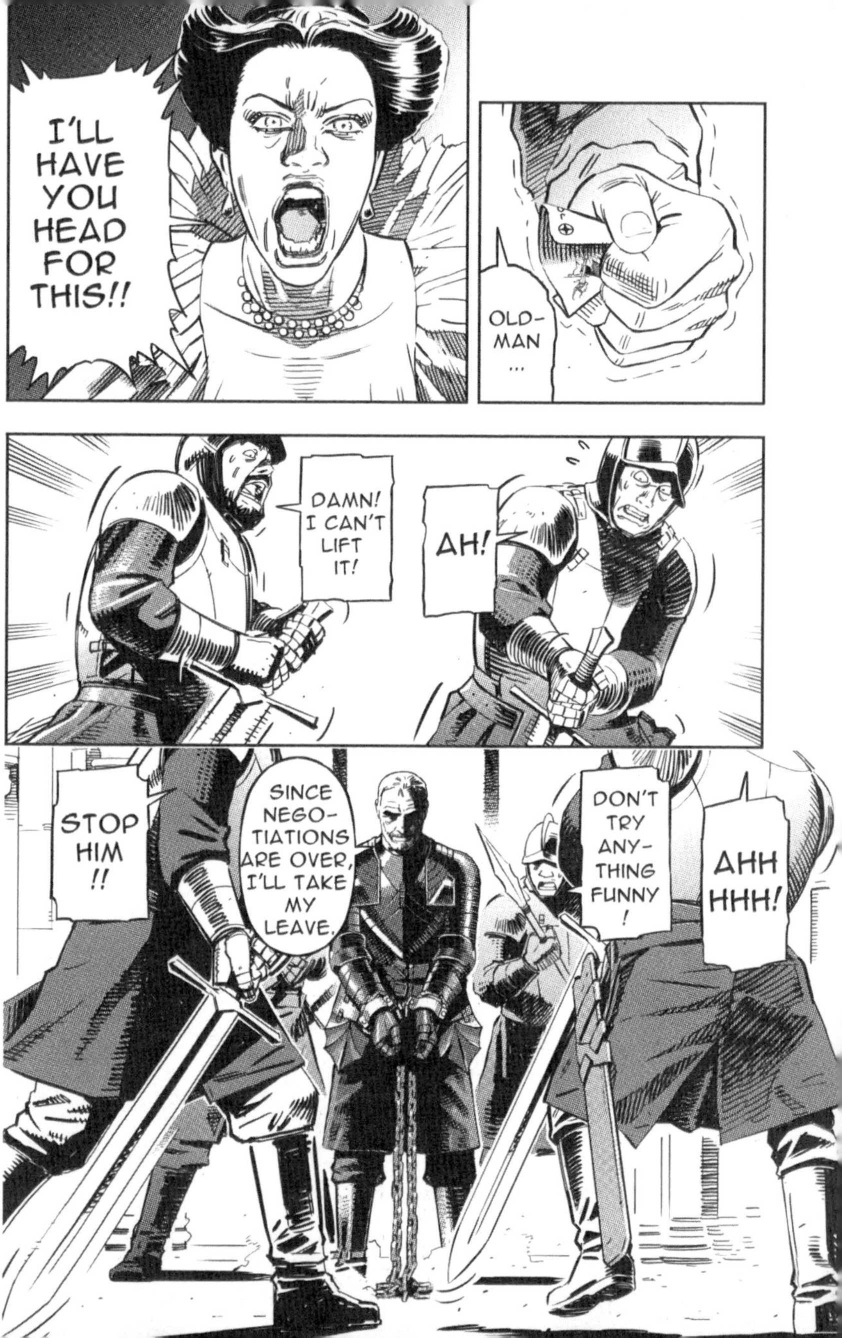
OLD-MAN...
I'LL HAVE YOU HEAD FOR THIS!!
AH!
DAMN! I CAN'T LIFT IT!
AHH HHH!
DON'T TRY ANY-THING FUNNY!
SINCE NEGO-TIATIONS ARE OVER, I'LL TAKE MY LEAVE.
STOP HIM!!

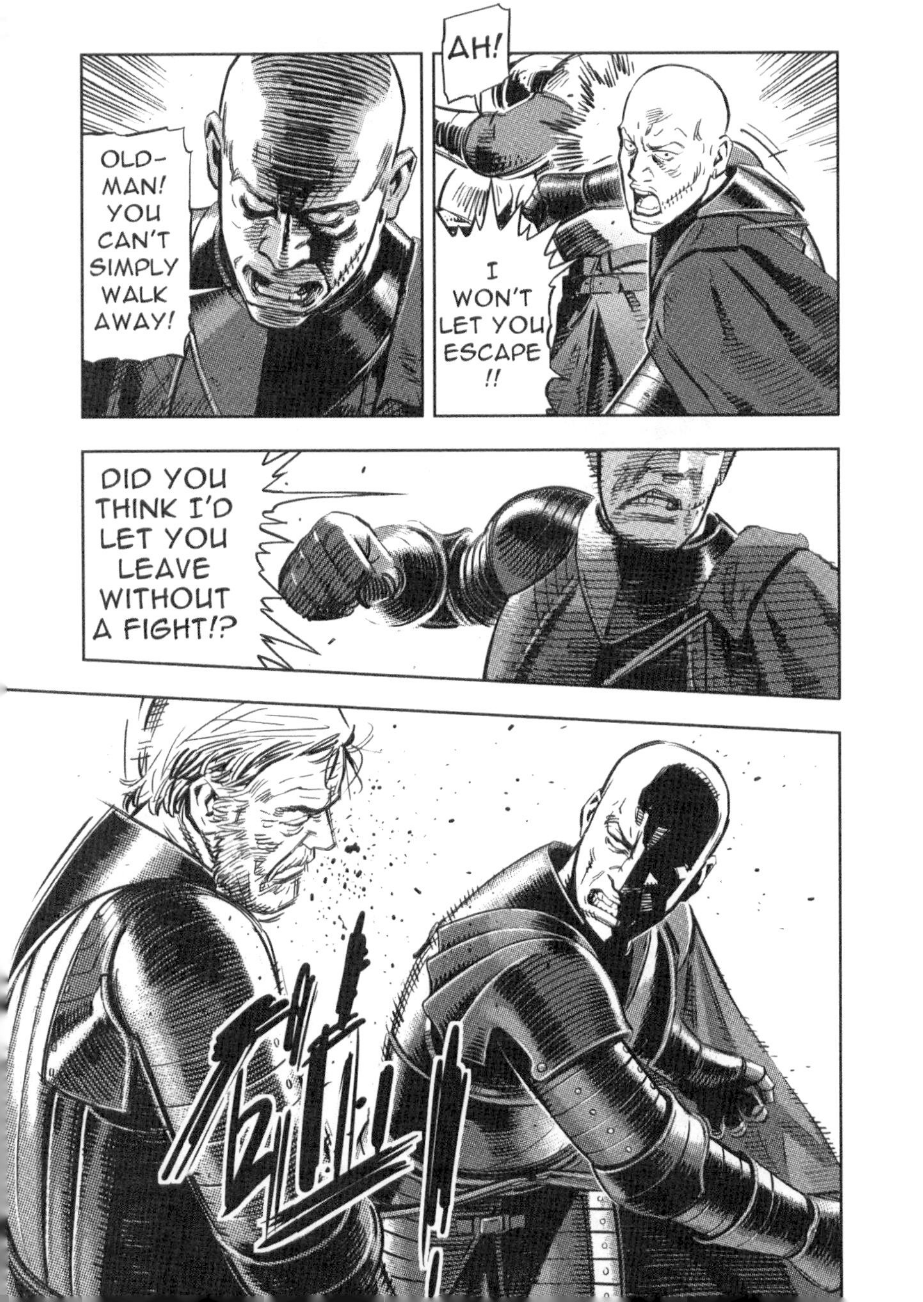
AH!
I WON'T LET YOU ESCAPE !!
OLD-MAN! YOU CAN'T SIMPLY WALK AWAY!
DID YOU THINK I'D LET YOU LEAVE WITHOUT A FIGHT!?

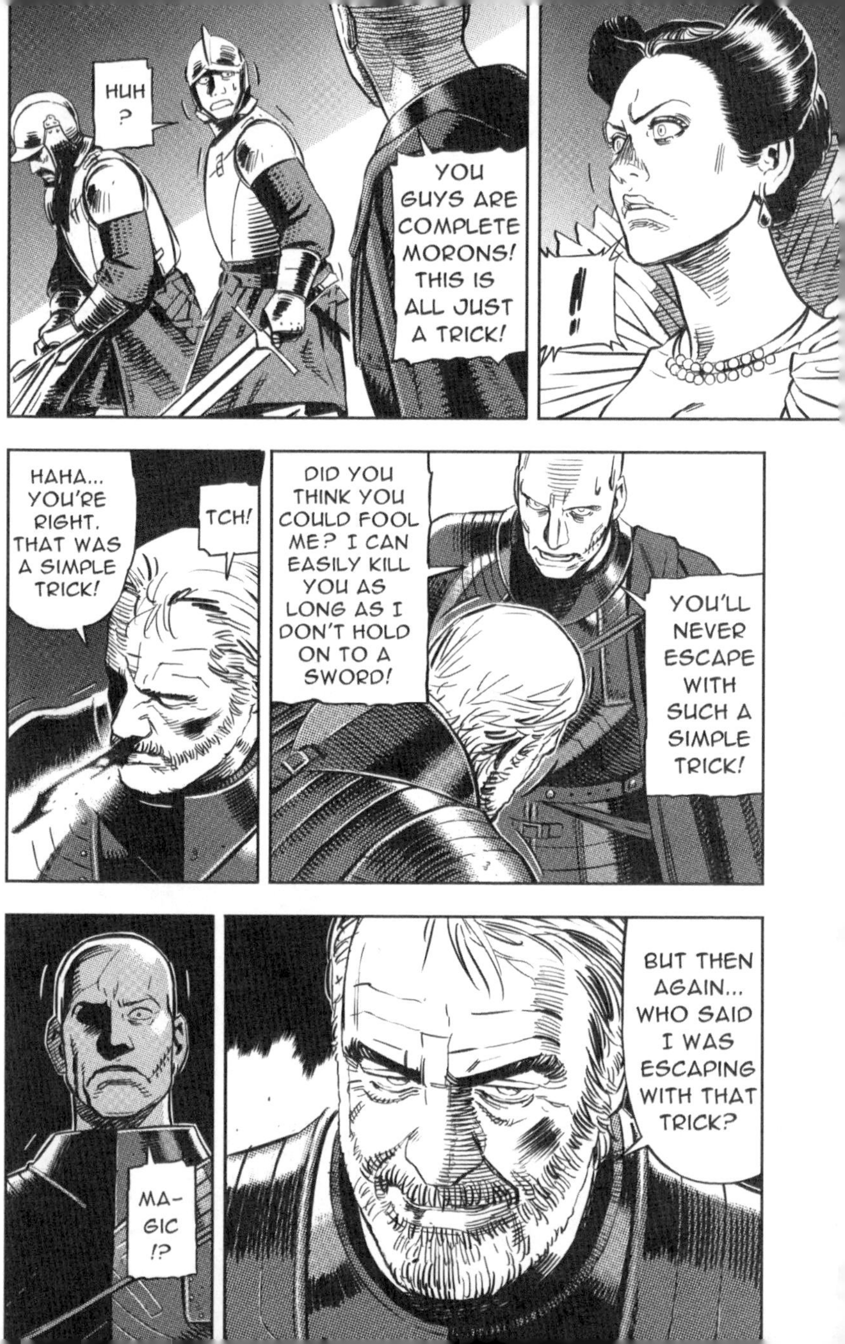
!!
YOU GUYS ARE COMPLETE MORONS! THIS IS ALL JUST A TRICK!
HUH?
DID YOU THINK YOU COULD FOOL ME? I CAN EASILY KILL YOU AS LONG AS I DON'T HOLD ON TO A SWORD!
YOU'LL NEVER ESCAPE WITH SUCH A SIMPLE TRICK!
TCH!
HAHA... YOU'RE RIGHT. THAT WAS A SIMPLE TRICK!
BUT THEN AGAIN... WHO SAID I WAS ESCAPING WITH THAT TRICK?
MA-GIC!?

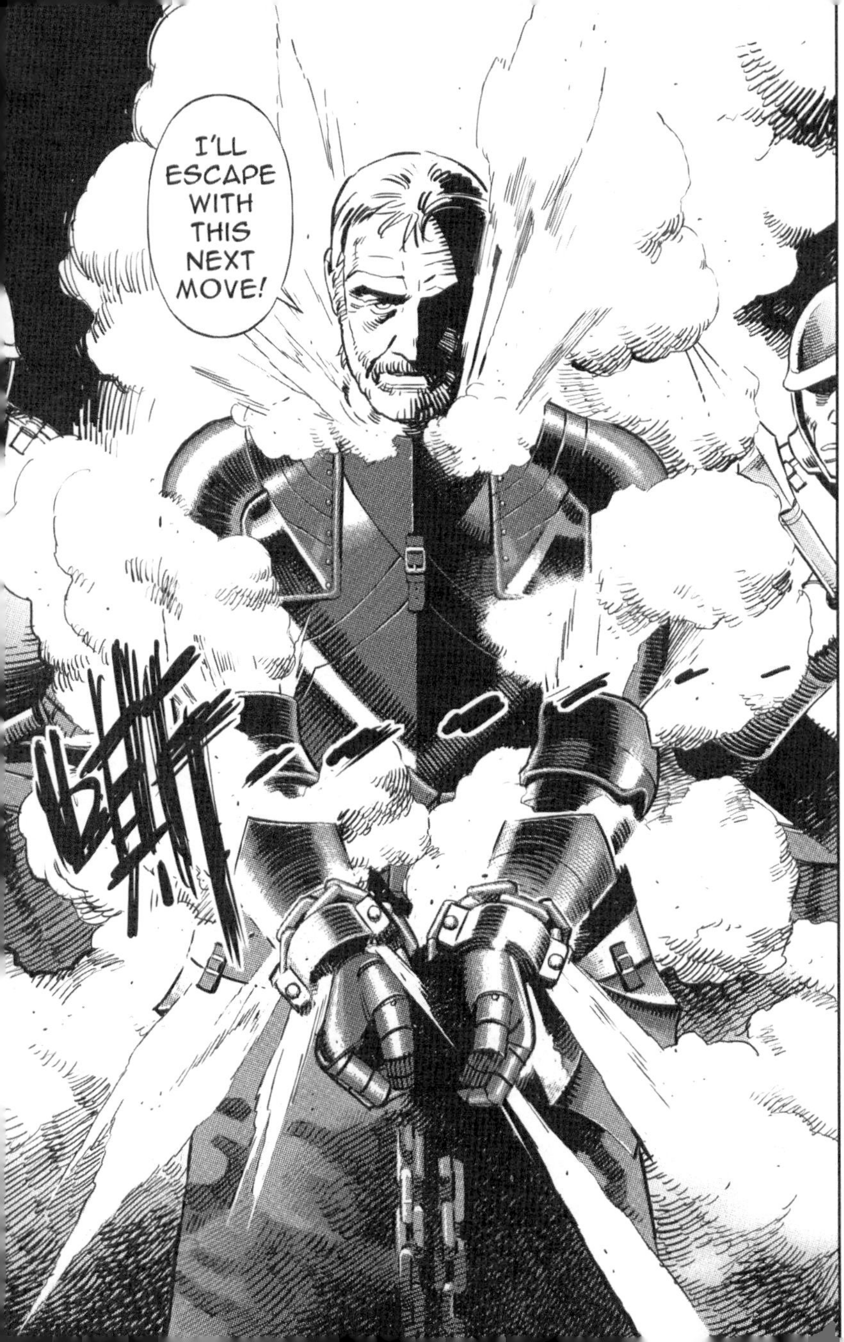
I'LL ESCAPE WITH THIS NEXT MOVE!

CHAPTER 9
LOOKING FOR SOMEONE

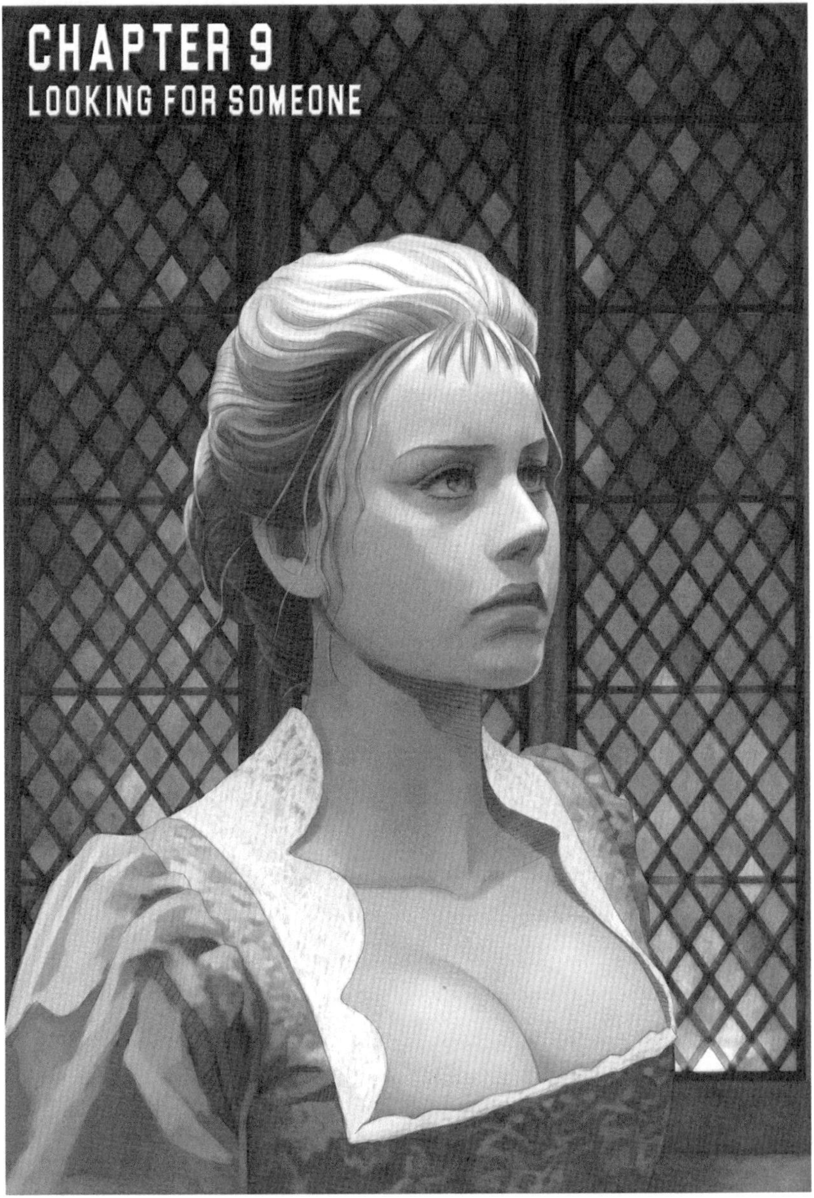

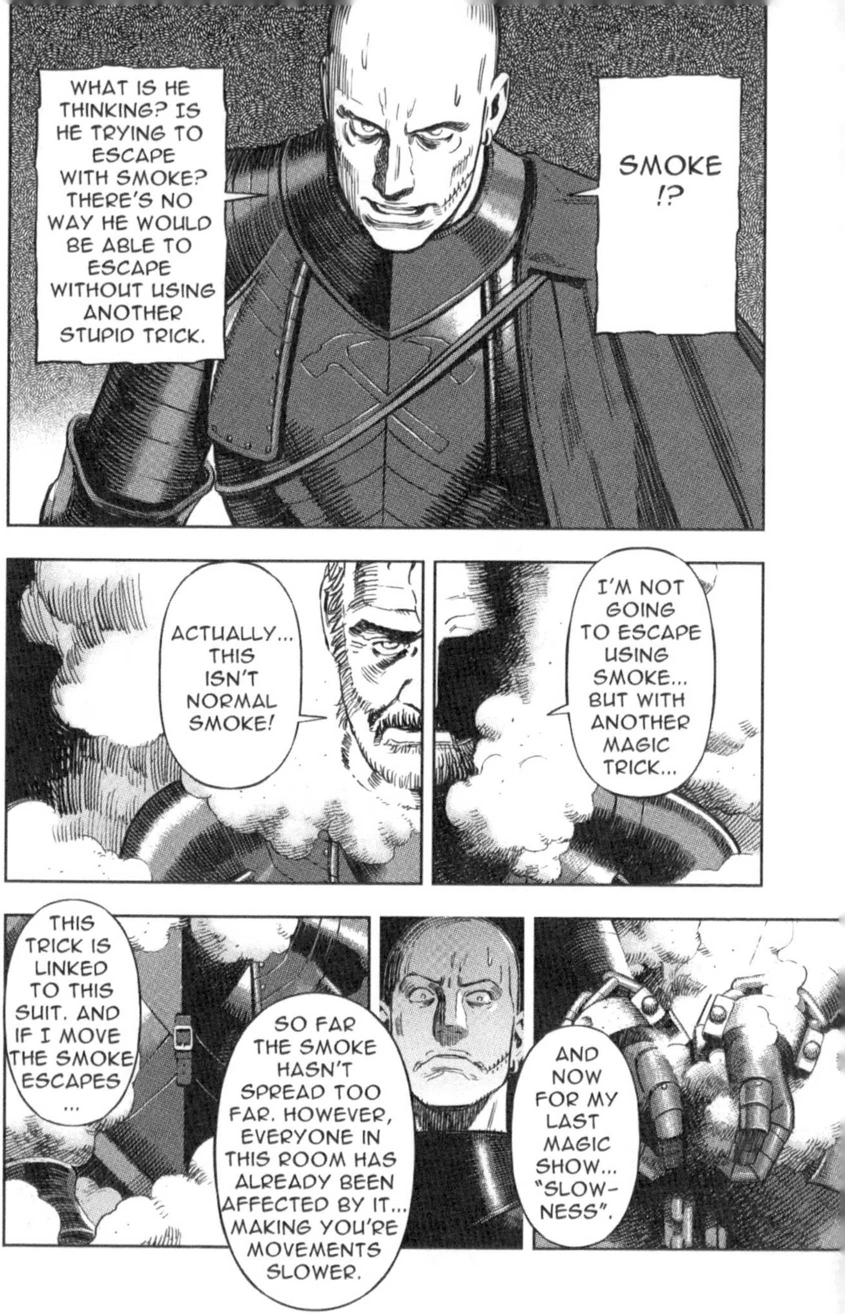
SMOKE !?
WHAT IS HE THINKING? IS HE TRYING TO ESCAPE WITH SMOKE? THERE'S NO WAY HE WOULD BE ABLE TO ESCAPE WITHOUT USING ANOTHER STUPID TRICK.
I'M NOT GOING TO ESCAPE USING SMOKE... BUT WITH ANOTHER MAGIC TRICK...
ACTUALLY... THIS ISN'T NORMAL SMOKE!
AND NOW FOR MY LAST MAGIC SHOW... "SLOW-NESS".
SO FAR THE SMOKE HASN'T SPREAD TOO FAR. HOWEVER, EVERYONE IN THIS ROOM HAS ALREADY BEEN AFFECTED BY IT... MAKING YOU'RE MOVEMENTS SLOWER.
THIS TRICK IS LINKED TO THIS SUIT. AND IF I MOVE THE SMOKE ESCAPES ...

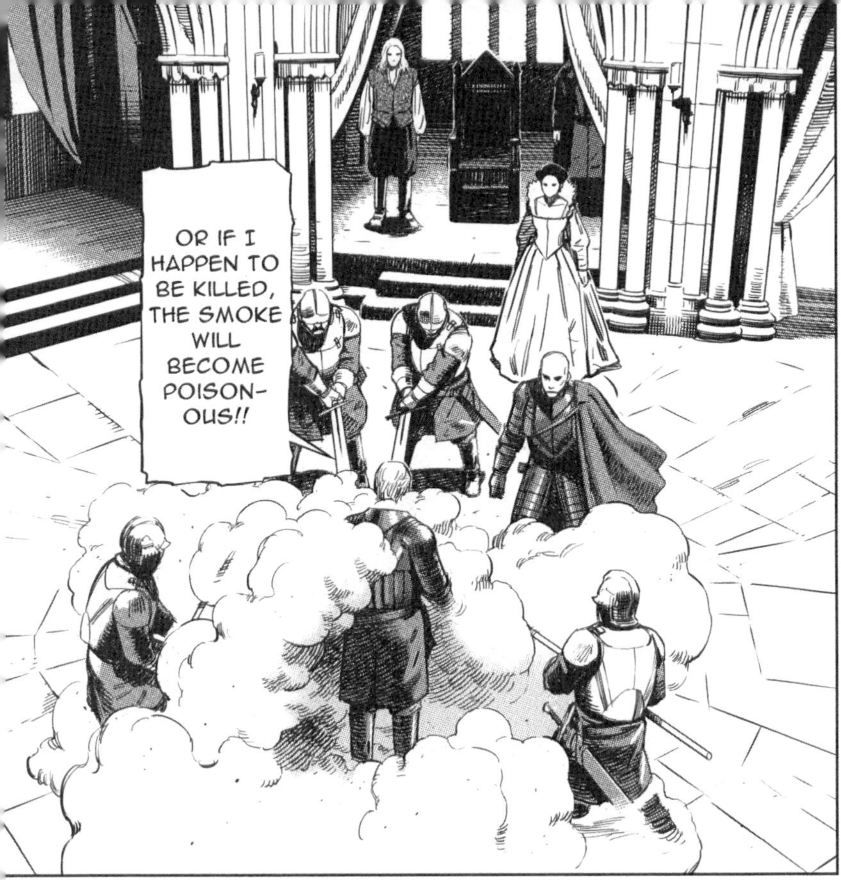
OR IF I HAPPEN TO BE KILLED, THE SMOKE WILL BECOME POISONOUS!!
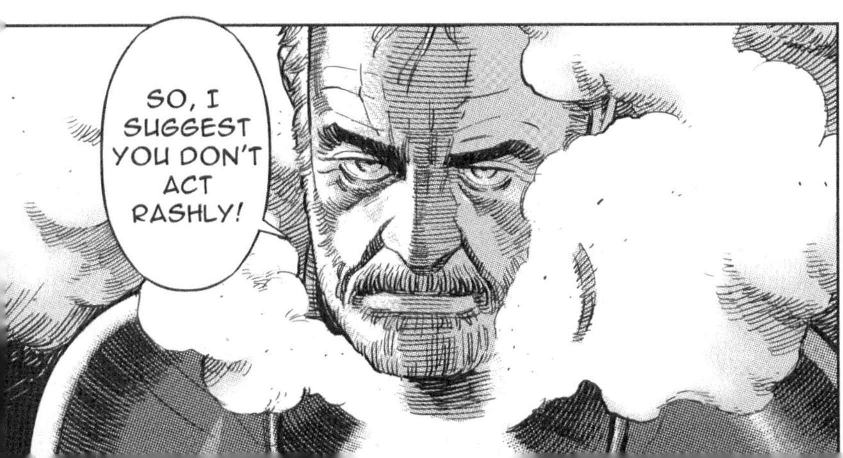
SO, I SUGGEST YOU DON'T ACT RASHLY!

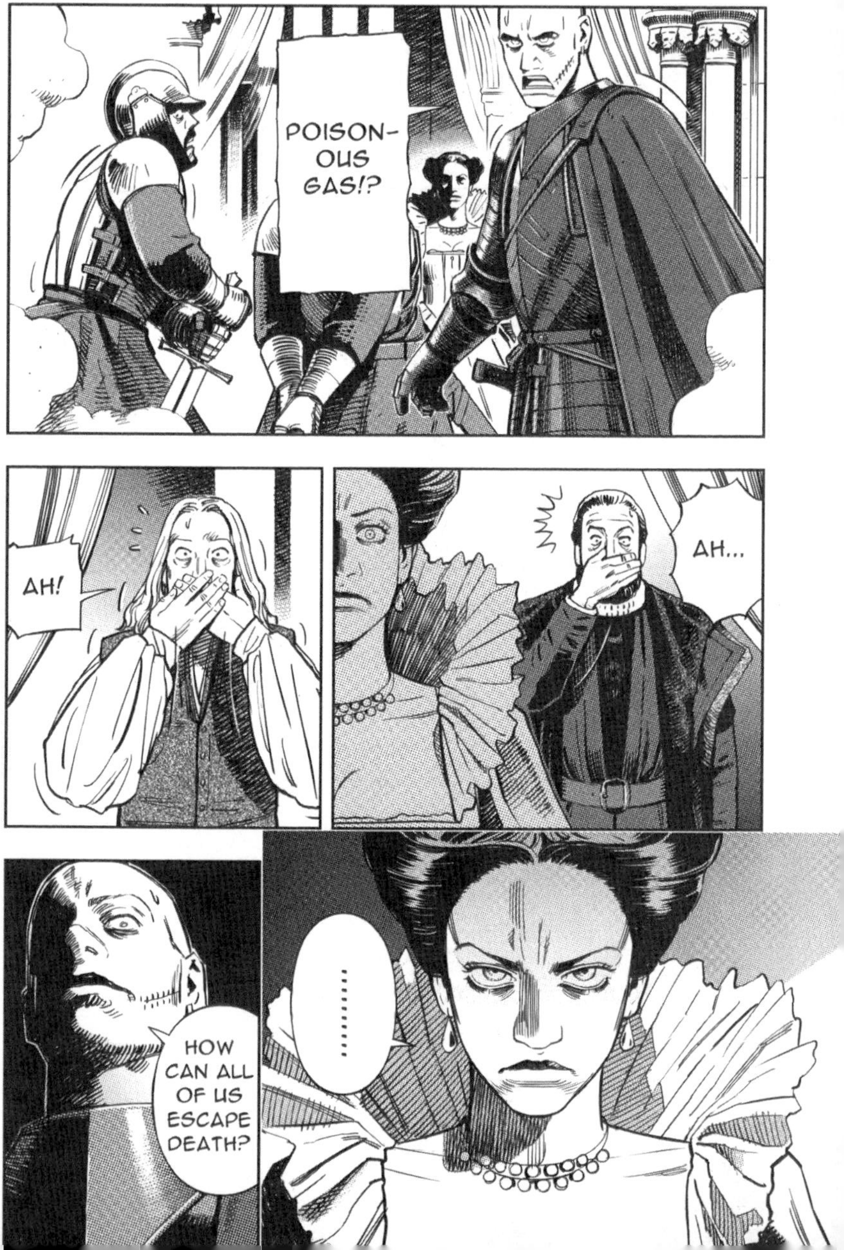
POISON-OUS GAS!?
AH...
AH!
....
HOW CAN ALL OF US ESCAPE DEATH?

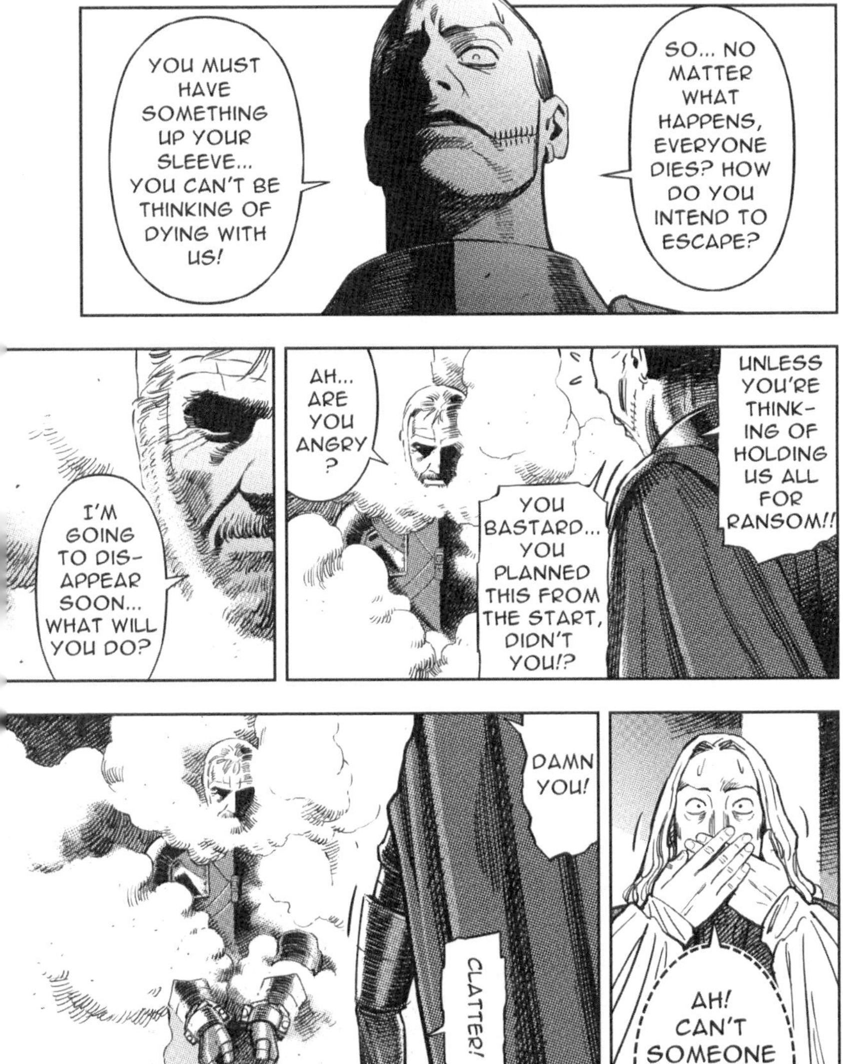
SO... NO MATTER WHAT HAPPENS, EVERYONE DIES? HOW DO YOU INTEND TO ESCAPE?
YOU MUST HAVE SOMETHING UP YOUR SLEEVE... YOU CAN'T BE THINKING OF DYING WITH US!
UNLESS YOU'RE THINKING OF HOLDING US ALL FOR RANSOM!!
AH... ARE YOU ANGRY?
YOU BASTARD... YOU PLANNED THIS FROM THE START, DIDN'T YOU!?
I'M GOING TO DISAPPEAR SOON... WHAT WILL YOU DO?
AH! CAN'T SOMEONE DO SOMETHING?
DAMN YOU!
CLATTER!

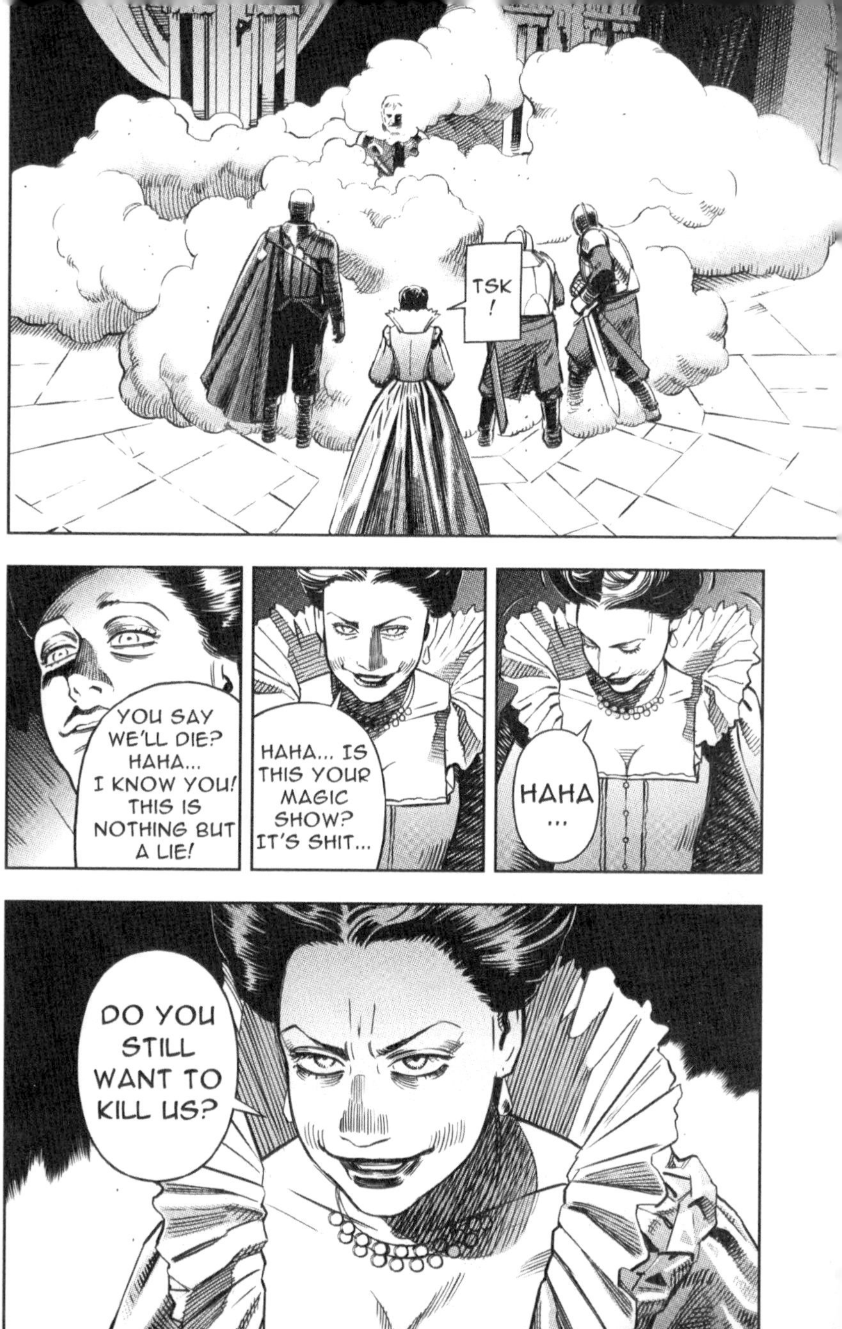
TSK!
HAHA...
HAHA... IS THIS YOUR MAGIC SHOW? IT'S SHIT...
YOU SAY WE'LL DIE? HAHA... I KNOW YOU! THIS IS NOTHING BUT A LIE!
DO YOU STILL WANT TO KILL US?

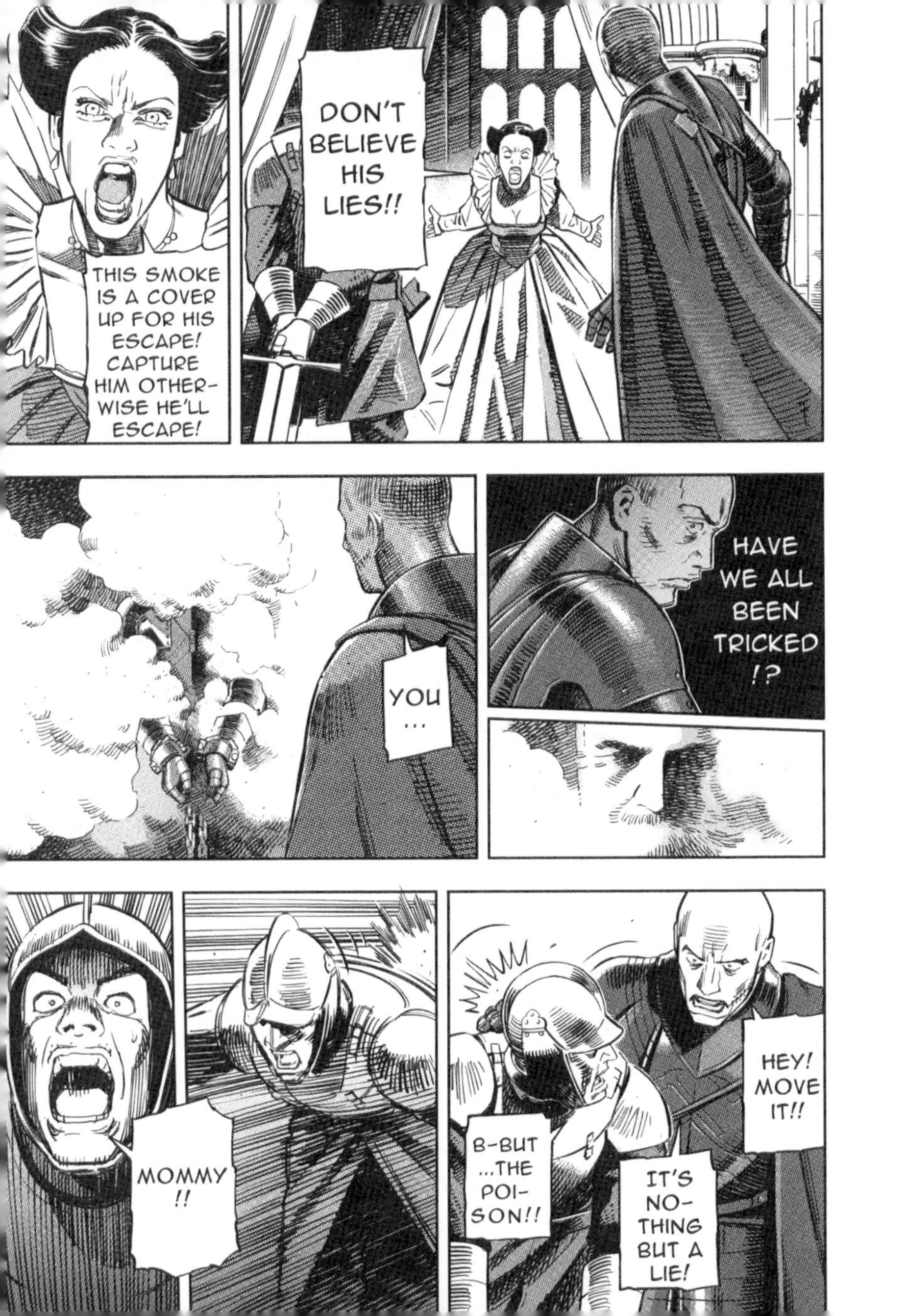
DON'T BELIEVE HIS LIES!!
THIS SMOKE IS A COVER UP FOR HIS ESCAPE! CAPTURE HIM OTHER-WISE HE'LL ESCAPE!
HAVE WE ALL BEEN TRICKED !?
YOU ...
HEY! MOVE IT!!
B-BUT ...THE POI-SON!!
IT'S NO-THING BUT A LIE!
MOMMY !!

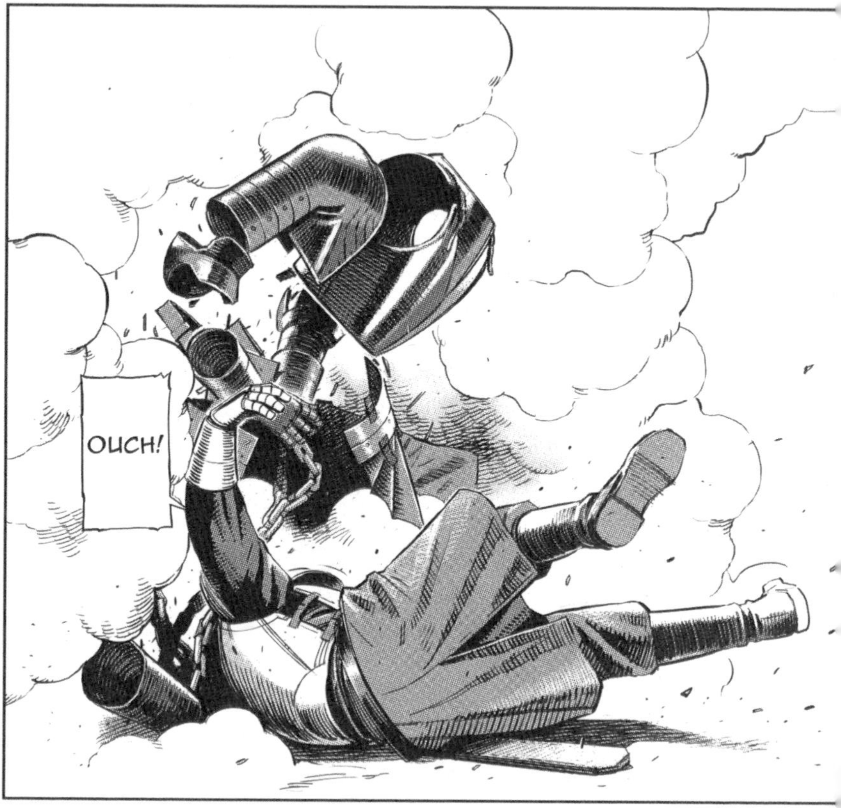
OUCH!

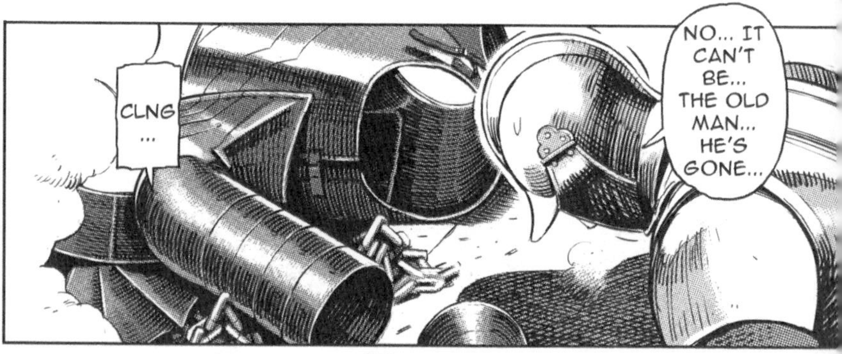
NO... IT CAN'T BE... THE OLD MAN... HE'S GONE...
CLNG ...

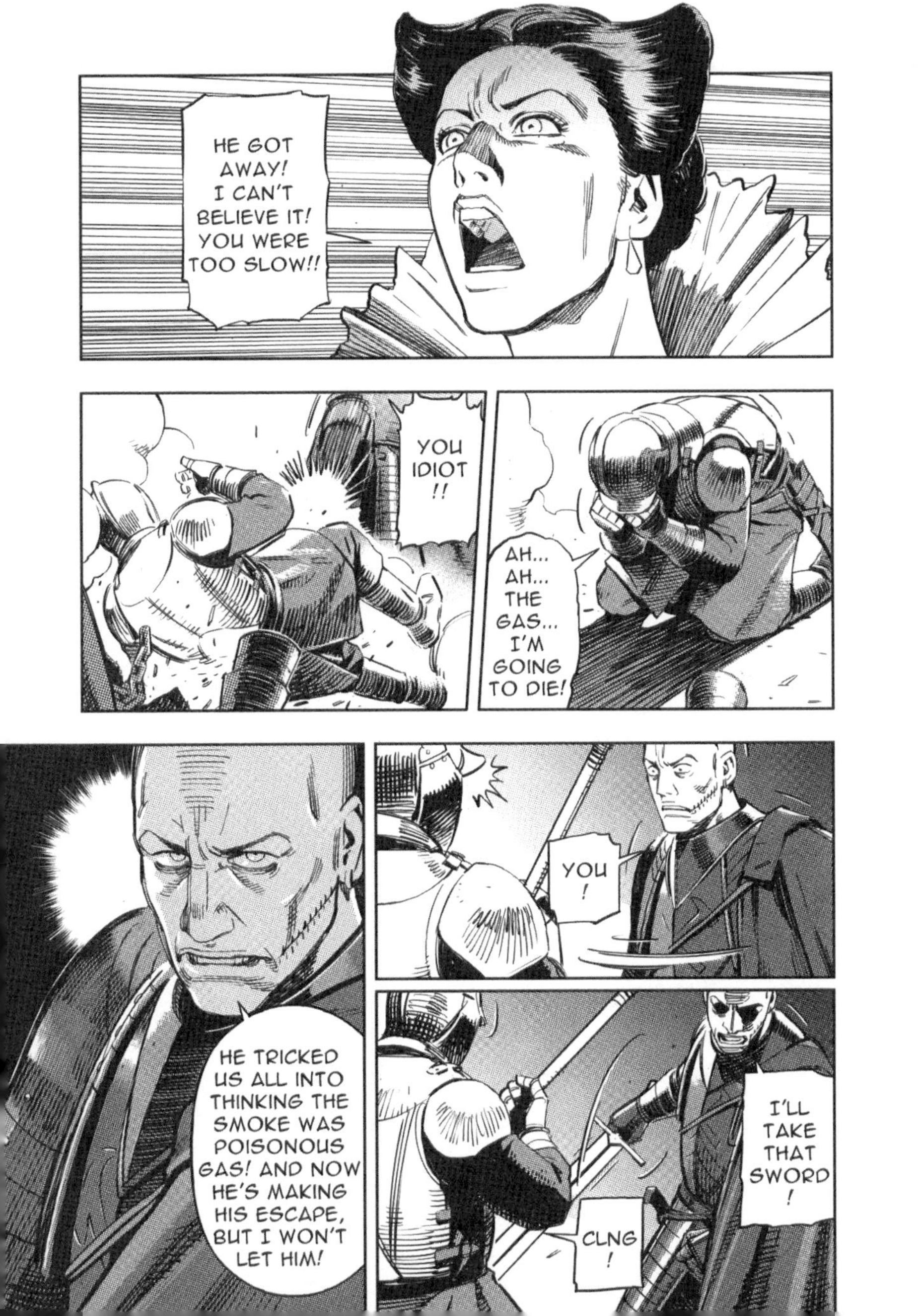
HE GOT AWAY! I CAN'T BELIEVE IT! YOU WERE TOO SLOW!!
AH... AH... THE GAS... I'M GOING TO DIE!
YOU IDIOT!!
YOU!
I'LL TAKE THAT SWORD!
CLNG!
HE TRICKED US ALL INTO THINKING THE SMOKE WAS POISONOUS GAS! AND NOW HE'S MAKING HIS ESCAPE, BUT I WON'T LET HIM!

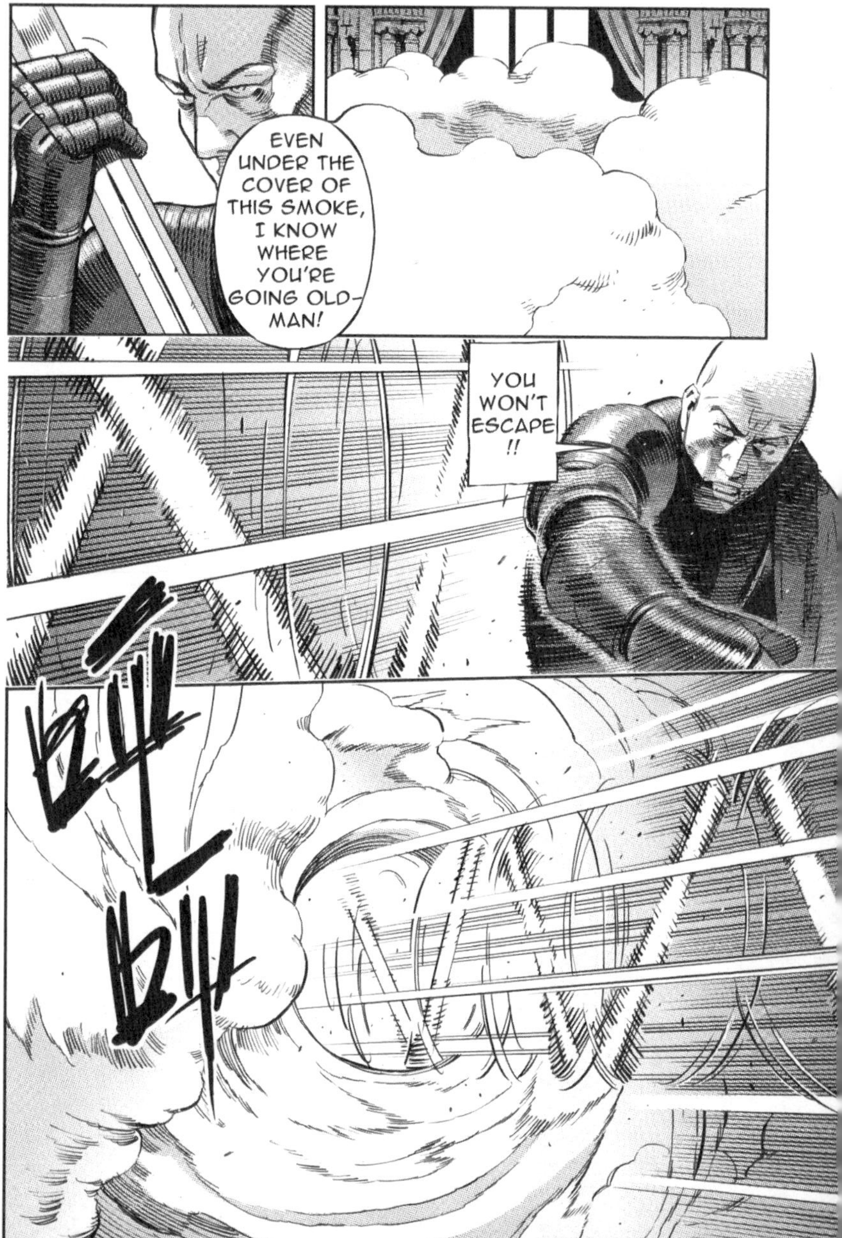
EVEN UNDER THE COVER OF THIS SMOKE, I KNOW WHERE YOU'RE GOING OLD-MAN!
YOU WON'T ESCAPE !!

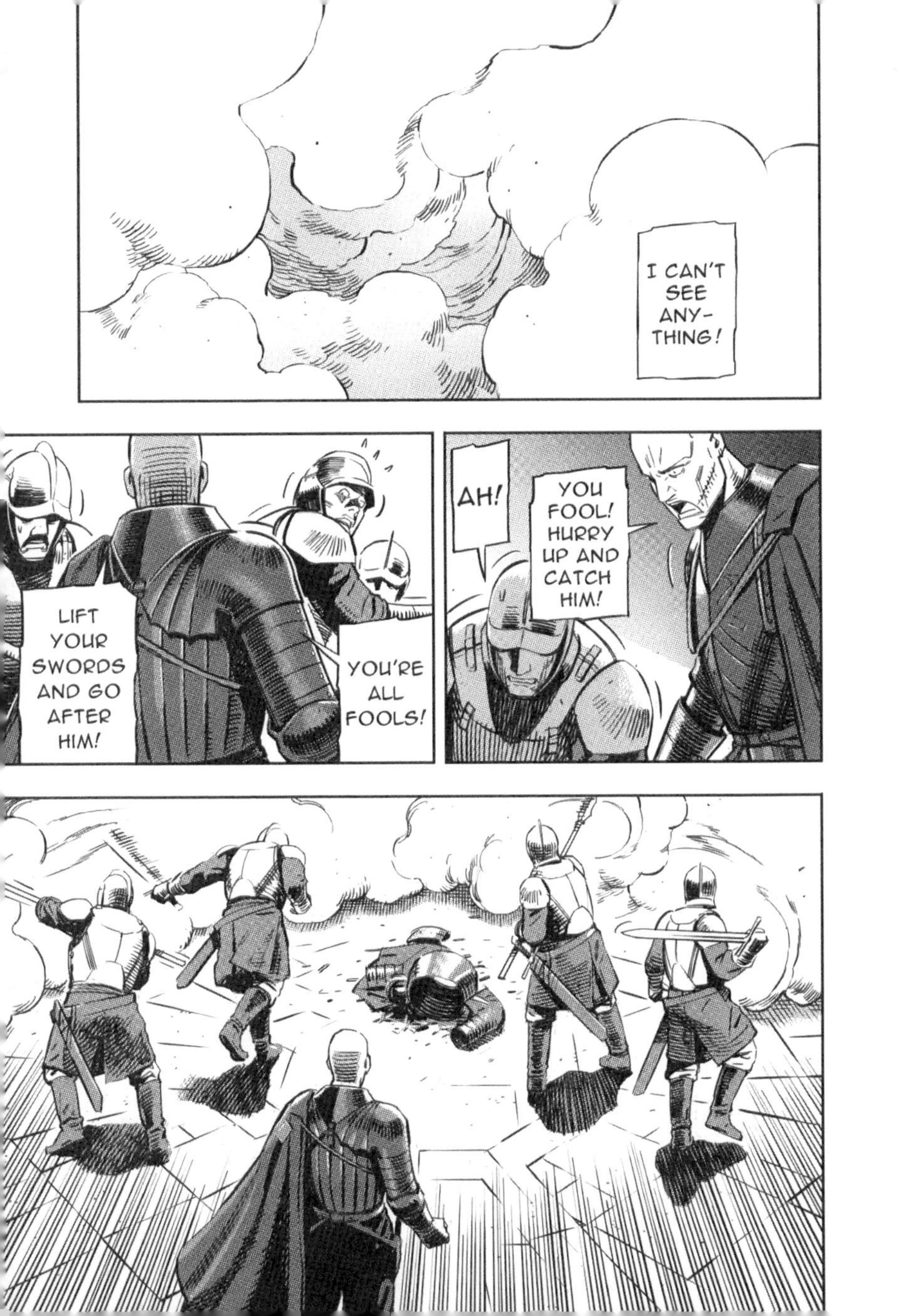
I CAN'T SEE ANY-THING!
YOU FOOL! HURRY UP AND CATCH HIM!
AH!
YOU'RE ALL FOOLS!
LIFT YOUR SWORDS AND GO AFTER HIM!

YOU MEN ARE USELESS! YOU'VE LET OLDMAN ESCAPE WHEN HE WAS RIGHT IN FRONT OF US... I'M FURIOUS!

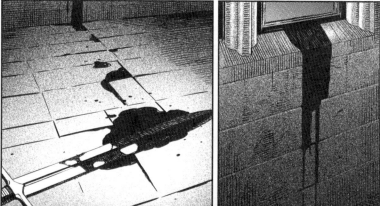

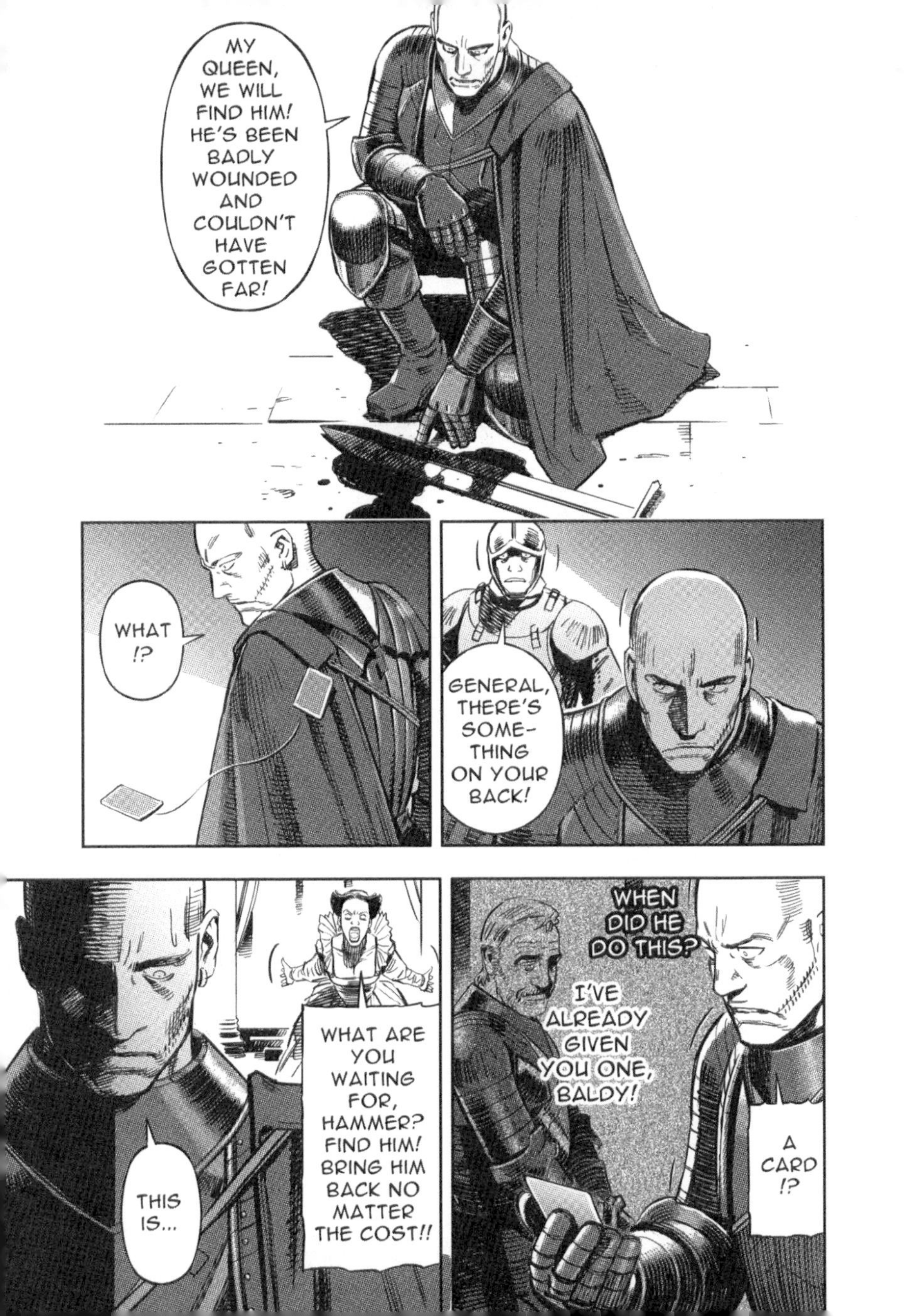
MY QUEEN, WE WILL FIND HIM! HE'S BEEN BADLY WOUNDED AND COULDN'T HAVE GOTTEN FAR!
GENERAL, THERE'S SOME-THING ON YOUR BACK!
WHAT !?
WHEN DID HE DO THIS?
I'VE ALREADY GIVEN YOU ONE, BALDY!
A CARD !?
WHAT ARE YOU WAITING FOR, HAMMER? FIND HIM! BRING HIM BACK NO MATTER THE COST!!
THIS IS...

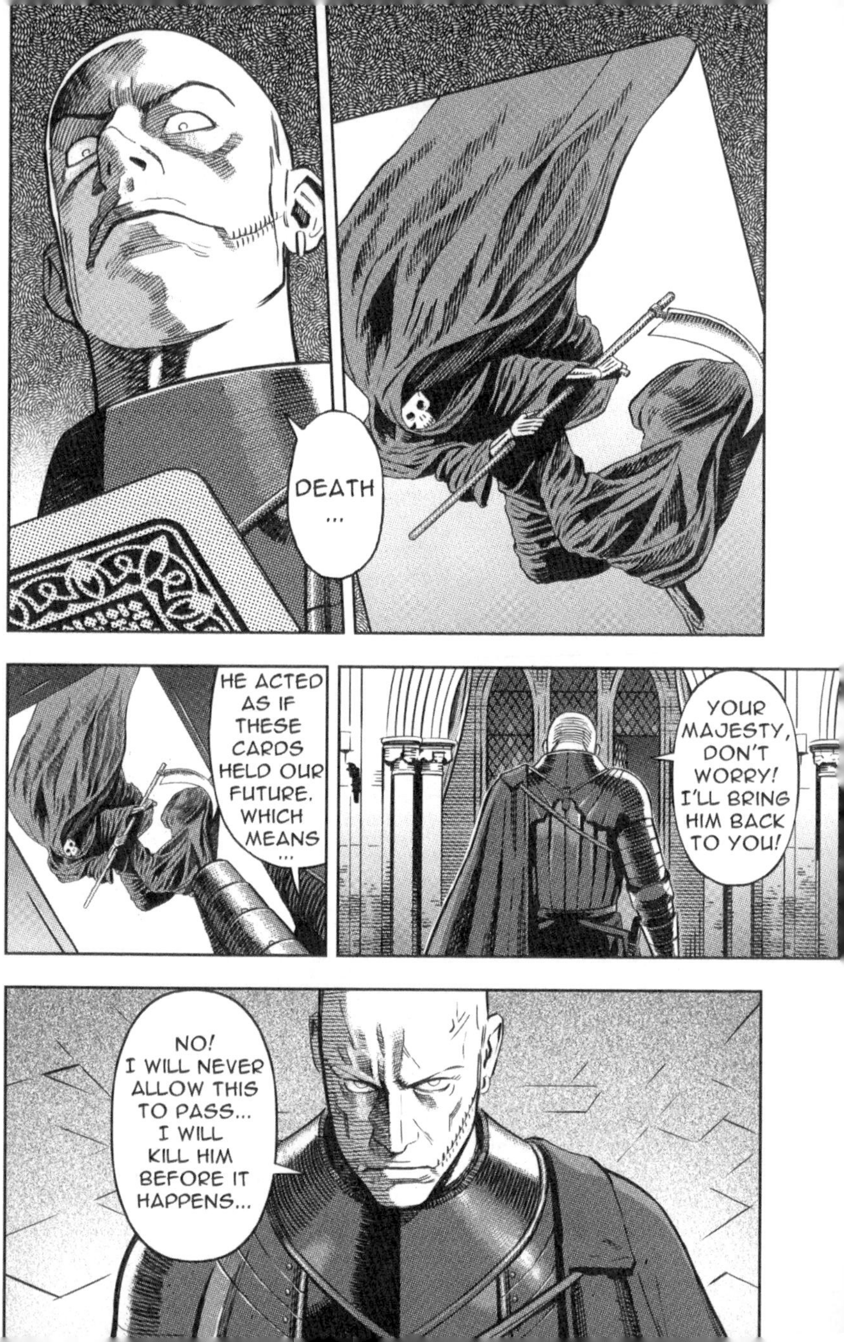
DEATH ...
YOUR MAJESTY, DON'T WORRY! I'LL BRING HIM BACK TO YOU!
HE ACTED AS IF THESE CARDS HELD OUR FUTURE. WHICH MEANS ...
NO! I WILL NEVER ALLOW THIS TO PASS... I WILL KILL HIM BEFORE IT HAPPENS...

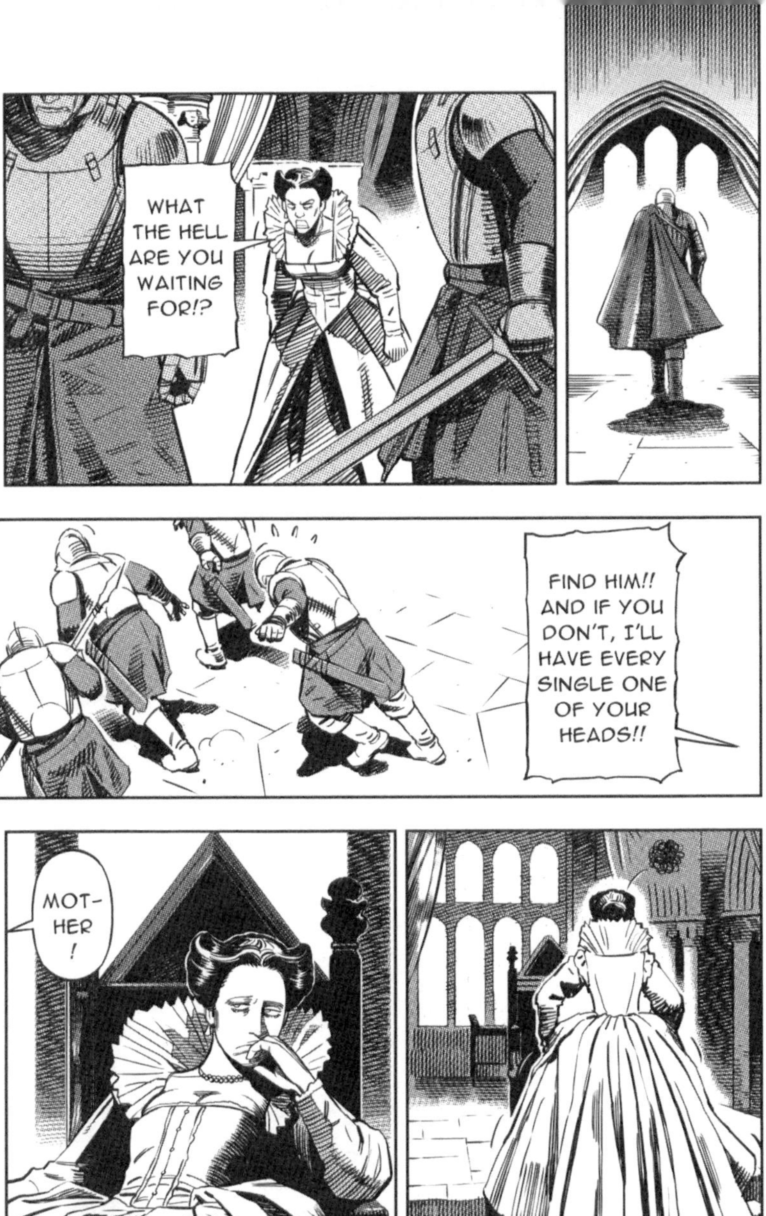
WHAT THE HELL ARE YOU WAITING FOR!?
FIND HIM!! AND IF YOU DON'T, I'LL HAVE EVERY SINGLE ONE OF YOUR HEADS!!
MOT-HER !

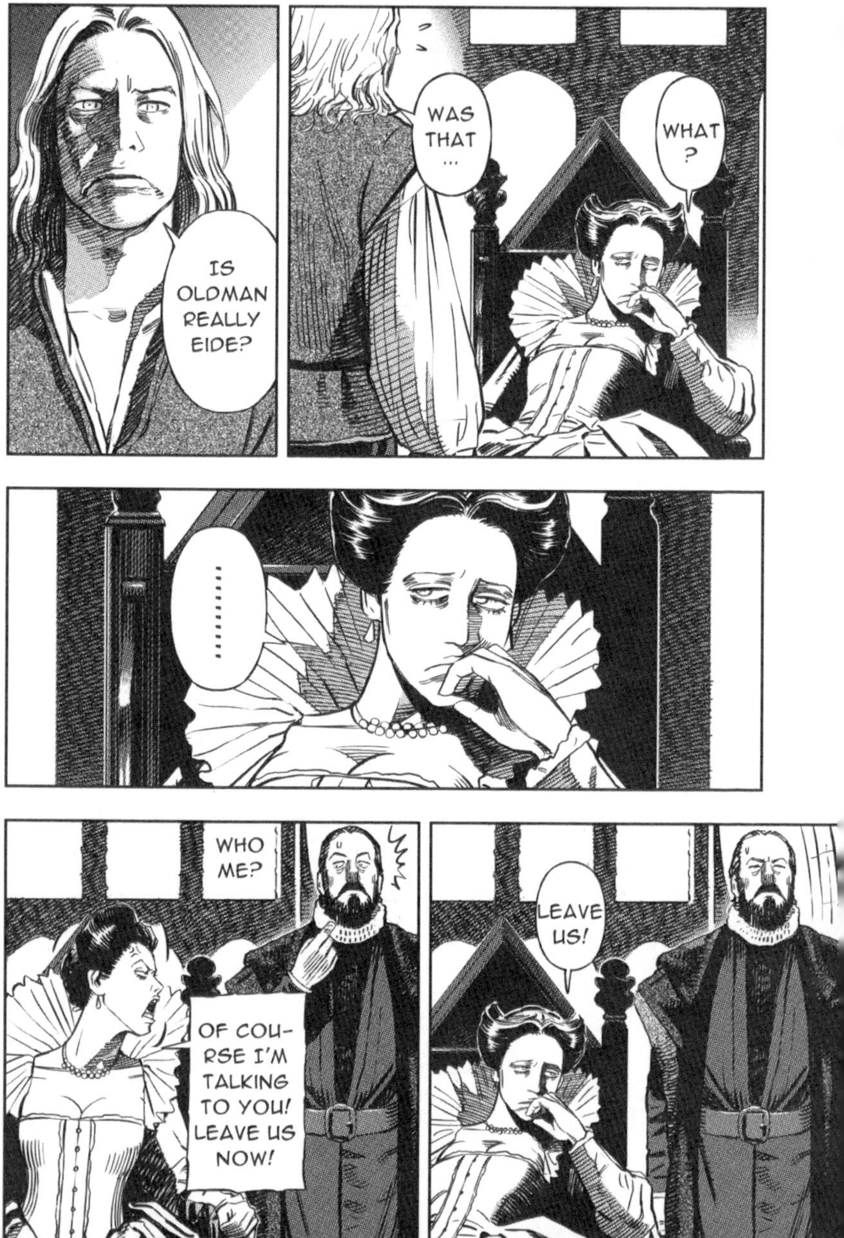
WHAT?
WAS THAT...
IS OLDMAN REALLY EIDE?
....
LEAVE US!
WHO ME?
OF COURSE I'M TALKING TO YOU! LEAVE US NOW!

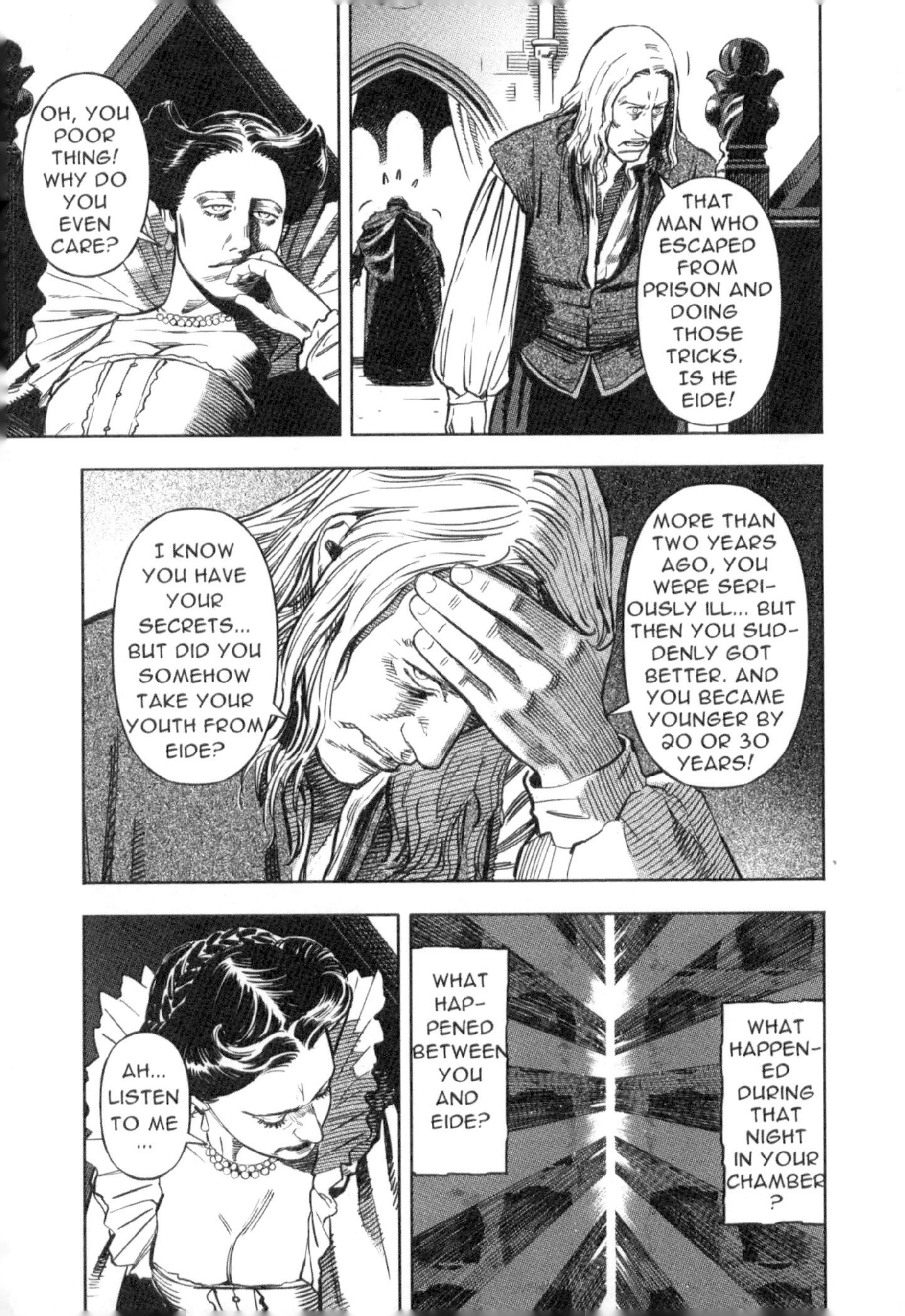
THAT MAN WHO ESCAPED FROM PRISON AND DOING THOSE TRICKS. IS HE EIDE!
OH, YOU POOR THING! WHY DO YOU EVEN CARE?
MORE THAN TWO YEARS AGO, YOU WERE SERI-OUSLY ILL... BUT THEN YOU SUD-DENLY GOT BETTER. AND YOU BECAME YOUNGER BY 20 OR 30 YEARS!
I KNOW YOU HAVE YOUR SECRETS... BUT DID YOU SOMEHOW TAKE YOUR YOUTH FROM EIDE?
WHAT HAPPEN-ED DURING THAT NIGHT IN YOUR CHAMBER ?
WHAT HAP-PENED BETWEEN YOU AND EIDE?
AH... LISTEN TO ME ...

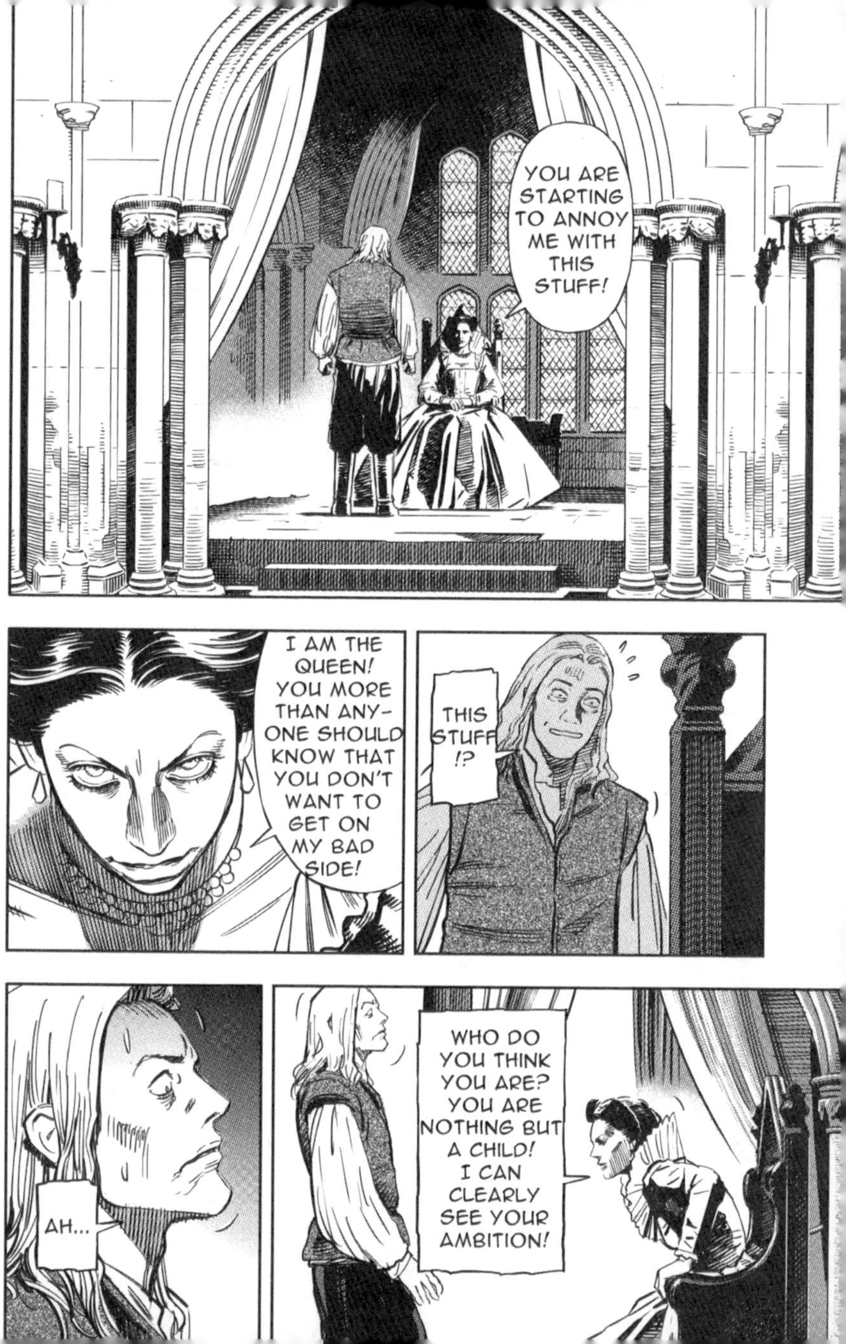
YOU ARE STARTING TO ANNOY ME WITH THIS STUFF!
THIS STUFF !?
I AM THE QUEEN! YOU MORE THAN ANY-ONE SHOULD KNOW THAT YOU DON'T WANT TO GET ON MY BAD SIDE!
WHO DO YOU THINK YOU ARE? YOU ARE NOTHING BUT A CHILD! I CAN CLEARLY SEE YOUR AMBITION!
AH...

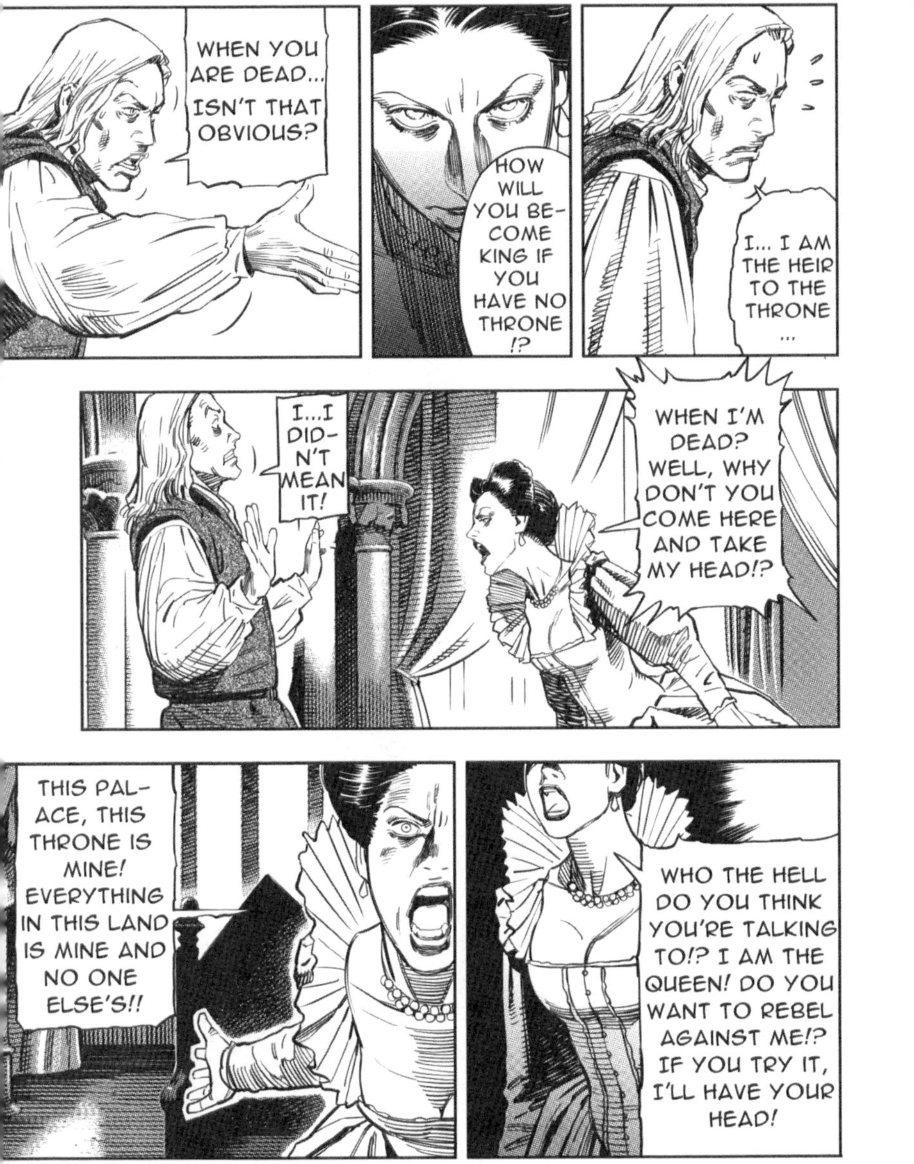
I... I AM THE HEIR TO THE THRONE ...
HOW WILL YOU BECOME KING IF YOU HAVE NO THRONE!?
WHEN YOU ARE DEAD... ISN'T THAT OBVIOUS?
WHEN I'M DEAD? WELL, WHY DON'T YOU COME HERE AND TAKE MY HEAD!?
I...I DIDN'T MEAN IT!
WHO THE HELL DO YOU THINK YOU'RE TALKING TO!? I AM THE QUEEN! DO YOU WANT TO REBEL AGAINST ME!? IF YOU TRY IT, I'LL HAVE YOUR HEAD!
THIS PALACE, THIS THRONE IS MINE! EVERYTHING IN THIS LAND IS MINE AND NO ONE ELSE'S!!

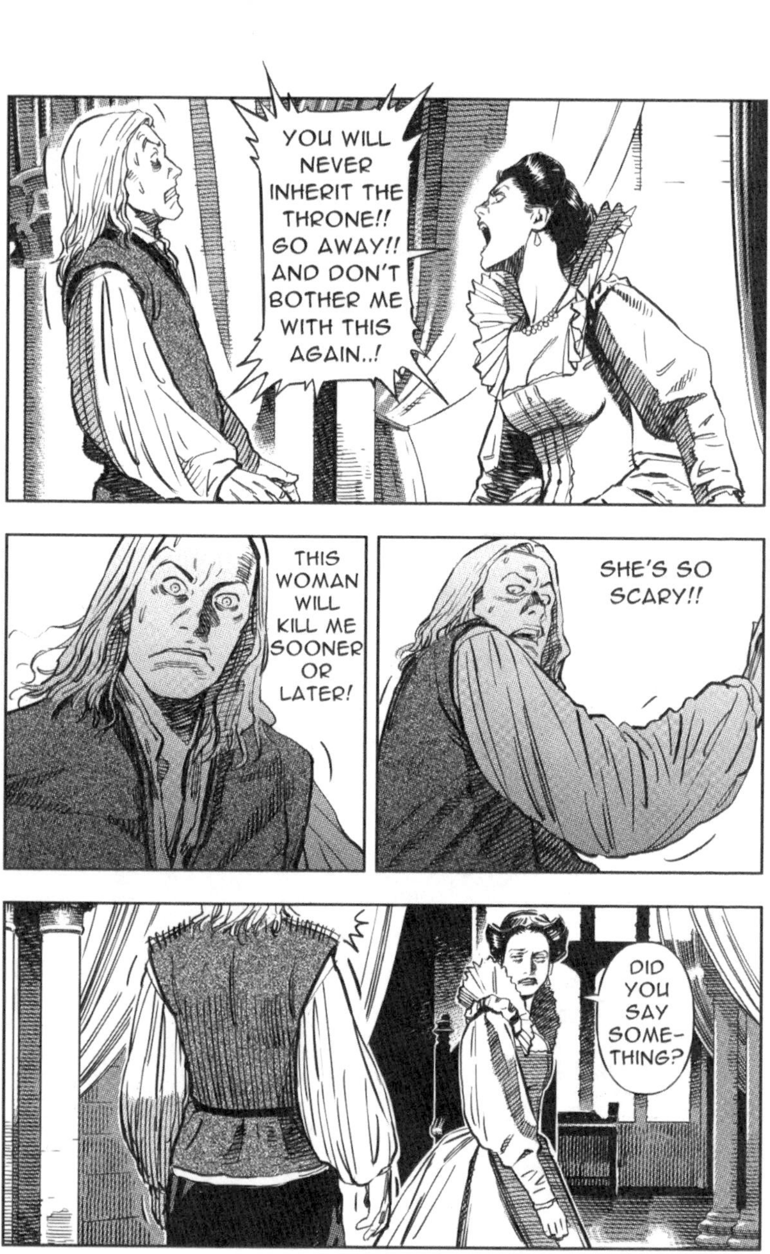
YOU WILL NEVER INHERIT THE THRONE!! GO AWAY!! AND DON'T BOTHER ME WITH THIS AGAIN..!
SHE'S SO SCARY!!
THIS WOMAN WILL KILL ME SOONER OR LATER!
DID YOU SAY SOME-THING?

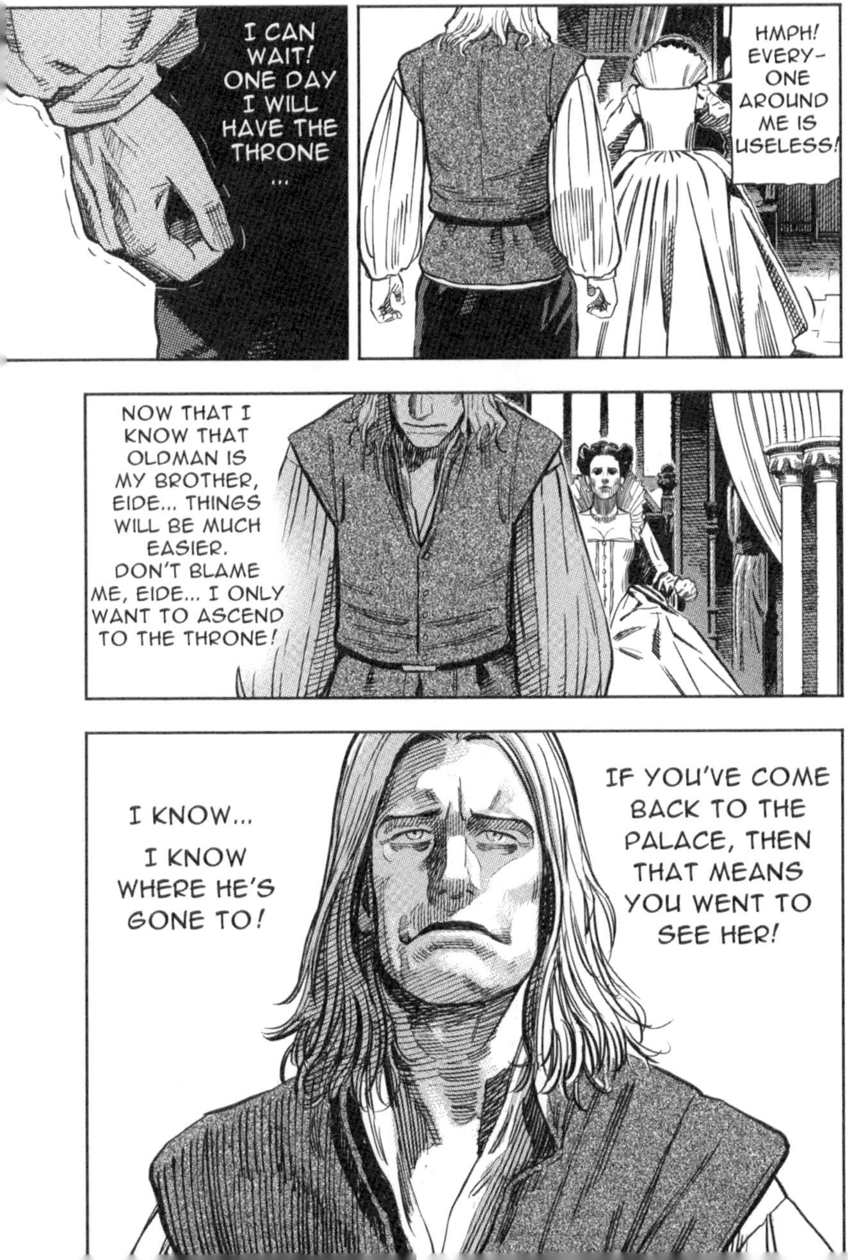
HMPH! EVERY-ONE AROUND ME IS USELESS!
I CAN WAIT! ONE DAY I WILL HAVE THE THRONE ...
NOW THAT I KNOW THAT OLDMAN IS MY BROTHER, EIDE... THINGS WILL BE MUCH EASIER. DON'T BLAME ME, EIDE... I ONLY WANT TO ASCEND TO THE THRONE!
IF YOU'VE COME BACK TO THE PALACE, THEN THAT MEANS YOU WENT TO SEE HER!
I KNOW...
I KNOW WHERE HE'S GONE TO!

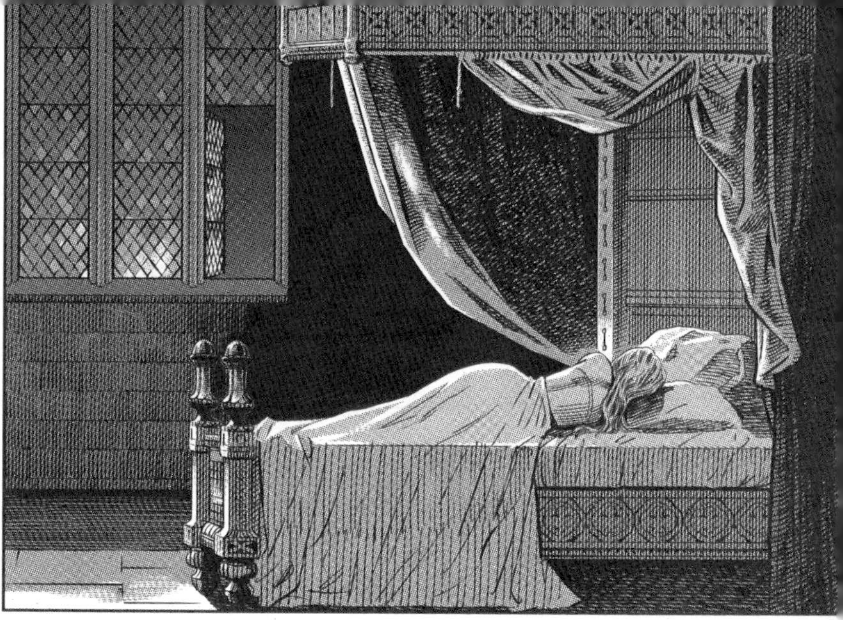
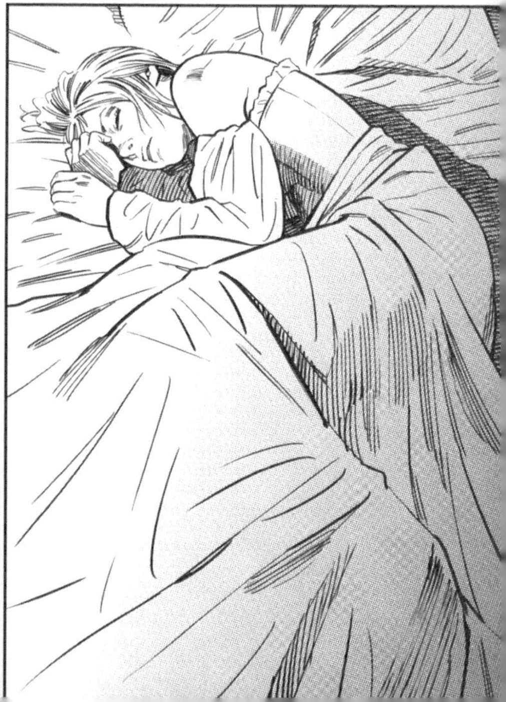
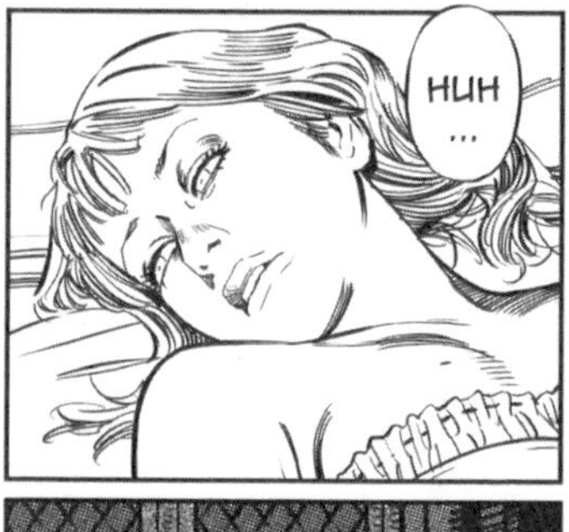
HUH
...
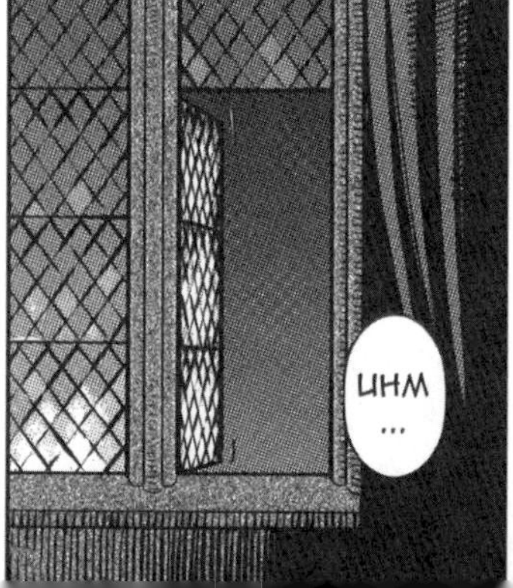
UHM
...

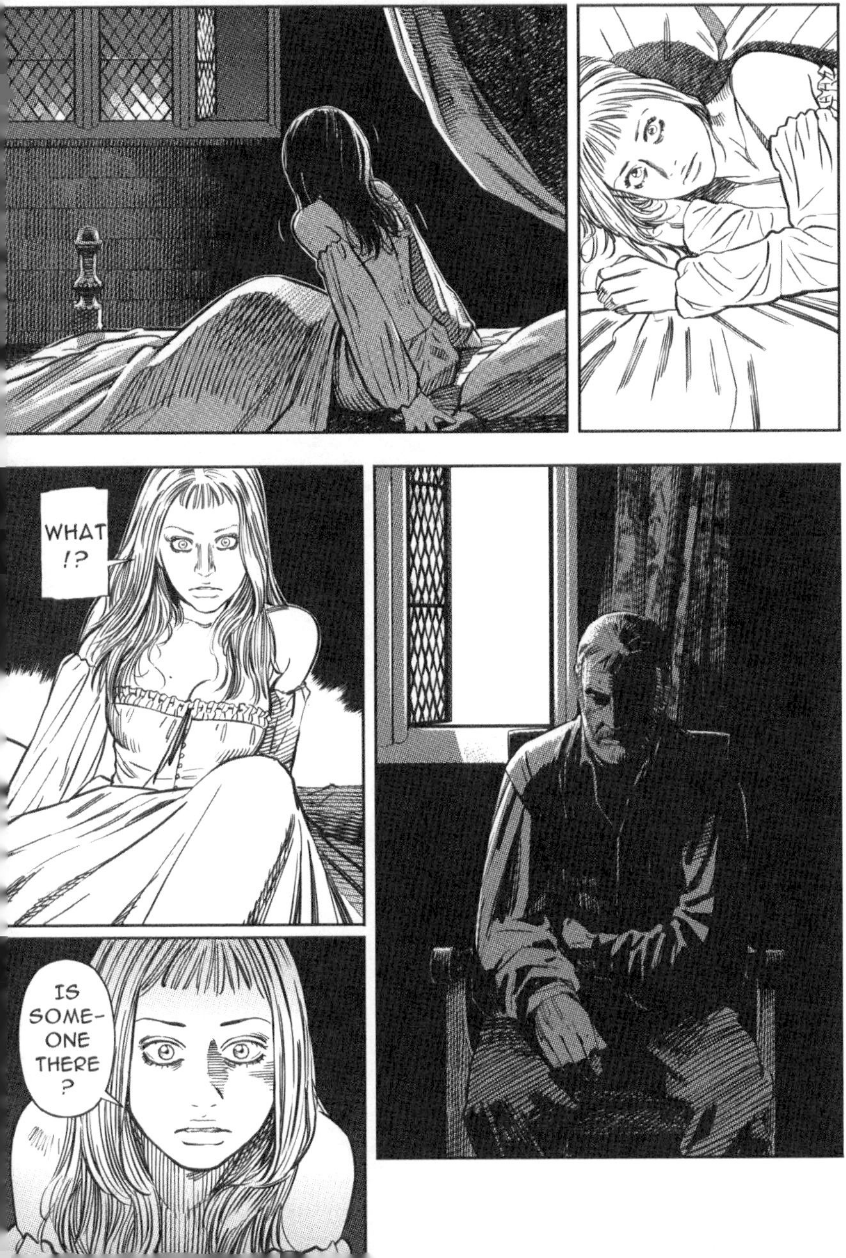
WHAT !?
IS SOME-ONE THERE ?

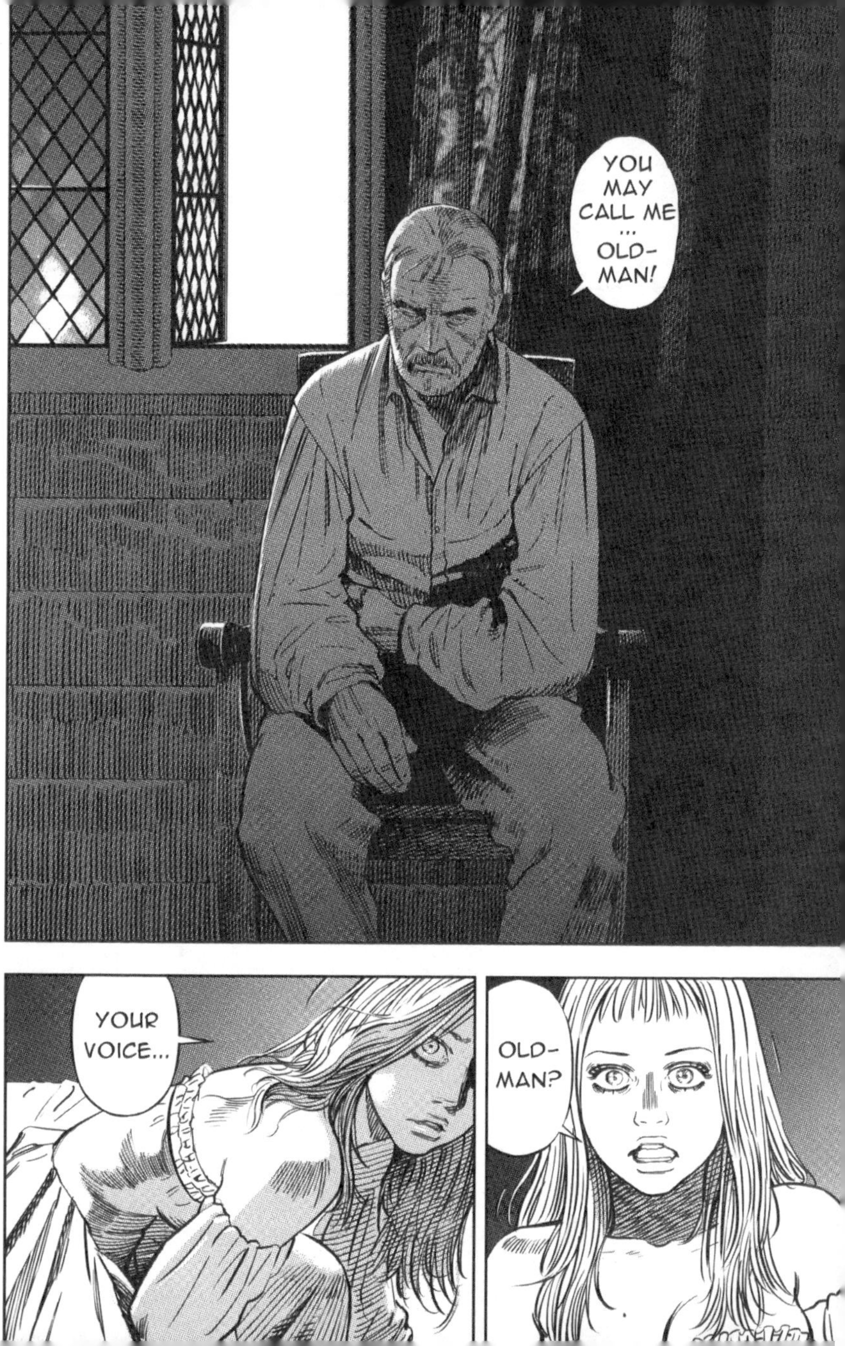
YOU MAY CALL ME ... OLD-MAN!
OLD-MAN?
YOUR VOICE...

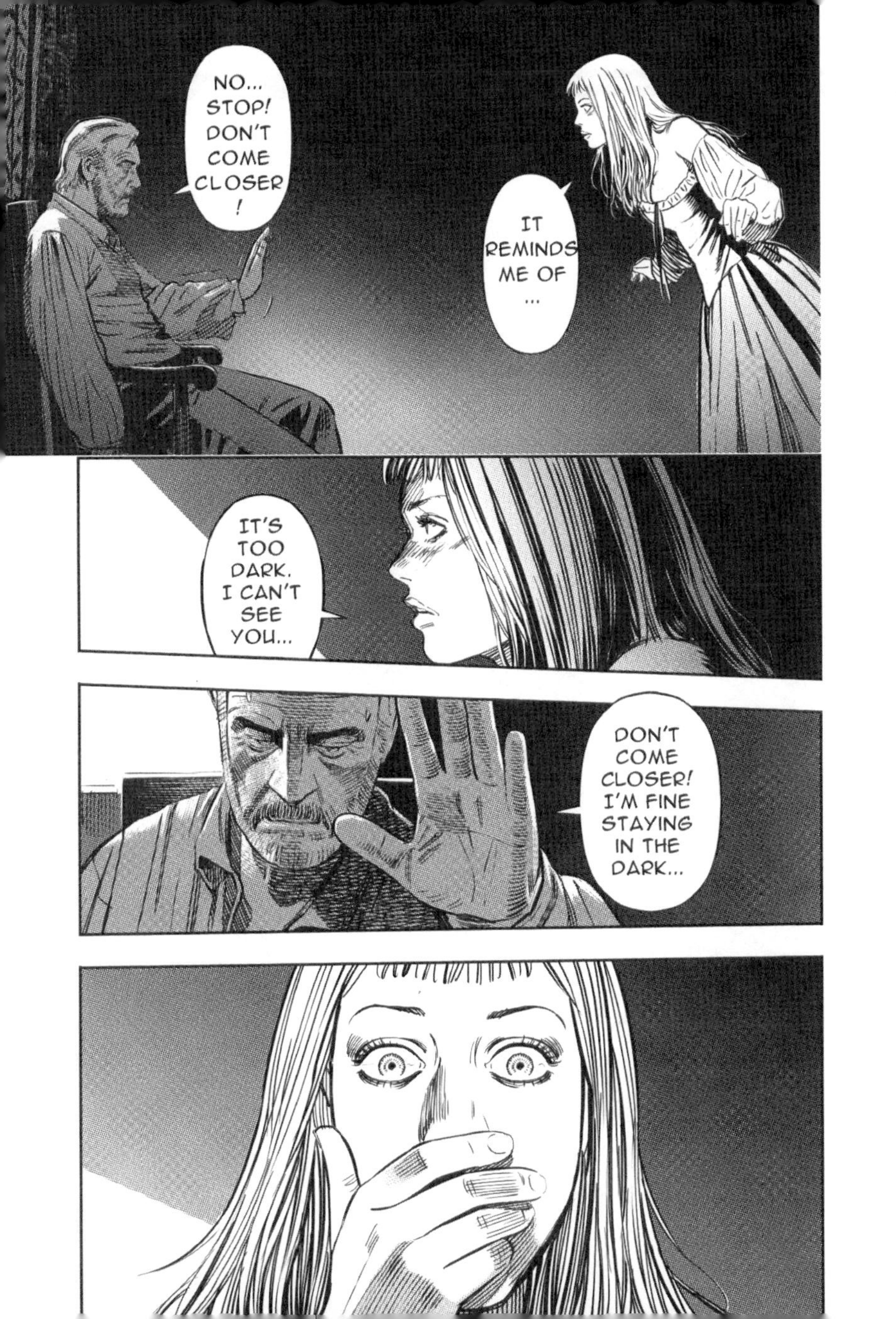
IT REMINDS ME OF ...
NO... STOP! DON'T COME CLOSER!
IT'S TOO DARK. I CAN'T SEE YOU...
DON'T COME CLOSER! I'M FINE STAYING IN THE DARK...

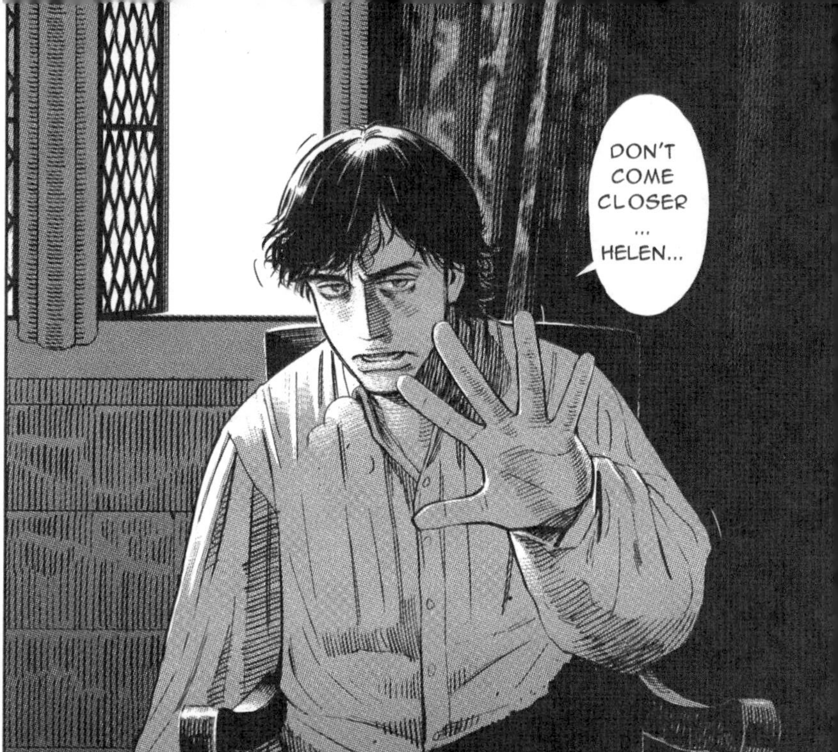
DON'T COME CLOSER ... HELEN...
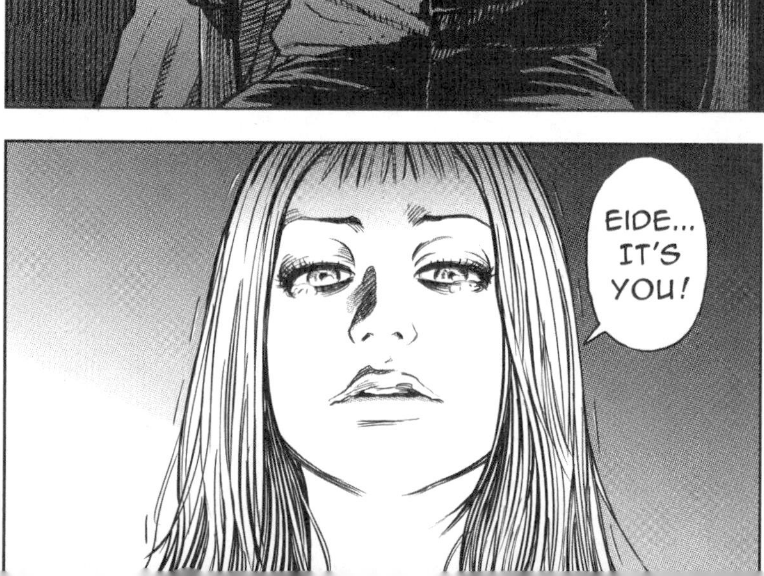
EIDE... IT'S YOU!

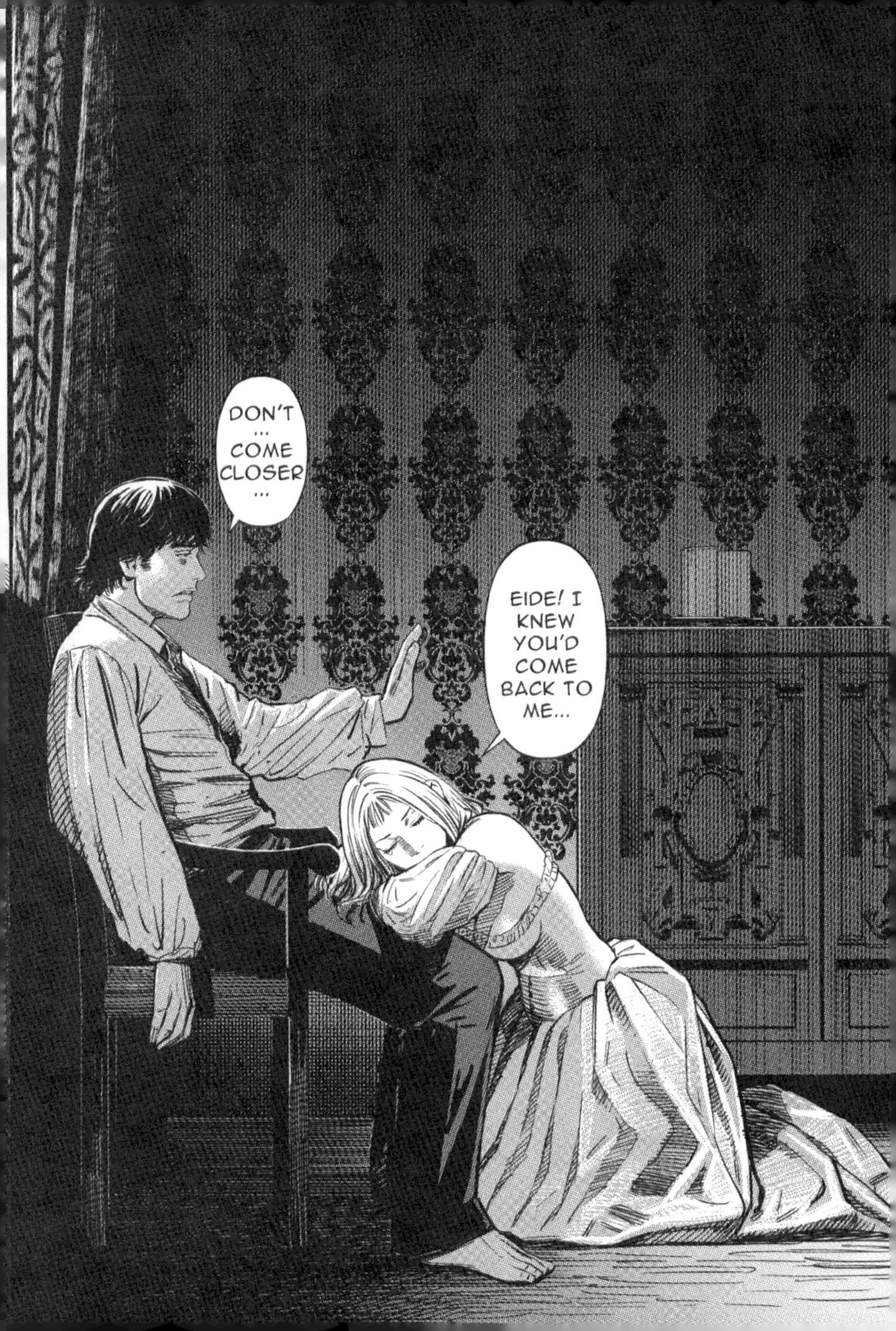
EIDE! I KNEW YOU'D COME BACK TO ME...
DON'T ... COME CLOSER ...

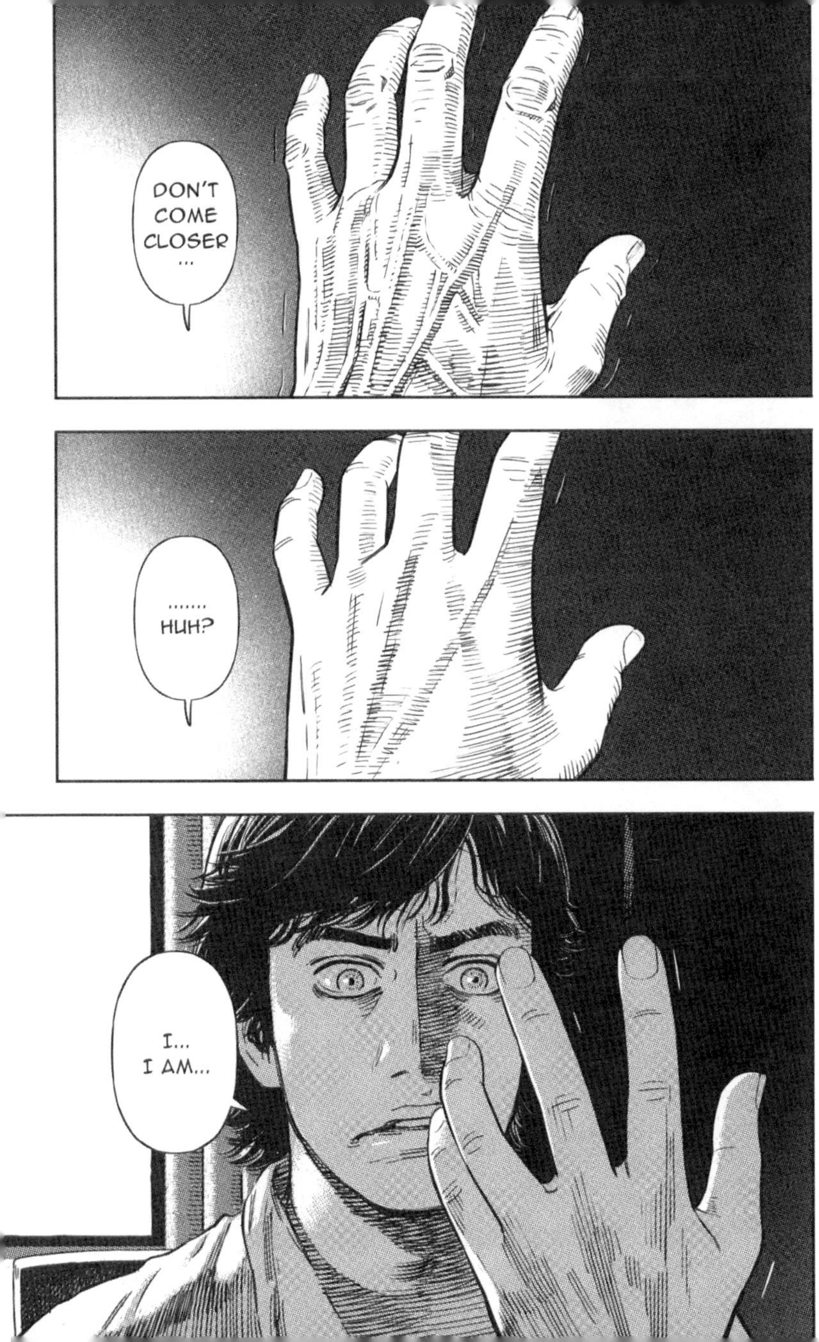
DON'T COME CLOSER …
……. HUH?
I… I AM…

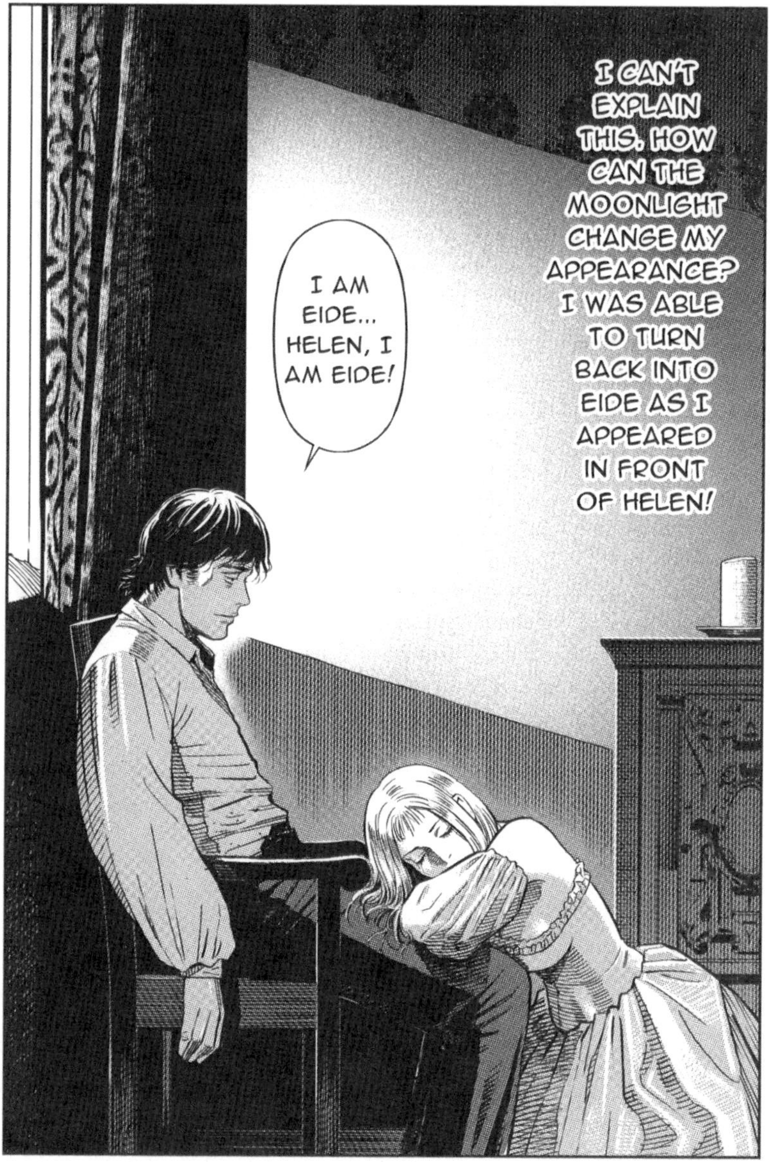
I CAN'T EXPLAIN THIS. HOW CAN THE MOONLIGHT CHANGE MY APPEARANCE? I WAS ABLE TO TURN BACK INTO EIDE AS I APPEARED IN FRONT OF HELEN!
I AM EIDE... HELEN, I AM EIDE!

CHAPTER 10
MOONLIGHT

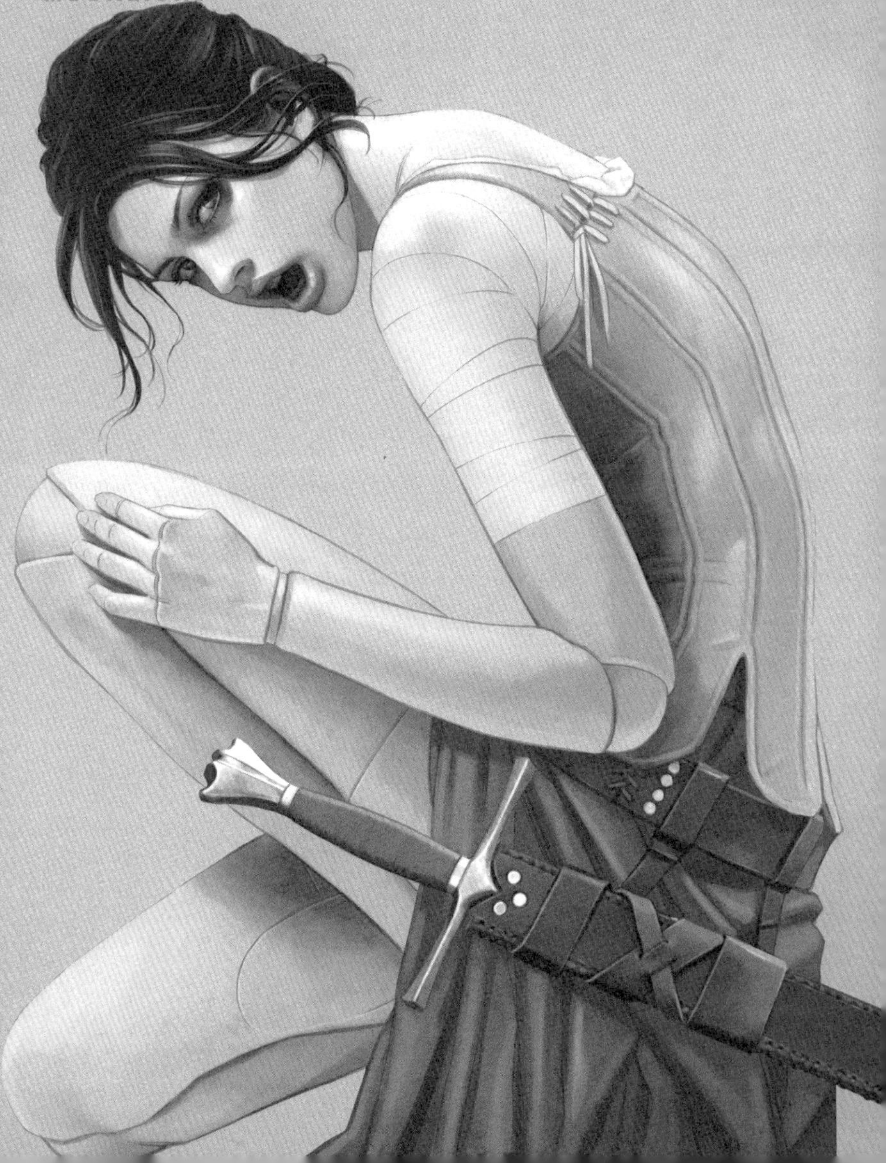

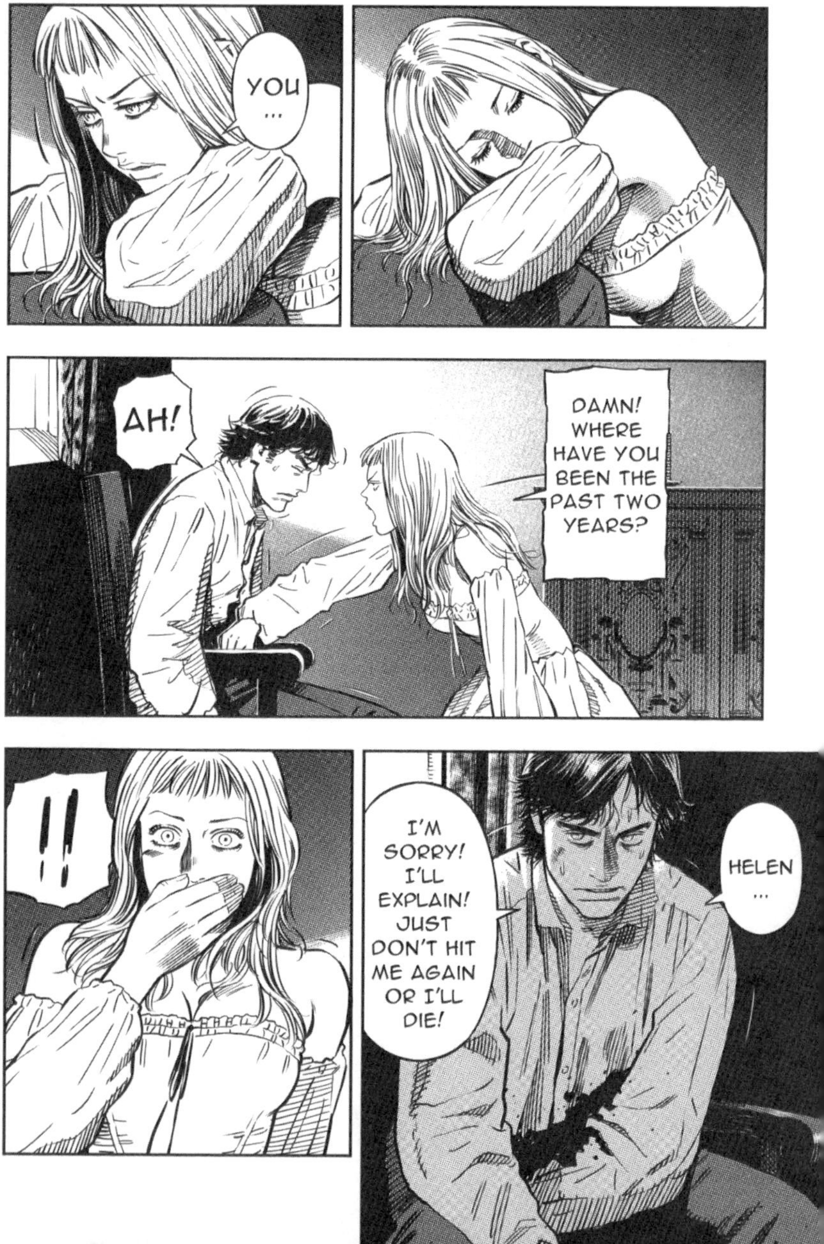
YOU ...
DAMN! WHERE HAVE YOU BEEN THE PAST TWO YEARS?
AH!
HELEN ...
I'M SORRY! I'LL EXPLAIN! JUST DON'T HIT ME AGAIN OR I'LL DIE!
!!

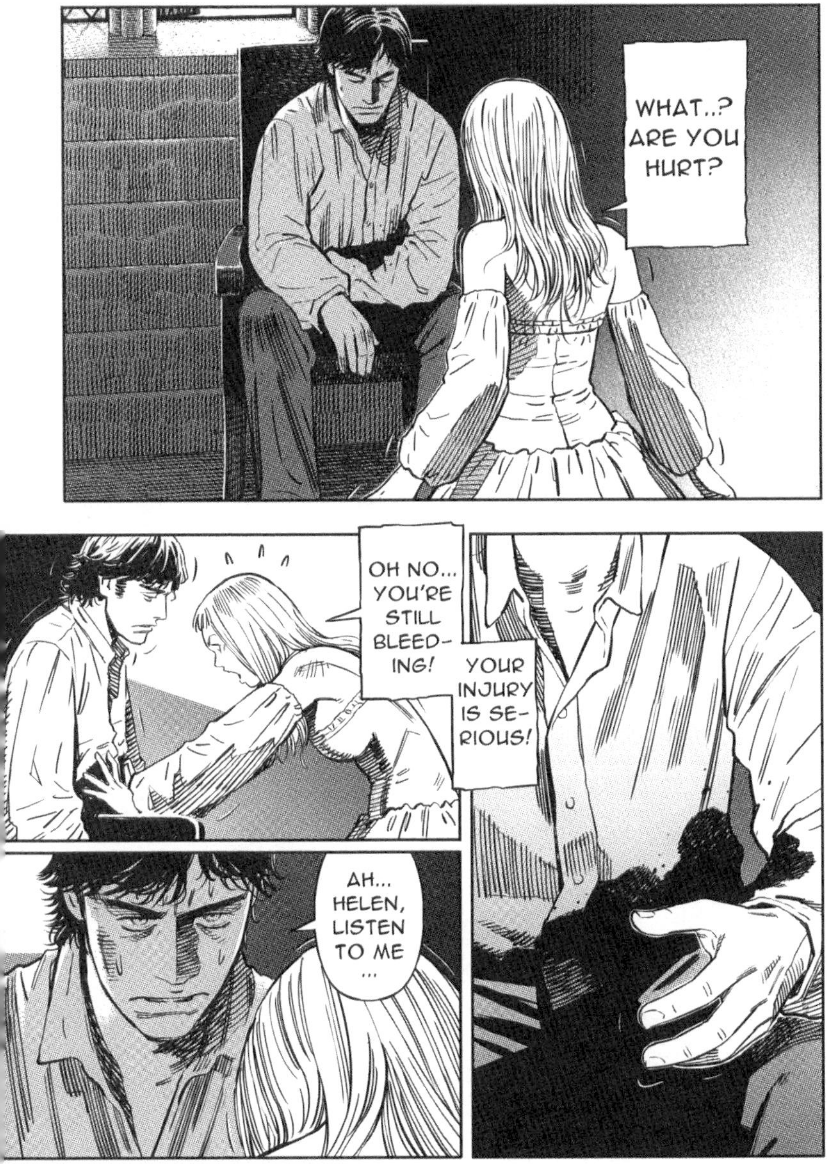
WHAT..? ARE YOU HURT?
YOUR INJURY IS SE-RIOUS!
OH NO... YOU'RE STILL BLEED-ING!
AH... HELEN, LISTEN TO ME ...

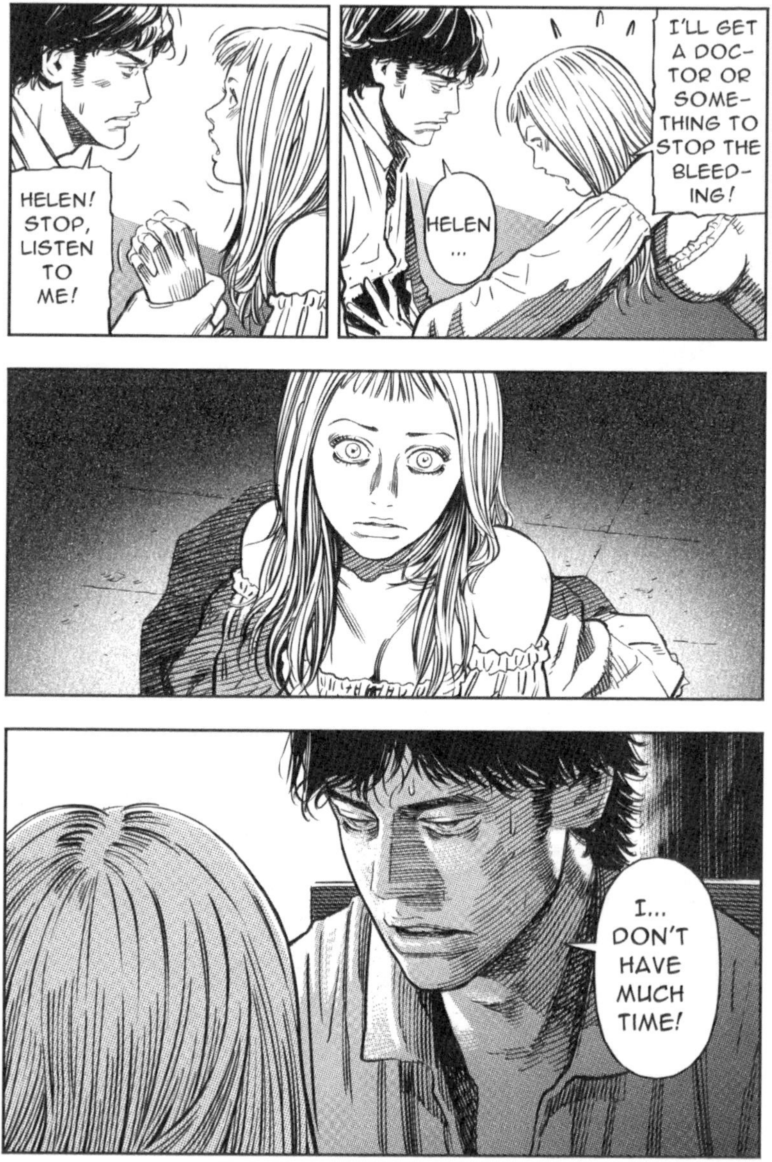
I'LL GET A DOCTOR OR SOMETHING TO STOP THE BLEEDING!
HELEN ...
HELEN! STOP, LISTEN TO ME!
I... DON'T HAVE MUCH TIME!

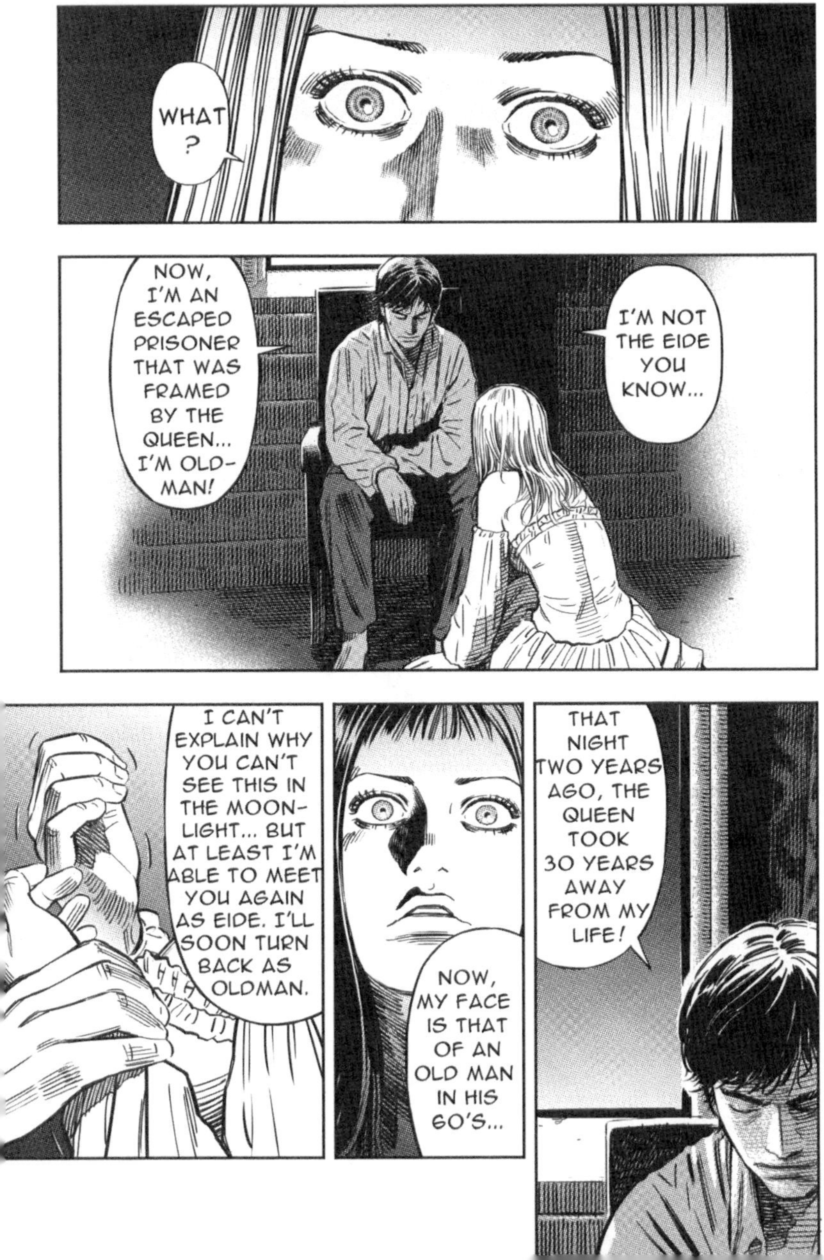
WHAT ?
I'M NOT THE EIDE YOU KNOW...
NOW, I'M AN ESCAPED PRISONER THAT WAS FRAMED BY THE QUEEN... I'M OLD-MAN!
THAT NIGHT TWO YEARS AGO, THE QUEEN TOOK 30 YEARS AWAY FROM MY LIFE!
NOW, MY FACE IS THAT OF AN OLD MAN IN HIS 60'S...
I CAN'T EXPLAIN WHY YOU CAN'T SEE THIS IN THE MOON-LIGHT... BUT AT LEAST I'M ABLE TO MEET YOU AGAIN AS EIDE. I'LL SOON TURN BACK AS OLDMAN.

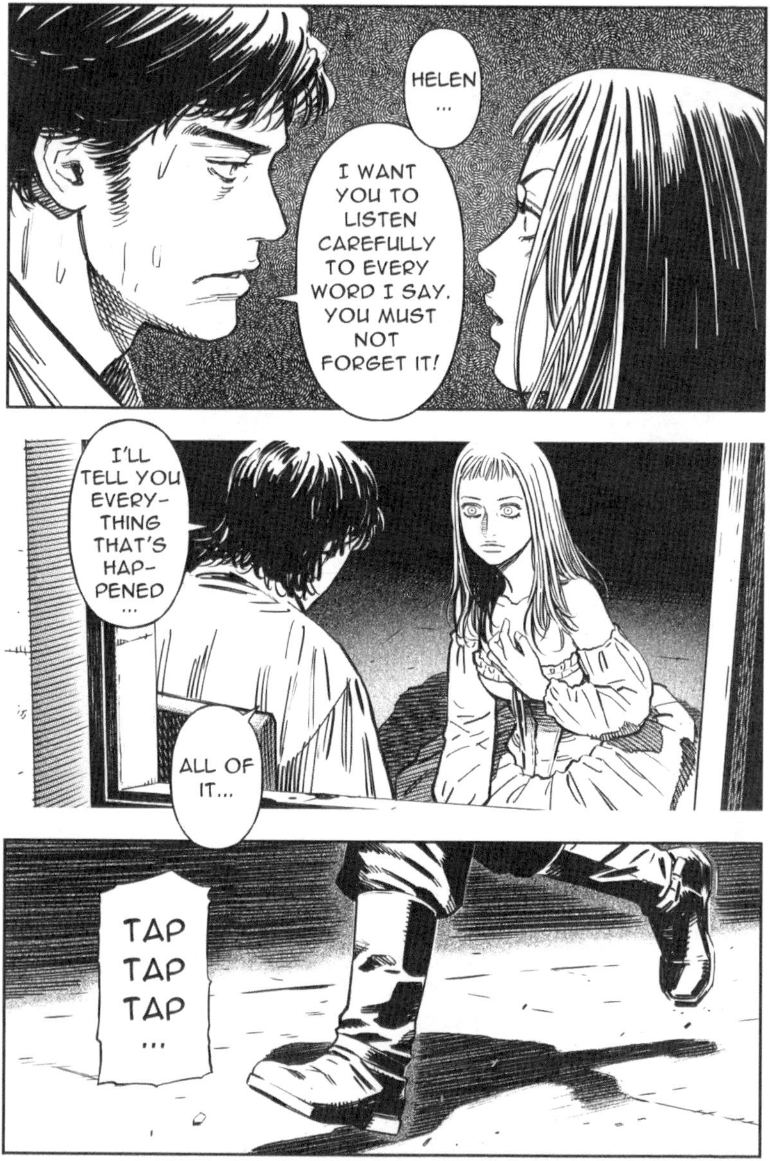
HELEN ...
I WANT YOU TO LISTEN CAREFULLY TO EVERY WORD I SAY. YOU MUST NOT FORGET IT!
I'LL TELL YOU EVERY-THING THAT'S HAP-PENED ...
ALL OF IT...
TAP TAP TAP ...

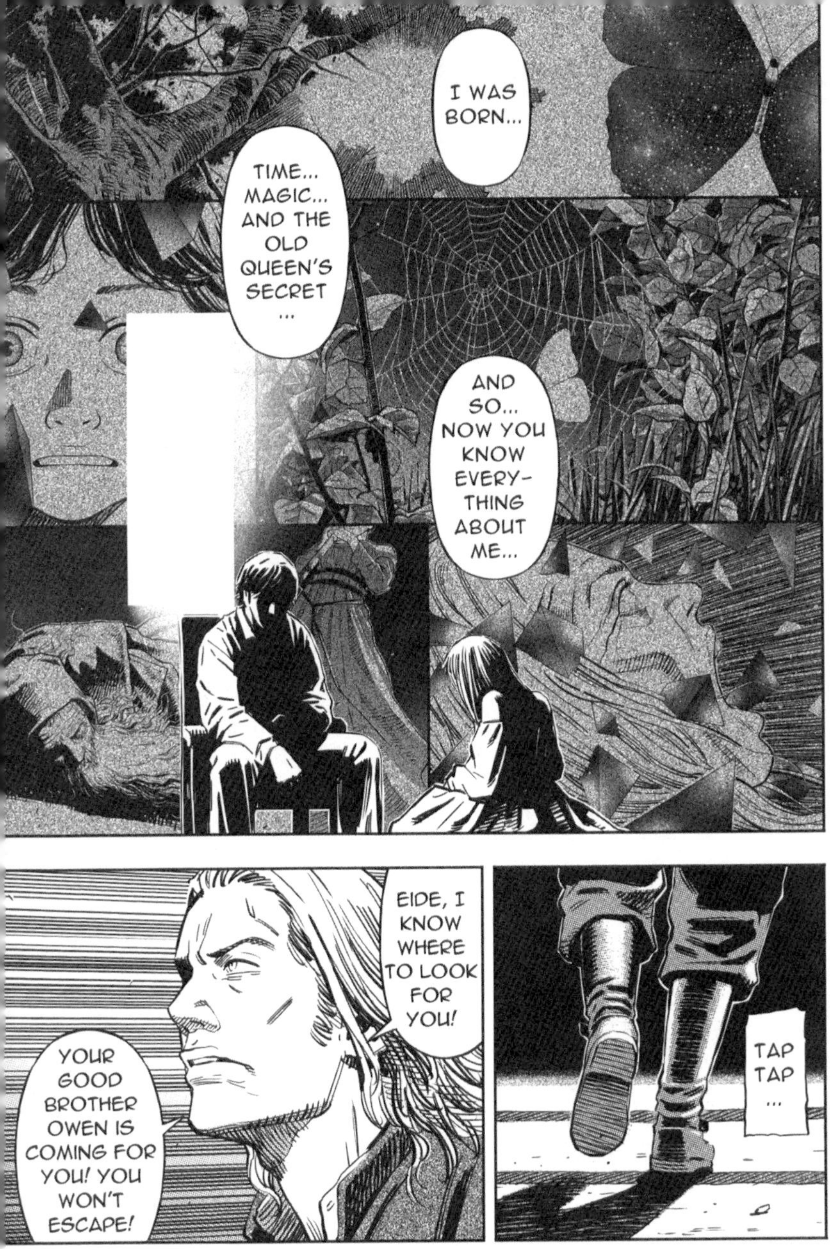
I WAS BORN...
TIME... MAGIC... AND THE OLD QUEEN'S SECRET ...
AND SO... NOW YOU KNOW EVERY-THING ABOUT ME...
TAP TAP ...
EIDE, I KNOW WHERE TO LOOK FOR YOU!
YOUR GOOD BROTHER OWEN IS COMING FOR YOU! YOU WON'T ESCAPE!

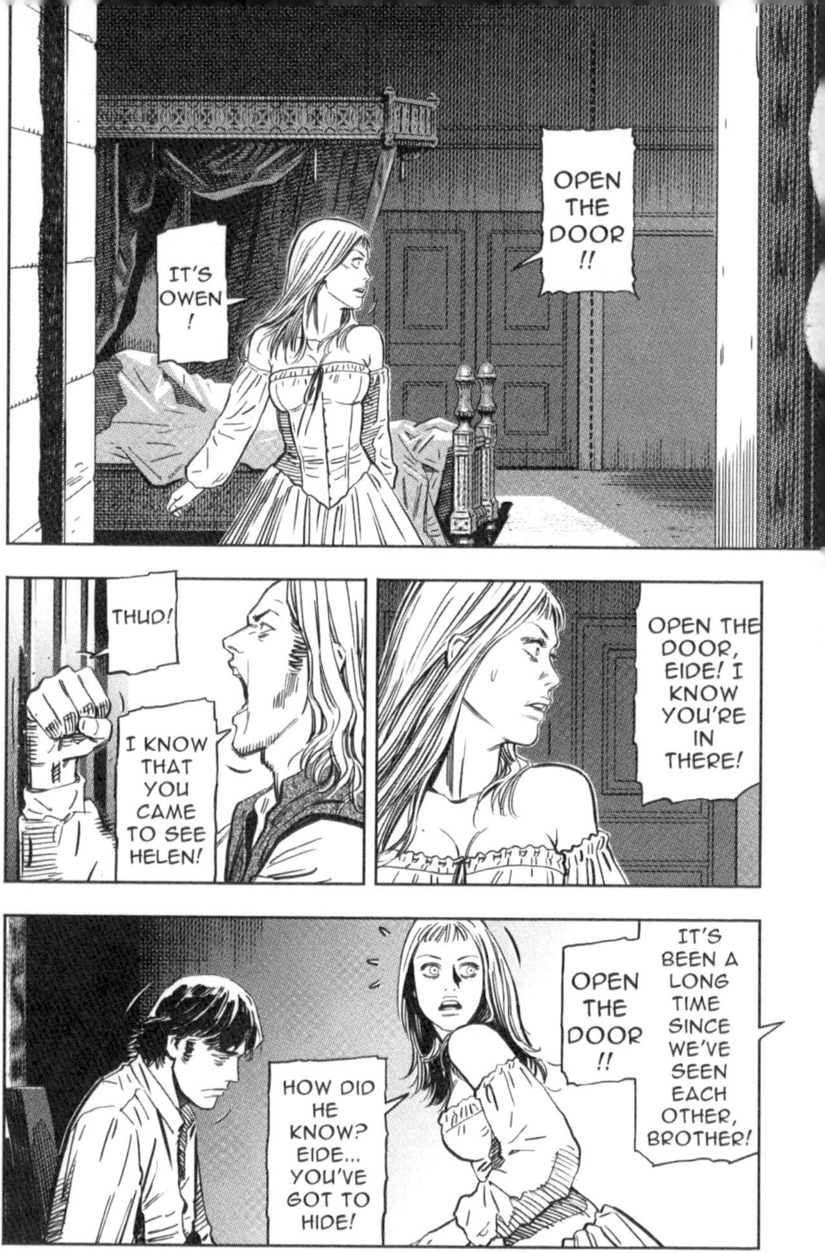
OPEN THE DOOR !!
IT'S OWEN !
OPEN THE DOOR, EIDE! I KNOW YOU'RE IN THERE!
THUD!
I KNOW THAT YOU CAME TO SEE HELEN!
IT'S BEEN A LONG TIME SINCE WE'VE SEEN EACH OTHER, BROTHER!
OPEN THE DOOR !!
HOW DID HE KNOW? EIDE... YOU'VE GOT TO HIDE!

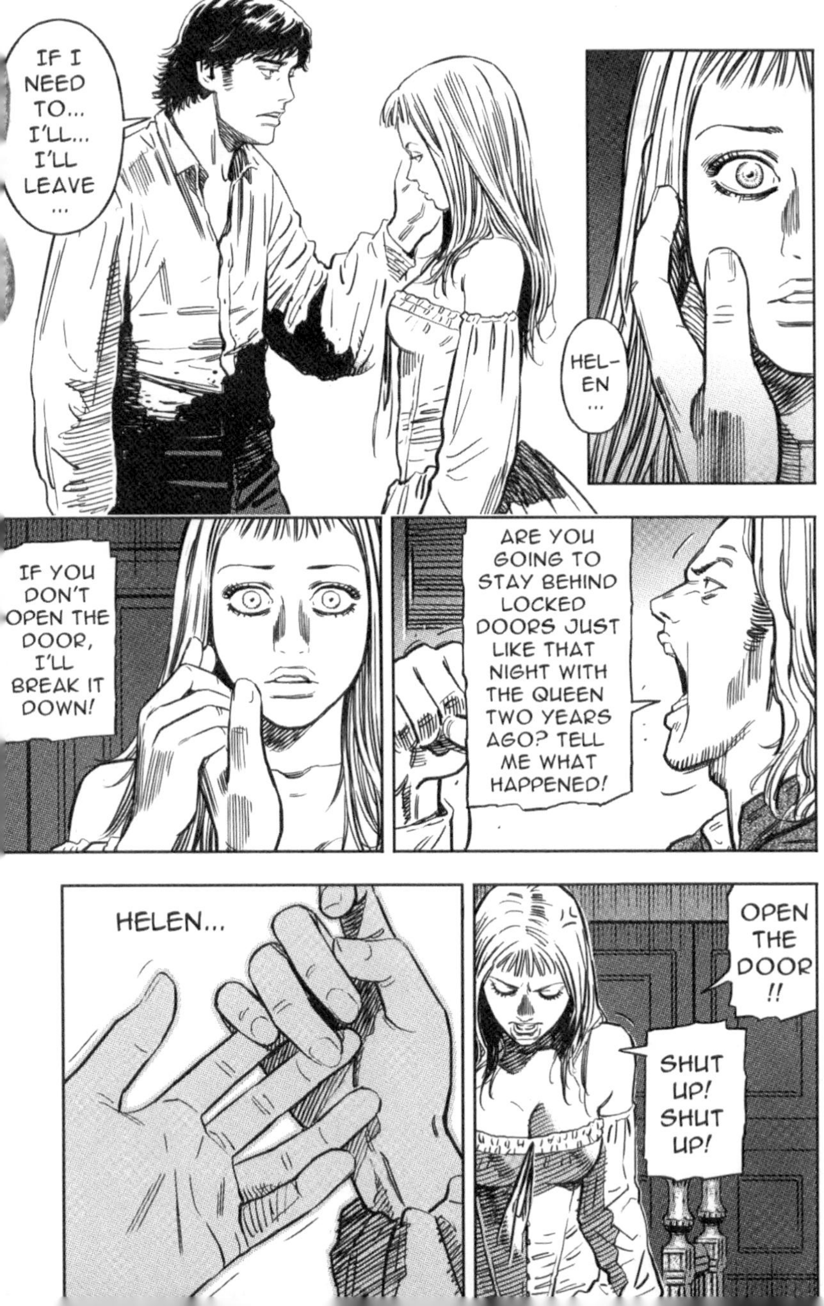
HEL-EN ...
IF I NEED TO... I'LL... I'LL LEAVE ...
ARE YOU GOING TO STAY BEHIND LOCKED DOORS JUST LIKE THAT NIGHT WITH THE QUEEN TWO YEARS AGO? TELL ME WHAT HAPPENED!
IF YOU DON'T OPEN THE DOOR, I'LL BREAK IT DOWN!
OPEN THE DOOR !!
SHUT UP! SHUT UP!
HELEN...

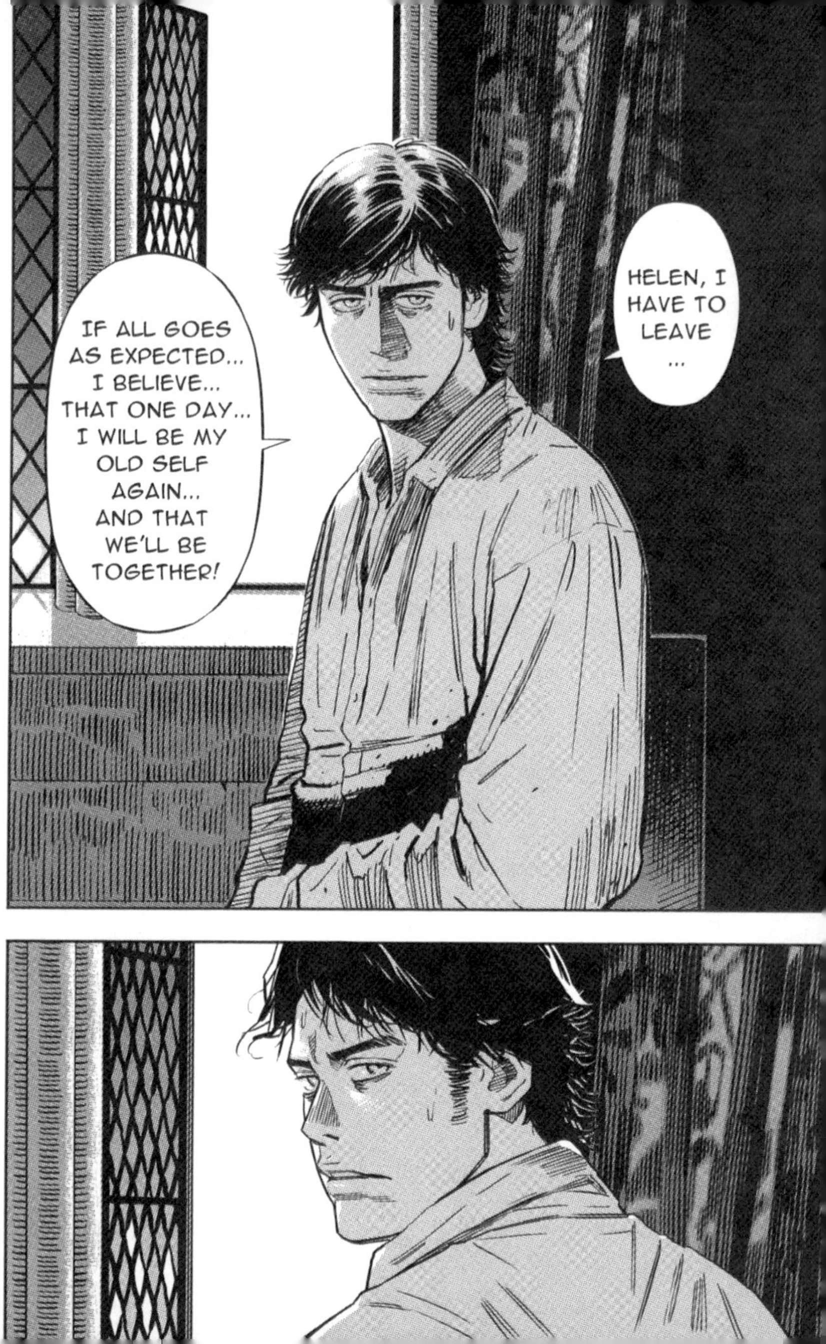
HELEN, I HAVE TO LEAVE ...
IF ALL GOES AS EXPECTED... I BELIEVE... THAT ONE DAY... I WILL BE MY OLD SELF AGAIN... AND THAT WE'LL BE TOGETHER!

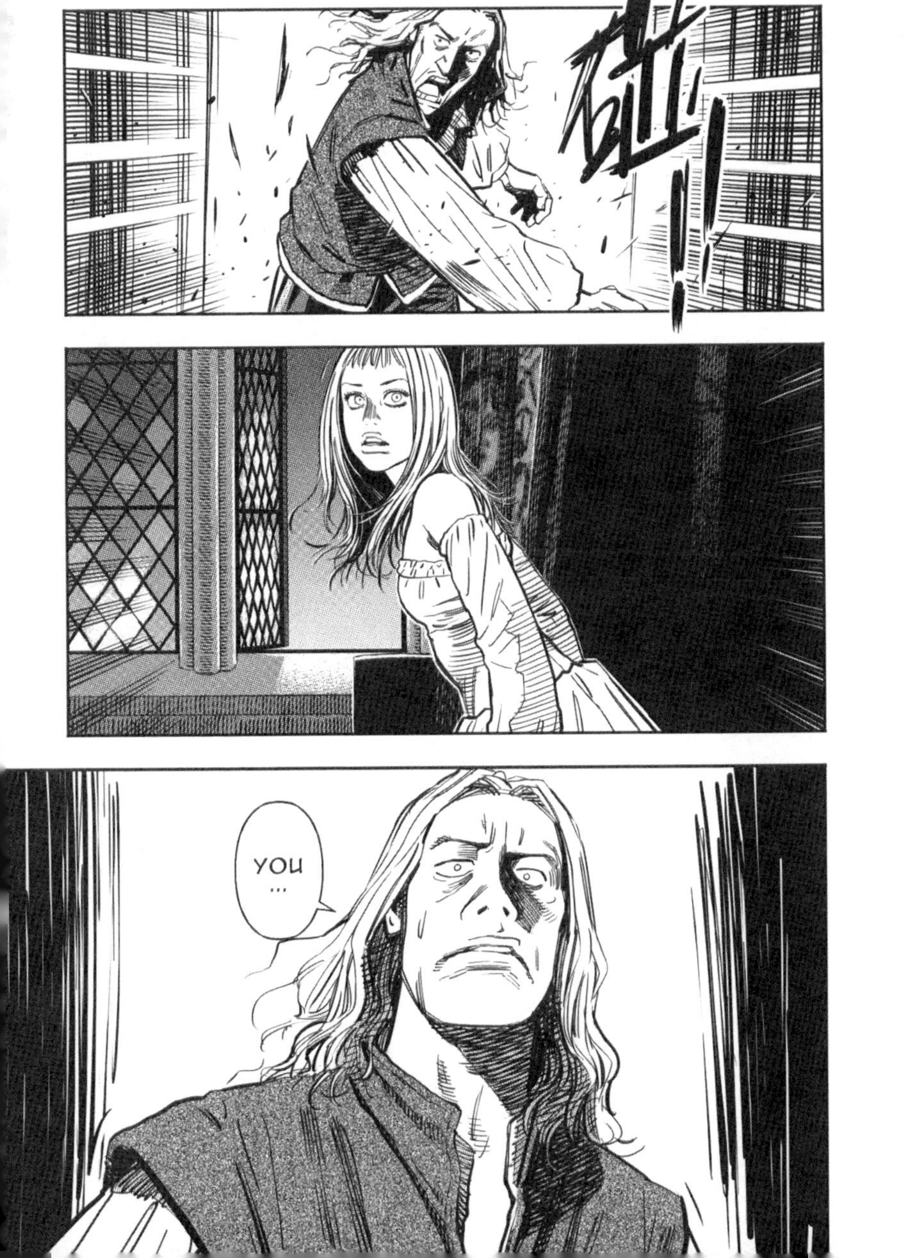
YOU ...

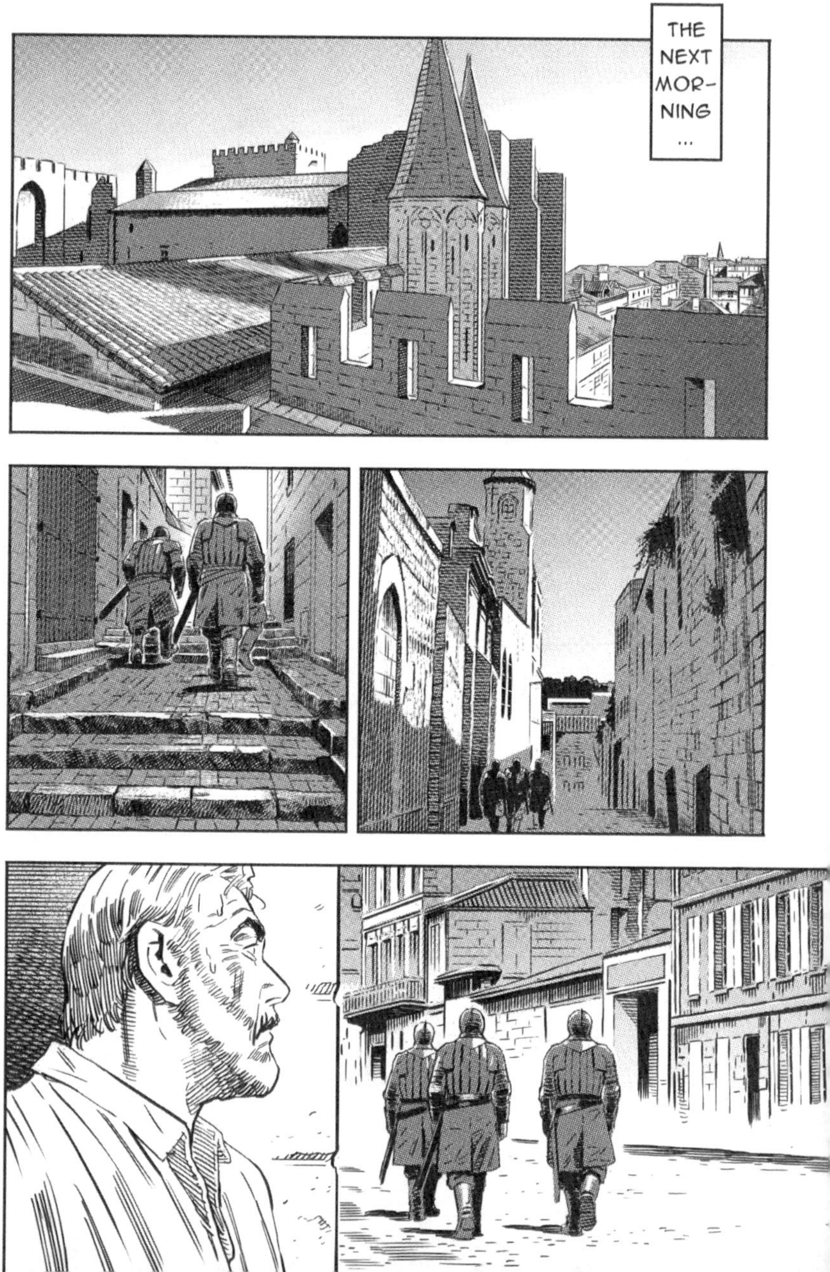
THE NEXT MOR- NING ...

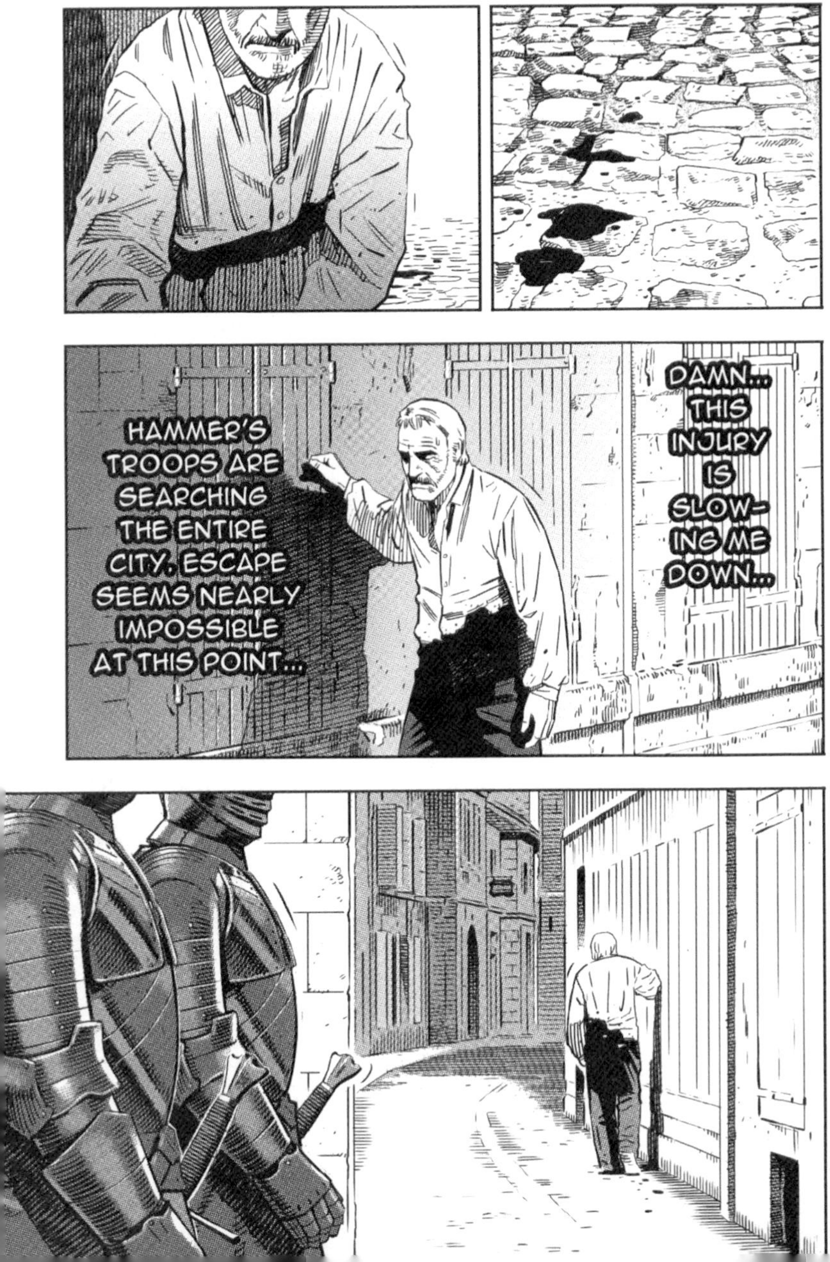
DAMN... THIS INJURY IS SLOWING ME DOWN...
HAMMER'S TROOPS ARE SEARCHING THE ENTIRE CITY. ESCAPE SEEMS NEARLY IMPOSSIBLE AT THIS POINT...

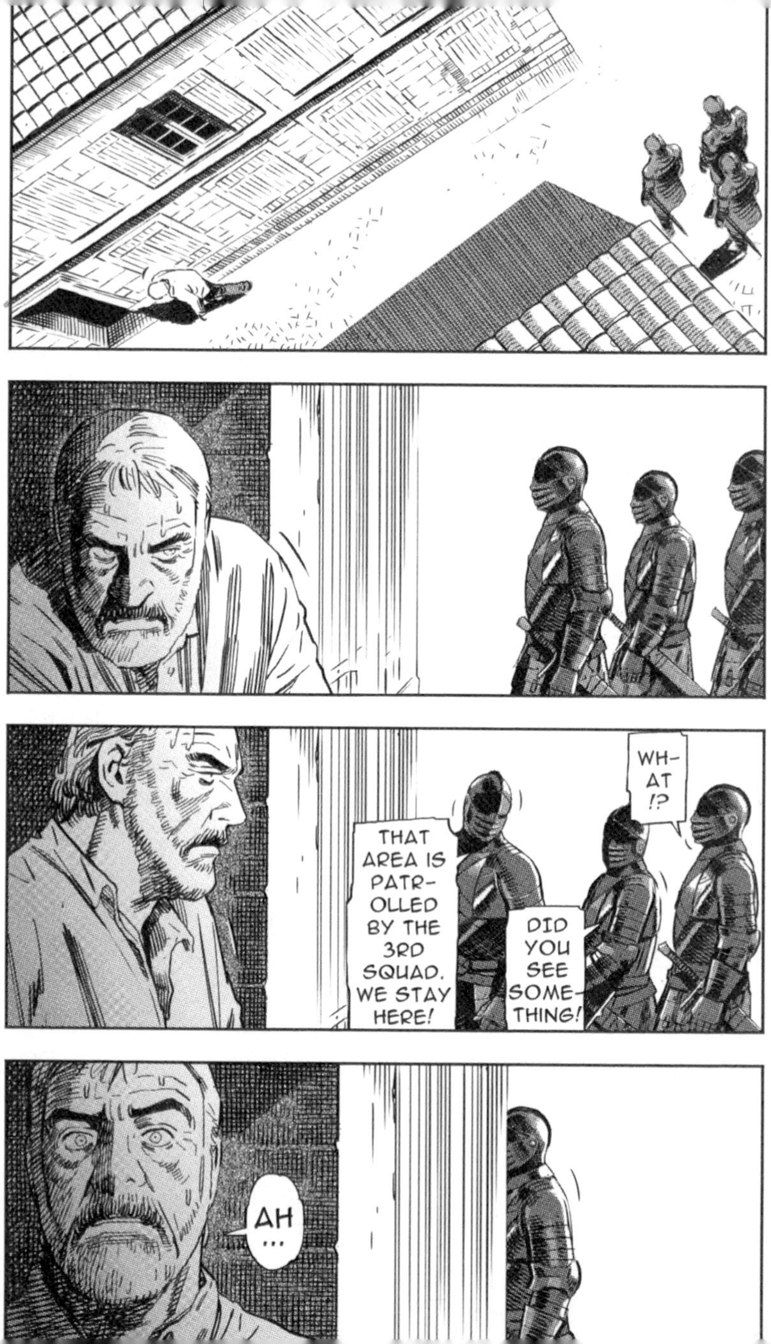
WH-AT!?
DID YOU SEE SOME-THING!
THAT AREA IS PATROLLED BY THE 3RD SQUAD. WE STAY HERE!
AH ...

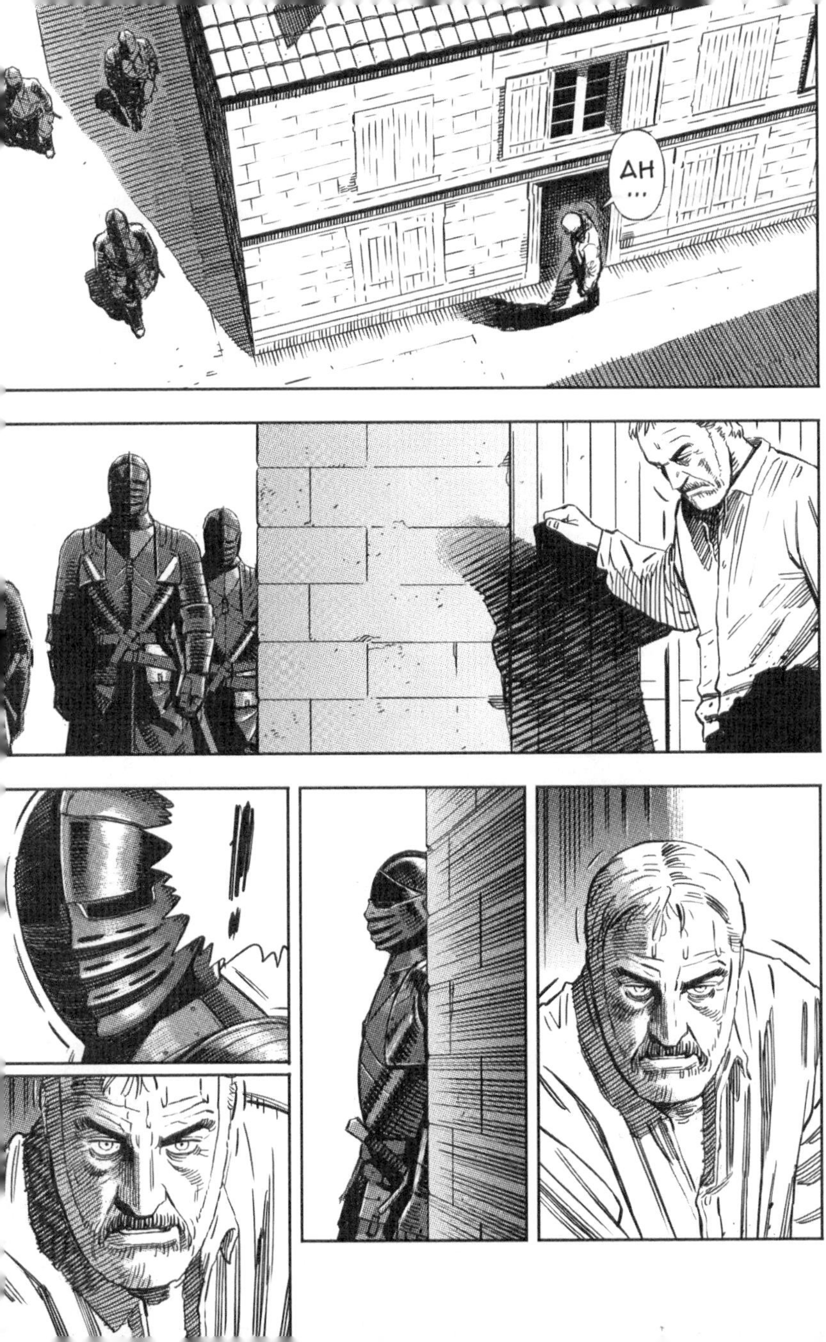
AH ...

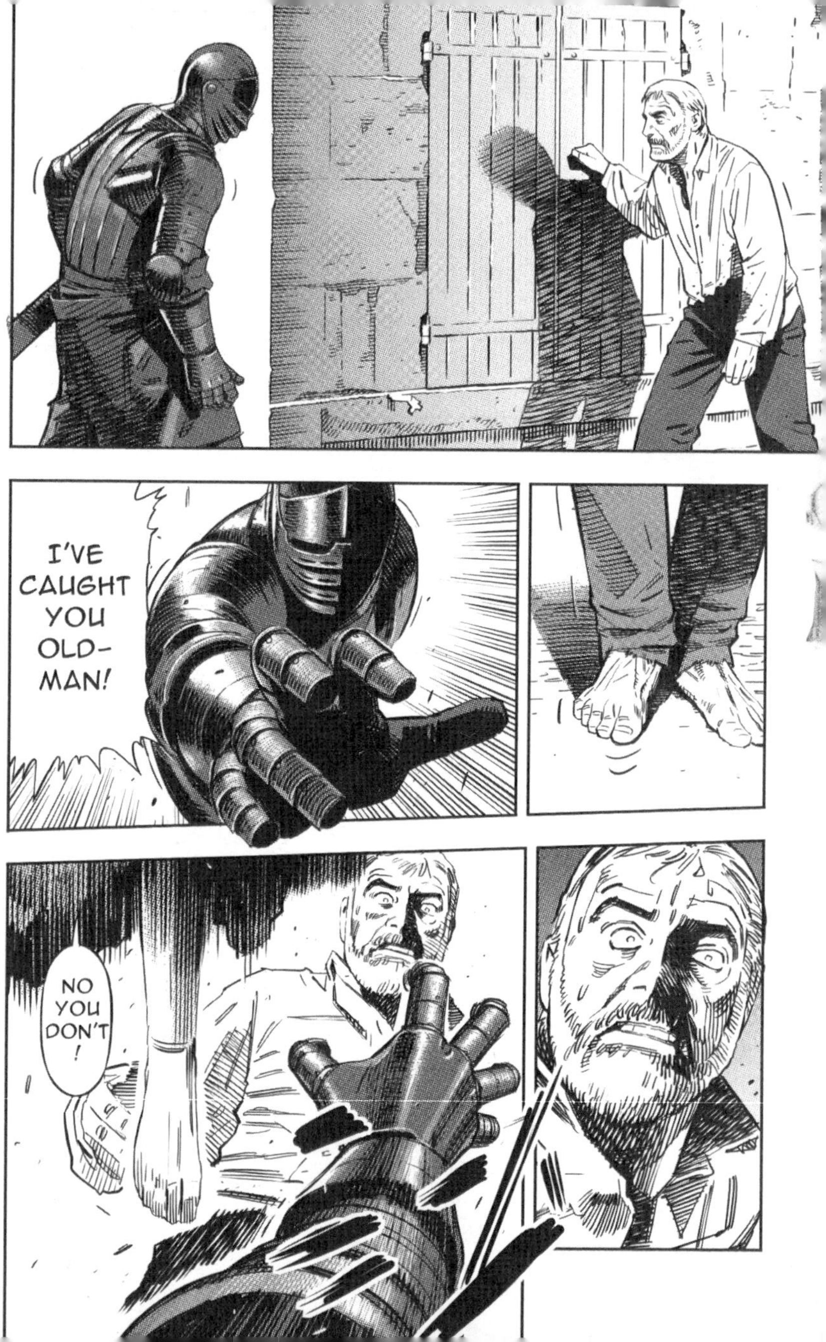
I'VE CAUGHT YOU OLD-MAN!
NO YOU DON'T!

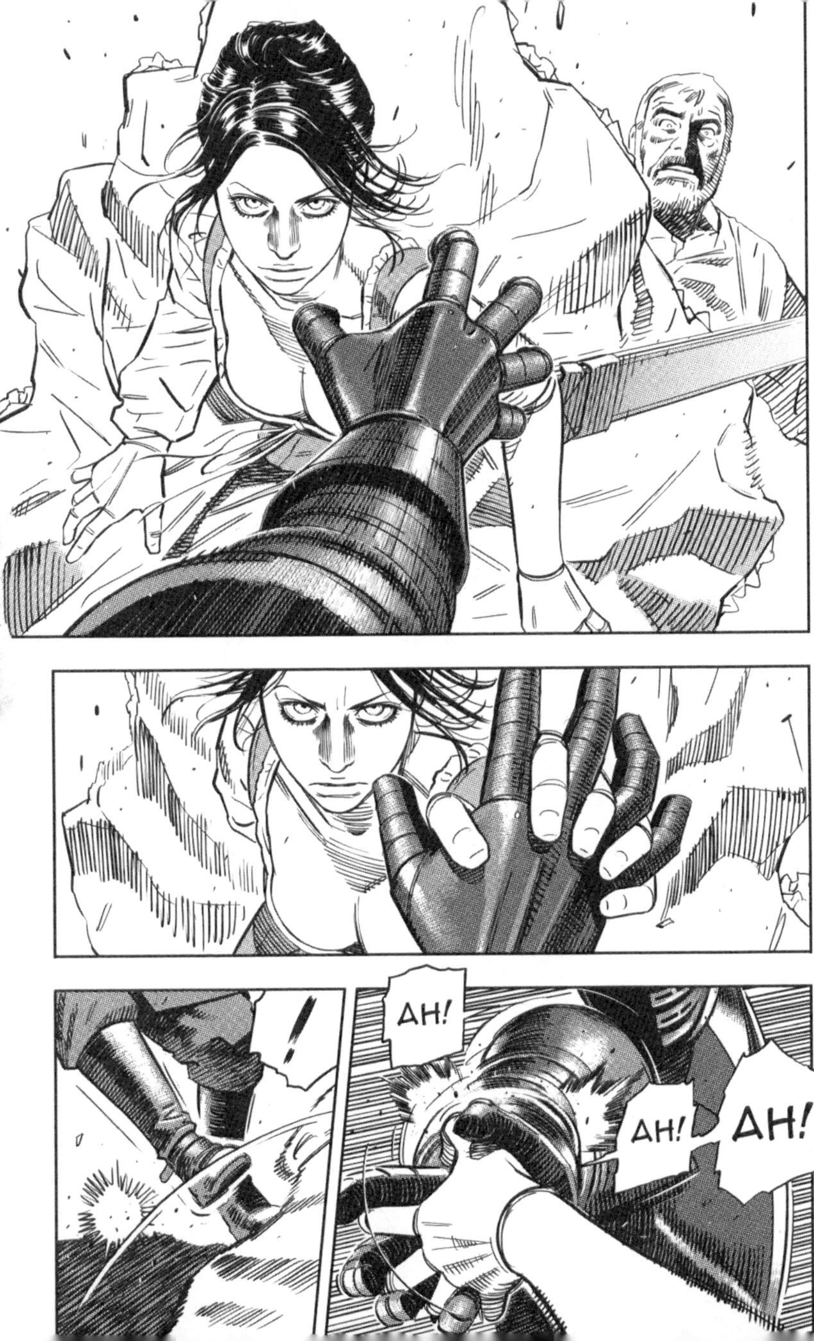
AH!
AH!
AH!
!

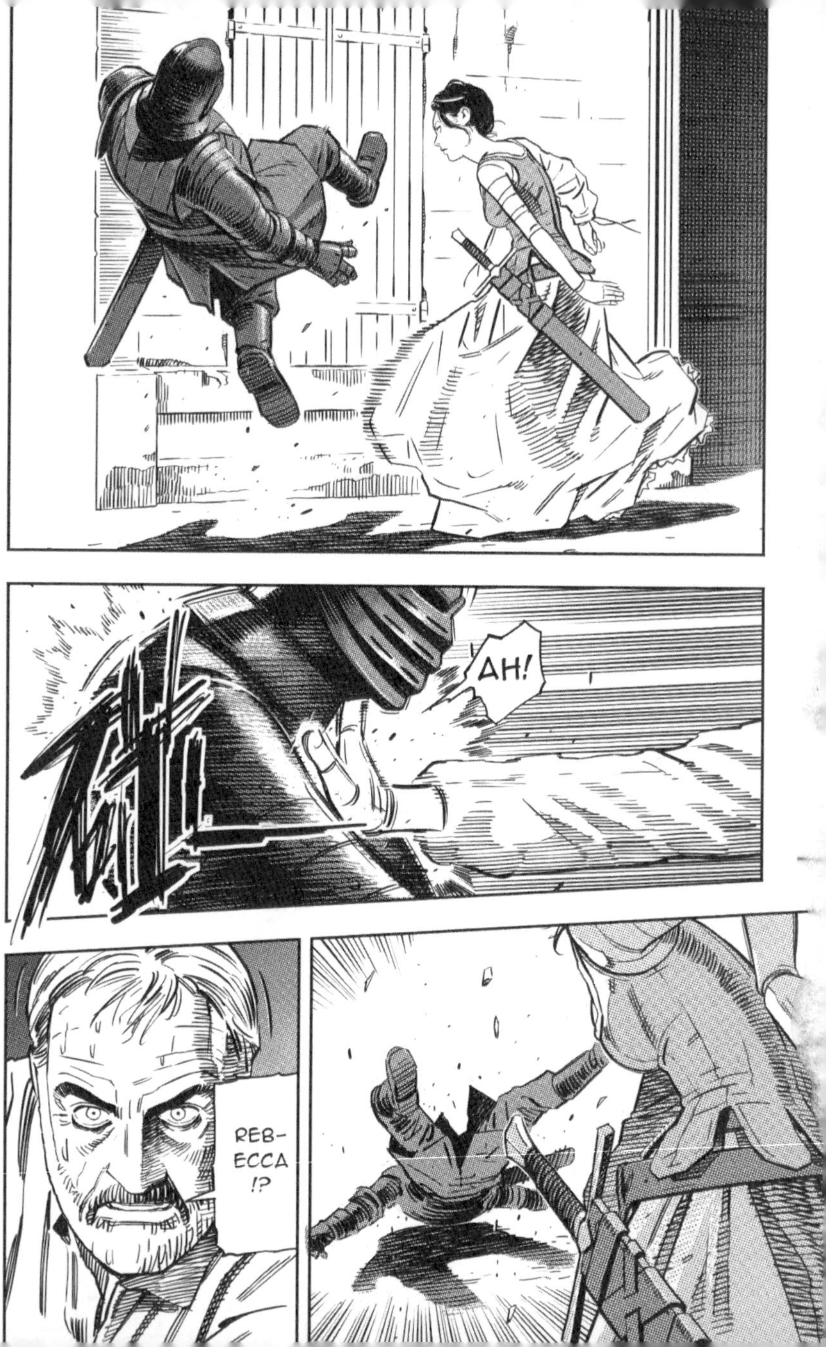
AH!
REB-ECCA !?

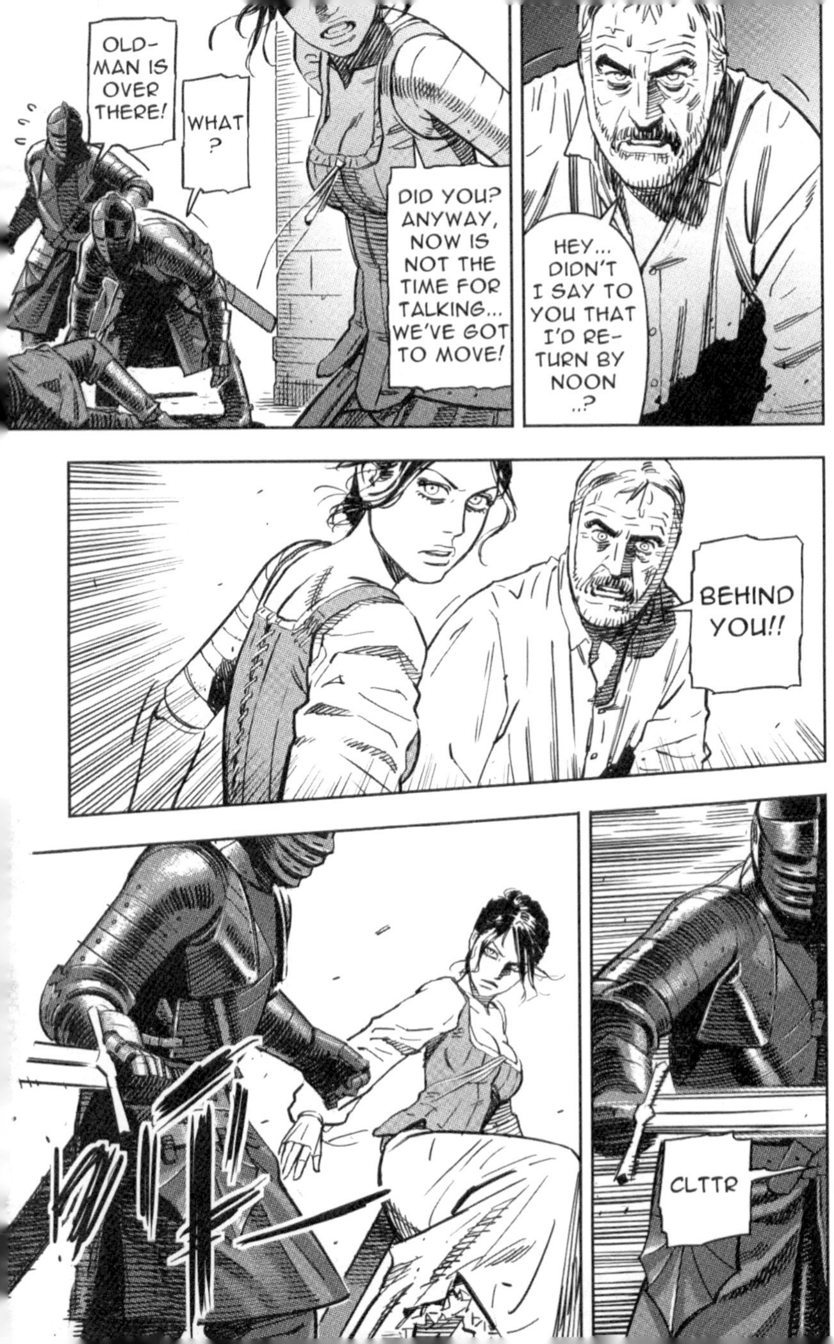
HEY... DIDN'T I SAY TO YOU THAT I'D RE- TURN BY NOON ..?
WHAT ?
DID YOU? ANYWAY, NOW IS NOT THE TIME FOR TALKING... WE'VE GOT TO MOVE!
OLD- MAN IS OVER THERE!
BEHIND YOU!!
CLTTR

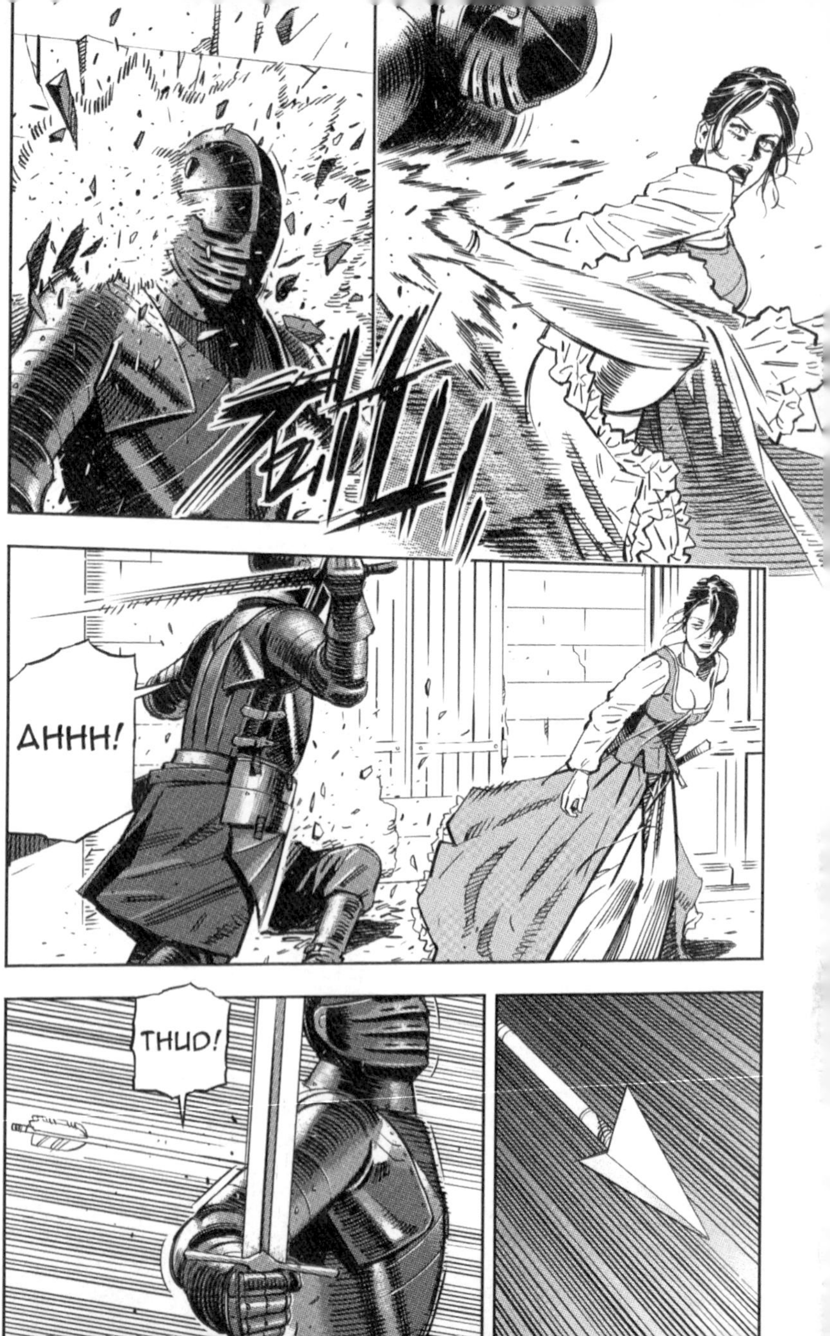
AHHH!
THUD!

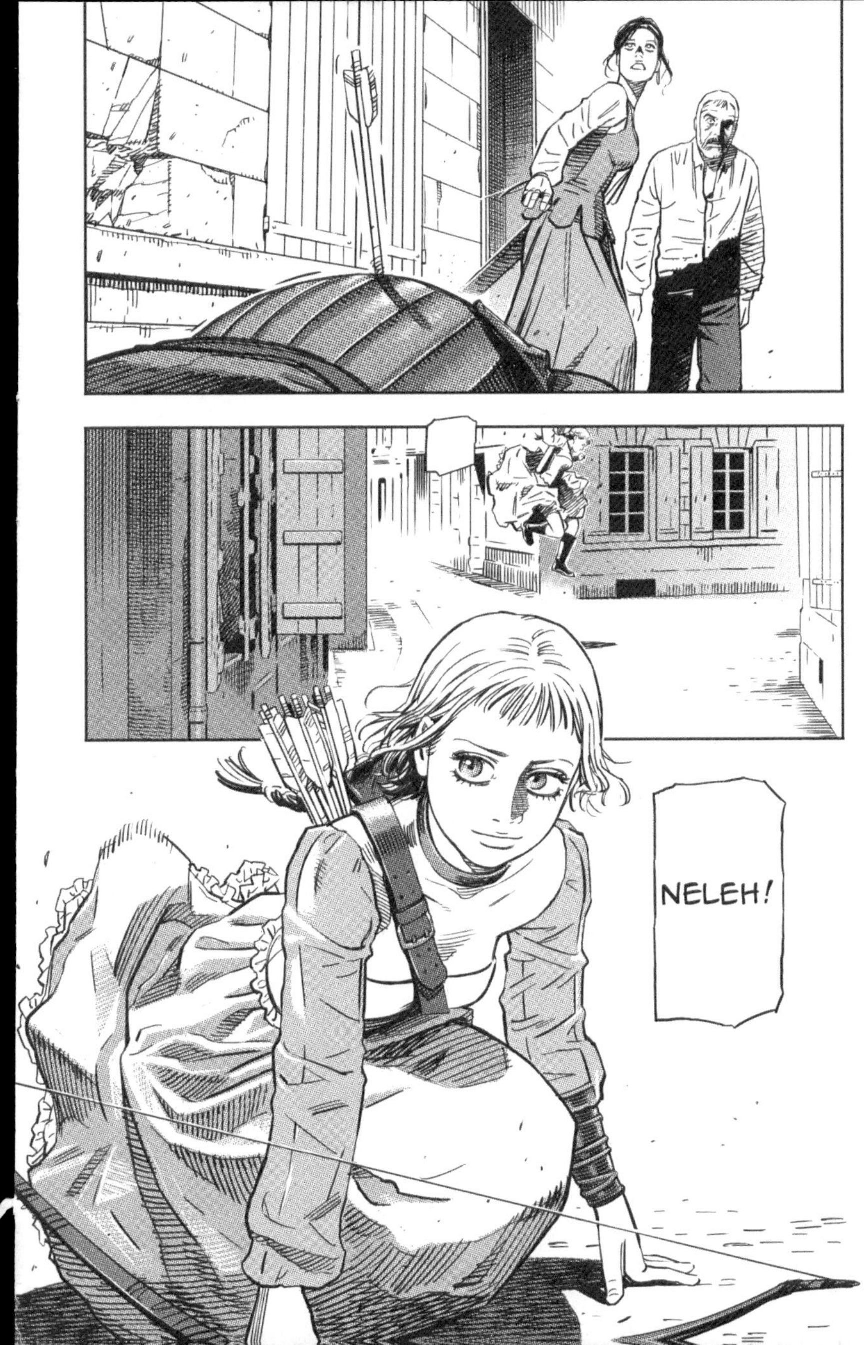
NELEH!

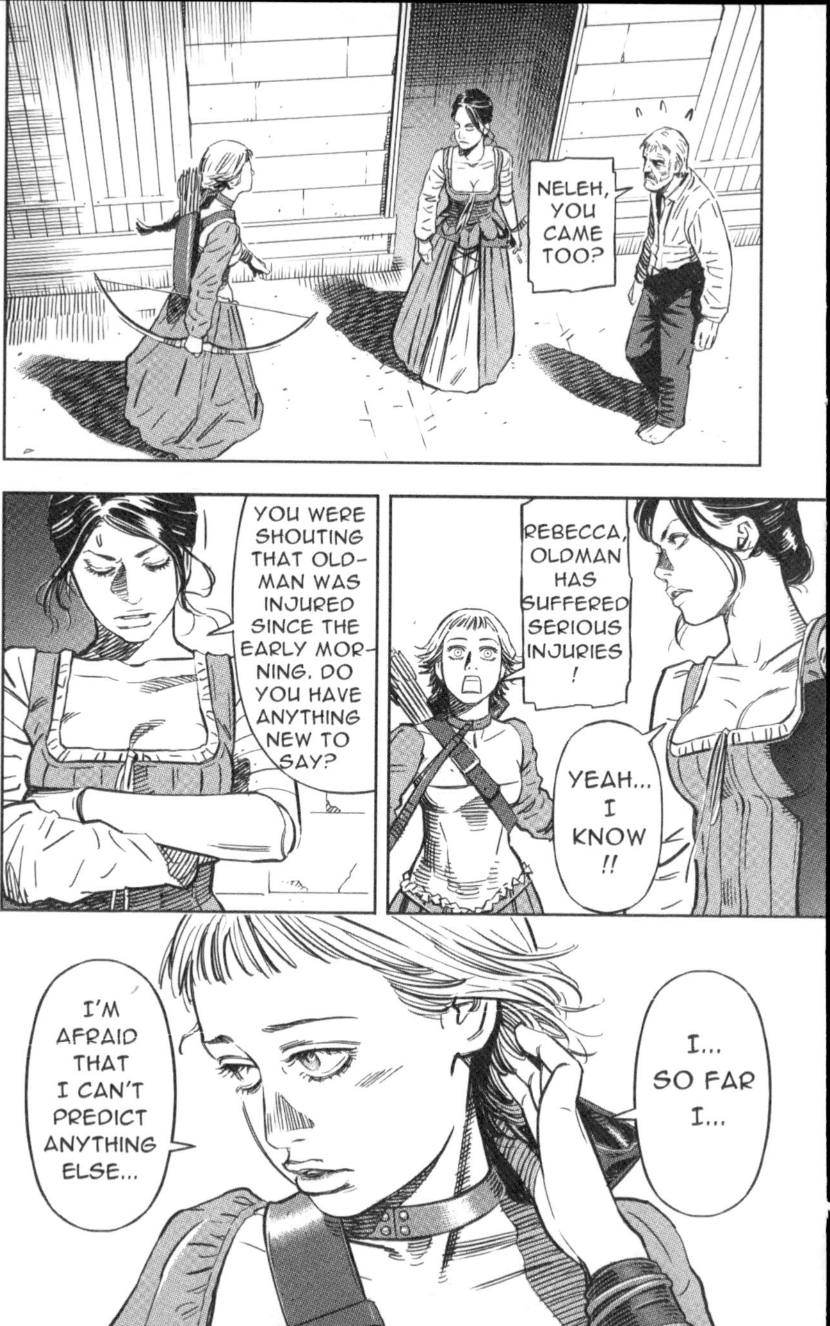
NELEH, YOU CAME TOO?
REBECCA, OLDMAN HAS SUFFERED SERIOUS INJURIES!
YEAH... I KNOW!!
YOU WERE SHOUTING THAT OLD-MAN WAS INJURED SINCE THE EARLY MOR-NING. DO YOU HAVE ANYTHING NEW TO SAY?
I... SO FAR I...
I'M AFRAID THAT I CAN'T PREDICT ANYTHING ELSE...

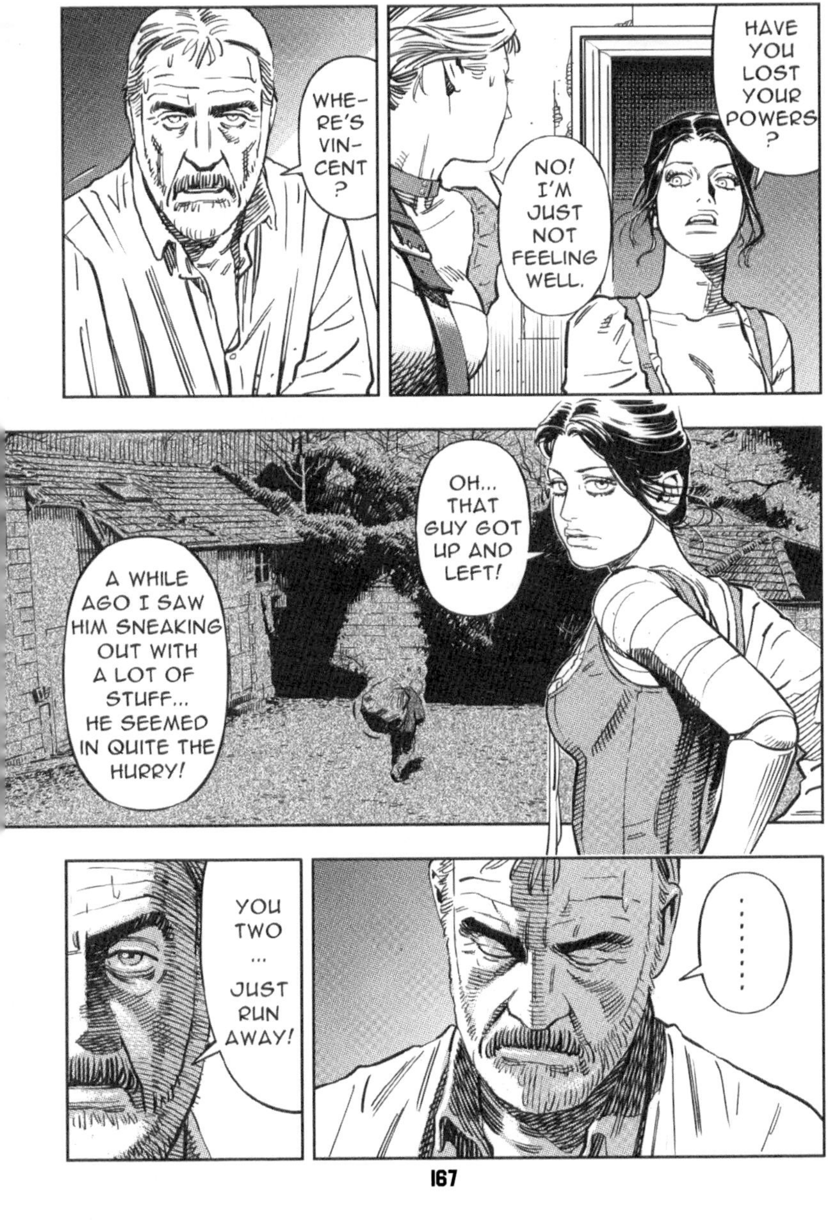
HAVE YOU LOST YOUR POWERS?
NO! I'M JUST NOT FEELING WELL.
WHERE'S VINCENT?
OH... THAT GUY GOT UP AND LEFT!
A WHILE AGO I SAW HIM SNEAKING OUT WITH A LOT OF STUFF... HE SEEMED IN QUITE THE HURRY!
......
YOU TWO ... JUST RUN AWAY!

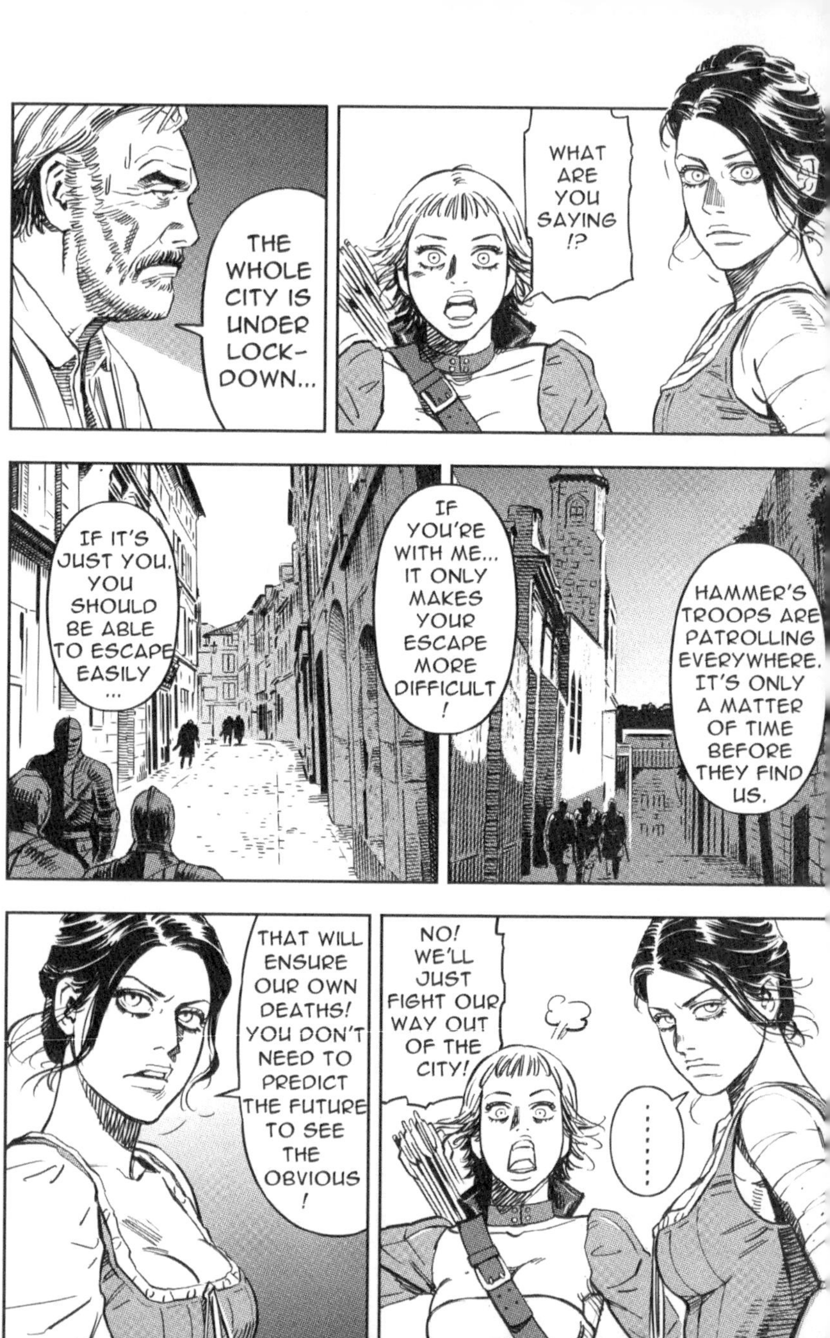
WHAT ARE YOU SAYING !?
THE WHOLE CITY IS UNDER LOCK-DOWN...
HAMMER'S TROOPS ARE PATROLLING EVERYWHERE. IT'S ONLY A MATTER OF TIME BEFORE THEY FIND US.
IF YOU'RE WITH ME... IT ONLY MAKES YOUR ESCAPE MORE DIFFICULT!
IF IT'S JUST YOU, YOU SHOULD BE ABLE TO ESCAPE EASILY...
NO! WE'LL JUST FIGHT OUR WAY OUT OF THE CITY!
......
THAT WILL ENSURE OUR OWN DEATHS! YOU DON'T NEED TO PREDICT THE FUTURE TO SEE THE OBVIOUS!

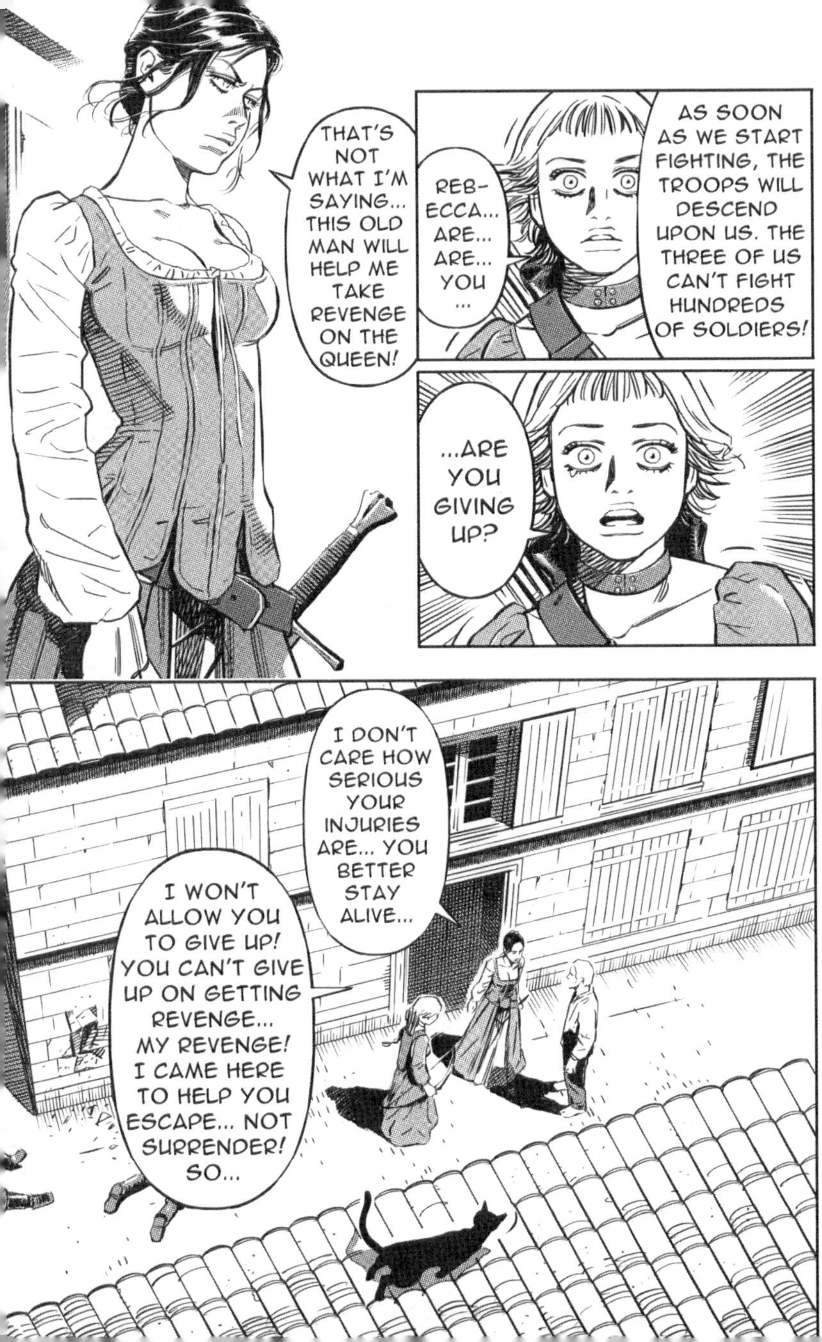
AS SOON AS WE START FIGHTING, THE TROOPS WILL DESCEND UPON US. THE THREE OF US CAN'T FIGHT HUNDREDS OF SOLDIERS!
REB-ECCA... ARE... ARE... YOU ...
...ARE YOU GIVING UP?
THAT'S NOT WHAT I'M SAYING... THIS OLD MAN WILL HELP ME TAKE REVENGE ON THE QUEEN!
I DON'T CARE HOW SERIOUS YOUR INJURIES ARE... YOU BETTER STAY ALIVE...
I WON'T ALLOW YOU TO GIVE UP! YOU CAN'T GIVE UP ON GETTING REVENGE... MY REVENGE! I CAME HERE TO HELP YOU ESCAPE... NOT SURRENDER! SO...

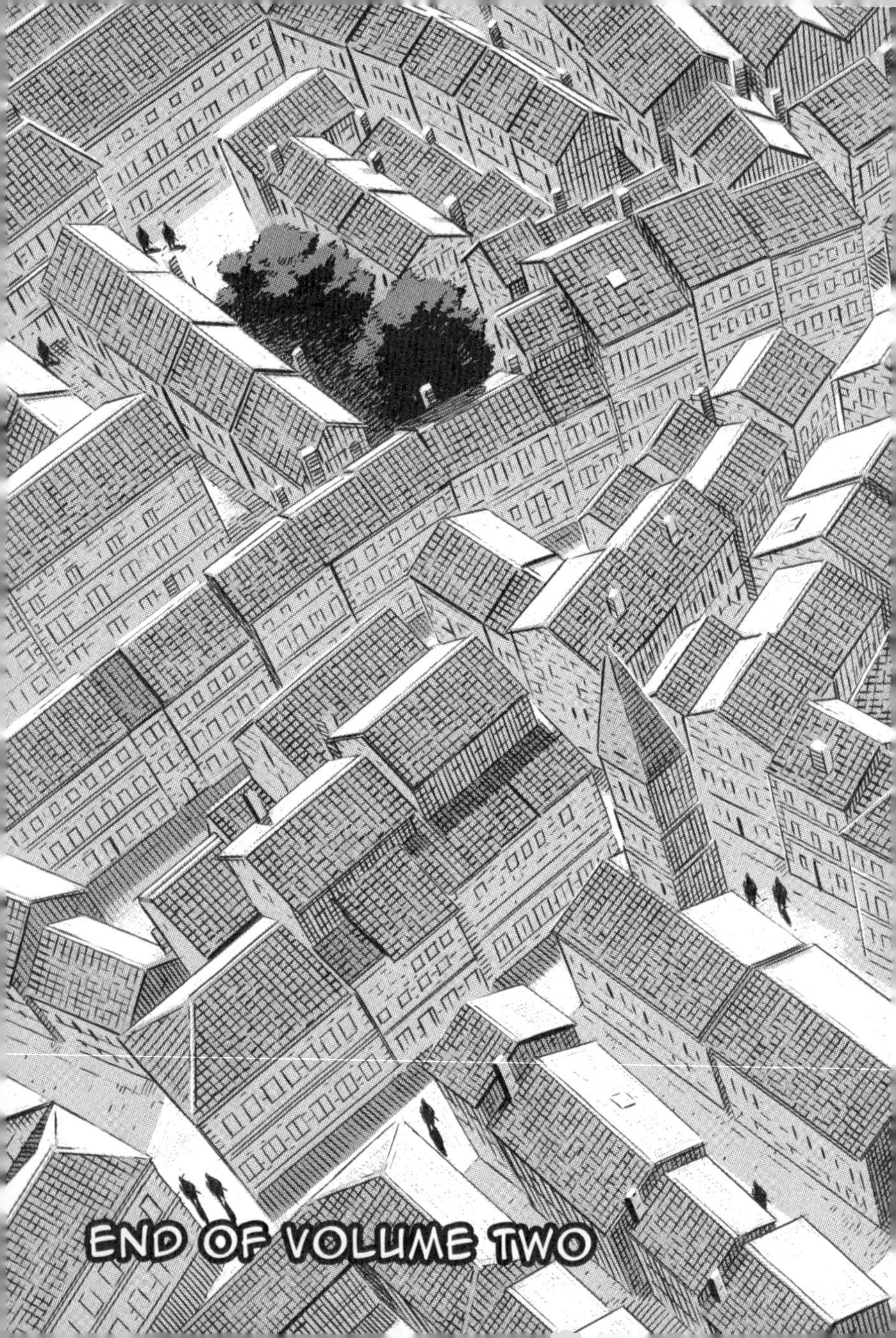
END OF VOLUME TWO

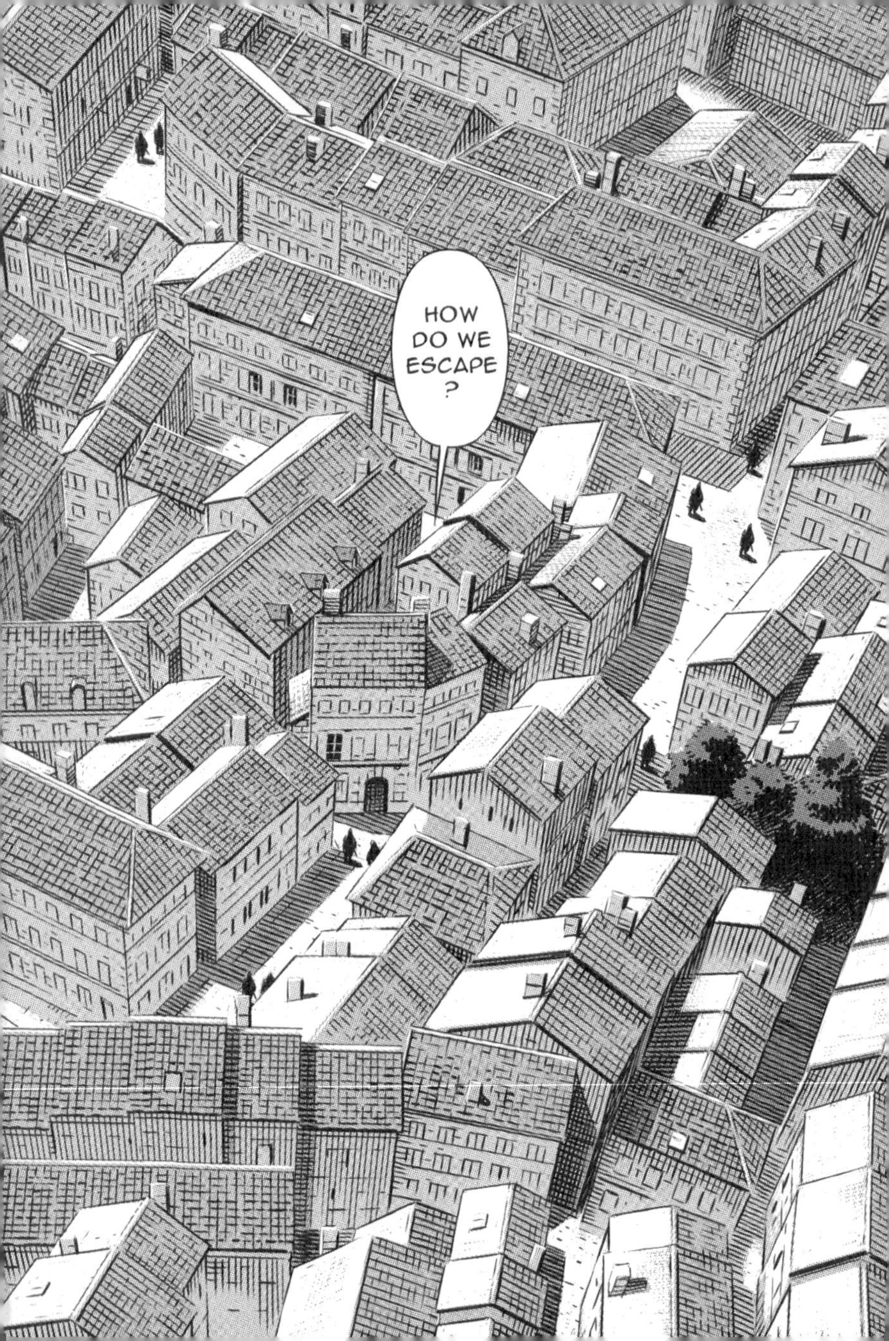
HOW DO WE ESCAPE ?